Intelligent Information Systems – Vol. 1

Advances in
Artificial Intelligence
for Privacy Protection and Security

INTELLIGENT INFORMATION SYSTEMS

Series Editors: Da Ruan *(Belgian Nuclear Research Centre (SCK.CEN) &*
Ghent University, Belgium)
Jie Lu *(University of Technology, Sydney, Australia)*

Intelligent Information Systems – Vol. 1

Advances in
Artificial Intelligence
for Privacy Protection and Security

editors

Agusti Solanas • Antoni Martínez-Ballesté
Rovira i Virgili University, Spain

 **World Scientific**

NEW JERSEY · LONDON · SINGAPORE · BEIJING · SHANGHAI · HONG KONG · TAIPEI · CHENNAI

Published by

World Scientific Publishing Co. Pte. Ltd.

5 Toh Tuck Link, Singapore 596224

USA office: 27 Warren Street, Suite 401-402, Hackensack, NJ 07601

UK office: 57 Shelton Street, Covent Garden, London WC2H 9HE

British Library Cataloguing-in-Publication Data
A catalogue record for this book is available from the British Library.

ADVANCES IN ARTIFICIAL INTELLIGENCE FOR PRIVACY PROTECTION AND SECURITY
Intelligent Information Systems — Vol. 1

ISBN-13 978-981-279-032-3
ISBN-10 981-279-032-2

Printed in Singapore.

Preface

Security has become a key issue in modern life, both in the physical and the virtual worlds. For the physical world, the need for security was always there, even though in very small isolated and peaceful communities, like a hamlet where everyone knows each other, security might seem a far-fetched concern. However, in the virtual world, for good or evil there are no small isolated communities: global connectivity implies that we are all within reach of (probably unknown) remote malicious parties. Therefore, it is today beyond dispute that the information society is not viable without a certain degree of security; no entity (organization or individual) likes to engage in a transaction which might render it vulnerable to attacks. For example, no shop would sell on-line if payment systems were not secure and/or buyers could penetrate the shop's backoffice.

While the information society has to stay secure to survive, it must respect privacy to stay human. Just as organizations do not like insecurity, human beings need some privacy to feel comfortable. Privacy is not exactly secrecy: it rather means that an individual should be given the means to control what information about her is disclosed, as well as when and to whom it is disclosed. Being privacy-friendly in the information society is in many respects parallel to being environment-friendly in the physical society. In principle, neither of both properties has much commercial appeal: just as being environmentally friendly tends to increase manufacturing costs, being privacy-friendly implies that the ability of service providers to profile users (*e.g.* in view of customer relationship management or with more dubious aims) is substantially reduced. However, in the same way that green products are earning ever larger market shares, privacy-preserving services will follow the same trend as the awareness of consumers about potential abuses and about their own rights increases.

There are reasons for optimism: individual privacy is mentioned in the Universal Declaration of Human Rights (1948) and data privacy is explicitly protected by law in most Western countries. Now the challenge is to turn laws into technologies and to have those technologies deployed, without significant losses in security, functionality or operational efficiency. For the time being, though, the development of privacy technologies is still very dependent on sponsorship and awareness campaigns by the public sector, unlike the development of security technologies.

This book edited by Dr. Solanas and Dr. Martínez-Ballesté has the virtue of embracing both privacy and security technologies. Furthermore, its scope is very broad, thanks to the contributions of international experts in several different areas of information and communications technologies, not just security and privacy experts. Hence, it can be especially useful for readers with a general background in ICT to grasp the challenges, the solutions and the ramifications of adding security and privacy to ICT systems . The initial part is an introduction putting privacy and security in context. Then there is a part devoted to privacy, consisting of chapters going from methodology to specific applications like statistical disclosure control and medical databases. The final part comprises several chapters covering different aspects of security research.

Having had the pleasure to do research with the co-editors and with several chapter contributors of this book for a number of years, I can only recommend this work to anyone interested in the intertwined areas of security and privacy.

Tarragona, January 2009.

Prof. Dr. Josep Domingo-Ferrer
Chairholder
UNESCO Chair in Data Privacy
Department of Computer Engineering and Mathematics
Universitat Rovira i Virgili
Tarragona, Catalonia

Contents

Chapter 1

Introduction

Agusti Solanas and Antoni Martínez-Ballesté
UNESCO Chair in Data Privacy
Department of Computer Engineering and Mathematics.
Rovira i Virgili University
Av. Països Catalans 26, 43007 Tarragona, Catalonia, Spain
{agusti.solanas, antoni.martinez}@urv.cat

> *"If self-regulation and self-restraint are not exercised by all concerned*
> *with automatic data processing [...] the computer will become the*
> *villain of our society. It is potentially one of the greatest*
> *resources of our civilization, and the tragedy of*
> *slowing its development is unthinkable."*
> **Lance J. Hoffmann. 1969**

This excerpt from an article by Lance J. Hoffmann published in *Computing Surveys* in 1969 points out the importance of taking into account the security and privacy aspects related to the use of computers. In this book, we recognize the importance of those topics and seek to collect a number of recent advances for the protection of privacy and security by means of artificial intelligence techniques, namely evolutionary computation, clustering, computer vision, etc. This book considers the security and privacy problems, and focuses on the relation between them and the field of artificial intelligence from a modern point of view. Notwithstanding, we should not forget that privacy and security have been important issues long before the age of computers.

From the very beginning, humans have tried to protect their privacy and enhance their security. Probably, the first attempt of ancient humans to gain some privacy and security was the use of caves. The size of the caves and the size of the entrances were important, for example the entrance would be smaller if the caves were to be used for secret activities.[1,2]

1

As time passed ancient humans evolved and their intelligence and capabilities increased. The smarter they were the more sophisticated their privacy and security methods became. Among these sophistications, writing was an outstanding step forward for many ancient societies (*e.g.* Egyptians, Sumerians, Chinese, Assyrians, Greeks, Mayas, etc.) and it changed their view on many areas such as commerce, diplomacy and war. The way messages were transmitted from strategists to commanders in the battlefield evolved. It was no longer secure to send plain messages because if they were intercepted by the enemy vital operations could be endangered. As a result, cryptography, the art of secret writing, became essential to guarantee the confidentiality of communications. In recent decades, cryptography has expanded beyond confidentiality to include more sophisticated properties such as integrity, non-repudiation, authentication, etc (See[3] for a comprehensive study of the history of cryptography).

Nowadays, many security and privacy problems cannot be optimally solved due to their complexity. In these situations, heuristic approaches should be used and artificial intelligence has proven to be extremely useful and well-fitted to solve these problems. Artificial neural networks, evolutionary computation, clustering, fuzzy sets, multi-agent systems, datamining and pattern recognition are just a few examples of artificial intelligence techniques that can be successfully used to solve some relevant privacy and security problems.

Our main aim has been to gather high quality scientific articles that address privacy and security problems by using artificial intelligence techniques. It can be believed that privacy, security and artificial intelligence are like water and oil, and cannot be mixed. However, this book shows that security and privacy can extraordinarily benefit from artificial intelligence.

We hope that the book will spark the interest of researchers from both worlds (security and privacy, and artificial intelligence) in the investigation of future ways of collaboration that lead to a better understanding of the problems and their solutions.

1.1. Organization of the book

The book you are about to read has been structured in three main parts:

The first part "A brief introduction to privacy and security" comprises Chapter 2 and 3. The aim of this first part is to introduce the main problems related to the many aspects of security and privacy. In Chapter 2, Martínez and Solanas summarize some of the most relevant privacy threats related to the use of information and communication technologies, namely the Internet, ubiquitous computing and large databases. Similarly, Ribargorda et al. provide the reader with an overview of information security in Chapter 3.

The second part, which includes Chapters 4 to 8, is devoted to several artificial intelligence techniques used to protect privacy in different areas. In Chapter 4, Schmid considers the problem of finding the right balance between societal benefit and individual privacy. He introduces some basic concepts such as anonymity, data perturbation and microaggregation, which are later used in other chapters. In Chapter 5, Pont-Tuset et al. follow the line of the previous chapter and study how data can be *desemantized* using, for example, neural networks. Taking the problem from a different point of view, Dewri et al. propose the use of multi-objective evolutionary computation for statistical disclosure control in Chapter 6. Chapter 7 is devoted to the study of cluster-specific information loss measures. Torra reviews and compares some of them emphasizing the importance of clustering and fuzzy sets. The second part of the book concludes with Chapter 8, where Gibert et al. show how multi-agent systems can be used to preserve the privacy of medical records in health-care applications.

The third part, which comprises Chapters 9 to 14, tackles the security problem from a broad point of view that includes physical security, national security and intelligence, and network security. In Chapter 9, Lu et al. propose the use of acoustic signal recognition and nonlinear Hebbian learning to detect vehicles that may be loaded with explosives approaching restricted areas. In Chapter 10, Puig et al. propose the use of textures in autonomous surveillance vehicles. This chapter compares different state-of-the-art texture classifiers and proposes an efficient solution to the problem of per-pixel classification of textured images with multichannel Gabor wavelet filters. Chapter 11 is devoted to the detection of aggressions in train compartments. Yang et al. present an efficient aggression detection system that integrates several aggression detection systems, including recognition of face patterns and one of the bests detectors *i.e.* human beings. In Chapter 12, Decherchi et al. consider the problem of text-mining for homeland security. They present a system for clustering documents that combines pattern-recognition grouping algorithms with semantic-driven processing. In Chapter 13, Zarza et al. address the problem of defining network security protocols for sensor or mobile ad-hoc networks where thousands of nodes can be involved by means of genetic algorithms. Finally, Chapter 14 focuses on the problem of securing mobile ad-hoc networks against selfish behaviors. Seredynski et al. propose a method that uses concepts concerning co-operation developed in evolutionary biology and tools like genetic algorithms and evolutionary game theory.

References

1. H. Holderness, G. Davies, A. Chamberlain, and R. Donahue. A conservation audit of archaeological cave resources in the peak district and yorkshire dales. Technical Report 7, CAPRA, (2006). URL http://capra.group.shef.ac.uk/7/743Research.pdf.
2. P. Arosio and D. Meozzi. The home-hunting habits of prehistoric britons. http://www.stonepages.com/news/archives/002329.html.
3. D. Kahn, *The Codebreakers: The Comprehensive History of Secret Communication from Ancient Times to the Internet.* (Scribner, December 1996).

PART 1
A Brief Introduction to Privacy and Security

Chapter 2

An Introduction to Privacy Aspects of Information and Communication Technologies

Antoni Martínez-Ballesté and Agusti Solanas

Rovira i Virgili University of Tarragona, UNESCO Chair in Data Privacy
Av. Països Catalans 26, 43007 Tarragona, Catalonia, Spain
{antoni.martinez, agusti.solanas}@urv.cat

Information and Communications Technologies (ICT) are fostering the appearance of a plethora of new services and applications. On the one hand, ICT will improve the efficiency of a variety of processes and will provide users with amazing amounts and varieties of services. On the other hand, the universal deployment of these new technologies and the world-wide access to them may lead to the invasion of users privacy.

In this chapter, we introduce the reader to a number of relevant aspects of privacy in ICT. We elaborate on the use of the Internet as a potential threat to users privacy, since the web and their modern services pave the way for the gathering of large amounts of data. Also, ICT allow the management of databases, which entail privacy concerns: for example, sensitive data from individuals can be stored in these databases and, moreover, administrators can track queries of the database users so the latter can be profiled. Finally, new trends in ubiquitous computing that look promising (e.g. location based services and radio-frequency identification) are also analyzed from a privacy-aware point of view.

Contents

2.1. Introduction

Information and communication technologies (ICT) are the fundamental tool for the proper development of the Information Society. These technologies allow the automatic collection, storage and processing of large amounts of data. Most of these data are related to human activities: e.g. processing census data, electricity bills, payslips, medical records, etc. The processing of these data by governments or companies has always entailed discussions about privacy. Even the Universal Declaration of Human Rights[1] states that *"no one shall be subjected to arbitrary interference with his privacy"* and that *"everyone has the right to the protection of the law against such interference or attacks"*. The privacy threat entailed to computer systems was already pointed out by Hoffman in 1969.[2]

The Internet is the world-wide platform for communication, information search and other activities, namely shopping, expressing opinions, sharing pictures, etc. Since the mid 1990s, millions of people from different cultures and education levels interact with a plethora of interconnected information systems. The Internet and ubiquitous computing involve an easier interaction between information systems and their users. Hence, the collection of data by service providers has become straightforward and, consequently, the amount of collected data has dramatically increased. This allows, for instance, the rapid creation of profiles for customer relationship management. However, data collection and analysis come into conflict with users privacy, since their habits can be profiled by third parties and their actions tracked as well. The following are some examples:

- *Digital Rights Management systems* require the users to identify themselves when subscribing or paying for some content. Hence, their tastes and preferences are being exposed.[3]
- *Authentication and identification of users* in a variety of services (e.g. transportation, e-mail services, online banking, etc.) allow the tracking of their activities.
- *Computerized video surveillance* entails several privacy concerns. Its wide deployment clashes with a diversity of data protection laws. Hence, several techniques must be applied to guarantee the privacy of individuals.[4]

The access to these data must be limited by governmental regulations to ensure confidentiality and guarantee the privacy of the users.[5]

In that sense, the Organization for Economic Co-operation and Development published in 1980 a set of guidelines on the protection of personal data.[6] They mentioned that information should only be collected with the *consent of the individuals* and *should not be disclosed to third parties*. These guidelines have been adopted as legal initiatives in several countries.

In Europe, the Directive 95/46/EC on the protection of personal data[7] develops the aforementioned guidelines. In addition, the Directive 2002/58/EC on privacy and electronic communications[8] elaborates on data collection and processing by means of ICT. According to the directive, the public and massive access to ICT gives rise to requirements concerning the protection of the privacy of their users. It states that *"the successful cross-border development of these services is partly dependent on the confidence of users that their privacy will not be at risk"*. It is observed in this directive that publicly available electronic communication services over the Internet open new possibilities for users but also new risks for their personal data and privacy. As a result, service providers should take appropriate measures to safeguard the security of their services and take care of the privacy of their users. Since Directive 95/46/EC also remarks that invading privacy may be necessary to safeguard national security, the Directive 2006/24/EC on data retention[9] provides a framework for legislation on the collection and storage of data with the purpose of detecting and prosecuting serious crime. Japan, Russia, the United States and Canada[a] currently have no comprehensive privacy laws.[10]

However, owing to the increasing availability and ubiquity of ICT, these legal initiatives will only result effective if users are concerned with ICT privacy threats and privacy enhancing technologies are widely deployed.

In order to clarify what providers can do with users' information, *privacy policies* were introduced. They are published by service providers and users make a decision on asking for the service based on these policies. Hence, if service providers do not properly follow their privacy policies, users have the right to take legal action against providers. These policy-based schemes are widely used on the Internet by e.g. e-commerce sites that define their privacy policies in e.g. P3P (Platform for Privacy Preferences).[11]

In this chapter we present a summary of the privacy concerns related to ICT. We also point out how ICT can contribute to enhance the privacy

---

[a]The non-European countries in the *Group of Eight*.

of their users. The following topics are addressed:

- Privacy of Internet users.
- Privacy in databases.
- Privacy in ubiquitous computing.

2.2. Privacy and the Internet

Internet is used by millions of people 24 hours a day to access all kinds of information. In addition, Internet technologies allow people to create and share a variety of content. Since the spread of broadband network access technologies, most Internet users are almost permanently connected to the network. This makes them more vulnerable to several attacks and perils, namely viruses and system hacking. Current operating systems include a firewall and antivirus or, at least, give the users advice on installing security software. Fortunately, computer users realize that only with these tools installed and updated their systems may remain safe. However, *users are not concerned about privacy risks*.

In this section we elaborate on some aspects of the privacy of Internet users.

2.2.1. *Monitoring User Activity*

As mentioned before ICT can be used to create personal profiles. The collection of traces from Internet services (e.g. visited websites, frequency of browsing, queries at search engines, etc.) allows the monitoring of user activity. Clearly, using Internet services entails the logging of some data, usually the Internet address of the user and a timestamp. Moreover, some Internet services explicitly ask for personal data in order to proceed with the service. Users are informed about security aspects and information sharing policies of the service. Hence users are conscious of the secure management of their personal data.

Surfing the Internet gives users the impression of a *high degree of privacy*.[5] As a result, most of them do not realize that their activity can be *monitored*.[12] Next, we describe several techniques used to monitor the activity of Internet users.

2.2.1.1. *Tracking Cookies*

Cookies are small pieces of information that web servers are allowed to put into user computers. They are retrieved from user computers to achieve several purposes, e.g. keeping user preferences, remembering the identity of the user and making web sessions feasible. Moreover, a web server is able to collect some information about user habits, since cookies allow the storage of the necessary information.

Tracking cookies[b] are not handled by the websites being visited, but by a central third party (usually an Internet marketing company). Hence, this third party will be able to track users browsing across several websites and, as a result, to build accurate profiles about the interests of these users. This information will be mainly used to deliver advertisements targeted to the interests of the user. Since the activity of users can be monitored, cookies are considered a potential privacy threat.[13,14]

With regard to this, the United States *Online Profiling Recommendations*[15] state that Internet users may be totally unaware of the monitorization of their activities. Fortunately, almost all the Internet marketing companies offer the so-called *optout* options to prevent their cookies from tracking the Internet user.[16] Furthermore, security software may also remove tracking cookies from users systems.

2.2.1.2. *Spyware*

Spyware are small pieces of software installed in a computer without the consent of the user. Their main task is to send information to remote databases so that it can be used to infer user habits. In addition, the worst side of spyware is that they can be programmed to send chat sessions or even passwords to the remote database, undermining confidence in online activities and the effectiveness of transport layer security.[17]

They do not spread like computer viruses do: they can be downloaded and installed by users themselves, because, for instance, they have clicked on a link that promises faster Internet browsing or even protection against spyware. Spyware can come bundled with free software and, potentially, any software behave as spyware. They may also be installed as *browser helpers* or toolbars. Besides tracking browsing habits, spyware may slow down the system and pop-up advertisements randomly. Hence, spyware are annoying and negatively impact the use of Internet.[18]

---

[b]Or third party cookies.

Although a plenty of security tools are intended to clean computer systems, spyware removal is not straightforward.

2.2.1.3. *Social Engineering Attacks*

The aim of social engineering attacks is to manipulate people into disclosing private information. *Phishing* is a social engineering attack that makes use of massive sending of fraudulent e-mails on behalf of trusted entities (e.g. online banking services or Internet service providers). In these e-mails, users are requested to visit a link that points to a fake website. These websites contain a form asking for several information (including private information such as passwords) that must be filled in order to avoid "*serious security problems*".

The prevention of phishing relays on the successful detection of fraudulent e-mails and fake websites. Current versions of web browsers and e-mail managers are capable of warning the user in case of detecting a site or e-mail suspicious of phishing. Besides, fake websites are not authenticated by trustworthy certificate authorities and, in addition, they often present misspellings and grammar errors. In that sense, only the *shrewdness* and *training* of users may prevent them from becoming victims.[19]

2.2.2. *Privacy in Modern Web Services*

During several years, the web has merely been a large public-access database allowing easy information search and retrieval. In contrast, only skilled users were able to create websites. Current Web 2.0[20] services allow the creation and sharing of content in a straightforward manner. In addition, these services provide users with tools to *collaborate* and express opinions. As a result, there is a huge amount of information from individuals in the Internet: comments on a blog post, opinions about a product, pictures in a sharing service, etc. This information is published in social network services, e-commerce sites, etc. Some of these services act as *mashup services*,[21] which gather and analyse the information from several other services. The popular use of these technologies raises new questions on privacy, specially in social networks and e-commerce services.

2.2.2.1. *Privacy in Social Networks*

Social network services allow people to be connected to an online community. Widely used social networks gather millions of users whose goal is to build large groups of *friends*. The use of these large communities has dramatically increased in the last years[c]. In these online services, users publish a profile that includes personal facts, i.e. their birth date, religious and sexual orientation, etc.[d], and can also share pictures and inform of their daily activities. This information can be accessed by virtually every member of the social network.

Social networks have developed privacy policies in which users are responsible for controlling the information they post and deciding who can access it.[23] Hence, most users are aware of the importance of controlling their information. However, there are some situations in which the privacy of non-members is exposed. As an example, if a user posts a picture of her with other people which are not members of the social network, the latter cannot control who views this picture. Moreover, there are some critical situations which are difficult to overcome: e.g. dishonest users creating fake profiles with harmful intentions such as monitoring their friends.[24] As a conclusion, only the consciousness of the users and informing them of a *code of ethics* may mitigate the privacy threats in social networks.

2.2.2.2. *Privacy in E-Commerce*

In e-commerce services the retailer knows what products have been purchased by their customers. This is feasible in real-world shopping as well. Moreover, online vendors store a large amount of data about their customers and their preferences, opinions and purchases. In addition, service providers ask customers for their e-mail address and other personal data. These personal data are transferred to third parties to perform a variety of functions on behalf of the service provider, e.g. delivering packages, sending advertisement e-mails, data analysis for marketing strategies, etc. Online shopping services specify the data collection and management by means of privacy policies that *users implicitly accept when they use the service.*

In online shopping, service providers make use of customer's data to inform about the popularity of their products or to recommend additional purchases to the customers. Moreover, *collaborative filtering* techniques are used to provide online shopping services with complex *recommendation*

---

[c]For example, in January 2008, the most popular social networks had more than 100 million users.

[d]In a recent study[22] on how a large community of students were using a social network, authors claim that a 28% of profiles posted contained a cellphone number and the majority of users disclosed their dating preferences, current relationship status or political views.

systems based on the preferences of their users. If service providers do not handle customer's data properly, users may give biased opinions to the recommendation system or even refrain from using it.[25] In that sense, several privacy-preserving collaborative filtering techniques are proposed: e.g. data perturbation,[26] distributed architectures[27] and data obfuscation.[28]

Modern web services also provide Internet users with social networks specialised in shopping, namely *social commerce* and *social shopping* networks. These networks gather thousands of users with the aim of knowing from each others shopping habits. Hence, users comment on real-world or Internet shopping and rate products, stores and even restaurants. In these cases, privacy threats are similar to those in social networks. Moreover, social commerce networks involve emerging collaborative commerce services, e.g. *group buying* (a model in which several buyers cooperate and buy at a discount price). These new services must rely on privacy enhancing technologies, so as to guarantee their proper development and rapid growing.

2.2.3. *The Big Brothers of Internet*

We have mentioned that data are collected with several purposes: from *cybercrime* acts made by individuals to *marketing strategies* to improve customer service. In this case several marketing companies reach an agreement with some Internet services so they can gather the data from the latter. By means of data mining, marketing and Internet advertising companies are aware of different customer needs.

However, these companies may have only the picture of a specific kind of Internet users. In contrast, the few companies that produce and manage the most popular software and Internet services are able to track the activity of the majority of ICT users. These companies offer several services that can collect information from *virtually every activity done by means of ICT*. In addition to operating systems and productivity software suites, these companies provide users with efficient Internet search engines and offer access to widely used e-mail and instant messaging services. They also offer location-based applications, multimedia sharing and searching engines, calendar managers, etc. Due to the large amount of information collected by these companies, some privacy concerns have arisen.[29,30] These companies have become *the Big Brothers of Internet*.

Regarding search engines, the queries of the users are stored and analyzed to improve search results and to provide *personalized advertisements*. In addition to that, the queries that users send to a search engine can disclose their interests and even their political views or sexual dispositions.[5]

With respect to Internet communications, e-mail and instant messaging services manage the information flow among millions of users. Although most of these communications are private, they can be *scanned* to track offenders and spammers. In order to comply with data retention policies, *instant communications can be stored and e-mail messages retained* even when users have deleted them from the servers. The information in blog services and opinion forums may also be retained and scanned with similar purposes.

Naturally, users are warned by the service providers that all the data collected and stored in their large information services will be managed according to the legislation.

2.3. Privacy in Databases

Most information systems and information technologies rely on databases. They store a variety of data and provide users with several tools for their management. In this section we describe the privacy aspects of databases and how this privacy can be preserved.

The privacy in databases is an ambiguous concept, whose meaning is context-dependent.[31] For instance, in statistical databases containing information from individuals, it refers to *respondent privacy*. In querying search engines, the concern is about preventing service providers from profiling users (hence, it refers to *user privacy*). In this section, we elaborate on both aspects.

2.3.1. *Privacy of the Respondents*

The main goal of respondent privacy in statistical and administrative databases is to prevent the re-identification of the respondents to which the records of a database correspond. If an statistical agency releases or publishes the raw data, there could be a serious privacy loss. It could be thought that deleting the direct identifiers (*e.g.* the name of the respondents) from the data before their release could be enough to guarantee respondent privacy. Unfortunately, protecting the privacy of the respondent is not so straightforward.

Data attributes can be classified as direct identifiers, quasi-identifiers, sensitive information and non-sensitive information. Table 2.1 shows an example data set where *Weight* and *Height* are quasi-identifiers and *Salary*

Table 2.1.   Example data set, where *Name* is an identifier to be suppressed before publishing the data set

Name	ZIP	Weight	Height	Salary	Cancer
John Doe	43152	85	182	26000	Yes
Maggie Simpson	43152	100	165	17000	Yes
Robert Smith	43132	85	183	32000	No
Mary Martin	43152	56	165	22000	No
Brian Johnson	43152	84	205	17400	Yes
Luisa Lopez	43121	65	198	23000	No
James Dawson	43122	66	160	18500	Yes
Peter Petrelli	43144	102	195	43500	Yes
Bridget Jones	43152	108	180	21600	Yes

and *Cancer* are sensitive attributes. We can build a dataset without sensitive information and another one with no direct identifiers, hence the latter can be public. However, if intruders having the data set without sensitive information make queries to the public data set, they will be able to disclose sensitive information (e.g., Maggie Simpson, with *ZIP*=43152, *Weight*=100 and *Height*=165, earns a salary of 17,000 and has cancer[e]). Moreover, intruders can disclose the salary of the "tallest man in a town" simply by querying the public data set.

To protect the privacy of the respondents *statistical disclosure control* (SDC) techniques must be applied to databases before releasing them. There are a variety of SDC techniques to protect databases. For instance, if quasi-identifiers achieve the k-anonymity property[32] (i.e., if a quasi-identifier is indistinguishable from other $k-1$ identifiers), it will become harder to link sensitive attributes with identifiers. k-Anonymity can be achieved by means of several methods, e.g. micro-aggregation. When micro-aggregation is applied, the set of original records is partitioned into several groups in such a way that records in the same group are *similar* to each other and the number of records in each group is at least k. An aggregation operator (for example, the mean for numerical data) is used to compute a centroid for each group. Then, each record in a group is replaced by the group centroid. Table 2.2 shows the data set without identifiers once quasi-identifiers have been masked with $k = 3$. Unfortunately, k-anonimity may not be enough to protect the privacy of the respondents, e.g. if records sharing a combination of quasi-identifiers have the same value for the sensitive attribute. Hence, several properties complement k-anonimity to improve respondent privacy.[33]

---

[e]If the intruder belongs to a health insurance company, the latter may not be interested in offering their products to Maggie Simpson.

Table 2.2. The example data set with identifiers suppressed and attributes *Weight* and *Height* micro-aggregated with $k = 3$

ZIP	Weight	Height	Salary	Cancer
43152	84.6	181.6	26000	Yes
43152	*103.3*	*163.3*	*17000*	Yes
43132	84.6	181.6	32000	No
43152	62.3	163.3	22000	No
43152	84.6	199.3	17400	Yes
43121	62.3	199.3	23000	No
43122	62.3	163.3	18500	Yes
43144	103.3	199.3	43500	Yes
43152	103.3	181.6	21600	Yes

Naturally, applying *masking methods* such as micro-aggregation results in some *information loss*. Thus, SDC techniques look for the best trade off between information loss and *disclosure risk*.[34] That is, both the risk of disclosing private information and the loss of data utility should be kept below reasonable thresholds.

2.3.2. *User Privacy*

User privacy is about guaranteeing the privacy of queries to dynamic databases in order to prevent user profiling and re-identification, for instance:

- Preventing the users of Internet search engines or location-based services from being profiled. As mentioned in Section 2.2.3, Internet search engines claim this profiling is to improve search results.
- Preventing the administrators of the database from getting important information from the queries sent by users. For example, if someone having a great idea queries a database to know if it has already been patented, the administrator, who is aware of the query, is able to patent the idea first.

A naive approach to achieve user privacy is the downloading of the entire database, so the user could query the database locally. Naturally, this is not applicable in large databases such as Internet search engines. *Private Information Retrieval* (PIR) techniques allow the retrieving of information from a database while maintaining the query hidden from the database administrators.

The first PIR proposal[35] uses at least two copies of the same database which do not communicate with each other. A second proposal allows single-database PIR by means of public-key encryption.[36] In these proposals, the database is modeled as a vector from which the user wants to retrieve the i-th component while keeping the index i hidden from the database administrator. Hence it is assumed that the user knows the physical address of the item. On the other hand, these models assume that the server cooperates in the PIR protocol. However, the users are those really interested in their own privacy, whereas the motivation for servers is dubious since PIR limits their profiling capabilities. As a result, these proposals may be unpractical in many real-world scenarios and, hence, new feasible protocols are being proposed.

In *collaborative PIR* schemes, users collaborate with each other in order to be cloaked in a user community[37] or to seek assistance by a peer-to-peer community who submits queries on their behalf. Another strategy, targeted to Internet search engines, consists of a client application that *adds fake keywords* to disguise the real query.[38]

2.4. Privacy in Ubiquitous Computing

Ubiquitous computing allows the integration of information systems to a variety of environments. In addition, it provides the Information Society with a wide range of new applications. In this section we discuss some privacy aspects of two significant and emerging technologies related to ubiquitous computing: *location-based services* and *radio-frequency identification*.

2.4.1. *Location-Based Services*

Location-Based Services (LBS) are gaining importance due to the advances in mobile networks and positioning technologies. They provide users with highly personalised information accessible by means of a variety of mobile devices that are able to locate themselves, e.g. by using a GPS or a fixed network infrastructure with GSM. Mobile devices are ubiquitous and services related to the user's current location proliferate. Examples of LBS are location-based tourist information, route guidance and location-based advertising, etc.

The simplest form of communication in a location-based information transaction involves a user and a provider. The former sends a simple query that includes her location. When users send their current locations, they are implicitly trusting the provider: They assume that the provider manages their location data honestly. Hence service providers can set up their own privacy policies, such as those of Section 2.1.

However, providers may not always be trusted and, consequently, new techniques to achieve the same goals without assuming mutual trust are needed. Next, we review the most significant proposals and we classify them regarding the use of *trusted third parties* (TTPs), i.e. entities that are completely trusted and, hence, theoretically guarantee the privacy of their users.

2.4.1.1. *TTP-Based Schemes*

Most of the solutions to address the privacy problems in LBS are based on TTPs. They are common because they are easy to understand/implement and because they offer a good trade-off between efficiency, accuracy and privacy. Moreover, some of the ideas used in these schemes appeared in more mature fields like e-commerce. Providers are no longer aware of the real locations of their users since trust is handed over to the TTP. Thus, these solutions move users' trust from providers to those TTPs.

Pseudonymisers receive queries from users and, prior to forwarding them to providers, they replace the real identities of the users by fake ones. Note that users must completely trust pseudonymisers, because they know all the information (i.e. identity and location) of the users. The main problem of this approach is that an attacker can infer the real identity of a user by linking a user's location with e.g. a public telephone directory.[39]

Moreover, *anonymisers* perturb real locations to achieve the k-anonymity property (already discussed in Section 2.3.1), so that it becomes harder to bind locations to users. In this context, the location of a given user is k-anonymous if it is indistinguishable from the location of $k - 1$ other users. Many examples of this approach and other similar ones based on cloaking can be found in the literature.[39–41]

2.4.1.2. *TTP-Free Proposals*

From the users' point of view, trusting an intermediate entity may be a problem in some situations. In addition, due to the fact that intermediate entities concentrate the queries of many users, communication delays can appear and the risk of failure is increased. With the aim to overcome these limitations, TTP-free schemes have been proposed. We distinguish those based on collaboration between users/providers from those based on obfuscation.

A first method based on *collaboration between users* is to generate *cloaking areas* in which the real locations of the users remain hidden.[42] The main problem of this approach is that users have to trust other users[f]. On the contrary, k users can add Gaussian noise with null average to their locations so they can freely share their perturbed locations and compute a *global centroid*,[43] which is used to represent them all[g]. Unfortunately, if users repeat this protocol several times without changing their locations, they will be disclosed due to the noise cancellation. To solve this problem, an improvement over this method[44] suggests the use of privacy homomorphisms that guarantee the privacy of the users even when they do not change their location. This method was extended to support non-centralized communications[45] by adding a randomly generated chain of users that share location information to compute a global centroid that identifies them. Finally, users can self-organise in ad-hoc structures, which are used to mix their queries in their way to the providers.[37] This results in a *private location-based information retrieval scheme* in which the provider is unable to link queries with their originating users.

Instead of using privacy protocols between users a different approach based on *user-provider collaboration* is proposed.[46] In this approach, users and providers collaborate to implement a PIR protocol that guarantees the location privacy of the user. Although the idea of using PIR techniques is promising, requiring the provider to collaborate with users seems unrealistic and can be computationally costly.

Obfuscation is a TTP-free alternative to collaboration-based methods that can be understood as the process of degrading the accuracy of the users' location with the aim to protect their privacy. In[47] an obfuscation method based on imprecision is presented. The space is modeled as a graph where vertexes are locations and edges indicate adjacency. Hence, in order to obtain an imprecise location, users send a set of vertexes to the provider instead of a single vertex. The provider cannot distinguish which of the vertexes is the real one. Some other recently proposed obfuscation methods can be found in,[48] where the real locations of users are replaced by circular areas of variable centre and radius, and in,[49] where a method called *SpaceTwist* is proposed. This method generates an anchor (i.e. a fake point) that is used to retrieve information on the k-nearest points of interest. After successive queries, users can determine their closest interest

---

[f]A malicious user can easily obtain and publish the location of other users
[g]By using this procedure, the k users become k-anonymous

point while the provider cannot derive their real locations.

2.4.2. *Radio-Frequency Identification*

Radio-Frequency Identification (RFID) devices will become ubiquitous in the near future. The spectacular market push of RFID technology is due to the interest by large retailers, important manufacturers and governments.

Simple RFID tags can be seen as a proper substitute of bar codes since they are mainly used to identify objects. Almost every object is liable to carry an RFID *tag*[h]. Unlike bar codes, RFID devices allow objects to be identified without visual contact and help in improving and automating many processes. In addition, complex tags with computing hardware embedded open the door to a variety of applications, e.g. contactless authentication.

To integrate RFID tags with information systems, RFID *readers* are needed. A tag will send some information (e.g. the identifier of the product, the result of some cryptographic function, etc.) upon a request from a reader in its range. Consequently, an eavesdropper could collect several information from people carrying tags (e.g. the brand of their clothes, the amount of banknotes they have in their pockets, the use of prosthesis, etc.) Moreover, making use of several readers strategically deployed, tags and the people carrying them can be tracked. Hence, *anonymity* and *untraceability* must be tackled in RFID technology if it is to be widely deployed.[50]

In that sense, several protocols for RFID take into account the privacy concerns of this technology. The very design of the tags can implement a command (i.e. *kill* or *sleep*) to permanently or temporarily disable its ability to answer requests from readers.[51] However, these proposals may not be adequate in many scenarios.

Juels suggested the use of *a collection of pseudonyms*[52] for a given tag with the idea of answering to each query with a different identifier (i.e. pseudonym). An *authorized reader* stores this collection of identifiers and, consequently, it is able to match the identifier with the tag. Thus, a *non-authorized reader* will only see different identifiers. However, if the same reader polls a tag a sufficient number of times, it will be able to collect the whole list of pseudonyms of a given tag. A possible solution to this attack consists in providing the tag with the ability of identifying the reader that is making the queries and refusing to answer when those queries are too frequent. Several other proposals are based on the use of pseudonyms.[53,54]

---

[h]Even banknotes.

As mentioned before, the use of RFID technology in authentication involves the deployment of tags equipped with a variety of *cryptographic hardware*. Hash functions and simple operations are sufficient for simple applications, whereas public key cryptography allows the deployment of more complex services and protocols. These cryptographic capabilities can also be used to provide identification and authentication applications with privacy. In this case, the challenge is to design protocols for *low-cost* tags (i.e. with a minimal set of cryptographic hardware).

As an example, in the *Improved Randomised Hash-locks* proposal[55] the tag uses a hash function to hide the identifier in the identification procedure. Several protocols based on simple cryptography operations can be found in the literature[56–60] and their privacy is analysed as well.[50] Some of these protocols suffer from scalability problems, which can be theoretically solved by means of the deployment of a *distributed structure of readers*.[61]

2.5. Conclusions

In this chapter, we have reviewed the most significant privacy concerns of Information and Communication Technologies. We have focused on privacy of Internet users, privacy related to the use and deployment of databases and privacy aspects of two promising technologies: RFID and location-based services.

Regarding privacy in the Internet, we have shown that service providers are able to profile and track their users. We have also pointed out the privacy threats of social networks. In addition, we have considered spyware and social engineering attacks as powerful techniques to threaten the privacy and security of users. We have illustrated the importance of protecting statistical databases so as to protect the privacy of respondents. Moreover, we have elaborated on privacy preserving techniques when using databases and on preventing queryable information services from profiling their users. Finally, we have reviewed the current trends in protecting the location privacy in location-based services and have pointed out current research topics in privacy in RFID.

In order to guarantee the proper development and universalization of the Information Society, Information and Communication Technologies must offer a set of easy-to-deploy techniques to succeed in protecting the privacy of their users.

Disclaimer and Acknowledgements

The authors are solely responsible for the views expressed in this paper, which do not necessarily reflect the position of UNESCO nor commit that organization. This work was partly supported by the Spanish Ministry of Education through projects TSI2007-65406-C03-01 "E-AEGIS" and CON-SOLIDER CSD2007-00004 "ARES", and by the Government of Catalonia under grant 2005 SGR 00446.

References

1. Universal Declaration of Human Rights. http://www.unhchr.ch/udhr/lang/eng.htm.
2. L. J. Hoffman, Computers and privacy: A survey, *ACM Computing Surveys*. 1(2), 85–103, (1969).
3. J. E. Cohen, DRM and privacy, *Communications of the ACM*. 46(4), 46–49 (Apr., 2003).
4. F. Coudert and J. Dumortier. Intelligent video surveillance networks: Data protection challenges. In *The Third International Conference on Availability, Reliability and Security – ARES*, pp. 975–981. IEEE Computer Society, (2008).
5. L. Kluver et al. ICT and Privacy in Europe: Experiences from technology assessment of ICT and Privacy in seven different European countries. http://epub.oeaw.ac.at/ita/ita-projektberichte/e2-2a44.pdf, (2006).
6. Guidelines on the Protection of Individuals with regard to Automatic Processing of Personal Data . http://eur-lex.europa.eu/.
7. Directive 95/46/EC on the Protection of Individuals with regard to the Processing of Personal Data and on the Free Movement of such Data. http://eur-lex.europa.eu/.
8. Directive 2002/58/EC on Privacy and Electronic Communications. http://europa.eu.int/eur-lex/pri/en/oj/dat/2002/201/20120020731en00370047.pdf.
9. Directive 2006/24/EC on the Retention of Data Generated or Processed in Connection with the Provision of Publicly Available Electronic Communications Services or of Public Communications Networks. http://eur-lex.europa.eu/.
10. Privacy International. The 2007 International Privacy Ranking. http://www.privacyinternational.org.
11. W3C. Platform for privacy preferences (P3P) project. Webpage (October, 2007). URL \url{http://www.w3.org/P3P/}. http://www.w3.org/P3P/.
12. M. Petković and W. Jonker, *Security, Privacy and Trust in Modern Data Management*. (Springer, 2007), 1st edition. ISBN 978-3-540-69860-9.
13. D. Kristol, Http cookies: Standards, privacy, and politics, *ACM Transactions on Internet Technology*. 1(2), 151–198, (2001).

14. E. Sit and K. Fu, Web cookies: Not just a privacy risk, *Communications of the ACM.* **44**(9), 120, (2001).
15. United States Federal Trade Commission. Online Profiling Recommendations. http://www.ftc.gov/os/2000/07/onlineprofiling.htm (July, 2000).
16. P. Dixon. Consumer tips: How to opt-out of cookies that track you. http://www.worldprivacyforum.org/cookieoptout.html (June, 2006).
17. Q. Hu and T. Dinev, Is spyware an internet nuisance or public menace?, *Communications of the ACM.* **48**(8), 61–66, (2005).
18. R. Thompson, Why spyware poses multiple threats to security, *Communications of the ACM.* **48**(8), 41–43, (2005).
19. P. Kumaraguru, Y. Rhee, A. Acquisti, L. F. Cranor, J. I. Hong, and E. Nunge. Protecting people from phishing: the design and evaluation of an embedded training email system. In eds. M. B. Rosson and D. J. Gilmore, *Proceedings of the SIGCHI conference on Human factors in computing systems*, pp. 905–914. ACM, (2007).
20. T. O'Reilly. What is web 2.0: Design patterns and business models for the next generation of software. http://www.oreillynet.com/pub/a/oreilly/tim/news/2005/09/30/what-is-web-20.html (September, 2005).
21. Mashup services (wikipedia). http://en.wikipedia.org/wiki/Mashup_(web_application_hybrid).
22. R. Gross, A. Acquisti, and H. J. H. III. Information revelation and privacy in online social networks. In eds. V. Atluri, S. D. C. di Vimercati, and R. Dingledine, *Workshop on Privacy in the Electronic Society*, pp. 71–80. ACM, (2005).
23. Facebook privacy policy. http://www.facebook.com/policy.php.
24. L. Schiffman. False friends: How fake facebook profiles open the door to monitoring. http://www.northbynorthwestern.com/2007/10/4687/facebook-friends/.
25. S. Berkovsky, N. Borisov, Y. Eytani, T. Kuflik, and F. Ricci. Examining users' attitude towards privacy-preserving collaborative filtering. In *Workshop on Data Mining for User Modeling, at the International Conference on User Modeling*, pp. 16–22, (2007).
26. Zhang, Ford, and Makedon. A privacy-preserving collaborative filtering scheme with two-way communication. In *CECOMM: ACM Conference on Electronic Commerce*, (2006).
27. W. Ahmad and A. A. Khokhar. An architecture for privacy preserving collaborative filtering on web portals. In *IEEE Industry Applications Society Annual Meeting*, pp. 273–278. IEEE Computer Society, (2007). URL http://doi.ieeecomputersociety.org/10.1109/IAS.2007.15.
28. R. Parameswaran and D. M. Blough. Privacy preserving collaborative filtering using data obfuscation. In *IEEE International Conference on Granular Computing – GrC*, pp. 380–386. IEEE, (2007). URL http://doi.ieeecomputersociety.org/10.1109/GRC.2007.129.
29. J. Hopkins, Once-brotherly image turns big brotherly, *USA Today* (December. 2005).

30. M. Malone. Is Google Turning Into Big Brother? http://abcnews.go.com/print?id=5727509 (September, 2008).

31. J. Domingo-Ferrer. A three-dimensional conceptual framework for database privacy. In eds. W. Jonker and M. Petkovic, *Secure Data Management*, vol. 4721, *Lecture Notes in Computer Science*, pp. 193–202. Springer, (2007).

32. P. Samarati, Protecting respondents' identities in microdata release, *IEEE Transactions on Knowledge and Data Engineering*. **13**(6), 1010–1027, (2001).

33. J. Domingo-Ferrer and V. Torra. A critique of k-anonymity and some of its enhancements. In *The Third International Conference on Availability, Reliability and Security - ARES*, pp. 990–993. IEEE Computer Society, (2008).

34. J. Domingo-Ferrer and J. M. Mateo-Sanz, Practical data-oriented microaggregation for statistical disclosure control, *IEEE Transactions on Knowledge and Data Engineering*. **14**(1), 189–201, (2002).

35. Chor, Goldreich, Kushilevitz, and Sudan. Private information retrieval. In *FOCS: IEEE Symposium on Foundations of Computer Science (FOCS)*, (1995).

36. E. Kushilevitz and R. Ostrovsky. Replication is not needed: Single database, computationally-private information retrieval (extended abstract). In *FOCS: IEEE Symposium on Foundations of Computer Science (FOCS)*, (1997).

37. D. Rebollo-Monedero, J. Forné, L. Subirats, A. Solanas, and A. Martínez-Ballesté. A collaborative protocol for private retrieval of location-based information. In *Proceedings of the IADIS International Conference on the e-Society*, (2009).

38. Goopir. http://crises-deim.urv.cat/unescoprivacychair/.

39. M. Gruteser and D. Grunwald. Anonymous usage of location-based services through spatial and temporal cloaking. In *Proceesings of MobiSys 2003: The First International Conference on Mobile Systems, Applications, and Services.*, pp. 31 – 42. USENIX Association, ACM, Sigmobile, ACM (May, 2003).

40. B. Gedik and L. Liu. A customizable k-anonymity model for protecting location privacy. In *Proceedings of the IEEE International conference on Distributed Computing Systems (ICDS'05)*, pp. 620 – 629, (2005).

41. B. Gedik and L. Liu, Protecting location privacy with personalized k-anonymity: Architecture and algorithms, *IEEE Transactions on Mobile Computing*. **7**(1), 1 – 18 (January, 2008).

42. C. Chow, M. F. Mokbel, and X. Liu. A peer-to-peer spatial cloaking algorithm for anonymous location-based services. In *GIS '06: Proceedings of the 14th annual ACM international symposium on Advances in geographic information systems*, pp. 171–178. ACM (November, 2006).

43. J. Domingo-Ferrer. Microaggregation for database and location privacy. In eds. O. Etzion, T. Kuflik, and A. Motro, *NGITS*, vol. 4032, pp. 106–116. Springer, (2006).

44. A. Solanas and A. Martínez-Ballesté. Privacy protection in location-based services through a public-key privacy homomorphism. In eds. J. Lopez, P. Samarati, and J. L. Ferrer, *EuroPKI*, vol. 4582, *Lecture Notes in Computer Science*, pp. 362–368. Springer, (2007).

45. A. Solanas and A. Martínez-Ballesté, A TTP-free protocol for location pri-

vacy in location-based services, *Computer Communications.* **31**(6), 1181–1191 (April, 2008).

46. G. Ghinita, P. Kalnis, A. Khoshgozaran, C. Shahabi, and K. Tan. Private queries in location based services: Anonymizers are not necessary. In *SIGMOD '08: Proceedings of the 2008 ACM SIGMOD international conference on Management of data*, pp. 121 – 132. Vancouver, BC, Canada, ACM (June, 2008).

47. M. Duckham and L. Kulit. A formal model of obfuscation and negotiation for location privacy. In *Pervasive Computing*, vol. 3468, *LNCS*, pp. 152–170. Springer Berlin / Heidelberg, (2005).

48. C. A. Ardagna, M. Cremonini, E. Damiani, S. De Capitani di Vimercati, and P. Samarati. Location privacy protection through obfuscation-based techniques. In eds. S. Baker and G. Ahn, *Data and Applications Security*, vol. 4602, *LNCS*, pp. 47 – 60. IFIP, (2007).

49. M. L. Yiu, C. S. Jensen, X. Huang, and H. Lu. Spacetwist: Managing the trade-offs among location privacy, query performance, and query accuracy in mobile services. In *IEEE 24th International Conference on Data Engineering ICDE'08*, pp. 366–375, (2008).

50. K. Ouafi and R. C.-W. Phan. Privacy of recent RFID authentication protocols. In *ISPEC*, vol. 4991, *Lecture Notes in Computer Science*, pp. 263–277. Springer, (2008).

51. A. Juels, R. L. Rivest, and M. Szydlo. The blocker tag: Selective blocking of RFID tags for consumer privacy. In *SIGSAC: 10th ACM Conference on Computer and Communications Security.* ACM, (2003).

52. A. Juels. Minimalist cryptography for low-cost RFID tags. In eds. C. Blundo and S. Cimato, *Security in Communication Networks*, vol. 3352, *Lecture Notes in Computer Science*, pp. 149–164. Springer, (2004).

53. C. Castelluccia and M. Soos. Secret Shuffling: A Novel Approach to RFID Private Identification. In *Conference on RFID Security*, pp. 169–180, Malaga, Spain (July, 2007).

54. J. Cichon, M. Klonowski, and M. Kutylowski. Privacy protection in dynamic systems based on RFID tags. In *International Workshop on Pervasive Computing and Communication Security (PerSec)*, pp. 235–240. IEEE Computer Society, (2007).

55. A. Juels and S. A. Weis. Defining strong privacy for RFID. In *International Workshop on Pervasive Computing and Communication Security (PerSec)*, pp. 342–347. IEEE Computer Society, (2007).

56. M. Ohkubo, K. Suzuki, and S. Kinoshita. Efficient hash-chain based RFID privacy protection scheme. In *International Conference on Ubiquitous Computing - Ubicomp, Workshop Privacy: Current Status and Future Directions*, (2004).

57. G. Tsudik. YA-TRAP: Yet another trivial RFID authentication protocol. In *PerCom Workshops*, pp. 640–643. IEEE Computer Society, (2006).

58. R. D. Pietro and R. Molva. Information confinement, privacy, and security in RFID systems. In *ESORICS*, vol. 4734, *Lecture Notes in Computer Science*, pp. 187–202. Springer, (2007).

59. M. Conti, R. Di Pietro, L. V. Mancini, and A. Spognardi. FastRIPP: RFID Privacy Preserving protocol with Forward Secrecy and Fast Resynchronization. In *33th Annual Conference of the IEEE Industrial Electronics Society (IEEE IECON 07)*, pp. 52–57, Taipei, Taiwan (November, 2007).

60. S.-C. Kim, S.-S. Yeo, and S. K. Kim. MARP: Mobile Agent for RFID Privacy Protection. In eds. J. Domingo-Ferrer, J. Posegga, and D. Schreckling, *International Conference on Smart Card Research and Advanced Applications – CARDIS*, Lecture Notes in Computer Science, Tarragona, Spain (April, 2006). IFIP, Springer-Verlag.

61. A. Solanas, J. Domingo-Ferrer, A. Martínez-Ballesté, and V. Daza, A distributed architecture for scalable private RFID tag identification, *Computer Networks*. **51**(9), 2268–2279, (2007).

Chapter 3

An Overview of Information Security

Arturo Ribagorda Garnacho, Ana Isabel González-Tablas Ferreres,
* Almudena Alcaide Raya

*Universidad Carlos III de Madrid, Computer Science Department,
Avda. de la Universidad 30, 28911 Leganés, Madrid, Spain*
{*árturo, aigonzal, aalcaide*}*@inf.uc3m.es*

At the same time as information security has become a critical issue when deploying information and communication systems, it has also required more and more, the collaboration of other computer science fields such as artificial intelligence. This chapter begins with the description of several vulnerabilities present nowadays in information systems, as well as the threats that they represent and, the motivation behind the different attacks. In this chapter, we also describe the most common security countermeasures that are applied at each step of a system access point operation. Firstly, we consider authentication systems, with special attention to biometric and challenge-response systems, followed by access control models and the mechanisms used to implement them. After that, the classification of cryptosystems, their mathematical foundations and several possible attacks are shown. Following, the digital signature mechanism and the foundations of its operation, including also the concepts of public key certificates and Certificate Authorities are described. Finally, audit logs are considered and main aspects of physical security are reviewed.

Contents

3.1. Introduction

In the past fifteen years we have witnessed the rapid growth and consolidation of information security, as one of the fields that contributes to Information and Communication Technologies (ICT). The main reason for this evolution has been the spread of Internet in companies, governmental organizations and, in general, the whole society, which has resulted in a remarkable increase of the risks that ICT have to consider. There is no doubt that information systems were more secure when they were isolated and accessible only by a restricted and controlled set of professionals. Another reason, related to the former one, is that society has become more and more aware of the risks involved in the transmission of personal data through Internet, with or without the consent of data owners (these data may even refer to the most private aspects of people), and the processing of these data by companies and individuals.

Information security deployment has been accompanied by an in depth analysis of new techniques and security protocols which, in the past few years, has been strongly influenced by Artificial Intelligence (AI). Research in this field is showing an increasing interest on security. Biometric and intrusion detection systems, cryptanalysis techniques and data mining computer audit logs are some of the growing number of examples, where AI techniques are being applied to information security. It is clear that, at least in the foreseeable future, both fields will be collaborating closely.

3.2. Vulnerabilities

Despite the consciousness of the value of the data being processed and the need of protecting these data in an adequate manner, it does not appear that we are succeeding in building more secure systems and products. The number of vulnerabilities in our systems increases every year, as US-CERT (US Computer Emergency Response Team) annual reports show and, it appears that we are not able to end this trend despite the efforts of developers. In 1995, 171 vulnerabilities were reported whereas, in 2007, they were 7.236: the resulting mean is 20 vulnerabilities per day. These statistics follow a yearly upward trend (with the exception of years 2003 and 2007) which does not seem to reverse.

There are several reasons for this evolution. On the one hand, some aspects are related to the transformation of systems and technologies from isolated and not very sophisticated ones to rather complex, interconnected and, what it is even worse, interdependent. On the other hand, the way in which people work and use IC Technologies has also influenced this trend. Firstly, it is very common to design, develop and implement software and, to a lesser extent hardware, in an inappropriate way; secondly, its use by people with null training and poor security awareness is quite common. Moreover, criminals are more eager every day to find vulnerabilities which provide them profit and/or personal satisfaction, the first reason being more frequent in the past few years.

Beginning with the first reason, we have to confront the most complex systems that humanity has ever built. Why is this so relevant for security? The explanation is a basic principle of security which specifies that complexity is one of its worst enemies. Therefore, if we build simple systems, we will be able to control their risks whereas when building more complex systems their security gets rapidly out of our control. However, it is clear that the tendency is to build more and more complex systems. For example, the size of the first versions of Windows operating system consisted of a few millions of lines of code, while it is estimated that the size of the more recent Windows XP and Vista versions exceeds the quantity of 50 million. This trend is currently present in all products available in the market.

Moreover, it was relatively easy to protect isolated computers with controlled physical and logical access points. By contrast, networks with unlimited extension, variable topology and uncontrolled access points have turned computers into naive nodes. Consequently, malicious computers can silently attack our systems from any location, in an unnoticed way and, most of the time, with total impunity.

Besides, the rapid substitution of wired transmission channels (such as twisted pair, coaxial cable and optical fiber) with wireless ones poses additional difficulties on the task of securing our systems. Wireless transmission channels are more easily intercepted and, therefore, the communication protocols and technologies used (*e.g.*, Bluetooth, Wi-Fi, Wi-Max, etc.) are more vulnerable to unauthorized access, denial of service and impersonation attacks, etc.

The continuous increase of vulnerabilities in systems does not only depend on technological factors but also on human ones. Firstly, the inexperience of some computer science engineers often results in not taking into account security aspects during system design and analysis phases. Later on, developers may attempt to integrate security mechanisms during the coding phase or, once vulnerabilities are noticed after the system has already been implemented. This lack of prevision leads to incorporate security as a system patch, instead of considering it during the whole system development process. Secondly, users' lack of training, or at least, conscientiousness, gives rise to involuntary mistakes that put their systems and the data they maintain into risk. Some examples of actions that cause vulnerabilities are the usage of poor quality passwords, the careless way of browsing the Web, the incompetence to distinguish a secure connection from an insecure one, the negligent opening of electronic mails, etc.

3.3. Threats

Individuals and organizations have taken advantage of all these vulnerabilities to obtain relevant information about people or organizations. Traditionally, individual attackers behaved this way to satisfy their ego, while organizations were motivated by the possibility of obtaining commercial advantage over their competitors (industrial espionage). Nowadays, both kinds of attacker seek financial profit, being that the main motivation behind this type of crime.

To achieve their goals, highly sophisticated attacks, conceptual and technically, have been designed. Most of the time, attacks are combined with social engineering techniques, which take advantage of users' ignorance, naivety or ambition, by using psychological methods. Even worse, some of these attacks are published on the Internet where everyone can access them freely or after payment. Consequently, attack methods have spread across the world and any Internet user might become a potential criminal independently of their skills, making the number of possible attackers grow exponentially.

Among these attacks, those performed by malicious software (*i.e.*, malware) stand out. Well-known types of malware are viruses, worms, backdoors, Trojan horses, etc. Nowadays, it is rather unusual to design malware that falls exclusively in one of the aforementioned categories; instead, current malware is usually built as a combination of them. Also remarkable are those kind of attack whose aim is to collapse a service (*e.g.*, distributed denial of service attacks, DDoS), to intercept communications (*e.g.*, using sniffers), to alter data (*e.g.*, spoofing and pharming attacks), or to generate fraudulent information (*e.g.*, hijacking attacks).

3.4. Countermeasures

To face such a high number of serious threats , several countermeasures have been developed. These countermeasures attempt to guarantee information confidentiality (information is known only by the authorized users), integrity (information is precise and complete) and availability (information is accessed exclusively by authorized users in a predetermined way and time).

According to what a countermeasure consists of and at what stage it is applied, they can be classified as prevention, detection, correction and recovery. Prevention measures try to prevent attacks before they happen, detection measures attempt to detect attacks at an early phase, correction measures aim at thwarting attacks while they are taking place and finally, recovery measures attempt to restore the system to its previous state. Some examples of these countermeasures are firewalls, intrusion detection systems (IDS), honeypots and contingency plans.

According to the nature of a countermeasure they can be classified as technical, physical, administrative and organizational. Technical countermeasures are those that act from within the system that is being protected. Physical countermeasures act on the protected system and its surrounding systems to prevent attacks that come from the outside. Finally, those that are implemented with policies, rules and procedures fall within the administrative and organizational category.

Focusing on technical countermeasures, it is worth remarking that they are commonly referred to as security services (mainly in network security contexts). In this case they are seen as abstract concepts that specify the kind of protection a system or product should provide. Some examples of security services are confidentiality, entity authentication, integrity, availability, non repudiation, etc.

These security services are implemented by what is referred to as mechanisms. Mechanisms act from within the protected system to provide a specific security service. More precisely, a security mechanism is a physical or logical device that is responsible for providing a security service or implementing a security model. Some mechanisms provide a single security service while others provide several of them. The other way round, it can happen that a certain service can be provided by several mechanisms. Some of the most important security mechanisms are authentication systems, data cipher systems (they provide confidentiality services), hash functions (they provide integrity services), digital signatures (they provide integrity and non repudiation services), etc.

3.5. Authentication mechanisms

Authentication mechanisms are the first barrier that a user has to overcome to enter a system. For that reason, and because once a user is inside the system, an attacker has many more opportunities to achieve his goal; it is one of the most important mechanisms to be applied. Authentication mechanisms are often combined with identification mechanisms and it is usual to refer to this combination as authentication. Identification means that an entity (the claimant) alleges to a second entity (the prover) to have certain identity, whereas authentication means to prove this identity to the prover. Although they are commonly used together, the strength of a combined mechanism relies on the authentication part, which we will describe in the next paragraphs.

Authentication implies that the claimant shows some credential to the prover. Traditionally, three types of credentials have been used: some information that is shared between the user and the system ("something you know"), some object that is owned by the user ("something you have") or some biometric characteristic or individual behaviour ("something you are"). Each type of credential results on a different method of authentication.

Authentication systems can be seen as the front door to information systems which has brought about an increasing interest in reinforcing this type of mechanism. It is possible to combine several of these methods to have stronger authentication systems, which are known as two or three factor authentication systems; for example, having a smart card and also knowing some password. Two and, to a less extent, three factor authentication systems are more common every day.

3.5.1. *Something you know*

Knowing something, such as a password or a PIN, is the most commonly used method of authentication. However, careless password selection (easily guessable) and the difficulties for remembering strong passwords raise a problem difficult to solve: passwords easy to recall are easily guessable and passwords difficult to guess are recalled with difficulty. Despite its weaknesses, this method still stands as the most frequent form of authentication, mainly because it is very easy to implement and well accepted by all users.

However, using the same password for a long period (they are usually changed after several months of use) is completely inappropriate when authentication is done to access a server or a network node. The transmission of a password through a network, either in clear or in an encrypted mode, involves a high risk of interception and, therefore, of impersonation. One time passwords (OTP) can be used to overcome this problem as they are credentials that change every time that a user attempts to enter the system.

There are several methods to build one time passwords systems. For example, in the method used in GSM communications, each user and the server share a password that is used to encrypt a random number (a challenge) which is sent in every connection from the server to the user. In every connection attempt, the server sends a new challenge, so its encryption will be different each time. If an attacker intercepts the transmitted credential, it will not imply an identity theft. The reason is that, in the next connection attempt, the server will send a different challenge and the attacker, not knowing the key to encrypt it, will not be able to send back the appropriate credential.

However, the current trend to build authentication systems is to use digital signatures. The server sends a challenge to the user, who signs the challenge and sends it back to the server. The server only has to verify the signature of the user.

3.5.2. *Something you are*

The disadvantages of basing authentication systems on recalling a string of characters (difficulties for remembering correctly, the need of changing them periodically, etc.) has raised the interest in automatizing some of the ancient authentication methods that are used by human beings (and also by animals): our anthropological characteristics, which include biological ones. Indeed, the credentials that we have mainly used throughout history have been our biometric characteristics: our face, our voice, our eyes, etc. However, the development of biometric authentication systems has been slower than expected, mainly because of the difficulties to achieve their goals and also because of the cost of the necessary equipment. On the other hand, current progress in artificial intelligent techniques is helping to increase the use of biometric systems and their development.

Biometric systems may be of different types but all of them have the advantage of not requiring the recalling of long character strings, as authentication data is incorporated in the user itself. Biometric data can be physiological or behavioral and, once it is measured, it is compared with biometric data that has been previously collected and stored. Some examples of biometric data, beyond the already mentioned, are the typing style, the characteristics of handwritten signature, mouse movements, etc.

Among the first type of characteristics, the properly called biometric, the fingerprints are the most used, followed by the iris and retinal vein pattern, hand geometry, palm prints, voice, face, etc. In all of them, a pattern with the most distinctive characteristics is constructed from a set of images or recordings of the biometric feature in consideration. Usually, the pattern has a notably smaller size in bytes compared to the size of the original images or recordings. During the authentication process, a new image or recording is obtained and a fresh pattern is deduced and compared with previously stored ones.

Although there are unquestionable advantages, there also exist several obvious disadvantages. First of all, these credentials are not secret: face, voice, fingerprint and, to less extent, iris and retina can be registered by anyone. Additionally, unlike passwords, these credentials cannot be changed (obviously except for the use of surgery) once there exist any suspicion that they have been jeopardized. For this reason, it is not advisable to send the patterns through any network for its comparison with other biometric data stored in a remote database.

Secondly, many of the strictly biometric systems are not easily accepted by the users. Main reasons are the apprehension of presenting the ocular globe, the hand, etc. to the authentication system and the users' reluctance to give this kind of personal data to companies or organizations even when the purpose asserted by the companies is user authentication exclusively.

Furthermore, biometric authentication devices are complicated to adjust. The main reason is that their most relevant parameters, rate of false acceptance (percentage of impostors that are accepted) and rate of false rejection (percentage of legitimate users that are rejected), are inversely proportional. Therefore, reducing the first one implies an increase of the second one, and vice versa. This situation has increased interest in multi-modal systems which combine several biometric authentication methods.

Finally, it is worth emphasizing that biometric credentials are often not used for authentication purposes but for both identification and authentication simultaneously. In that case, the credential presented by the user (his biometric data) is compared with the data stored in a database that contains the biometric data of all users until a match is found. This procedure is called 1:N, because one pattern is compared with N. It is more time consuming than purely biometric authentication procedures, which do not aim to identify the user using the biometric data. In purely biometric authentication procedures (excluding identification), the user first introduces an identification code that is used as an index to retrieve certain authentication data from the database. Then, the retrieved data is compared with the credential presented by the user. This procedure is called 1:1 because one pattern is compared exclusively with another one, and it is the only type of biometric system used when the number of users is high. Although rare, 1:1 authentication systems based on passwords can also be found.

3.5.3. *Something you have*

With regard to the last kind of authentication systems, those based on the possession of an object, it is worth mentioning that nowadays, there is only one system of this type being used and, it is based on the possession of a smart card, usually with cryptographic capacities. In two factor authentication systems (those that combine two of the three types of credentials), the possession of a smart cards is complemented with the knowledge of some data shared between the user and the card, or the matching of some user's biometric characteristics with a biometric pattern stored in the card. Systems that combine the possession of a smart card with some biometric measure stored exclusively in the smart card present the advantage of maintaining users' biometric data under his own control (and not under the control of a company or organization), which prevents all possible concerns related to personal data privacy.

3.6. Access control mechanisms

After user authentication, and provided that it has been successful, access
control service takes place. This service is implemented by mechanisms
with the same name. Access control services have the goal to allow users
to access the system resources which they are authorized to use. For this
reason, they are sometimes named as authorization services. It is common
that a user must pass through several access control points before access
is granted. For example, a user wishing to access certain registries of a
database should probably have to pass first the operating system access
control mechanism and afterwards, the database one.

3.6.1. *Access control policies*

A central aspect in access control services is the access control policy which
is comprised by the rules that define who, under which conditions and
what data can be accessed. The rules can be specified in high or low levels
according to the desired grade of granularity.

There are two main types of high level policies: open and closed. In
the first one, access is granted by default except otherwise stated. On
the contrary, in the second one, access is denied by default except if it is
explicitly allowed. Obviously, the second ones are much more reliable than
the first ones and, they are actually the only ones which have been broadly
implemented. For example, firewalls are usually configured by default to
deny all connections but those specifically directed to some port or services.

In other words, access control services establish a filter between the
subjects and the objects they want to access. This filter has to be applied
in all access attempts and cannot be avoided in any case. Firewalls are
again a good example of this concept.

3.6.2. *Access control models*

The terms subject, object and right to access have a specific meaning in
the access control models proposed to provide access control services. A
subject is any active entity that may access any resource in the system;
users, processes or programs are the usual subjects in the context of access
control models. An object is any passive entity that can be accessed by
another entity; examples of objects are physical resources, pages of memory,
registries, data, etc. Note that a program may be either a subject or an
object. Finally, a right or privilege to access is the authorization that a

subject has on certain object; some examples of rights of access are reading, writing, execution, etc.

3.6.2.1. *Access matrix model*

The most widely spread access control model is the access matrix model. It was first proposed by Graham and Denning[1] in 1972 and by Lampson[2] in 1974, and it was later improved by Harrison, Ruzzo and Ullman[3] in 1976. In this latter model, the names of the subjects identify the rows of the matrix and the names of the objects identify the columns. Each entry of the matrix contains the access rights of the corresponding subject (row) on the corresponding object (column).

The implementation of this model can be very problematic if the system, as it is most common, has a high number of subjects and objects. In this situation, a very large matrix must be created and its storage can result unfeasible. Instead, each column or row is independently stored, keeping only the entries that contain some access right.

If columns are used, the mechanism is known as Access Control List (ACL). For each object, the subjects that are allowed to access it with an indication of the specific rights are specified. This is the access control mechanism that was first implemented and currently the most broadly spread.

If rows are used, the mechanism is known as list of capabilities. It specifies, for each subject, the set of objects that the subject can access with an indication of the specific rights. Implementations of this model are less common because its maintenance is more tedious, given that it is usually the set of subjects the one that suffers more changes during a system normal operation (insertion and deletion of users, update of responsibilities, etc.)

The access matrix model and the mechanisms used to implement it regulate the access of subjects to the objects but they do not take care of what these subjects do with the objects once the subjects have access to them. Thus, once a subject has acquired some information, the models do not prevent him from spreading such data. In other words, the owner of an object has the discretional right of granting other subjects to access that object. This is the reason why this model is also called discretionary access control model.

3.6.2.2. *Mandatory access control models*

Mandatory or non-discretionary access control models appear to counteract the possible diffusion allowed by discretionary models. Mandatory models aim to control the flow of information. These models are specified by the objects, the subjects and a set of ordered security levels used to classify objects and subjects. First, mandatory access control models classify objects and subjects into a set of categories, which are assigned certain security level regarding confidentiality or integrity . Therefore, each object and subject has a security label comprised by a category and a security level. When a subject wants to access certain object, access is granted depending on the comparison of their security labels. Since the appearance of the Bell and LaPadula model[4] in 1973 and the Biba model[5] in 1977, numerous mandatory models have been and are being proposed.

3.7. Data encipherment mechanisms

Data encipherment has been, par excellence, the security mechanism mostly used since ancestral times. There are solid evidences of its use back in the Classical Antiquity and even before. However, because of the lack of formal theoretical foundations, up until 1949 data encryption had not been considered a scientific area.[6]

The discipline that addresses data encryption is called cryptography (from kryptos and grapho, which mean covered, or hidden and writing respectively), and it is defined as the study of the principles, methods and means to hide the meaning of a message but not the message itself. It is important to remark this distinction as there is another discipline, steganography (from steganos and grapho, which mean hidden and writing respectively), which addresses the study of the principles, methods and means to hide a message. Thus, cryptography allows to see the message but not to interpret it, whereas steganography makes the message itself invisible.

In detail, a cryptosystem is comprised by:

- A sender (usually known by Alice and represented by A) that creates a message in clear or plaintext that belongs to a space of messages $M = \{m_1, m_2, ...\}$. Plaintexts are formed using a given alphabet and must follow a set of syntactic and semantic rules.
- An encryption device, which transforms the plaintext in an unintelligible message known as ciphertext or cryptogram. The ciphertext belongs to a space of ciphertexts or cryptograms $C = \{c_1, c_2, ...\}$. The alphabet used

to form ciphertexts can be the same as the one used for plaintexts or a different one. An encryption function belongs to the family $E_k : M \to C$ and is determined by an encryption key $k \in K = \{k_1, k_2, ...\}$.

- A storage or transmission channel.
- A decryption device who works inversely to the encryption device, that is, it produces the plaintext from the ciphertext. The decryption function belongs to the family $E_k^{-1} : C \to M$ and is determined by a decryption key $k^{-1} \in k^{-1} = \{k_1^{-1}, k_2^{-1}, ...\}$.
- A receiver (usually known by Bob and represented by B).

Moreover, a protocol to convey the interchange or negotiation of keys must be added. Additionally, it is assumed that there exists an attacker who wants to intercept the message and decipher it using cryptanalysis techniques.

The fundamental elements of a cryptosystem are the encryption and decryption devices, which can be implemented by hardware or by software. An encryption device consists of an encryption algorithm which depends on a parameter called encryption key. Similarly, a decryption device consists of a decryption algorithm that depends on a decryption key. Sometimes, the encryption device also includes a key generator system which is in charge of creating the encryption and decryption keys.

The encryption algorithm must be computationally irreversible; that is, it should be very difficult to reverse with the current processing power unless some additional information is known, ideally the decryption key. Thus, any entity knowing this information will be able to decrypt the ciphertext and obtain the plaintext (provided that the decryption algorithms are publicly known, as it usually happens). Even knowing the algorithms, it should still be very difficult to infer the plaintext from the ciphertext without knowing the required information.

Ideally, the key generator must produce random keys, although if it relies on an algorithm it will produce, at most, pseudorandom data which in the best case scenario will pass pseudorandomness criteria, among which Golomb's postulates stand out.

According to Simmons,[6] the era of scientific cryptography began with Claude Shannon. Shannon establishes the two general principles which must inspire the construction of an encryption algorithm: the diffusion and the confusion.[7]

Confusion means that the statistical properties of the symbols in the ciphertext do not reveal any information about the statistical properties of the symbols in the plaintext. This is done to prevent a cryptanalyst to gain information about the plaintext from the ciphertext.

Diffusion means that the influence of a symbol of the plaintext affects as many symbols as possible in the ciphertext. Thus, the statistical properties of one of the symbols in the plaintext diffuse over the majority of the ciphertext, which leads to a concealment of the statistical properties of the plaintext given the ciphertext. Provided that plaintext and ciphertext are represented as binary numbers, this principle is exemplified by making each bit in the ciphertext to depend on all the bits in the plaintext.

Extending these ideas about the diffusion, it is also desirable that the alteration of any symbol of the key, influences as many symbols as possible in the ciphertext.

Another two concepts frequently used in the design of binary algorithms are the avalanche criterion and the strict avalanche criterion. The first one is satisfied by those algorithms in which, if a bit in the plaintext is changed, a percentage of the bits in the ciphertext changes. The second criterion implies that each bit of the ciphertext must change with one-half probability whenever a bit in the plaintext changes.

3.7.1. *Attacks*

The science that addresses the study of systematic methods to decrypt encrypted information is called cryptanalysis. Attacks with this goal are denoted as cryptanalytical and its practitioners are called cryptanalysts. In some sense, cryptanalysis and cryptography can be considered opposite sciences.

One of the assumptions taken when studying the defensive methods against cryptanalysts is that they have access to at least a whole cryptogram. It is also assumed that cryptanalysts know the encryption algorithm but not the decryption key. This assumption relies on Kerchoffs' principle that establishes that the security of an encryption algorithm must be based exclusively on the secrecy of the key and not on the algorithm that has been used.[8] Therefore, a cryptanalyst's main goal is to obtain the decryption key so he can not only produce the plaintext that corresponds to the ciphertext he knows, but also to decrypt every ciphertext he may intercept. A less ambitious goal is to produce the plaintext that corresponds to a certain ciphertext. In any case, if it is possible to find out one of both, a plaintext for a given ciphertext or the decryption key, the encryption algorithm is said to be vulnerable or broken.

There are several situations that a cryptanalyst may face, and therefore, several types of attacks which he may elaborate. Next we will describe the most relevant of these attacks.

The most unfavorable case scenario for a cryptanalyst is that in which he has access only to the ciphertext. In this case, the attack is denominated ciphertext-only attack. Under this assumption, and even knowing the encryption algorithm, the only options left to the attacker are to statistically analyze the ciphertext (usually, in order to search repeated patterns) or to try all possible decryption keys in the space K^{-1}. For obvious reasons, the latter attack is known as exhaustive search or brute force attack; the attacker's probability of success increases as the size of the decryption key space decreases.

A second case, more advantageous for the attacker, takes place when he knows a cryptogram and the corresponding plaintext, as well as the encryption algorithm. To infer the plaintext which corresponds to certain parts of a ciphertext can be quite easy. For example, messages transmitted by means of standard protocols have the same symbols in the same positions and, certain fields (sender, receiver, etc.) can be easily guessed. This type of cryptanalysis is called known-plaintext attack.

The best situation for the cryptanalyst is that in which he can chose a plaintext of any length and can obtain the corresponding ciphertext. This kind of attack is denoted as chosen-plaintext attack. This attack may take place when an attacker has access to a file in a computer containing the encrypted passwords of its users (as it happened in Unix); the attacker can collect a high number of plaintext-ciphertext pairs by introducing a number of different passwords.

Finally, another common attack is the one called chosen-ciphertext attack. In this case, the cryptanalyst chooses a ciphertext (for example, a chain of zeroes) and decrypts it to study the characteristics of the plaintext and, thus infer the key. A typical example of this type of attack may take place when the key is stored in a secure device and it cannot be accessed by users. This attack may also take place in public key cryptosystems as we will explain in the following sections.

3.7.2. *Cryptosystems classification*

Cryptosystems and by extension the encryption algorithms can be classified according to several criteria of which the most important ones are:

(1) According to the type of transformation applied to the plaintext in

order to produce the ciphertext, they can be classified into substitution, transposition or product ciphers.

(2) According to the type of key, they are divided into symmetric (secret) key cryptosystems or asymmetric (public) key cryptosystems.
(3) According to the number of plaintext symbols encrypted at the same time, they can be categorized as block or stream ciphers.

Next, we will describe in more detail each of these systems.

3.7.2.1. *Substitution, transposition and product ciphers*

Substitution ciphers replace each symbol of the plaintext alphabet by another symbol from the ciphertext alphabet, according to a rule specified by the encryption key. By contrast, transposition ciphers change the position of the symbols in the plaintext; such a permutation is also determined by the encryption key. Finally, product ciphers apply transposition and substitution consecutively, being this an effective manner of obtaining high levels of diffusion and confusion.

3.7.2.2. *Symmetric or secret key cryptosystems*

Symmetric or secret key cryptosystems have been known before Common Era; their most prevalent characteristic is that the decryption key is the same as the encryption key; more precisely, one can be inferred one from the other in reasonable bounds of time. Assuming that the keys are equal ($k = k^{-1}$), which is quite common in this kind of cryptosystems, the system can be represented as:

$$E(k, m) = c \qquad (3.1)$$
$$E^{-1}(k, c) = m \qquad (3.2)$$

Then, it is obvious that the key must be a secret, shared exclusively between Alice and Bob, as its knowledge by a third party would lead to the discovery of the plaintext. For this reason, these systems are denoted as secret key cryptosystems. Additionally, they present an absolute symmetry when Alice transmits a message to Bob and when it is Bob who transmits a message to Alice. For this reason these systems are also known as symmetric cryptosystems.

There is a high number of examples of this kind of algorithms, some of the most relevant are AES (Advanced Encryption Standard),[9] which is the encryption standard of the U.S. government, IDEA (International

Data Encryption Standard), the RC-X family (with X ranging from 2 to 6), Twofish, Blowfish, A5 (used in GSM cellular networks), and DES (Data Encryption Standard),[10] which is the former encryption standard of the U.S. government and still the most popular and extensively used, despite its age and obsoleteness.

The key length is a very important aspect of these algorithms and, in general of all encryption methods. It is a bound to the strength of the algorithm as, if no other vulnerability exists, the only way to attack the cryptosystem is trying all possible keys, which will be more difficult as the key space grows. Obviously, as computer power still follows Moore's law, key lengths that are considered as appropriate today, will be insufficient tomorrow. For example, 56-bit DES keys, which were extensively used a few years ago, now provides a ridiculous strength. Nowadays, the most common algorithms use key lengths ranging from 128 ($|K| = 2^{128}$) to 256 ($|K| = 2^{256}$), although there are some algorithms that use larger ones.

Symmetric cryptosystems have been the mechanism mainly used to provide data confidentiality and it is predictable that this situation continues as their speed is higher to that of asymmetric ones.

3.7.2.3. *Asymmetric or public key cryptosystems*

The main problem of symmetric cryptosystems has been the transmission of the secret key from Alice to Bob. The key could not be transmitted through the same channel as the message because it must remain secret and the channel is assumed to be dangerous. Therefore, firstly, it is necessary to find a secure channel in order to transmit the key which poses important logistic problems. This problem has been present from the antiquity till the decade of the seventies.

Indeed, at the end of the seventies, Diffie and Hellman discovered a new type of cryptosystems that used a pair of different encryption-decryption keys which were such that it was not feasible to infer one from the other, without knowing some additional information.[11] This discovery supposed a landmark in the history of cryptography, which began the public key cryptography era.[6]

Actually, the way of operation of these systems is the following one. First of all, Alice (who wishes to receive encrypted messages from Bob and other users) creates two keys (an encryption key and a decryption key) and discloses one which becomes the encryption key and, it is known as the public key. The other key must remain secret only known by Alice; this key becomes the decryption key and it is known as the private key.

It must be noticed that in the great majority of this type of cryptosystems, once the key pair has been generated, any one of them can be chosen to be the public or the private key. This fact is important for digital signature mechanisms built on public key cryptosystems.

From the moment in which Bob obtains Alice's public key, he can send her encrypted messages by using her public key. The messages encrypted this way can be decrypted only with the corresponding private key, which is assumed to be exclusively known by Alice. If Alice's public and private keys are denoted with pk_A y sk_A, the described communication can be represented as:

$$E(pk_A, m) = c \qquad (3.3)$$

$$D(sk_A, c) = m \qquad (3.4)$$

Reciprocally, if Alice wishes to send Bob an encrypted message, she will need to use Bob's public key and Bob can in turn decrypt the message using his private key. If Bob's public and private keys are denoted with pk_B y sk_B, the described communication can be represented as:

$$E(pk_B, m) = c \qquad (3.5)$$

$$D(sk_B, c) = m \qquad (3.6)$$

This way of functioning, which clearly distinguishes these schemes from those of secret key, is the reason why the former are known as public key cryptosystems. Additionally, the asymmetry between the operations performed by Alice and Bob when they exchange an encrypted message (they have to cipher and decipher with different keys) is what makes these systems be known as asymmetric cryptosystems.

The powerfulness of asymmetric cryptosystems relies on the difficulty of deducing the private key from the public one unless some additional information is known. This additional information cannot be deduced either from knowing the encryption algorithm or from the public key. This consideration led Diffie and Hellman to consider one-way trap door functions as ideal candidates for implementing public key cryptosystems. Mathematically, a one-way function $y = f(x)$ with $x \in A$ and $y \in f(A)$ is such that:

(1) For every $x \in A$, $f(x)$ is very easy to calculate.
(2) For almost every $y \in f(A)$, it is very difficult to find x such that $x = f^{-1}(y)$.

In other words, one-way functions are easy to compute but its inverse is virtually impossible to find. The existence of such functions is a conjecture, although its existence is quite an extended belief. In particular, a common view is that one-way functions currently used in cryptography are indeed one-way functions. An example of such functions is the modular exponentiation:

$$y = g^x mod(p) \tag{3.7}$$

being g and x integers, and p a large prime number (more than 200 decimal digits). Its complexity is $O(y = log(p))$. On the other hand, the inverse function, the discrete logarithm:

$$x = log_g(y)mod(p) \tag{3.8}$$

has a complexity of $O(e^{\sqrt{ln(p)ln(ln(p))}})$ provided that the most efficient algorithm known till now is used. Furthermore, it is believed that it does not exist a more efficient algorithm for its resolution. Nonetheless, some particular values of p allow solving it in polynomial time. Analogously, a one-way trap door function (whose existence has neither been proven) is a function easy to compute but, its inverse is practically impossible to find unless some additional information is known (the trap). This information cannot be deduced from the knowledge of $f(x)$. Formally, a family of one-way functions depending of a parameter z, $f(x, z)$, is also a trap door function if:

(1) Once z is known, it is very easy to produce algorithms E_z and E_z^{-1} to compute $y = f(x, z)$ and $x = f^{-1}(y, z)$, respectively.
(2) If z is unknown, for almost every $y \in f(A)$, it is virtually impossible to find an algorithm E_z^{-1} to compute $x \in A$ such that $x = f^{-1}(y, z)$ even knowing E_z.

In other words and regarding public key cryptosystems, the knowledge of the trap (z) allows computing the encryption and decryption keys and, consequently, the encryption and decryption algorithms respectively, but its ignorance makes unfeasible to find E_z^{-1} even knowing E_z.

Despite the great advantages that this public key cryptosystems have, mainly because they do not need a secure channel to exchange the keys, they are extraordinarily slow when compared with symmetric schemes. This is the reason why its use is restricted to very small messages (some tens of characters) either for providing confidentiality or for implementing digital signatures.

Another important disadvantage is the absence of authentication of the sender of an encrypted message. Indeed, as any sender uses the same key to encrypt messages for Bob (all of them use Bob's public key), Bob cannot deduce who is the sender of any of the messages he receives. Contrarily, in secret key cryptosystems, it is possible to authenticate the sender of a received ciphertext as it is usual that, in this type of systems, each pair of users share a different key.

Leaving digital signatures for the following section, the main application of public key cryptosystems is to provide a secure channel for secret key cryptosystems. This way, secret key cryptosystems keep being used almost exclusively to provide confidentiality. Indeed, an elegant and simple way to establish such a channel is that Alice generates a fresh secret key and sends it encrypted with Bob's public key to Bob. This operation is feasible even with slow asymmetric algorithms, because of the small size of symmetric keys. Once Bob receives the encrypted secret key, he can decrypt it with his private key and use it, from then on, to exchange confidential messages with Alice by using a symmetric key cryptosystem. Additionally, there will be no restrictions on the size of the messages imposed by asymmetric paradigms. Therefore, the combination of asymmetric and symmetric cryptosystems allows taking the maximum advantage from both; the first one contributes to create a secure channel and the second one to encrypt large amounts of data.

Contrarily to secret key cryptosystems, in public key cryptosystems there is only one extensively used encryption algorithm, the RSA algorithm,[12] even when it was the first one to be proposed. Although more rarely, the Diffie-Hellman public key algorithm described in their seminal paper is also used; nevertheless, the goal of this algorithm is to negotiate a secret key, which can be used afterwards in a secret key cryptosystem over insecure channels. These systems require quite large keys to provide a strength equivalent to the one obtained by secret key cryptosystems with much smaller keys; for example, RSA would require at least a 1024-bit key. The use of larger keys and the fact that these algorithms rely on number theory makes them much slower than secret key ones.

In recent years, interest on certain public key cryptosystems based on a new paradigm has grown; they are based on elliptical curves instead of on number theory. Although they are not completely trusted by all because of their youth (number theory exists since the antiquity while elliptical curves are relatively recent in comparison), they require much smaller key sizes compared to other public key algorithms. Thus, they are rather suitable for applications that need light cryptographic algorithms.

3.7.3. *Stream and block cryptosystems*

Stream ciphers are built on algorithms that transform the symbols from the plaintext into symbols of the ciphertext one at a time. Usually, after decomposing the plaintext into symbols, the sequence of symbols is encrypted with a sequence of keys $K = \{k_1\ k_2\ k_3\ ...\}$ or keystream.[13] Sometimes, the symbols of the key sequence depend on the symbols of the plaintext previously encrypted. The key sequence can be periodic or not; in the first case, the cipher is known as periodic stream cipher and non-periodic otherwise.

The simpler but most used stream cipher is comprised by a keystream generator that produces a sequence of bits that are used one at a time to apply the exclusive-or operation on one bit of the plaintext. Thus, if the keystream is represented by $\{k_1\ k_2\ k_3\ ...\}$ and the bits of the plaintext by $\{m_1\ m_2\ m_3\ ...\}$, then the bits of the ciphertext, $\{c_1\ c_2\ c_3\ ...\}$, are calculated as follows:

$$c_i = m_i \oplus k_i \tag{3.9}$$

By the properties of the exclusive-or operation, the corresponding decryption function is the following:

$$m_i = c_i \oplus k_i \tag{3.10}$$

If the keystream has a period larger than the length of the plaintext, the key generator is also known as running key generator. Provided this, if the generated keystream is a random bit sequence, the cipher provides perfect secrecy,[7] property that is only provided by this kind of ciphers.

Keystream generators can be classified into random or pseudorandom. First ones obtain the keystream by registering random processes which can be natural or not, and second ones build the keystream by means of a pseudorandom algorithm.

Random key stream generators fulfill the second condition for perfect secrecy. However, they have the disadvantage of requiring a continuous key exchange to avoid keystream reuse. Therefore, this type of generators is used in rare occasions, usually if maximum security is required and for infrequent communications.

Amongst these generators, the most used is the one based on the white noise created by a resistance at ambient temperature (the lower the temperature, the less the quantity of white noise). The noise is amplified and made the input of a logic gate pulse generator; the output is stored in a one-bit counter and sampled periodically to obtain the random bit stream. Other natural processes which are random in its magnitude or at the moment of happening and are used as sources to obtain random data are the following: the radioactive decay, the atmospheric noise, the differences of potential between very close capacitances, etc. Nevertheless, there are also some sources of randomness in computers that can be used to produce keystreams: the clock of the system, the amount of used memory, the number of occupied blocks in the disc, the time between a user's consecutive pulsations when writing a random text, etc.

On the contrary, pseudorandom keystream generators do not produce a random sequence but they can generate it as large as desired without the logistic problems of the random ones. The pseudorandom algorithm depends on a parameter, the random seed, which determines the keystream and must be changed every time a new message is encrypted or when the message size exceeds the period of the cipher.

In any case, although no finite algorithm can generate real random sequences, it does not mean that pseudorandom sequences are unacceptable, in fact, some of them are sufficiently good to be used as running keys.

In practice, if a real random keystream is desired, some unpredictable, and usually natural phenomena should be registered and communicated to the ciphertext receiver. Obviously, in the case of very large plaintexts, as the key cannot be reused, an enormous storage capacity is needed, which makes this approach unfeasible for most scenarios. In this situation, it is necessary that sender and receiver use generators based on deterministic phenomena, that is, pseudorandom generators that produce the same keystream.

Unlike stream ciphers, block ciphers divide plaintext in relatively large blocks equal in size and encrypt each of them separately using the same key. The block size depends on the encryption algorithm; some of them require a specific size while others let the user choose it. Similarly, the key length also depends on the encryption algorithm, sometimes it can be chosen by the user and it is fixed other times.

Moreover, while the main problem for building stream ciphers is the design of the keystream generator (the encryption algorithm was a simple exclusive-or operation), in block ciphers the principal difficulty is the design of the encryption algorithm (the key in this case is the same for all blocks and finite).

The mode of operation described for block ciphers presents some disadvantages because the encryption of a block of plaintext does not have any effect in the rest of blocks. Thus, the repetition of a block of ciphertext provides valuable clues for cryptanalysts. Moreover, an active attacker may change the order of ciphertext blocks, delete or copy some of them without being detected. To counteract these vulnerabilities, other modes of operations have been proposed; the most common are known by the acronyms CBC, OCB and OFB.

On the other hand, as the overall length of the plaintext must be a multiple of the block size, some padding may have to be added to the last block such as white spaces, zeroes or any other suitable character. Thus, the length of the resulting ciphertext will be larger than the length of the plaintext. Still worse, if the padding symbols are very numerous and equal, the last ciphertext block can provide priceless information to cryptanalysts. Implementations of each algorithm must anticipate specific solutions to address this issue.

In general, all block ciphers present the same structure:

(1) An initial transformation that may depend or not on the key.
(2) A cryptographic algorithm built as the product of substitutions (lineal and non lineal) and permutations; it is iterated a number of times, usually 4, 8, 16 or 32.
(3) An expansion key algorithm.
(4) A final transformation which is the inverse of the initial one.

Besides, in the second step, the majority of ciphers divide the block into two equal parts, the right one and the left one. In every iteration, only one half is encrypted and then permuted with the other half before the next iteration takes place. This way of functioning is known as Feistel structure[14] and has dominated the design of block ciphers for a long time.

Some well known examples of block ciphers are DES, IDEA, AES, etc.

3.8. Digital signature mechanism

Although asymmetric cryptosystems can be used to provide confidentiality of messages, due to their slowness, its fundamental utility, besides the encryption of secret keys, is to provide origin authentication and message integrity by means of the cryptographic mechanism known as digital signature. To achieve this, the author of the message (Alice) has to encrypt it with her private key. Since what is encrypted with the private key can only be decrypted with the public key and the former cannot be inferred from the later, any receiver (Bob) can decrypt the message with Alice's public key and have guarantees that the sender of the message is Alice.

In other words, if Alice wishes to sign a message, the only thing she has to do is to encrypt it with its private key sk_A. In turn, the receiver of such a message, Bob, will have to decrypt it with Alice's public key pk_A, to verify that it has been sent by Alice. If this operation is successful, Alice could not deny that she is the author of the message. Moreover, as the digital signature depends also on the message, if the message changes, the signature will be different (contrarily to what happens with handwritten signatures) therefore, this feature allows proving the message's integrity or the absence of alterations. In summary, such a digital signature mechanism is stronger than handwritten signatures, because it allows proving message integrity and origin authentication whereas handwritten signature, which depends only on the calligraphic characteristics of the signer, can only provide origin authentication.

The processes just described are one of the possible implementations of the generation and verification transformations of digital signature mechanisms. In the described case, digital signatures are built using a specific type of public key cryptosystems, but it is not the only way to construct them. General digital signature mechanisms are defined by a signing process and a verification process. The signing process is specified by a secret key known to the signer (also known as private key) and outputs a digital signature given a message. The verification process is public and, given a signed message and a digital signature, establishes whether the given digital signature has been generated on the given message by a specific signer.

As some of the cryptographic functions underlying digital signatures may be very slow and expensive (more if public key cryptosystems are used), digital signature creation is usually preceded by an additional step. Firstly, a summary of the message is computed. This summary is supposed to be much smaller than the message itself and, consequently, it is assumed that the signing operation will be less time consuming. It is this summary what it is signed using the private key of the signer. As a conclusion, the process comprises the following steps:

(1) First, the signer of a message M, Alice, calculates its summary R (also known as digital fingerprint or hash) by using a cryptographic hash function. This type of functions must satisfy two conditions.

    The first one establishes that it is highly improbable that two different messages result in the same hash. In other words, if M_1 and M_2 are two different messages and their hashes are R_1 and R_2 respectively, the probability of R_1 being equal to R_2 is negligible.

The second condition establishes that given a message M_1 and its hash R, it is very difficult to find another message M_2 that has the same hash R.

(2) Then, Alice creates a digital signature on the hash R using a digital signature generation algorithm and her private key.

(3) Finally, Alice attaches the message to the digital signature and sends both to Bob.

Bob, the receiver, upon reception of the message and the digital signature of its hash, performs the following steps:

(1) First, he separates the message and computes its hash using the same hash function used by Alice.

(2) Then, he applies the verification algorithm using Alice's public key, the received digital signature and the hash obtained in step 1.

If this process finishes successfully, Bob has corroborated the following:

(1) The received message M was the one that Alice actually sent (and she cannot deny it).

(2) The message M has not been modified from the moment it was signed to the moment the signature has been verified.

It is interesting to remark that digital signature mechanisms do not provide confidentiality (as it happens with handwritten signature) because the message is usually sent in clear along with the signature or it can be easily obtained applying the verification transformation on the digital signature (everyone may know the signer's public key necessary to perform this process). In synthesis, digital signature mechanisms do not have as aim to provide confidentiality but message integrity and origin authentication.

There are only a few signature and hash algorithms that are used in daily practice. Among the first ones, RSA[11] (from its authors' surnames: Rivest, Shamir and Adlemann) and DSA (Digital Signature Algorithm, upon which is built DSS, the Digital Signature Standard used in U.S. government[15]) can be remarked. Among the second ones, MD-5 (Message Digest, by RSA Data Security Inc.) and the family of SHA algorithms (Secure Hash Algorithm, on which SHS, the Secure Hash Standard used also in U.S. government, is built[16]) stand out.

3.9. Digital certificates

From what has been said up until now it can be understood that, public key mechanisms are of extraordinary relevance in a globalised world that operates more and more every day, by means of electronic transactions. Nevertheless, there is still another problem that must be overcome. How can one be sure that a public key purportedly owned by Alice does actually belong to her? Obviously, if Alice repudiates this public key and the corresponding private one, it is not possible to attribute her any responsibility (legal or not) derived from the use of that pair of keys to create digital signatures. It is necessary a mechanism that guarantees that a public key belongs to a certain entity. This is the aim of public key certificates or identity certificates.

In synthesis, a public key certificate or identity certificate is an electronic document digitally signed by a Trusted Third Party (TTP) known as Certification Authority (CA). The public key certificate vouches for the binding between a public key and its owner, who is identified by its name or any other data that allows his identification. Therefore, the user who wishes to obtain a certificate must first identify and authenticate himself to the CA. This process is more or less strict according to the intended use of the certificate; thus, it can vary from an on-line identification (in this case the association is usually established only between an email address and the public key) to a physical identification corroborated by a personal identification document. Naturally, in the first case, the messages signed with the private key corresponding to such a public key will lack of complete reliability. Public key certificates and their corresponding private keys can be stored in smart cards, thus preventing its replication although, in this case, a specific reading device is necessary to access them.

Consequently, if Bob wishes to verify the authorship and integrity of a message signed by Alice, he should follow the following steps:

(1) First, he will obtain Alice's public key certificate which is usually attached to the message and should be signed by certain CA.
(2) Then, he will extract Alice's public key pk_A from the certificate.
(3) Finally, he will verify the authenticity of the key by verifying the CA's signature on Alice's public key certificate.

If everything is correct, the CA, which is trusted by Bob, attests that the obtained public key is actually owned by Alice. From what has been said, public key certificates can be stored and transmitted without requiring confidentiality because the information they contain is public and its fraudulent modification will be detected during the verification of the CA signature.

In summary, the main benefit for a user is that he can obtain in a trustworthy and reliable way, the public keys of several signers provided that he knows a unique public key, the one of the CA, which is a trusted entity to vouch for the relation between a public key and certain user.

It is worth to remark that public key certificates are issued not only for physical persons but also for entities and computers. The main additional types of public key certificates are those that attest the public key of Certification Authorities (signed by themselves or by other CA), servers (usually used to establish SSL connections), software developers (that allow their users to verify the integrity and authorship of downloaded software) and physical persons.

Although there are several certificate formats, the most frequently used is the one defined in the X.509 recommendation by the ITU-T (Telecommunication Standardization Sector Of the International Telecommunication Union) and the ISO/IEC (International Organization for Standardization/International Electronic Commission).[17]

3.10. Audit logs

Audit logs store all the accesses or attempts of access of all users to a given system. In every case, the user identification, the terminal and the starting time are registered. In addition, if access is granted, other data such as the finishing time, the accessed objects and information about programs, data and physical resources may also be registered.

This mechanism differs from the ones exposed in previous sections, as it has a posteriori effect when the registered data is inspected (routinely or because an incident happened) and unauthorized accesses or behaviors are noticed. Therefore its function is dissuasive provided that its existence is known, as non expert attackers may desist in their actions if they do not know how to elude it.

Operating systems always include this type of logs although information systems usually maintain others of their own. For example, it is very common that database management systems have their own one. Thus, the operating system knows which database has been acceded but not the specific actions the user has done once he has been granted access to the database; these actions are registered by the database management system audit log.

In all cases, the great problem of these mechanisms is the high volume of information that they may have to store for each access operation. In large systems, which accumulate numerous daily accesses, this problem makes audit logs routine examination (for example, weekly or monthly) almost impossible. For this reason, they are only used to persecute the actions of a particular user when there are indications of unauthorized activities. Thus, the potential of this mechanism to discover intrusions is wasted when there are no suspicions of illegal actions.

It is at this point where artificial intelligence techniques can be of great aid. They allow the automatic analysis of great volumes of information and, although some developments already exist, there are still lots more to do.

3.11. Physical security

Physical security addresses the security of hardware and auxiliary installations from material, natural or human threats that come from the equipment operational environment. In the sixties and seventies, when computers were being introduced into companies and governmental organizations, physical security was the main concern. The reasons were the high price of hardware, the small quantity of processed data, the limited number of automated processes and the usual concentration of equipment in data processing centers.

This way, the kind of incidents that people were more concerned about were fires, floods, earthquakes, thefts and sabotages. Consequently, the more deployed security mechanisms were fire and floods prevention, detection and extinction, constructional (like choosing locations far away from geologic faults), access control of objects and individuals, etc.

The progressive decrease of equipment prices, the increase of automated data and processes, and the generalization of distributed computing, with the consequent fragmentation risk, have dramatically modified the attention paid to physical countermeasures (it has decreased in comparison with the higher concerns placed on protecting data and software) and their focus.

3.11.1. *Intrusion prevention*

A physical security aspect that is on the increase nowadays is intrusion prevention. We can already find very antique security mechanisms with this goal in the Ancient Egypt, as pharaohs and other high dignitaries placed tramps in their tombs to avoid their desecration and plundering. More recently, encryption devices have been designed to be destroyed when the enemy is about to capture them and encryption keys have been written with water soluble inks (mainly the ones used in warships) or over easily inflammable materials to facilitate their rapid elimination. Some examples of this kind of mechanisms appear in current fiction, as the cryptex of The Da Vinci Code or the ingenious systems that are common in the Indiana Jones films.

Today, physical countermeasures have focused on the problems caused by intrusions on equipments under the control of isolated individuals or on equipments placed at inherently compromised locations. This has led to the development of tamper resistant systems, which have as goal to prevent intrusions on the equipment. The National Institute of Standards and Technology (NIST) has even published a standard that specifies several levels of protection that encipherment equipments may offer against intrusions.[18] Besides tamper resistant equipments, another type of devices whose goal is to detect intrusions but not to prevent them has also been developed. This type of equipment is denoted as tamper evident.

A well-known example of system frequently located at potentially hostile locations is Automatic Teller Machines (ATM), which store cash and confidential data (cryptographic keys). Protection systems range from temperature sensors and accelerometers (to detect the opening of the equipment and its movement) to encryption algorithms deployed on the very same keyboard (to avoid its manipulation in order to capture the characters typed in before they are encrypted). In some type of ATM, cryptographic keys are stored in memory cards that erase their content when an intrusion is detected.

Currently, the main concern is the prevention of physical intrusions in smart-cards that have cryptographic capabilities, specially, those that can generate digital signatures. This kind of smart-cards generate signatures inside the card, therefore the private key does not need to leave the card, action that would compromise it. It is a requirement to strongly protect this type of smart cards against physical intrusions that have as a goal to obtain the private key. The minimum required security level is EAL 4+ when evaluated according to standard ISO 15408.[19]

3.11.2. *Electromagnetic emanations*

Another issue that has attracted great attention in the past years is the electromagnetic radiations emitted by electronic devices, peripheral equipments, power lines and communication cables. These radiations can be intercepted using not very sophisticated or expensive devices from outside the rooms where the attacked equipment is located, in order to obtain information that is being processed (or transmitted) or data stored in the equipment (such as cryptographic keys).

The optimal solution is to shield the room where the electronic devices are placed (that is, to build a Faraday cage) or to use equipments (computers, printers, scanners, etc.) that have obtained TEMPEST certification according to NATO and U.S. standards. Devices that comply with TEM-. PEST requirements usually protect themselves by shielding their radiations or, more rarely, by perturbing them with spurious signals. Traditionally, monitors based on cathode ray tubes as well as, transmission channels that connect them to computers and electric power networks were especially vulnerable in this regard. Fortunately, modern flat screens and optical fiber cables reduce to a great extent the amount of emissions facilitating, therefore, their TEMPEST certification.

Devices protected against the interception of electromagnetic emissions are nearly exclusive to diplomatic or military contexts. This type of protection may increase the price by 300% and make rather difficult to upgrade the equipment.

3.11.3. *Physical access control systems*

Finally, a third issue that has raised the attention of security researchers is physical access control systems. Although it is not usual for companies to concentrate all their computer equipment in a single room, some of them, such as telecommunication or Internet service providers and banks, still keep large data centers (rooms or buildings) whose criticality makes necessary to deploy rigorous physical access control systems. Nowadays, this problem must also be considered when protecting critical infrastructures such as airport installations or water and energy supply systems.

Biometric systems used as authentication mechanisms are playing a fundamental role in this context. When implementing physical access control systems, the most frequently used biometric mechanisms are those based on the characteristics of iris, hand geometry, palm prints, voice and face, leaving fingerprint systems aside.

It is worth mentioning that there exist several experimental systems whose objective is not to authenticate individuals but to detect some specific emotional or physiological state as a symptom of dangerous behavior, to avoid their access to critical places. It is of common use in this kind of systems, to apply artificial intelligent techniques to deduce anxiety levels from the measurement of body temperature variations, facial expressions, pulse, respiration frequency, etc. This kind of systems is especially convenient for airports, legal courts, governmental buildings or critical infrastructures. However, some psychologists doubt that the relation between high anxiety levels and potential dangerous behaviors is so clear, specially, if it is considered that, our modern society has a high number of anxiety sources, which do not always imply future criminal behaviors.

References

1. G. Graham and P. Denning. Protection: Principles and practice. In *Proc. Spring Join Comp. Conference*, vol. 40, pp. 417–429, Montvale, N. J., (1972). AFIPS Press.
2. B. Lampson. Protection. In *Proc. 5th Princeton Conf. on Information Sciences and Systems*, Princeton, (1971). Reprinted in ACM Operating Systems Rev. 8, 1, pp 18–24. (Jan. 1974).
3. M. A. Harrison, W. L. Ruzzo, and J. D. Ullman. Protection in operating systems. In *Comm. ACM*, number 8 in 19, pp. 461–471 (Aug., 1976).
4. D. E. Bell and L. J. LaPadula. Secure computer systems: Mathematical foundation. Technical Report 2547, Mitre Corp (mar, 1973).
5. K. J. Biba. Integrity considerations for secure computer systems. Technical Report 3153, Mitre Corp, Bedford, MA, (1977).
6. G. J. Simmons, *The Science of Information Integrity*. (Contemporary Cryptology, New York, 1992).
7. C. Shannon, Communication theory of secrecy systems, *Bell Systems Technical Journal*. **28**, 656–715, (1949).
8. A. Kerckhoffs, *La cryptographie militaire*. 1883.
9. NIST, *FIPS PUB 197: Advanced Encryption Standard (AES)*. Nov. 2001.
10. NIST, *FIPS PUB 46: Data Encryption Standard (DES)*. 1977.
11. W. Diffie and M. E. Hellman, New directions in cryptography, *IEEE Transactions in Information Theory*. **IT-22**, 664–654 (nov, 1976).
12. R. L. Rivest, A. Shamir, and L. Adleman, A method for obtaining digital signature and public-key cryptosystems, *Communications of the ACM*. **21** (2), 120–126 (feb, 1978).
13. G. S. Vernam, Cipher printing telegraph system for secret wire and radio telegraphic communications, *J. American Institute of Electrical Engineering*. **55**, 109–115, (1926).

14. H. Feistel, Cryptography and computer privacy, *Scientific American.* **228**(5) (may, 1973).
15. NIST, *FIPS PUB 186-2: Digital Signature Standard (DSS).* Jan. 2000.
16. NIST, *FIPS PUB 180-3: Secure Hash Standard (SHS).* Oct. 2008.
17. ITU-T. Recommendation x.509 - the directory: Public-key and attribute certificate frameworks, (2005).
18. NIST, *FIPS PUB 140-2: Security Requirements for Cryptographic Modules.* May 1977.
19. ISO/IEC JTC1/SC27. Information Technology - Security techniques - Evaluation Criteria for IT Security, ISO/IEC 15408:2005 - Common Criteria, (2005).

PART 2
Privacy Protection by means of Artificial Intelligence

Chapter 4

Data Mining in Large Databases — Strategies for Managing the Trade-Off Between Societal Benefit and Individual Privacy

Matthias Schmid

Department of Medical Informatics, Biometry and Epidemiology,
Friedrich-Alexander-University Erlangen-Nuremberg
Waldstrasse 6, D-91054 Erlangen, Germany
matthias.schmid@imbe.med.uni-erlangen.de

Over the last decades, the development of empirical research in the social and economic sciences has led to an increasing demand by researchers for access to data. At the same time, the capacity of modern computer systems has grown considerably, so that now enormous amounts of data can easily be stored and processed. Evidently, there is a trade-off between gaining knowledge from large databases and protecting the privacy of individuals, organizations and companies. This chapter contains an overview of the various aspects related to this problem. It is outlined how privacy issues can be measured and quantified, and how confidential data sets or outputs can be masked such that the confidentiality of respondents is maintained. In addition, a survey of techniques for assessing the analytical validity of masked data sets and outputs will be given.

Contents

4.1. Introduction

The past decades have seen a constantly increasing demand from society, economy and research organizations for access to accurate information. The principal reason for this demand is that society has become more and more information-based, so that statistical analyses based on large amounts of collected data are increasingly used for governing all kinds of societal and economic processes. Therefore, it is commonly accepted that providing sufficient information to government agencies, researchers, etc., is necessary for the common good.

Collecting and processing information for societal and economic purposes is not a new issue at all. However, due to the enormous advances in technology, statistical information nowadays has a much higher quality than it used to have 10 or 20 years ago. As an example, the capacity of databases and information systems has grown considerably over the last decades, so that now huge amounts of data can easily be stored and processed.[1,2] At the same time, powerful data mining tools and statistical methods for analyzing high-dimensional data have been developed.[3]

Although it is unquestionable that society benefits to a large extent from the advances in information technology, it is equally unquestionable that the available information should not be disseminated without restriction. In fact, it is a basic ethical principle that the privacy of individuals, organizations and companies should be protected as far as possible. In most countries and supranational organizations, this principle is expressed in a number of data protection laws and regulations (notable examples are the Directive on the Protection of Personal Data[a] enacted by the European Union and the Convention for the Protection of Individuals with regard to Automatic Processing of Personal Data[b] enacted by the Council of Europe). As a consequence of these laws and regulations, there is an obvious trade-off between delivering information to data users and protecting the privacy of individuals, *i.e.*, between the common good and the individual good. This trade-off, which is known as the *statistical disclosure control problem*, concerns all kinds of data holders, *e.g.*, statistical offices, non-governmental organizations, companies (collecting consumer data) and private owners of databases.

On the other hand, there is a variety of groups of data users that are

---

[a]http://ec.europa.eu/justice_home/fsj/privacy/index_en.htm
[b]http://conventions.coe.int/Treaty/en/Treaties/Html/108.htm

affected by the statistical disclosure control problem. Typical examples of data users are governments, researchers, companies and the media. For each combination of data holders and data users, it is necessary to develop a strategy for accessing confidential data in order to extract the largest possible amount of information without violating privacy and data protection laws. Consequently, methods for measuring and quantifying terms such as "privacy", "confidentiality", "data utility" and "information content" have to be developed.

This chapter contains an overview of various aspects related to the trade-off between privacy and data access. In Section 4.2 some typical examples of data holders (collecting and storing information) and data users (demanding access to this information) will be presented. Section 4.3 outlines the most commonly used strategies for regulating the access to confidential information. In particular, it is explained how privacy issues can be quantified and measured, and how confidential data sets or outputs can be masked such that the privacy of individuals is maintained. In Section 4.4 it will be outlined how the utility and the information content of a published data set or output can be measured. A summary of the chapter will be given in Section 4.5.

4.2. Examples of data-collecting institutions and data users

In this section some typical examples of data holders and data users are considered. Each of these examples is characterized by a data collecting institution, a (possibly large) number of individuals whose data are collected and stored (and whose privacy has to be maintained), and various kinds of legitimate data users whose aim is to access the collected data (and to use data mining tools for analyzing them). In addition, each example involves so-called "data attackers" (also termed "data snoopers") that might benefit illegally from the information published by the data holder.

(1) *Official statistics.* Most countries and political communities (such as the European Union) have established statistical offices that collect and store large amounts of data about their citizens. In many cases, citizens are even committed by law to provide these institutions with confidential information. A typical example of officially collected data are census data, which are collected by many countries in various forms. As a consequence, statistical offices possess large databases containing highly accurate information on many aspects of society. This infor-

mation could, for example, be used by governments (that could adjust their policy according to the collected information), intelligence services (that could use the collected information for detecting terrorist activities), the media or researchers at universities. On the other hand, statistical offices are committed by law to guarantee confidentiality when they release data collected from citizens or companies, so that data snoopers are prevented from using sensitive information for their purposes (as an example, officially collected data could be misused by companies for analyzing competitors). Consequently, guidelines on the safe release and dissemination of officially collected data have to be developed. This has been accomplished by a number of officially-organized research projects.[4,5]

(2) *Medical data.* Storage and dissemination of medical data is considered to be a particularly sensitive issue with respect to privacy maintenance.[6] Medical data are collected by pharmaceutical companies, but also by health insurance companies, hospitals and epidemiologists, where e-health systems have led to an enormous increase in electronically stored data. Similar to officially collected data, providing accurate personal information to health organizations and insurance companies is mandatory in many countries. Also, recent advances in DNA sequencing have led to large databases containing highly sensitive information on genetic codes. This information can be used for identifying individuals (and their patient characteristics) almost uniquely. Sharing the information contained in medical databases clearly leads to an enormous societal benefit, since it may result in improved diagnostics, medical care, prevention of diseases, and also in a reduction of administrative costs. On the other hand, patient data can easily be misused for commercial purposes. Typical examples are insurance companies that might discriminate employees or customers because of their patient histories. As a consequence, strict regulations have to be imposed on data users (*e.g.*, researchers at universities) working with medical data.

(3) *Consumer data collected by companies.* Recent advances in hardware technology, along with the development of credit card, loyalty card and e-commerce systems have led to an enormous amount of data on consumer and customer behavior. These databases constitute a valuable source of information for marketing companies and advertising agencies (*i.e.*, for legitimate data users applying consumer profiling techniques to the data). It is unquestionable that a large group of customers might

benefit from the analysis of their data, since it may lead to customized information, recommendations or discount campaigns. On the other hand, data snoopers could misuse customer data for illegal advertising or profiling activities. It is therefore necessary to regulate the data transfer between data-holding companies and data-processing companies, so that sensitive customer information is not made available to a broader public and is not diverted from its intended use.

Clearly, this section cannot provide a comprehensive overview of all kinds of privacy problems but is rather focused on discussing some typical examples of data-collecting institutions and data holders. It is important to note that the *differentiation* between data users and data holders might not even be easy in many practical situations. This is, *e.g.*, the case when a data-collecting company is subdivided into several departments, where each department could at the same time be a data holder (providing information to other departments) and a data user (demanding information from other departments). In these cases, it is often advisable to partition the collected data, so that different departments either possess different sets of observations containing the same attributes (*horizontal partitioning*) or possess different attributes of the same sets of observations (*vertical partitioning*).[7]

4.3. Strategies for controlling privacy

This section contains a brief introduction to various strategies for solving the problem of providing data users with sufficient information while maintaining the privacy of individuals. All strategies involve a reduction of the information content of published data sets and outputs (*i.e.*, query results), and thus also an inevitable reduction of the utility of published data and outputs. For this reason, privacy-controlling strategies should be designed such that the highest possible quality of published data and query results is guaranteed, since only in this case data users will be able to benefit from the release of the information.

4.3.1. *Input control and masked data sets*

A popular strategy to balance data protection and data utility is to release *anonymized data*, *i.e.*, to control the input of statistical analyses.[5,8,9] This strategy is as follows: First, the confidentiality level of a particular set of data is assessed. Thereafter, the data are masked (or *anonymized*), where anonymization is accomplished by applying so-called "disclosure control techniques" (also called "anonymization techniques") to the data. Disclosure control techniques should be applied such that

(1) confidentiality requirements are satisfied, and
(2) the masked data differ from the original data as little as possible, so that data utility is preserved to a maximum extent.

After the data have been masked, they are made available to the data users. The types of disclosure control techniques that have been applied to the data might also be communicated to the data users (provided that confidentiality requirements are not affected).

A consequence of applying disclosure control techniques to confidential data is that data users have to rely on masked data sets with a reduced information content. This, however, implies that the results of subsequent statistical analyses based on the masked data will be perturbed to a certain extent. It is therefore necessary to conduct a thorough analysis of the impact of disclosure control techniques on the results of statistical analyses, *e.g.*, on explorative methods, estimation, hypothesis testing, etc. Otherwise, conclusions drawn from the masked data might be invalid.

Generally, disclosure control techniques can be *perturbative* or *non-perturbative*. When a *non-perturbative* disclosure control technique is applied to a data set, the information content of the data is reduced without any distortion of the data values. Popular non-perturbative disclosure control techniques include *subsampling of observations*, *suppression* and *generalization*. With data suppression, sensitive data values or attributes are removed from a data set. Generalization techniques either involve the aggregation of confidential data values and attributes or the combination of a particular set of categories of qualitative attributes (*global re-coding*[8]).

When a *perturbative* disclosure control technique is applied to a data set, small errors are artificially introduced into the data. Popular perturbative masking techniques are:

- *Microaggregation.*[10,11] With this technique, the data values of small groups of observations are replaced by a summary statistic such as the group mean. Obviously, microaggregation implies that small errors (*i.e.*, the deviations of the original data values from their group mean) are added to the original (confidential) data. A key concept of microaggregation techniques, which is also the basis of non-perturbative techniques such as re-coding, is the concept of k-anonymity:[12] A data set is said to satisfy k-anonymity if any combination of values of a number of confidential attributes occurs at least k times in the data set (where $k > 1$). Consequently, if the group size used for microaggregation is equal to k, k-anonymity is achieved for the microaggregated data. Clearly, the smaller the value of k is chosen, the higher the information content of the masked data will be. Extensions and refinements of the k-anonymity concept have been developed by Machanavajjhala et al. and Li et al.[13,14]

- *Addition or multiplication of random noise.*[15,16] With this technique, small error terms drawn from a pre-specified random distribution are added to (or multiplied with) the original data values. These random errors should either be zero on average (if random noise is added to a data set) or one on average (if random noise is multiplied with the original data values).

- *Post randomization and data swapping.*[17,18] With data swapping techniques, a fraction of data values is swapped randomly between observations. Post randomization (PRAM) uses a predetermined probability mechanism for "misclassifying" a fraction of data values of the qualitative attributes.

- *Imputation and simulation of artificial data.*[19,20] These techniques are used for masking confidential data by imputing a number of artificially generated data values or attributes. A typical example of imputation techniques is the replacement of sensitive outliers by a threshold value (such as the 25%- or 75%-quantile of the corresponding data distribution).

4.3.2. *Output control*

In contrast to input control techniques, output control techniques are used for restricting or masking the results of queries and statistical analyses (*e.g.*, association rules or classification rules) based on a confidential data set. The basic principle of output control techniques is that the original data should not physically "leave" the data holders. Instead, only the results of queries or statistical analyses obtained from the data are made available to the data users. As an example, consider a statistical database that receives a particular query. The output of this query could either be the data values of a subset of observations contained in the database or a statistical model estimate (*e.g.*, an aggregate statistics computed from the data). After the output of the query has been computed from the original data, its level of confidentiality is investigated. If disclosure risk is above an acceptable level, the output is restricted or perturbed before publication ("query output perturbation"[21]).

Typical examples of anonymization strategies for outputs are:

- The *controlled remote data processing strategy*, which is, *e.g.*, used by the German statistical offices.[22] This strategy requires data users to send a self-produced software syntax to the data holder (*e.g.*, to a statistical office). Employees of the statistical office then apply the syntax to the original (confidential) data set. If the results obtained from the original data comply with data protection laws, they are sent back to the data users. Otherwise, suppression or generalization techniques are applied to the output.

- The release of *macrodata sets*, *i.e.*, contingency tables which are produced from an original (confidential) data set. These tables include aggregate values and summary statistics of different kinds of attributes, where the cells of a contingency table are defined by the value combinations of some qualitative attributes (which might also be included in the original data set). After a contingency table has been produced, the level of confidentiality of each of its cells is investigated. This is necessary because (despite of aggregating the original data) cells could still reveal sensitive information on the observations contributing to the value of the cell. If a cell is considered to be sensitive, it has to be suppressed or masked. For this purpose, various strategies and algorithms have been developed.[23] A related strategy would be to hide sensitive *association rules* in the original data set before computing a contingency table.[24]

4.3.3. *Query auditing*

In addition to input or output control, query auditing is a widely used technique for preventing data attackers from disclosing confidential information. The key idea behind query auditing is that data attackers are potentially able to submit a large number of different queries to a database in order to accumulate knowledge and to identify observations. This identification could in turn lead to a disclosure of sensitive information. With query auditing, the queries submitted to a particular database are controlled and regulated, so that information associated with a particular individual cannot be revealed by narrowing down its identity.[25] Query auditing involves a restriction of both the number of successive queries (in order to prevent accumulation of knowledge about observations) and the combinations of different kinds of queries (in order to prevent identity disclosure). Query auditing can generally be combined with the output control strategies presented above. Examples of query auditing techniques are given in Kenthapadi et al. and Nabar et al.[26,27]

Obviously, all strategies for regulating the access of data users to confidential information require data holders to investigate the level of confidentiality of observations contained in their data bases. A key requirement for this is that terms such as "re-identification risk" and "disclosure risk" of observations are properly measured and quantified. In the next subsections, a variety of methods that can be used for operationalizing confidentiality and privacy are outlined.

4.3.4. *Measuring privacy and disclosure risk in published data sets*

This subsection considers techniques for investigating the confidentiality level of published data sets (*i.e.*, the inputs of statistical analyses). Attributes contained in an original (confidential) data set can be classified into identifiers, quasi-identifiers and outcome attributes.[28] Identifiers are those attributes that unambiguously define an observation (such as name of a respondent, social security number, address of a company, etc.). Clearly, the values of these attributes have to be removed before publication. Quasi-identifiers (also termed *key variables*) are attributes that can be linked with an external database (or other external sources of information) in order to identify observations included in a data set. Unlike identifiers, however, they cannot be removed from the original data set, as, in principle, any attribute of a data set can be a quasi-identifier (this depends on the external database under consideration). Outcome attributes contain the most sensitive information included in a data set. The objective of a data attacker will typically be to get hold of the values of the outcome attributes, so if he uses the key variables for identifying individuals in the published data set, he will be able to draw conclusions on the values of the corresponding outcome attributes. This type of attack is commonly referred to as a *background knowledge attack*.[29]

Following these considerations, it is necessary for data holders to construct so-called "scenarios of attack". By a scenario of attack, the motives and the strategy of a data attacker can be modeled.[30] Typical scenarios of attack are:

(1) *The database cross match*: In this case, data attackers aim at identi-

fying as many observations of a data set as possible (in order to gain a maximum amount of knowledge about the outcome attributes contained in the data set).

(2) *The match for an individual:* In this case, the objective of a data attacker is to identify a particular observation in the data set (in order to get hold of the data values of its outcome attributes).

In order to construct a scenario of attack, data holders have to specify appropriate sets of key variables and outcome attributes. Also, they have to make assumptions about the external sources of information available to a data attacker. Depending on the scenario of attack, privacy issues are either investigated on the individual level ("personalized privacy preservation") or on the mass level. The most common strategies for measuring the level of confidentiality are:

- *The concept of uniqueness.*[31] With this approach, it is assumed that all key variables in a data set are qualitative. An individual is considered to be sensitive if it is the only observation in the population to have a particular combination of values in the key variables (*i.e.*, if it is a *population unique*). Clearly, a population unique can easily be identified if it is included in a sample. Consequently, the re-identification risk can be measured by considering the *sample uniques*, *i.e.*, those observations in the original data set that are unique with respect to the key variables. Note that an observation is not necessarily unique in the population if it is unique in the sample data. A commonly used measure of population uniqueness is the probability $P(F_i = 1 | f_i = 1)$, where f_i denotes the frequency of a particular value combination i of the key variables in the sample and F_i denotes the frequency of this combination in the population. Various strategies for estimating $P(F_i = 1 | f_i = 1)$ have been developed in the literature.[32–34]

- *Matching techniques.* Here the re-identification risk of a data set is measured by simulating database cross matches. It is assumed that data attackers possess a re-identification file extracted from an external database. This file is assumed to include the values of a set of key variables. The concept of matching techniques is as follows: First, the re-identification file is matched with the original data set, in the sense that pairwise comparisons between the observations included in the original data set and the observations included in the re-identification data set are performed. These comparisons typically result in a number of correctly linked observations, a number of falsely linked observations and a number of observations where no link is possible. The percentage of correctly linked observations can then be used as a measure of the re-identification risk of the observations contained in the original data. In the literature, various approaches on how to match a re-identification data set with the original data have been suggested. Most of these approaches use record linkage techniques for performing pairwise comparisons of observations[35–37] or statistical matching techniques based on distance measures.[38]

It is important to note that both the concept of uniqueness and matching techniques do not only allow for analyzing the level of confidentiality in the original data set but also for measuring the impact of disclosure control techniques on the confidentiality level of the published data set. The latter issue can be investigated by replacing the original data set with the masked data set. In particular, if it is possible to identify a set of observations contained in the masked data set, an additional analysis for investigating how *closely* the disclosed data values resemble the original values should be carried out. A detailed example on how to develop anonymization strategies for officially collected data sets can, *e.g.*, be found in Hafner and Lenz.[39]

4.3.5. *Measuring privacy and disclosure risk in published outputs*

As outlined above, the output of a database query can either be a subset of observations contained in the database or the result of a statistical analysis (such as a contingency table or a number of association rules). If the output is a subset of observations, the techniques for investigating privacy in published data sets (as described in the previous subsection) can be used. If the output of a database query is the result of a statistical analysis, privacy problems typically occur in the following situations:

- The number of individuals contributing to a statistical output is smaller than a natural number n. For example, if the mean of a subgroup containing $n = 1$ observations is published, disclosure of that observation is highly likely. This problem is associated with measuring the confidentiality level in contingency tables.[40]
- The statistical output is heavily influenced or dominated by the data values corresponding to a particular individual. As an example, if the value of a particular individual dominates the mean of a subgroup of individuals, data attackers can closely approximate the value of the

individual by using the group mean. This is one of the reasons why "outliers", *e.g.*, individuals with very large or small unique data values are considered to be particularly sensitive.

- The statistical output can be used to obtain close predictions of the values of sensitive attributes. A typical example of this type of privacy problem is a regression relationship between a non-confidential predictor variable and a highly confidential outcome attribute. If (a) the prediction error of this relationship is small and if (b) the coefficients of the corresponding regression model are published, data attackers can use the statistical output for obtaining close predictions of the confidential outcome attribute.

4.4. Measures of the utility of published data sets and outputs

In this section, the problem of measuring the information loss due to privacy regulations will be discussed. Clearly, both input and output control techniques reduce the utility of published information. This reduction can have the following consequences:

- Practical problems cannot be investigated any more by analyzing masked data or by interpreting masked outputs.
- It is not possible any more to apply to a masked data set all sorts of estimation techniques or inferential statistical methods that could have been applied to the original data. Similarly, since a number of estimation techniques or inferential statistical methods might lead to highly sensitive results, a number of query results or statistical outputs cannot be published any more.
- The results of statistical methods based on a masked data set might differ strongly from the results based on the original data. Similarly, a masked output might differ strongly from the original output obtained from analyzing the original data. Both cases might lead to wrong conclusions drawn by the data users.

For these reasons it is necessary to ensure that data users can draw the same (or at least very similar) conclusions from a masked output or from a masked data set as they would have drawn from the original data set or output. Concerning the release of masked data sets, this implies that the *analytic potential* of the masked data has to be investigated before publication. According to the authors of a major research project conducted by the German statistical offices,[5] the analytic potential of a data set comprises "all possibilities to analyze practical problems by means of applying descriptive or inferential statistical methods to the data". It should thus be guaranteed that data users obtain the same results (or at least similar results) from the published data as they would have obtained from an analysis of the original (confidential) data. Similar arguments hold true when masked results of database queries or masked outputs are made available to data users.

The aspects outlined above should be reflected by any measure of data utility. Commonly used strategies for measuring data utility are:

(1) The *index-based approach*. With this approach, the effect of input or output control techniques on data utility is measured by a set of indices that characterize the multivariate distribution of a data set. Typical examples are means, variances and higher-order moments, which are either contained in a masked output or have been computed from a masked data set. Generally, disclosure control techniques should not lead to a large bias in these indices. In the same way, cost measures (such as variance or entropy) can be used for measuring the effect of anonymization techniques on data utility.[41]

(2) The *application-based approach*. This approach can be regarded as an extension of the index-based approach. The effect of disclosure control techniques is investigated by considering the results of several types of statistical analyses (such as regression, clustering and classification methods, significance tests, etc.). These results are either obtained from a masked data set or are contained in a masked output. If the results obtained from the original data differ largely from the published results, there is evidence for a strong reduction in data utility. To obtain realistic measures of data utility via the application-based approach, it is required that the types of statistical analyses applied to the data represent a comprehensive summary of relevant practical problems.

(3) The *theory-based approach*. With this approach, the properties of masking techniques and their effect on the results of statistical analyses are investigated analytically. By deriving theoretical results (*e.g.*, on the unbiasedness or consistency of statistical estimators based on a masked data set), it is possible to assess the impact of masking techniques on data utility. In addition, in some cases it is possible to develop correction procedures that remove the bias caused by masking techniques. As an example of the theory-based approach, consider the addition of

random noise to confidential data: From measurement error theory, it is known that adding random noise to data may cause a bias in linear model estimators. However, this bias can be removed by applying specially developed correction techniques[42] to the masked data. In the same way, the bias caused by microaggregation can be removed in a number of situations.[43]

4.5. Conclusion

As outlined in the previous sections, societal benefit can be increased tremendously by an efficient usage of information stored in large databases: Resources can be allocated more efficiently, administrative costs can be reduced, and the needs of society can be investigated more thoroughly. On the other hand, storing and processing information should not compromise the privacy of individuals, organizations and companies. It is important to note that data protection laws and regulations do not only help to maintain privacy but also lead to high standards on data quality. In fact, data quality heavily relies on the willingness of respondents to provide correct information, so that accurate information is more likely to be obtained if the privacy of respondents is not compromised.

Clearly, in many cases, "absolute" anonymity can only be ensured by publishing no data or outputs at all, while the utility of published data and outputs is maximized by applying no anonymization techniques at all. In each of these two "extreme" situations, either the common good or the individual good is compromised to a large degree. Therefore, the goal of any strategy for publishing data sets and outputs must be to find the proper balance between privacy and data utility. Since it is difficult to measure terms such as "privacy", "disclosure risk" and "data utility" unambiguously and in an objective way, the needs of data users and data holders have to be investigated carefully. Realistic scenarios of attack have to be developed, while, in addition, data holders have to be aware of the needs of legitimate users of their data. The process of creating masked data sets and outputs for publication is summarized in Figure 4.1.

It is further important to note that both the technology for storing and processing information and the development of statistical software and data mining tools are subject to continuous improvement. By using artificial in-

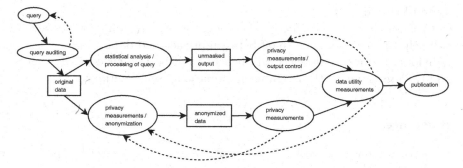

Fig. 4.1. The diagram shows the various steps involved in creating masked data sets and outputs.

telligence techniques (*e.g.*, neural networks, genetic algorithms or methods for image analysis), data mining tools are now able to generate highly accurate detection and prediction rules, even from moderately large databases. These tools should be designed such that relevant statistical patterns can be recognized without compromising the privacy of unaffected respondents. As an example, pattern-based discovery tools for detecting terrorist activities should be able to accurately identify suspicious persons but should also have an integrated privacy-protection mechanism to safeguard civil rights.

The relationships discussed above imply that research in privacy and disclosure control has to go hand in hand with the development of information technology. As a consequence, various branches of science are concerned with improving the existing methods for dealing with privacy issues: *Computer scientists* have to develop efficient techniques for investigating privacy and disclosure risk on both the mass level and the individual level. In addition, techniques and algorithms for dealing with "privacy-compromising" queries and for anonymizing large amounts of data have to be improved. On the other hand, expert knowledge of various groups of data users is necessary for investigating disclosure risk and the analytic potential of a data set. For example, the expertise of *econometricians*, *social scientists* and *medical researchers* can be used for identifying groups of data attackers and for developing realistic scenarios of attack. Finally, *mathematicians* and *statisticians* have to investigate the properties of anonymization techniques and privacy measures. For example, the efficiency loss caused by the application of disclosure control techniques to a data set has to be investigated and quantified, either via simulation or analytical techniques. In addition, methods on how to correct a possible "anonymization" bias have to be improved.

A close cooperation between the above-mentioned branches of science will help to manage the trade-off between privacy and data utility, so that individual members of society will benefit from both knowledge discovery and the protection of their right of informational self-determination.

References

1. J. Domingo-Ferrer and V. Torra, *Privacy in Statistical Databases.* (Springer, Berlin, 2004).
2. C. C. Aggarwal and P. S. Yu, *Privacy-Preserving Data Mining: Models and Algorithms.* (Springer, New York, 2008).
3. T. Hastie, R. Tibshirani, and J. Friedman, *The Elements of Statistical Learning: Data Mining, Inference, and Prediction.* (Springer, Berlin, 2001).
4. CASC. Computational aspects of statistical confidentiality. European Project IST-2000-25069. http://neon.vb.cbs.nl/casc, (2004).
5. G. Ronning, R. Sturm, J. Höhne, R. Lenz, M. Rosemann, M. Scheffler, and D. Vorgrimler, *Handbuch zur Anonymisierung wirtschaftsstatistischer Mikrodaten.* Statistik und Wissenschaft 4, (Statistisches Bundesamt, Wiesbaden, 2005). In German.
6. L. Sweeney. *Computational Disclosure Control: A Primer on Data Privacy Protection.* PhD thesis, Massachusetts Institute of Technology, (2001).
7. C. Clifton, M. Kantarcioglu, J. Vaidya, X. Lin, and M. Zhu, Tools for privacy-preserving distributed data mining, *SIGKDD Explorations.* **4**(2), 28–34, (2003).
8. L. Willenborg and T. de Waal, *Elements of Statistical Disclosure Control.* (Springer, New York, 2001).
9. P. Doyle, J. Lane, J. Theeuwes, and L. Zayatz, *Confidentiality, Disclosure, and Data Access.* (North-Holland, Amsterdam, 2001).
10. D. Defays and P. Nanopoulos. Panels of enterprises and confidentiality: The small aggregates method. In *Proceedings of the 1992 Symposium on Design and Analysis of Longitudinal Surveys,* pp. 195–204, Ottawa, (1993). Statistics Canada.
11. J. Domingo-Ferrer and J. M. Mateo-Sanz, Practical data-oriented microaggregation for statistical disclosure control, *IEEE Transactions on Knowledge and Data Engineering.* **14**(1), 189–201, (2002).
12. L. Sweeney, K-anonymity: A model for protecting privacy, *International Journal of Uncertainty, Fuzziness and Knowledge-Based Systems.* **10**(5), 557–570, (2002).
13. A. Machanavajjhala, J. Gehrke, D. Kifer, and M. Venkitasubramanian. l-Diversity: Privacy beyond k-anonymity. In *Proceedings of the 22nd IEEE International Conference on Data Engineering (ICDE '06)*, Atlanta, GA, USA, (2006).
14. N. Li, T. Li, and S. Venkatasubramanian. t-Closeness: Privacy beyond k-

anonymity and *l*-diversity. In *Proceedings of the 23nd IEEE International Conference on Data Engineering (ICDE '07)*, Istanbul, Turkey, (2007).
15. R. Brand. Microdata protection through noise addition. In ed. J. Domingo-Ferrer, *Inference Control in Statistical Databases*, pp. 97–116. Springer, Berlin, (2002).
16. J. J. Kim and W. E. Winkler. Multiplicative noise for masking continuous data. Statistical Research Division Report RR 2003/01, U.S. Bureau of the Census, Washington, (2003).
17. T. Dalenius and S. P. Reiss, Data-swapping: A technique for disclosure control, *Journal of Statistical Planning and Inference.* **6**(1), 73–85, (1982).
18. J. M. Gouweleeuw, P. Kooiman, L. Willenborg, and P.-P. de Wolf, Post randomisation for statistical disclosure control: Theory and implementation, *Journal of Official Statistics.* **14**(4), 463–478, (1998).
19. R. J. A. Little and D. B. Rubin, *Statistical Analysis with Missing Data.* (Wiley, New York, 2002), 2. edition.
20. T. E. Raghunathan, J. Reiter, and D. B. Rubin, Multiple imputation for statistical disclosure limitation, *Journal of Official Statistics.* **19**(1), 1–16, (2003).
21. A. Blum, C. Dwork, F. McSherry, and K. Nissim. Practical privacy: The SuLQ framework. In *Proceedings of the 24th Symposium on Principles of Database Systems*, pp. 128–138, (2005).
22. R. Sturm, Faktische Anonymisierung wirtschaftsstatischer Einzeldaten, *Journal of the German Statistical Society.* **86**(4), 468–477, (2002). In German.
23. S. Giessing. Survey on methods for tabular data protection in argus. In eds. J. Domingo-Ferrer and V. Torra, *Privacy in Statistical Databases*, pp. 1–13. Springer, Berlin, (2004).
24. V. S. Verykios, A. Elmagarmid, E. Bertino, Y. Saygin, and E. Dasseni, Association rule hiding, *IEEE Transactions on Knowledge and Data Engineering.* **16**(4), 434–447, (2004).
25. N. R. Adam and J. C. Wortmann, Security-control methods for statistical databases: A comparative study, *ACM Computing Surveys.* **21**(4), 515–556, (1989).
26. K. Kenthapadi, N. Mishra, and K. Nissim. Simulatable auditing. In *Proceedings of the 24th Symposium on Principles of DatabaseSystems*, pp. 118–127, (2005).
27. S. Nabar, B. Marthi, K. Kenthapadi, N. Mishra, and R. Motwani. Towards robustness in query auditing. In *Proceedings of VLDB Conference 2006*, pp. 151–162, (2006).
28. J. Domingo-Ferrer and V. Torra, Ordinal, continuous and heterogeneous *k*-anonymity through microaggregation, *Data Mining and Knowledge Discovery.* **11**(2), 195–212, (2005).
29. D. Martin, D. Kifer, A. Machanavajjhala, J. Gehrke, and J. Halpern. Worst-case background knowledge for privacy-preserving data publishing. In *Proceedings of the ICDE Conference 2007*, pp. 126–135, (2007).
30. M. J. Elliot and A. Dale, Scenarios of attack: The data intruder's perspective on statistical disclosure risk, *Netherlands Official Statistics.* **14**, 6–10, (1999).

31. J. G. Bethlehem, W. J. Keller, and J. Pannekoek, Disclosure control of microdata, *Journal of the American Statistical Association.* **85**(409), 38–45, (1990).

32. C. J. Skinner, C. Marsh, S. Openshaw, and C. Wymer, Disclosure control for census microdata, *Journal of Official Statistics.* **10**(1), 31–51, (1994).

33. C. J. Skinner and D. J. Holmes, Estimating the re-identification risk per record in microdata, *Journal of Official Statistics.* **41**(4), 361–372, (1998).

34. S. E. Fienberg and U. E. Makov, Confidentiality, uniqueness, and disclosure limitation for categorical data, *Journal of Official Statistics.* **14**(4), 385–397, (1998).

35. M. A. Jaro, Advances in record-linkage methodology as applied to matching the 1985 census of Tampa, Florida, *Journal of the American Statistical Association.* **84**(406), 414–420, (1989).

36. W. E. Winkler. Matching and record linkage. In ed. B. G. Cox, *Business Survey Methods*, pp. 355–384. Wiley, New York, (1995).

37. W. E. Yancey, W. Winkler, and R. H. Creecy. Disclosure risk assessment in perturbative microdata protection. In ed. J. Domingo-Ferrer, *Inference Control in Statistical Databases*, pp. 135–152. Springer, Berlin, (2002).

38. J. Bacher, R. Brand, and S. Bender, Re-identifying register data by survey data using cluster analysis: An empirical study, *International Journal of Uncertainty, Fuzziness and Knowledge-Based Systems.* **10**(5), 589–607, (2002).

39. H.-P. Hafner and R. Lenz. Anonymization of linked employer employee datasets using the example of the German Structure of Earnings Survey. In *Proceedings of the Joint UNECE/Eurostat Work Session on Statistical Data Confidentiality*, Manchester, United Kingdom, (2007).

40. S. Giessing. Nonperturbative disclosure control methods for tabular data. In eds. P. Doyle, J. Lane, J. Theeuwes, and L. Zayatz, *Confidentiality, Disclosure, and Data Access*, pp. 185–213. North-Holland, Amsterdam, (2001).

41. J. Domingo-Ferrer and V. Torra. A quantitative comparison of disclosure control methods for microdata. In eds. P. Doyle, J. Lane, J. Theeuwes, and L. Zayatz, *Confidentiality, Disclosure, and Data Access*, pp. 111–133. North-Holland, Amsterdam, (2001).

42. R. J. Carroll, D. Ruppert, L. A. Stefanski, and C. Crainiceanu, *Measurement Error in Nonlinear Models: A Modern Perspective.* (Chapman & Hall, London, 2006), 2. edition.

43. M. Schmid, H. Schneeweiss, and H. Küchenhoff, Estimation of a linear regression under microaggregation with the response variable as a sorting variable, *Statistica Neerlandica.* **61**(4), 407–431, (2007).

Chapter 5

Desemantization for Numerical Microdata Anonymization

Jordi Pont-Tuset[1], Jordi Nin[2], Pau Medrano-Gracia[1],
Josep-Ll. Larriba-Pey[1] and Victor Muntés-Mulero[1]

[1] *DAMA-UPC, Data Management, Universitat Politècnica de Catalunya*
{jpont,pmedrano,larri,vmuntes}@ac.upc.edu
[2] *IIIA, Artificial Intelligence Research Institute, CSIC,*
Spanish National Research Council
jnin@iiia.csic.es

Many situations demand for publishing confidential data without revealing the identity of data owners. For this purpose, anonymization methods are specially important in order to minimize both the disclosure risk and the information loss of the released data.

In this chapter, we describe a methodology for numerical data anonymization based on a novel strategy for preprocessing data. The key point of this strategy is to *desemantize* the data set, *i.e.* to gather all the values together in a single vector regardless of the attribute they belong to. Data anonymization is achieved by modeling the preprocessed data in a way that it is accurate enough to be representative of the original data, but sufficiently dissimilar not to reveal the confidential information.

In order to prove the validity of our methodology, we present four different approaches for the modeling step of the anonymization process. Those approaches outperform some of the best methods available in the literature in terms of the trade-off between privacy preservation and information loss.

Contents

5.1. Introduction

Manipulating large data volumes is an increasingly common practice in many organizations in this Information Era. The sharp rising in the use of the Internet, for instance, provides companies with a vast amount of personal data. In many cases, this information may be sensitive and thus, there is a growing public concern about how it is managed. On the other hand, however, these data may be interesting to be analyzed for several purposes such as medical research, public security, decision support, market analysis, etc.

In view of this state of the art, it is clear that some data must be publicly released but as far as to whom the sensitive and private information is concerned should not be revealed. In order to protect data confidentiality it is necessary to *anonymize* the data, *i.e.*, to perturb or summarize them in some manner so that the individual respondent cannot be identified. With this process, however, the statistical usefulness of the resulting data are likely to be lessened.

Therefore, we can assert that there exists a trade-off between the statistical usefulness of data and the protection of individual privacy. According to this, a wide range of anonymization methods has developed which aim at guaranteeing an acceptable level of protection for the confidential data, while preserving their statistical significance.

These methods are classified depending on the form and type of data they handle and the way they modify it in order to achieve the protection. Firstly, in this work we assume to manipulate *microdata* that refer to individual units as opposite to *aggregated* data. Microdata are formed by individual records that contain values of variables for a single person, a business establishment, or any other individual unit. Microdata files are useful for research or analytical purposes and, therefore, third parties have increased their demand for statistical data in microdata format. Secondly, the *type of data* that an anonymization method is intended to handle is relevant to its characteristics: numerical or categorical attributes. Finally, taking into account the *effect on the original data*, protection methods can be classified into three different categories: perturbative, non-perturbative, and synthetic data generators: (i) *Perturbative methods* distort the original data set slightly modifying the original data values. In this way, the combinations of values which unambiguously identify an individual (or respondent) in the original data set disappear, and new combinations appear in the protected data set. This obfuscation makes it difficult for an intruder to link the values of the protected data set to its owner. (ii) *Non-perturbative methods* do not distort the original data set. Instead, they make partial suppressions or detail reductions in it. Due to this, the combinations of values that originally identified an individual may be changed into a more general composition that is likely not to be specific of a respondent. And finally, (iii) *Synthetic data generators* build a data model from the original data set, and afterward, a new (protected) data set is randomly generated constrained by the model computed. Although these methods allow us to have a certain control over the statistical information we preserve, privacy might not be guaranteed.

This chapter tackles the creation of a new methodology for *anonymizing numerical microdata*. Thus, we will handle data sets consisting only of numerical attributes that refer to individual units.

Given that the original microdata set may contain confidential information, one of our goals will be to *assure that third parties are not able to reveal the identity of the individuals in the released data set*. In other words, our methods have to give some certainty about the privacy protection achieved.

On the other hand, since microdata files are increasingly used for statistical purposes in many areas, *the protected data set must be as statistically accurate as possible*. Our methods have to assure, therefore, sufficient fidelity of the released data to the original one.

Anonymization methods aim at guaranteeing a certain balance in this trade-off, depending on the value of some parameters. Hence, the majority of these methods allows us to modify their results in order to give more importance to statistical accuracy or privacy protection.

Our main objective is not the creation of an anonymization method itself, but of a general methodology. This methodology will allow us to weight the balance of the trade-off not only by changing the value of some parameters, but by allowing the user the freedom of completely designing some of its parts.

As a result, this methodology may accept both perturbative methods and synthetic data generators, whereas the complexity of the resulting data protection method may range between a very simple approach and the most intricate algorithm.

In order to prove the validity of the proposed methodology, we present different approaches based on artificial intelligence techniques to the its parts that are designable by the user. These are adequate for several scenarios and in some aspects outperform the existing methods. They range in complexity from the simplicity of an average to the intricacy of an artificial neural network.

All the anonymization methods presented in this chapter are extracted from the artificial intelligence (AI) literature. Specifically, microaggregation, a type of perturbative protection method, ONN and PoROP-k are based on typical AI techniques, such as clustering. the use of artificial neural networks for data anonymization or polynomial regressions, a well-known tool for data mining and data analysis.

This chapter is organized as follows. In Section 5.2 we present some preliminaries needed later on. Section 5.3 presents the overview of the methodology employed in this chapter. Next, in Section 5.4, we expound the details of the preprocessing block of our methodology. Section 5.5 depicts some approaches to the second block of our methodology, the data fitting. Section 5.6 gives the details about the experiments performed in order to evaluate our methodology. Finally, in Section 5.7 we draw some conclusions related both to the specific approaches presented and the general aspects of our methodology proposal.

5.2. Background and State of the Art

In this section we explain some concepts on which we base our methodology. Namely, we first detail the scenario where a microdata protection method is applied to preserve the privacy of the owners of some statistical data. Next, we describe the ways the quality of a microdata protection method may be measured, according to the levels of privacy and statistical utility that it provides. Later, we present two state-of-the-art anonymization methods:

rank swapping and *microaggregation*. Finally, we give a brief description of a general *artificial neural network* and we point out the basic characteristics of the *backpropagation algorithm*.

5.2.1. *Microdata protection scenario*

We will consider a microdata set X as a matrix with n rows (*records*) and k columns (*attributes*). Each row contains the values of the attributes for an individual. The attributes in a data set can be classified into three non-disjoint categories: (i) *Identifier attributes* unambiguously identify the individual, *e.g.*, the passport number; (ii) *Quasi-identifier attributes* may identify the individual when some of them are combined. For instance, age, postal code or job do not generally identify unambiguously an individual, but the set of people working at DAMA-UPC, living in a certain town and being born in 1984 contains a single individual; (iii) *Confidential attributes* contain sensitive information about the individual, *e.g.*, the salary.

Considering this classification, a data set X is divided into $X = id \parallel X_{nc} \parallel X_c$, where id are the identifiers, X_{nc} are the non-confidential quasi-identifier attributes, X_c are the confidential attributes, and $\parallel$ denotes concatenation. As introduced previously, before releasing a dataset X with confidential attributes, some anonymization methods ρ may be applied, leading to a protected dataset X'.

We will assume the following scenario, similar to the framework presented in.[1] Firstly, identifier attributes in X are either removed or encrypted, and therefore, we will consider $X' = X'_{nc} \parallel X'_c$. Confidential attributes X_c are not modified, and so we have $X'_c = X_c$. This is done in order to have the best accuracy in the information that third parties are really interested in. Finally, the anonymization method itself is applied to non-confidential quasi-identifier attributes, in order to preserve the privacy of the individuals whose confidential data are being released. Thus, we have $X'_{nc} = \rho(X_{nc})$. This scenario allows third parties to have precise information on confidential data without revealing whom these data belongs to.

In this scenario, an intruder might have obtained the non-confidential quasi-identifier data (X_{nc}), together with the identifiers (id), of the individuals represented in our microdata set, from another source. Note that it is not difficult to obtain, for instance, the address, age and name of an individual, together with its passport number. Once we release the protected data set X'_{nc}, the intruder has access to these data set and thus he has both the protected data set $(X'_{nc} \parallel X_c)$ and part of the original data set (id and X_{nc}).

Record linkage (RL) is defined as the process of linking pairs (or groups) of records from a set of databases. A simple criterion to link two of them may be finding the closest pairs under a given distance. Typical applications of record linkage may include de-duplicating a database or deciding which two records from different sources refer to the same person.

By means of record linkage, the intruder (let us refer to him as Ben) might be able to link some individuals represented in X'_{nc} with some in X_{nc}. Let us suppose that Ben has linked the non-confidential attributes referring to a specific individual (Kate), *i.e.*, he already knows which record in X'_{nc} refers to her. Since the released data set contains X_c, Ben is apprised of the confidential data about Kate, for instance, her income. Figure 5.1 shows a schema of this process, followed by an intruder to discover the identity of some individuals.

This situation is what the anonymization methods try to avoid, so one of their aims is to make re-identification of individuals hard to achieve, or at least, make its result uncertain.

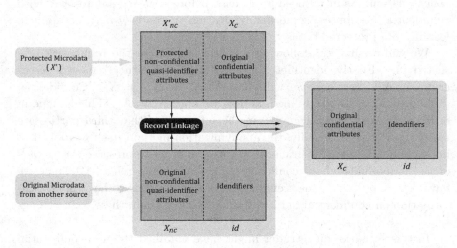

Fig. 5.1. Process followed by an intruder in order to disclose confidential values through record linkage in our scenario

5.2.2. *Information loss and disclosure risk*

The main objective of all anonymization methods, as introduced formerly, is to guarantee a good level of privacy protection while preserving the statistical usefulness of the released file. In other words, they aim at minimizing both the *disclosure risk* (DR) and the *information loss* (IL) of the protected data set. Disclosure risk measures the capacity of an intruder to obtain some information about the original data set from the protected one, by means of techniques like record linkage. Information loss measures the reduction of the statistical utility of the protected data set with respect to the original one.

However, the higher one of these parameters, the lower the other is, and thus finding the optimal combination of these two measures becomes a difficult and challenging task. Moreover, in some situations an organization could be interested in releasing the data by fixing a desirable level for one of the parameters. For these two reasons it becomes necessary to compute both measures very accurately before releasing the protected data set, ensuring enough protection level and statistical utility.

Some approaches are presented in the literature to calculate the information loss. In[2] the authors compute the average difference between some statistics calculated on both the original and the protected microdata. A probabilistic variation of this measure was presented in.[3] A different approach may be found in,[4] where some measures (accuracy, completeness, and consistency) are calculated over the protected data to evaluate the information loss.

In order to compute the disclosure risk, many works as[2,5,6] use record linkage methods[2,7,8] to evaluate the amount of links an intruder is capable of discovering. Alternatively, in[9] the authors define a framework for privacy protection where the intruder can only query the database by using propositional sentences. If the database answers these queries with enough level of generalization, it is difficult for the intruder to infer any confidential information of a specific individual. The measure of disclosure risk in this scenario is the percentage of individuals for which an intruder is able to discover the value of a confidential attribute.

Normally, information loss and disclosure risk are combined to obtain an overall value about a specific protection method, that weights the relation between information loss and disclosure risk. One approach was presented in,[2] where the authors combine both IL and DR in a *score* using an arithmetic mean. Another approach is the *risk-utility* (R-U) maps,[10,11] that show graphically the relation between a numerical measure of statistical disclosure risk (R) and data utility (U).

Among all of these possibilities, we selected the measures presented in,[2] mainly because a lot of protection methods have been evaluated using this score, and therefore, we can compare our results with many other works easily. In addition, this measure allows modifications of the IL computation and the DR computation. Particularly, we compute the IL value by weighting five different measures reflecting statistical loss, and the DR by combining the result of three methods that reflect the privacy protection.

5.2.3. *State of the art in microdata anonymization methods*

This section describes two state-of-the-art microdata anonymization methods: rank swapping and microaggregation. We will pay special attention to the latter, since it is specifically compared to one of our approaches in the experiments section.

5.2.3.1. *Rank swapping*

Rank swapping is a widely used microdata protection method, which was originally described in.[12] In the comparisons made in,[13] it was ranked among the best microdata protection methods for numerical attributes.

Rank swapping with parameter p and with respect to an attribute $attr_j$ (*i.e.*, the j-th column of the original data set X) can be defined as follows. Firstly, the records of X are sorted in increasing order of the values x_{ij} of the considered attribute $attr_j$. For simplicity of notation, assume that the records are already sorted, *i.e.*, $x_{ij} \leq x_{\ell j}$ for all $1 \leq i < \ell \leq n$. Then, each value x_{ij} is swapped for another value $x_{\ell j}$, randomly and uniformly chosen in a certain limited range depending on the value of p. Finally, the sorting step is undone. Rank swapping of a data set usually consists in running the algorithm explained above for each attribute to be protected, in a sequential way. We will refer to Rank Swapping with parameter p as RS-p. The parameter p is used to control the swap range, and is normally defined as a percentage of the total number of records in X. Intuitively, when p increases, the difference between x_{ij} and $x_{\ell j}$ may increase, and thus, the re-identification may be more difficult. On the other hand, the differences between the original and the protected data set are higher, decreasing in this way its statistical usefulness.

5.2.3.2. *Microaggregation*

In the recent years, microaggregation[14,15] has emerged as one of the most promising protection methods. Given a data set of a attributes, microaggregation builds small clusters of at least k elements and replaces the original values with the centroid of the cluster to which the record belongs to (interpreting each record as a point in $\mathbb{R}^a$). In this case, privacy is ensured because at least k elements of the original data set are mapped to the same value in the protected data set. This property is known as k-anonymity.[16-18] The construction of the cluster is aimed at minimizing the sum of squared errors of the original values with respect to the cluster centroids, in order to achieve the better statistical usefulness of the protected data.

A simpler approach for microaggregation is to protect each attribute separately. This corresponds to *univariate microaggregation*. It was rapidly replaced with the *multivariate microaggregation*, where microaggregation is applied to blocks of attributes. This method is referred to as MIC-vm-k where v stands for the size of the blocks of attributes and k for the size of the clusters. The main drawback of these approaches is that it is not assured that every protected record has at least k equal values in the protected data set (and k-anonymity is not ensured anymore), to the detriment of their privacy protection, since two records which are in the same cluster for one block of attributes may be in different clusters for other blocks.

A possible way of computing the real level of anonymity achieved by a microaggregation method is to consider the ratio between the total number n of records and the number of protected records which are different. This gives the average size of each "global cluster" in the protected data set. We denote this *real anonymity* measure by k'. It was introduced in[19] and used in other papers like.[20] We will use this measure to compare one of our approaches to microaggregation.

Finding the optimal multivariate microaggregation (in the sense that minimizes the sum of the square error) has been proved to be NP-Hard.[21] Thus, considering large blocks may be very costly, and so, many heuristic methods may be found in the literature that solve the problem with an acceptable efficiency, but may lead to a sub-optimal solution. In this work, we consider the heuristic microaggregation algorithm called *Maximum Distance to Average Vector* (MDAV).[15]

Regarding information loss, we presented some general measures in the previous section, which may be applicable to any protection method. Since multivariate microaggregation aims at minimizing the Sum of the Squared Errors (SSE), but there are no optimal solutions in polynomial time, the actual value of SSE for a given method is a measure of its quality with regard to information loss.

To sum up, increasing the size of the attribute blocks guarantees a better privacy protection, but the resulting algorithm tends to be less efficient. In this chapter, we use specific privacy protection and information loss measures to evaluate microaggregation methods.

5.2.4. *Artificial neural networks*

An *artificial neural network* (ANN) is an interconnected network of simple processing elements which are also called *neurons*. Each artificial neuron computes the output by weighting all of its inputs and then applying a final output function called *activation function*. By changing the values of these connection weights, the network can collectively produce a complex overall behavior. The process of changing these values is called *training* or *learning*. In this work, we use the *backpropagation algorithm* presented in[22] for the training phase. Later in this subsection, we outline the main aspects of this algorithm.

Neurons are arranged in groups called *layers*. Generally, the pth network layer contains M_p neurons and each processing element ($k = 1, ..., M_p$) computes a single stimulated response as follows:

$$o_k^p = f_k^p(net_k^p) \qquad\qquad net_k^p = \sum_{j=1}^{M_{p-1}} w_{jk}^p i_j + \theta_k^p$$

where o_k^p is the final output value returned by each neuron in the pth layer, f_k^p is the activation function, w_{jk}^p is the weight assigned to the connection between neurons j and k, and θ_k^p is called *bias* and it is further detailed in.[23] Note that f_k^p is applied to the net_k^p value that each neuron receives from the neurons of a previous layer ($i_j, j = 1, ..., M_{P-1}$) weighted with a certain w_{jk}^p.

For all layers and for $k = 1, ..., M_p$, we consider a *sigmoid* activation function:

$$f_k^p(x) = \frac{1}{1 + e^{-cx}} \qquad c \geq 0 \qquad\qquad (5.1)$$

where parameter c modifies the shape of this function and it is directly proportional to the slope at the origin of the activation function. Thus, increasing c, the ability of the ANN to separate patterns tends to be higher, but the stability of the iterative algorithm may decrease.

Although they have the same structure, layers are classified into three types: the input layer, that receives the external values; the hidden layers, that receive the information from a previous layer in the ANN and pass the results to the next layer; and the output layer, that returns the results of the ANN. The number of hidden layers is arbitrary and depends on the scenario.

The number of neurons in the hidden layers influences the complexity of the patterns that the net will be able to learn. The larger the number of neurons considered, the larger the complexity of the patterns an ANN is able to recognize. Note that, increasing the number of neurons, the complexity of the ANN structure becomes larger.

We assume in our work that there are neither feedback connections between neurons nor layer-bypassing connections. This means that the inputs of each layer depend exclusively on the previous layer outputs.

5.2.4.1. *The backpropagation algorithm*

The *backpropagation algorithm* allows the ANN to learn from a predefined set of input-output example pairs. The basic idea of this method is to adjust the weights of each processing element iteratively.

After initializing the network weights using uniformly distributed random numbers, the input data are propagated throughout the ANN. An error value is then computed at the output layer (first cycle) and, afterward, at all the hidden layers (second cycle). In this work, for the lth training vector, the error (E_l) is computed as the sum of the squared difference between the desired and the actual output of each neuron. The overall error (E) for all the training set is then the sum of all these errors $(E = \sum_l E_l)$.

Based on this error, connection weights are updated using an *iterative steepest descent* method. To apply this method we consider the direction of the gradient $(-\nabla E_l)$ and the learning-rate parameter η, so that weights are updated from step t to step $t + 1$ as follows:

$$w_{jk}(t + 1) = w_{jk}(t) - \eta \frac{\partial E_l}{\partial w_{jk}} \tag{5.2}$$

Note that parameter η tunes the norm of the vector that modifies the weight values. This parameter has an effect on the range of the weights explored and the probability of divergence. Weights in hidden layers are similarly adjusted.[22]

Here, we assume that the learning process is complete when the overall error E diminution from step to step is below a certain tolerance threshold. When the learning process is complete, the ANN has theoretically internalized the hidden patterns in the provided examples, meaning that it should be able to approximate them.

5.3. A New Desemantization Methodology

This chapter proposes a new generic methodology that aims at helping any anonymization method to be able to produce a protected set, diminishing the information loss and the disclosure risk as much as possible. In this section, we present an overview of our proposal.

As we have seen in the previous section, the number of attributes in a data set increases the complexity of a protection method and diminishes its ability to achieve the desired quality for its output. In general, increasing the number of attributes rises either the disclosure risk, the information loss, or both. Our work poses a solution to leverage the impact of the data semantics on the protection methods. The key idea of our proposal is to break the semantics of the values in the data set. An overview of the proposed methodology is depicted in Figure 5.2. The whole process is divided into two different phases: (i) the *Data Preprocessing* phase where the data set is transformed and normalized to make the protection process more straightforward; and (ii) the *Protection* phase, where a protection method is applied after preprocessing the data to obtain the final protected data set to be released. In the following sections we detail both phases separately, proposing also three new protection methods for the protection phase.

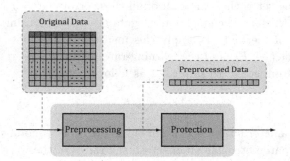

Fig. 5.2.   Global overview of the desemantization methodology

5.4. Data Preprocessing

As introduced in previous sections, our methodology proposal is divided into two main blocks. This section goes into further detail about the data preprocessing block. Particularly, we describe how the two main goals of this procedure are achieved: to ease the fitting of a model to the original data and to *desemantize* the microdata set.

As shown in Figure 5.3, the preprocessing block can be decomposed in several steps, namely: vectorization, sorting, partitioning, and normalization. At the end, sorting, partitioning, and normalization steps are repeated once. Then, we go into further detail about these steps and illustrate the process by means of an example.

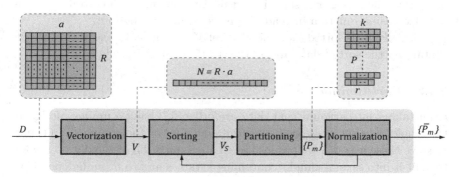

Fig. 5.3.   Data preprocessing schema

5.4.1. *Vectorization*

The vectorization step gathers all the values in the data set in a single vector, regardless of the attribute they belong to. In this way, we ignore the attribute semantics and, therefore, the possible correlation between two different attributes in the data set. In other words, we *desemantize* the microdata set. This process will play a central role in later discussions about the results of our methods.

Formally speaking, let $\mathcal{D}$ be the original data set to be protected. We denote by R the number of records in $\mathcal{D}$. Each record consists of a numerical attributes or fields. We assume that none of the registers contains blanks. We denote by N the total number of values in $\mathcal{D}$. As a consequence, $N = R \cdot a$.

Let V be a vector of size N containing all the values in the data set. Our methods treat values in the data set as if they were completely independent. In other words, the concepts of record and field are ignored and the N values in the data set are placed in V.

The effect of this step on a certain database is depicted in the upper half of Figure 5.3.

5.4.2. *Sorting*

Since the values in the vectorized data set belong to different source attributes, they present a pseudo-random aspect and it becomes very difficult to fit a model of them. In order to simplify the distribution of the data, the whole vector is sorted. In this way, our model has to fit an *easy* non-decreasing function instead of a more complex function.

Formally, V is sorted increasingly. Let V_s be the sorted vector of size N containing the sorted data and v_i the ith element of V_s', where $0 \le i < N$.

5.4.3. *Partitioning*

Even taking into account that data are ordered, fitting a unique model to the whole data set may not be accurate enough, or too complex. In order to solve these aspects, we propose to create a partition of the data set, *i.e.*, to split it into several chunks containing k values and to fit an independent model for each of them. Thus, modifying the value of k provides us with some control over the accuracy of the model by changing the size of the chunks of data being fitted. In other words, the higher the number of points per chunk k, the less accurate the model, and vice-versa. Note that if the data set was not sorted, k would not have this property. We go into further detail about the influence of this parameter in Section 5.6.

Formally, V_s is divided into smaller sub-vectors or chunks. We define k where $1 < k \le N$ as the number of values per chunk. Note that if k is not a divisor of N the last chunk will contain a smaller number of values. Let P be the number of chunks containing k values. We call r the number of values in the last chunk, where $0 \le r < k$. Therefore, $N = kP + r$. We will suppose that $r > 0$, so we have $P + 1$ chunks (note that $r > 0$ if and only if k does not divide N). We denote by P_m the mth chunk.

Let $v_{m,n}$ be defined as the nth element of P_m:

$$\begin{cases} v_{m,n} := v_{mk+n} & n = 0 \ldots k - 1 \quad m = 0 \ldots P - 1 \\ v_{P,n} := v_{Pk+n} & n = 0 \ldots r - 1 \end{cases}$$

The upper half of Figure 5.3 shows the effect of this step on a certain database.

5.4.4. *Normalization*

Since the range of the values in the different attributes could differ significantly among them, it is necessary to normalize the data to a certain predefined range of values.

There are many ways to normalize a data set. A possible solution would be to normalize each attribute separately before the application of the vectorization step. However, this normalization method could present problems with skewed attributes and, therefore, the attributes could not be merged in the sorting step. For this reason, we propose to normalize the data stored in each chunk independently. In this way, similar values are place in the same chunk and, therefore, the chances of avoiding the effect of skewness in the data are higher.

The range of normalization is usually not relevant to future steps of the methodology, so it is normally set to $[0, 1]$. Nevertheless, in some cases the result of the model we will fit in the next step is highly dependent on the boundaries of the normalized values. For instance, as discussed in Section 5.5.3.1, the result obtained by an artificial neural network is very sensitive to its input range and thus we will explain then how to adjust it.

Formally, we denote the normalized values by $\bar{v}_{m,n}$, the normalized chunks by $\bar{P}_m$, and the boundaries of the range we will fit all the data into by $[B_{min}, B_{max}]$. Let $\max_m$ and $\min_m$ be the maximum and the minimum values in the mth chunk:

$$\max_m := \max_{0 \le i < k} \{v_{m,i}\} \qquad \min_m := \min_{0 \le i < k} \{v_{m,i}\}$$

The normalized values are then defined as:

$$\begin{cases} \bar{v}_{m,n} := (B_{max} - B_{min}) \frac{v_{m,n} - \min_m}{\max_m - \min_m} + B_{min} & \text{if } \max_m \ne \min_m \\ \bar{v}_{m,n} := \frac{B_{max} + B_{min}}{2} & \text{if } \max_m = \min_m \end{cases}$$

where $0 \le m < P$ (or $0 \le m \le P$ if k does not divide N,) and $0 \le n < k$. Note that $\max_m = \min_m$ means that all the values in the chunk are the same. In this case, the normalized value is centered in the normalization range.

5.4.5. *Re-sorting and re-normalization*

One of the goals of the sorting process, apart from making data easier to fit, is to *desemantize* the data set, *i.e.*, to merge values from different attributes in order to break completely the semantic and, therefore, make the re-identification process more difficult. If the range of values of a certain attribute differs significantly from the others, it is likely that it is not merged in previous steps.

In order to appropriately mingle all attributes, once data has been sorted and normalized, we repeat these two steps. Since the range of values have been homogenized by normalization, attributes are conveniently mixed in the second sorting step and thus the data set is correctly preprocessed.

5.5. Data Fitting

Our data anonymization methodology is based on the construction of a model that fits the original numerical data set to be protected, once they have been preprocessed through the algorithm described in previous section. With this model we want to obtain a representation of the original data which is similar enough to be representative of the original data set, but different enough not to reveal the confidential information.

This step of our methodology is completely designable by the user, in the sense that any type of model may be applied in order to fulfill the requirements of a particular scenario. In this section we present different approaches to this process, *i.e.*, different data fitting models. First of all, we propose a model based on the computation of the mean value of each chunk of data. Next, we present a method based on a regression model. Finally, we present the use of a model based on artificial neural networks.

5.5.1. *Mean value model*

The first approach to the data fitting process is the computation of the mean value of each chunk. Therefore, the protected data set is obtained by substituting each original value of the mean value of the chunk it belongs to. We will call the resulting method *One Dimension Microaggregation* (Mic1D-k). Below, we describe this algorithm in detail.

Recalling the notation used in the previous section, for each chunk $\bar{P}_m$, the mean value of its components is computed:

$$\mu_m = \sum_{n=0}^{k-1} \frac{\bar{v}_{m,n}}{k} \qquad m = 0 \ldots P - 1 \qquad\qquad \mu_P = \sum_{n=0}^{r-1} \frac{\bar{v}_{P,n}}{r}$$

where the latter expression is applied to the last chunk if $r > 0$, *i.e.*, if k does not divide the total number of values in the data set.

The protected value $\bar{p}_{m,n}$ for $\bar{v}_{m,n}$ is then:

$$\begin{cases} \bar{p}_{m,n} = \mu_m & n = 0 \ldots k - 1 \quad m = 0 \ldots P - 1 \\ \bar{p}_{P,n} = \mu_P & n = 0 \ldots r - 1 \end{cases}$$

Finally, Mic1D-k de-normalizes the data into the original range, accordingly to the normalization and renormalization steps in the previous block. Note that, in this approach the range of normalized values is not relevant, in the sense that the protected values are independent of it. In this case, normalization process is just used to mix attributes, as explained before, and thus we will set the normalized range to $[0,1]$.

The protected values are placed in the protected data set in the same position held by the corresponding $v_{m,n}$ in the original data set. In this way, we are undoing the sorting and vectorization steps.

5.5.2. *Polynomial regression model*

The next approach to the data fitting process is to base our model on regressions. This section describes the use of least square error polynomial regressions in the data fitting step. We call the method that uses these regressions PoROP-k, that stands for *Polynomial Regression on Ordered Partitions.*

PoROP-k computes firstly the regressions for all the chunks of the partition obtained in the preprocessing step. Once data are modeled, the protected data set is obtained by adding noise to it. Now we precisely describe this algorithm.

For each chunk $\bar{P}_m$, polynomial fitting is computed over the following (X, Y) points:

$$(0, \bar{v}_{m,0}) \quad (1, \bar{v}_{m,1}) \quad (2, \bar{v}_{m,2}) \quad \cdots \quad (k-1, \bar{v}_{m,(k-1)})$$

When $r > 0$, the size of the last chunk $(\bar{P}_P)$ is $r < k$. In this case, the regression function of this chunk is computed differently: the nearest last k points of $\bar{V}_s$ are used, but only the r points held by $\bar{P}_P$ are actually protected. This guarantees that each polynomial regression is computed using the same number of points, so the level of accuracy is homogeneous. Therefore, in this case, the fitting for the last chunk is computed over the following (X, Y) points:

$$(0, \bar{v}_{m,N-k}) \quad (1, \bar{v}_{m,N-k+1}) \quad (2, \bar{v}_{m,N-k+2}) \quad \cdots \quad (k-1, \bar{v}_{m,N-1})$$

Next, we present the formulæ used to compute the coefficients of a linear regression, which is the simplest case. Assuming that the resulting polynomial regression is $l_{m,n} = \alpha_m + \beta_m n$ (where $n = 0 \dots k - 1$), then the expressions used to compute α_m and β_m are:

$$\alpha_m = \frac{2}{k(k+1)} \left[(2k-1) \sum_{n=0}^{k-1} \bar{v}_{m,n} - 3 \sum_{n=1}^{k-1} n \, \bar{v}_{m,n} \right]$$

$$\beta_m = \frac{2}{k(k+1)} \left[-3 \sum_{n=0}^{k-1} \bar{v}_{m,n} + \frac{6}{k-1} \sum_{n=1}^{k-1} n \, \bar{v}_{m,n} \right]$$

These results can be derived from the normal equations as presented in.[24] Although formulæ for quadratic and cubic degree regressions are used later in the experiments, the details about them are omitted for the sake of simplicity.

Later, PoROP-k methods add Gaussian noise to the polynomial regression to partially change the order of the points. With the addition of noise, re-identification will be more difficult for an intruder even knowing the values of some attributes.

PoROP-k methods may be considered both a protection method and a synthetic data generator depending on the way used to add noise. If the Gaussian noise is computed regardless of the original value to protect, PoROP-k methods can be considered synthetic data generators. We call this set of methods PoROP$_s$-k. An example of two different regression curves, quadratic and cubic, computed on the same data set is shown in Figure 5.4. On the other hand, if the noise addition is dependent on the point to be protected, PoROP-k methods must be considered perturbative. In this latter case, we call this method set *PoROP_p-k*. An example of these is presented in Figure 5.5.

Finally, both PoROP-k methods de-normalize the data into the original range, accordingly to the normalization and renormalization steps in the previous block. Note that, in this approach the range of normalized values is not relevant, in the sense that the result of the regression model is independent of it. In this case, normalization process is just used to mix

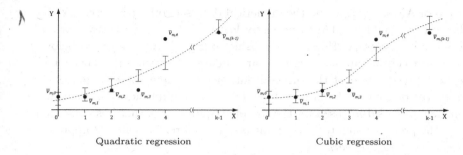

Quadratic regression · · · Cubic regression

Fig. 5.4. Example of different regression curves on a set of points from a chunk of data and the more probable intervals for the protected values when noise is added independently of the original values (synthetic method)

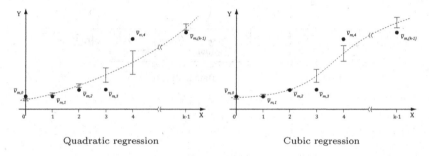

Quadratic regression · · · Cubic regression

Fig. 5.5. Example of different regression curves on a set of points from a chunk of data and the more probable interval for the protected values when noise is added taking into account the original value (perturbative method)

attributes, as explained before, and thus we will set the normalized range to $[0,1]$.

The protected values are placed in the protected data set in the same place held by the corresponding $v_{m,n}$ in the original data set. In this way, we are undoing the sorting and vectorization steps.

Finally, analogously to Mic1D-k, both PoROP-k methods de-normalize the data into the original range of data and undo the sorting and vectorization steps. Again, the normalized range is set to $[0,1]$, since the result of this method does not depend on it either.

5.5.3. *Neural networks*

The last approach we considered for the data fitting is the use of *Artificial Neural Networks* (ANNs). The basic idea of this approach is to use a group of ANNs for learning the numerical data set to be protected. ANNs themselves would be able to perfectly learn all data using a structure as complex as necessary. However, this is not our goal. As introduced before, we want to obtain an inaccurately learned data set which is similar enough to be representative of the original data set but different enough not to reveal the original confidential values. In order to fulfill these requirements, our new proposal is based on the use of simple ANN structures combined with the preprocessing techniques introduced before. We call this approach *Ordered Neural Networks* (ONN).

As shown in Figure 5.6, the data fitting process of ONN can be decomposed in two steps, namely *learning* and *data protection*.

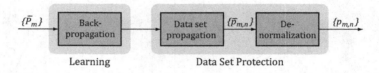

Fig. 5.6.   Data fitting ONN schema

Once data has been preprocessed as explained in previous sections, ONN applies the backpropagation algorithm taking as training set these data. Once the learning process finishes, data are protected according to the accuracy reached previously. Differently from the previous approaches presented in this chapter, for ONN the range of values after normalization is highly relevant, in the sense that the result of the model obtained by the ANNs is highly dependent on it, as we will show in the experiments.

Another restriction of this approach is that we must assure that all the chunks of the partition have k values. In other words, k must divide the number of points of the data set. If that is not the case, we can add dummy values to fulfill this requirement and erase them after the process.

Below, we firstly depict the influence the range of normalization has on the learning process and later we go into further detail about the learning and the data protection processes.

5.5.3.1. *Normalization range*

As introduced in Section 5.2.4, the ability of a neural network to learn depends, among other facts, on the range of values of the input data set and the activation function. In order to make the learning process possible, it is necessary to normalize the input data set. An input value x is desired to range between two fitted values $-B_{in}$ and B_{in}, where $B_{in} \in \mathbb{R}^+$, so that the output values of the activation function fall between a certain $B1_{out}$ and $B2_{out}$. The basic idea is to adjust the boundaries (B_{in}) in order to make the normalized input values fit in the range where the slope of the activation function is relevant, as explained in.[23] Figure 5.7 shows the activation function used and the ranges of normalization.

More formally, using Equation 5.1 we relate the input and output ranges:

$$B1_{out} = \frac{1}{1 + e^{c(B_{in})}} \qquad B2_{out} = \frac{1}{1 + e^{-c(B_{in})}}$$

According to this, we set the normalization and renormalization ranges in the preprocessing block to $[-B_{in}, B_{in}]$. Analogously, the desired output, which is denoted by $y_{m,n}$, where $0 \le m < P$ and $0 \le n < k$, is normalized between $B1_{out}$ and $B2_{out}$. The range of values of the desired outputs is then $[B1_{out}, B2_{out}]$. Notice that, in the input layer, the outputs fall in the same range, making the training process easier.

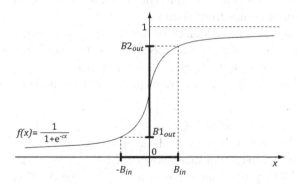

Fig. 5.7.   Activation function and ranges of normalization

5.5.3.2. *Learning process*

Finally, ONN creates an array of ANNs in order to learn the whole data set, where each ANN is associated to a chunk of data. Therefore, the array contains P ANNs. The objective for each ANN is to learn the values in its corresponding chunk, although a specific ANN is not only fed with the values in that chunk, but uses the whole data set to learn. In some sense, using the whole data set, we are adding noise to the learning process by using input data coming from a chunk that is not the one to be learned.

This learning process, in conjunction with the preprocessing techniques previously explained, make the ANNs internalize the data patterns distortedly. In this way, the reproduced data are resembling enough to the original, to maintain their statistical properties, but dissimilar enough not to disclose the original confidential values.

Specifically, the ANN that learns the values of a chunk $\bar{P}_m$ receives the nth value of that set, $\bar{v}_{m,n}$, together with the $P - 1$ nth values of the remaining chunks. Since the network is intended to learn all values $\bar{v}_{m,n}$ in $\bar{P}_m$, the desired output is set to $\bar{y}_{m,n} = \bar{v}_{m,n}$. This process is repeated iteratively until the learning process finishes.

In our proposal, each ANN contains three layers: the input layer, a single hidden layer, and the output layer, which can be described as follows:

- **Input Layer.** The input layer consists of $M_1 = P$ neurons. Each of them takes the data from a different chunk as input. That is, input of the ith neuron comes from chunk $\bar{P}_i$.
- **Hidden Layer.** The hidden layer has $M_2 = n_h$ neurons. As explained in,[23] n_h has an effect on the speed of the learning process and the ability of the network to learn complex patterns.
- **Output Layer.** The output layer consists of one single neuron ($M_3 = 1$).

The structure of the array of ANNs is shown in Figure 5.8.

All networks learn the original data updating their weights by using the iterative *backpropagation algorithm* explained in Section 5.2.4.1. The quality of the data protection depends mainly on the ANN structure and the preprocessing parameters.

5.5.3.3. *Data protection*

Once the ANNs have been trained, and therefore the weights updated, the last step obtains the protected values for the data set. This includes the

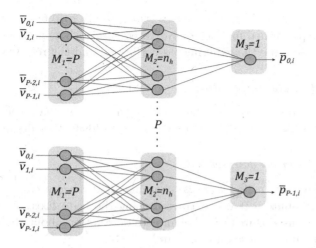

Fig. 5.8.   Array of ANNs used by ONN

data set propagation and the de-normalization, as explained below.

Let $\bar{p}_{m,n}$ be the protected value for $\bar{v}_{m,n}$. As mentioned before, the mth ANN of the array has been trained to reproduce $\bar{v}_{m,n}$ when the values in the P input neurons is $\bar{v}_{0,n}, ..., \bar{v}_{P-1,n}$. In this way, $\bar{p}_{m,n}$ is defined as the output obtained when having $\bar{v}_{0,n}, ..., \bar{v}_{P-1,n}$ as input of the mth already trained ANN.

Finally, the protected value $p_{m,n}$ for $v_{m,n}$ is obtained by de-normalizing $\bar{p}_{m,n}$ as explained in the previous approaches, in order to undo the normalization and renormalization steps in the preprocessing block.

As in the previous approaches, the protected values $p_{m,n}$ are placed in the protected data set in the same place held by the corresponding $v_{m,n}$ in the original data set in order to undo the sorting and vectorization steps.

5.6. Experiments

In this section, we present the experiments performed in order to test our methodology using real data sets available in the Internet and widely used for evaluation purposes of data protection methods. In order to prove the validity of our methodology, we test the three approaches presented in this chapter and highlight their main properties.

First of all, in Section 5.6.1, we describe the data sets used in the experiments. Each of the three next sections (5.6.2 to 5.6.4) presents the experiments performed for each of our three data fitting approaches. In all of them, we describe the experiments performed and the results obtained.

5.6.1. *Data sets description*

This section briefly describes the data sets used to evaluate the proposed methods. For each of them, a reference is given for further details.

5.6.1.1. *The Census data set*

The first data set, called *Census*, contains 1080 records consisting of 13 numerical attributes. It was extracted using the Data Extraction System of the U.S. Census Bureau.[25] A complete description about the details of the construction of these data set can be found in.[26]

5.6.1.2. *The EIA data set*

The second data set, called EIA, was obtained from the U.S. Energy Information Authority.[27] It contains 4092 records consisting of 15 attributes. We have discarded the 5 non-numerical attributes and the 5 identifier attributes.

5.6.1.3. *The Water-treatment data set*

The Water-treatment data set was extracted from the UCI repository[28] and contains 35 attributes and 380 entries. As we will explain in the next section, we have selected 9 out of the 35 attributes in these data set.

5.6.2. *Mic1D-k evaluation*

We have tested Mic1D-k and compared our results with those obtained by the MDAV microaggregation algorithm, using the *Census*[25] and *Water-treatment*[28] data sets presented previously. These data sets have been used in previous works[13,19] to compare different microaggregation techniques.

As shown in,[20] when protecting a data set using multivariate microaggregation, the way in which the data are split to form blocks is highly relevant with regard to the degree of privacy achieved (k' value). Similarly to this work, we have reduced both data sets to have 9 attributes. Note that, although Census has been used with 13 attributes in other experiments of this chapter, in this case we have selected attributes $a1$ to $a9$, in order to be able to make three blocks of three attributes, as we describe below.

In both data sets, attributes $a1, a2$ and $a3$ are highly correlated, as well as attributes $a4, a5$ and $a6$, and attributes $a7, a8$ and $a9$. On the contrary, attributes of different blocks are non-correlated. For our experiments, when protecting data using MDAV microaggregation, we assume attributes to be split into three blocks of three attributes each. Also, we consider two situations when protecting the data sets using MDAV microaggregation: blocking correlated attributes and thus non-correlated blocks, *i.e.*, $(a1, a2, a3)$, $(a4, a5, a6)$ and $(a7, a8, a9)$; or blocking non-correlated attributes but correlated blocks, *i.e.*, $(a1, a4, a7)$, $(a2, a5, a8)$ and $(a3, a6, a9)$. Testing these two cases will let us study the impact of the choice of the attributes for the microaggregation groups, based on their correlations.

For each data set and attribute selection method, we apply MDAV microaggregation using the same parameterizations as those in previous works.[19,20] Namely, we protect the data sets using MDAV with parameter $k = 5, 25, 50, 75, 100$ for the Census data set, and $k = 5, 10, 15, 20, 25$ for the Water-treatment data set. The selection of these values aims at covering a wide range of SSE values and, thus, studying scenarios with different *information loss* values.

For Mic1D-k, we use $k = 3000, 3200, 4000, 4400, 5000$ for the Census data set and $k = 300, 500, 800, 850, 900$ for the Water-treatment data set. Note that, since Mic1D-k *desemantizes* the data set, there is no point in considering different situations related to the correlation of the attributes and, therefore, we protect the data set just once for each parametrization. In order to make the comparison fair, we have chosen the values of k in Mic1D-k to obtain similar SSE values to those obtained by MDAV after protecting the data sets.

We consider that a possible intruder knows the value of three random attributes of the original data set. Different tests are performed assuming that the intruder knows different sets of three attributes. Depending on these attributes the intruder will have information coming from one or more groups (of those three created by microaggregation). Table 5.2 shows all the considered possibilities.

Firstly, we suppose that the three known attributes belong to the same MDAV microaggregated block (*e.g.* $(a1, a2, a3)$ in the correlated scenario or $(a1, a4, a7)$ in the non-correlated). Since the size of the three microaggregation blocks is 3, there are only three options to consider. We denote this case by 1G. Since the intruder only has access to data from one group,

Table 5.1. Types of nodes participating in the NTS and settings of test scenarios.

Type of player	Forwarding approach	Sleep mode	s_1[a]	s_2[b]	s_3[c]
Strategy-Based (SB)	reputation based	never	10	20	40
Adaptive Sleep (AS)	forward if in idle mode	if $sr > 0.4$	10	5	4
Adaptive Forwarding (AF)	if $sr < 0.4$	never	10	5	4
Cooperative (C)	always forward	never	10	5	4
Selfish 1 (SF1)	always discard	never	10	15	4
Selfish 2 (SF2)	forward with prob. 0.5	never	10	10	4

[a] distribution of players in scenario 1 (s_1), [b] distribution of players in scenario 2 (s_2), [c] distribution of players in scenario 3 (s_3).

Table 5.2. Different groups of variables known by the intruder in the Mic1D-k scenario

Correlated	1G	$(v1, v2, v3)$, $(v4, v5, v6)$, $(v7, v8, v9)$
	2G	$(v1, v2, v5)$, $(v1, v3, v7)$, $(v2, v3, v6)$, $(v1, v4, v5)$, $(v2, v4, v6)$ $(v5, v6, v9)$, $(v6, v7, v8)$, $(v1, v8, v9)$, $(v2, v7, v9)$
	3G	$(v1, v4, v7)$, $(v1, v5, v8)$, $(v1, v6, v9)$, $(v2, v4, v7)$, $(v2, v5, v8)$ $(v2, v6, v9)$, $(v3, v4, v7)$, $(v3, v5, v8)$, $(v3, v6, v9)$
Non-correlated	1G	$(v1, v4, v7)$, $(v2, v5, v8)$, $(v3, v6, v9)$
	2G	$(v1, v4, v5)$, $(v1, v3, v7)$, $(v4, v7, v8)$, $(v1, v2, v5)$, $(v2, v4, v8)$ $(v5, v8, v9)$, $(v3, v6, v8)$, $(v1, v6, v9)$, $(v3, v4, v9)$
	3G	$(v1, v2, v3)$, $(v1, v5, v6)$, $(v1, v8, v9)$, $(v2, v3, v4)$, $(v4, v5, v6)$ $(v4, v8, v9)$, $(v2, v3, v7)$, $(v5, v6, v7)$, $(v7, v8, v9)$

MDAV ensures the k-anonymity property (this is the best possible scenario for MDAV). However, note that, generally, the intruder cannot choose the attributes obtained from external sources and it might be difficult to obtain all the attributes coming from the same group. Secondly, we assume that the known attributes belong to two different MDAV microaggregated groups. There are many possible combinations of three attributes under this assumption, so nine of them were chosen randomly. We refer to this case as 2G. Finally, case 3G is defined analogously to 2G, and also nine possibilities of known attributes are considered. Note that, in both scenarios 2G and 3G, k-anonymity is not ensured by MDAV. Note also that, if the intruder had more than three attributes, it would not be possible to consider 1G. We are considering the case where the intruder only has three attributes to study a scenario where MDAV preserve k-anonymity.

The first column of Tables 5.3 and 5.4 presents the parameter that defines both methods (k for MDAV and k for Mic1D). In the second one we present the SSE values for all the parameterizations and situations described before. Note that the range of SSE covered by the two methods is similar, so this allows us to compare the disclosure risk of both methods fairly. For all these scenarios, we compute k' and the mean of all the k' values in each situation is presented in the remaining three columns. Note that, whereas MDAV is affected by the fact that the chosen attributes are correlated or not, this effect is not noticeable using Mic1D-k. Specifically, when the attributes in a group are not correlated, the information loss (SSE) using MDAV tends to be increased since we are trying to collapse the records in a single value, using three independent attributes or dimensions. Nevertheless, this effect can be neglected with our technique since, thanks to the data preprocessing (*desemantization*), the whole microaggregation process is performed on a single dimension (vector of values), the semantics of attributes are ignored and the effect caused by attribute correlations is avoided.

Table 5.3. SSE and real k' values using MDAV-k and Mic1D-k methods assuming that different groups of variables are known by the intruder using the Census data set

		SSE	k' 1G	2G	3G			SSE	k' 1G	2G	3G
MDAV-k	5	64.99	5.00	1.92	1.00	MDAV-k	5	58.49	5.00	1.96	1.02
	25	223.73	25.12	7.00	1.09		25	260.13	25.12	7.35	1.24
	50	328.31	51.43	14.66	1.41		50	356.47	51.43	15.86	2.05
	75	382.34	77.14	23.18	1.96		75	563.79	77.14	24.38	2.83
	100	428.68	108.00	35.00	3.33		100	721.91	108.00	36.14	4.62
Mic1D-k	3000	32.27	8.37	9.87	5.77	Mic1D-k	3000	32.27	5.63	8.51	8.04
	3200	89.18	11.97	13.76	8.26		3200	89.18	8.01	11.95	11.83
	4000	129.06	20.10	22.09	13.89		4000	129.06	13.53	19.45	19.19
	4400	310.63	23.15	26.94	17.01		4400	310.63	16.62	23.64	22.45
	5000	738.12	72.83	76.08	55.02		5000	738.12	59.77	67.72	67.25

Correlated attributes   Non-correlated attributes

Results show that, in general, Mic1D-k achieves lower disclosure risk levels (larger values of k') than those achieved by MDAV for similar information loss (SSE), especially when the attributes chosen come from different microaggregated groups (2G and 3G), which is the most common case. When the intruder has access to the three attributes coming from a single microaggregated group, MDAV presents k' values which are similar or, in some cases, even larger than those obtained by Mic1D-k (comparing cases with similar SSE). This is normal since MDAV preserves the

Table 5.4. SSE and real k' values using MDAV-k and Mic1D-k methods assuming that different groups of variables are known by the intruder using the Water data set

	k	SSE	k' 1G	2G	3G
MDAV-k	5	28.18	5.09	1.94	1.00
	10	46.14	10.00	3.14	1.01
	15	72.03	15.20	4.42	1.01
	20	94.24	20.00	5.75	1.04
	25	114.56	25.33	7.28	1.10
Mic1D-k	300	32.67	1.62	1.51	1.10
	500	65.89	3.25	3.39	1.76
	800	80.95	7.87	7.55	4.67
	850	132.13	9.65	10.03	6.65
	900	255.64	12.95	13.61	9.14

Correlated attributes

	k	SSE	k' 1G	2G	3G
MDAV-k	5	69.51	5.00	2.03	1.03
	10	126.21	10.00	3.55	1.16
	15	173.96	15.20	5.28	1.39
	20	259.07	20.00	7.00	1.53
	25	247.58	25.33	9.22	1.91
Mic1D-k	300	32.67	1.11	1.35	1.35
	500	65.89	1.78	2.58	2.63
	800	80.95	4.74	7.17	6.88
	850	132.13	6.54	9.77	8.67
	900	255.64	9.07	14.52	11.71

Non-correlated attributes

k-anonymity in this case. However, in the remaining scenarios (2G and 3G), that represent most of the cases, Mic1D-k achieves larger k' values than those obtained by MDAV when similar *SSE* values are compared. In other words, Mic1D-k is able to keep much better the statistical usefulness of data for a similar level of privacy protection.

5.6.3. *PoROP-k evaluation*

We test PoROP$_s$-k and PoROP$_p$-k methods using linear, quadratic and cubic regressions. The range of values for the number of points per chunk k has been defined in order to test a wide spectrum of cases ranging from low to high IL values. Since the distribution of values in each data set is different, values of k are specifically for each one, namely, for the Census data set k ranges from 2000 to 10000, while it ranges from 6000 to 18000 for the EIA data set. We execute each configuration five times performing 510 tests in total. The average IL, DR and score values for each configuration and both data sets are presented in Figure 5.9. Table 5.5 shows the detail of the scores obtained from the experiments. Note that the figures and tables presented in this section only show the results using the synthetic version (PoROP$_s$-k). The results obtained by PoROP$_p$-k are almost identical and are omitted for the sake of simplicity.

In general, being able to control the IL is important, especially when we are interested in keeping the statistics in the protected data set. As we can see in the first row of Figure 5.9, *PoROP-k* methods present a strong relation between IL and the value of parameter k. Normally, when parameter k increases, IL increases. Note that this can be observed regardless of the model regression and the data set. In our case, the preprocessing phase is very important to guarantee this strong relation, since by vectorizing, ordering, partitioning and normalizing $PoROP_p$-k makes it possible to find a regression model that accurately fits the data set.

Observing the same figure, we can see that the more complex the polynomial model, the lower the information loss. This happens because by increasing the complexity of the regression function, we also increase the fitting capabilities of the polynomial models.

A decrease in the information loss typically implies an increase in the disclosure risk. The second row of Figure 5.9 presents the evolution of the disclosure risk as a function of k. We can observe that, as the complexity of the regression model increases, $PoROP$-k methods generally present a larger DR.

Table 5.5. $PoROP_s$-k average scores using the Census and the EIA data set

k	Linear	Quadratic	Cubic
2000	42.1	42.2	42.3
3000	41.3	41.8	42.0
4000	40.3	41.9	42.0
5000	37.6	41.1	41.6
6000	42.1	41.4	41.9
7000	40.9	31.9	35.5
8000	41.1	34.0	37.6
9000	51.6	36.0	41.1
10000	61.5	40.4	42.9

Census

k	Linear	Quadratic	Cubic
6000	36.1	39.1	38.0
8000	34.0	35.2	35.6
10000	33.8	33.3	35.1
12000	43.4	33.0	33.7
14000	52.1	39.9	34.3
16000	40.7	38.1	33.2
18000	69.4	38.3	33.2

EIA

However, the overall decrease on the information loss compensate for the increase on the disclosure risk. This is shown in the last row of Figure 5.9, where we can observe that the score values obtained by quadratic and cubic regression models are in general lower than the values obtained by the linear regression models. This effect is clearer when the chunks of the partition have a large number of points. In these cases $PoROP$-k methods outperform the results obtained by the use of a simple regression model due to their greater fitting capabilities.

Table 5.5 shows that, by increasing the complexity of the regression functions, we achieve a better quality in the protection. Specifically, in the Census data set, the best scores are obtained using quadratic regression (31.9), while the best scores using linear regressions are 37.6. Analogously, when using the EIA data set the best scores are obtained using cubic re-

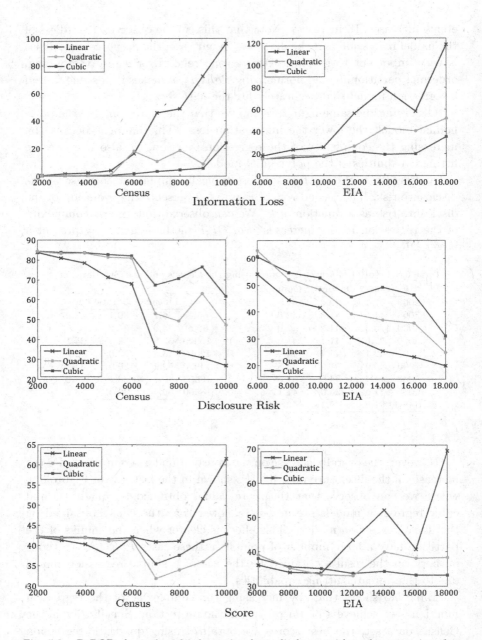

Fig. 5.9.   PoROP$_s$-k results of information loss, disclosure risk and score using the Census and the EIA data set

gressions instead of linear regressions.

5.6.4. *ONN evaluation*

In this section, we compare ONN with the best ranked protection methods presented in the literature. The survey in[13] reviews the most common protection methods concluding that *Rank Swapping* (RS-p) and *Microaggregation* (MIC-vm-k) are the two methods that obtain lower scores for numerical data protection. For this reason, we compare ONN with these two methods. Specifically, we have chosen the best five parameterizations for RS-p and MIC-vm-k. In order to test the three methods, we use the Census data set presented previously.

The ONN parameters are: number of chunks in the partition (P), normalization range size (B), learning rate parameter (E), activation function slope parameter (C), and number of neurons in the hidden layer (H).

Another parameter, regarding the disclosure risk evaluation, is the number of attributes used by an intruder to reveal data using RL techniques (V). We have divided our experiments into two different scenarios. Firstly, we assume that the intruder only has half of the original protected attributes ($V = 7$). This scenario was used in.[29] Secondly, we assume that the intruder is able to obtain all the original attributes ($V = 13$). This scenario could be considered to be the most favorable scenario for the intruder.

The values selected for each factor were chosen according to an exhaustive empirical search among a realistic set of parameters. The best-score parameter sets, for both cases of the V parameter, are presented in Table 5.6. These sets of configurations are later referred to as ONN-A, ONN-B, etc.

Table 5.6. ONN parameters used in the experiments

	P	B	E	C	H		P	B	E	C	H
A	8	0.8	0.4	4.0	8	A	8	0.8	0.4	4.0	8
B	10	0.8	0.1	3.5	8	B	8	0.8	0.3	4.0	8
C	10	0.8	0.1	3.0	8	C	8	0.8	0.1	4.0	2
D	10	0.8	0.1	4.0	8	D	10	0.8	0.1	3.5	8
E	8	0.8	0.1	4.0	2	E	8	0.8	0.1	3.5	2

We have also run RS-p and MIC-vm-k using their best five parameterizations, extracted from,[13] so we can fairly compare to them.

The left side of Table 5.7 shows the scores in the first scenario. As we can observe, the IL when protecting data using ONN is, in general, lower than that obtained using RS-p or MIC-vm-k. This means that ONN is able to fit the data set better than the other two approaches. These results are consistent with the methodology used by ONN to protect data. Since ONN is trained using the data set after being preprocessed, the patterns learned depend on values that come from different individuals in the original data set. Because of this, an intruder should know the values in each chunk to be able to understand the learned patterns. Since this information is no longer available after protecting the data, ONN can get lower IL while preserving relatively good rates of DR.

Table 5.7.   ONN average results for IL, DR, and score using $V = 7$ and $V = 13$ variables

	Param.	IL	DR	Score		Param.	IL	DR	Score
RS-p	$p=14$	23.83	24.21	24.02	RS-p	$p=14$	23.83	31.32	27.58
	$p=17$	27.40	21.87	24.64		$p=17$	27.40	28.43	27.92
	$p=12$	21.08	27.83	24.45		$p=12$	21.08	35.83	28.46
	$p=15$	27.44	23.62	25.53		$p=15$	27.44	30.51	28.98
	$p=13$	25.39	26.35	25.87		$p=13$	25.39	33.79	29.59
MIC-vm-k	$v=4\ k=17$	23.98	31.67	27.82	MIC-vm-k	$v=4\ k=17$	23.98	40.80	32.39
	$v=4\ k=19$	26.10	31.09	28.59		$v=4\ k=19$	26.10	40.10	33.10
	$v=4\ k=11$	21.27	36.22	28.74		$v=4\ k=11$	21.27	46.45	33.86
	$v=3\ k=20$	21.95	35.85	28.90		$v=3\ k=20$	21.95	46.70	34.33
	$v=3\ k=15$	18.98	39.33	29.15		$v=3\ k=15$	18.98	50.94	34.96
ONN	A	20.42	26.25	23.33	ONN	a	21.45	33.52	27.49
	B	20.59	26.95	23.77		b	22.23	32.99	27.61
	C	20.31	27.26	23.78		c	22.38	33.04	27.71
	D	20.66	26.96	23.81		d	20.59	34.88	27.73
	E	22.38	25.65	24.01		e	22.56	33.20	27.88
		$V = 7$					$V = 13$		

Regarding DR, the best disclosure risk corresponds to RS-p. These results make sense because when the intruder has a reduced set of variables, it is very difficult to re-identify individuals because, by swapping, RS-p mixes values from different individuals. ONN presents a good DR, better than that obtained by MIC-vm-k.

Observing the scores, ONN shows to be the best protection method among those compared in this work and, therefore, all the methods studied in.[13] Note that, although the DR is lower for RS-p, the scores show that ONN is better ranked, meaning that the benefits obtained by avoiding the IL compensate for the increase in the DR.

The left side of Table 5.7 shows similar results for the second scenario, where the intruder has all the variables. As we can observe, the results are very similar. It is important to notice though the larger the number of variables known by the intruder, the more similar the DR presented by

RS-p and ONN.

5.7. Conclusions

We have presented a new methodology for numerical microdata anonymization, *i.e.*, a methodology that aims at guaranteeing the privacy protection of a data set, while preserving its statistical significance.

Our methodology presents a new way of preprocessing the data based on their *desemantization*. We gather all the values in a single vector, independently of the attribute they belong to. Thanks to that, possible relations between attributes are omitted and, therefore, it is more difficult for an intruder to re-identify the individuals. The data in this vector are sorted in order to mix all the attributes and make a data modeling easier. Once data are preprocessed, our methodology fits a model to the sorted data. This step is completely designable by the user, allowing the resulting method to be adapted to a specific scenario, in order to fulfill some particular requirements.

We have presented and tested three approaches to these data fitting step, with the result of three different data protection methods in the same methodology framework: Mic1D-k, PoROP-k and ONN. These methods cover both perturbative methods and synthetic data generators, several scenarios and a wide range of complexity of their algorithms. In view of their results we can assert that our methodology, specifically the key point of data desemantization, is a valid and powerful approach to the numerical microdata anonymization problem.

Acknowledgments

The authors want to thank the Spanish MICINN for its support through projects TIN2006-15536-C02-02, ARES CONSOLIDER INGENIO 2010 CSD2007-00004 and eAEGIS TSI2007-65406-C03-02; the Government of Catalunya for grants 2005- SGR-00093 and GRE-00352 and both institutions plus UPC for the I3 grant of J. L. Larriba-Pey.

References

1. V. Torra, J. M. Abowd, and J. Domingo-Ferrer. Using mahalanobis distance-based record linkage for disclosure risk assessment. In *Privacy in Statistical Databases*, vol. 4302, *LNCS*, pp. 175–186, (2006).

2. V. Torra and J. Domingo-Ferrer, *Disclosure control methods and information loss for microdata*, In *Confidentiality, disclosure, and data access : Theory and practical applications for statistical agencies*, chapter 5, pp. 91–110. Elsevier, (2001).
3. J. M. Mateo-Sanz, J. Domingo-Ferrer, and F. Sebé, Probabilistic information loss measures in confidentiality protection of continuous microdata, *Data Mining and Knowledge Discovery.* **11**(2), 181–193, (2005).
4. E. Bertino, I. N. Fovino, and L. P. Provenza, A framework for evaluating privacy preserving data mining algorithms, *Data Mininig Knowledge Discover.* **11**(2), 121–154, (2005).
5. F. Sebé, J. Domingo-Ferrer, J. M. Mateo-Sanz, and V. Torra. Post-masking optimization of the tradeoff between information loss and disclosure risk in masked microdata sets. In *Inference Control in Statistical Databases*, vol. 2316, *LNCS*, pp. 187–196, (2002).
6. W. E. Yancey, W. E. Winkler, and R. H. Creecy. Disclosure risk assessment in perturbative microdata protection. In *Inference Control in Statistical Databases*, vol. 2316, *LNCS*, pp. 135–152, (2002).
7. W. E. Winkler. Data cleaning methods. In *Proceedings of the ACM Workshop on Data Cleaning, Record Linkage and Object Identification*, (2003).
8. W. E. Winkler. Re-identification methods for masked microdata. In *Privacy in Statistical Databases*, vol. 3050, *LNCS*, pp. 216–230, (2004).
9. D.-W. Wang, C.-J. Liau, and T. sheng Hsu, An epistemic framework for privacy protection in database linking, *Data and Knowledge engineering.* **61**, 176–205, (2007).
10. G. T. Duncan, S. E. Fienberg, R. Krishnan, R. Padman, and S. F. Roehrig. Disclosure limitation methods and information loss for tabular data. In *Confidentiality, Disclosure, and Data Access: Theory and Practical Applications for Statistical Agencies*, pp. 135–166, (2001).
11. G. T. Duncan, S. A. Keller-McNulty, and S. L. Stokes. Database security and confidentiality: Examining disclosure risk vs. data utility through the r-u confidentiality map. Technical Report 142, National Institute of Statistical Sciences, http://www.niss.org/, (2004).
12. R. A. Moore. Controlled data swapping techniques for masking public use microdata sets. U. S. Bureau of the Census, (1996).
13. J. Domingo-Ferrer and V. Torra, *A quantitative comparison of disclosure control methods for microdata*, In *Confidentiality, disclosure, and data access : Theory and practical applications for statistical agencies*, chapter 6, pp. 111–133. Elsevier, (2001).
14. D. Defays and P. Nanopoulos. Panels of enterprises and confidentiality: The small aggregates method. In *Proceedings of 92 Symposium on Design and Analysis of Longitudinal Surveys*, pp. 195–204. Statistics Canada, (1993).
15. J. Domingo-Ferrer and J. M. Mateo-Sanz, Practical data-oriented microaggregation for statistical disclosure control, *IEEE Transactions on Knowledge and Data Engineering.* **14**(1), 189–201, (2002).
16. P. Samatari and L. Sweeney. Protecting privacy when disclosing information: k-anonymity and its enforcement through generalization and suppression.

Technical report, SRI Intl. Tech. Rep., (1998).

17. L. Sweeney, Achieving k-anonymity privacy protection using generalization and suppression, *International Journal Uncertainty Fuzziness Knowledge-Based Systems*. **10**(5), 571–588, (2002).

18. L. Sweeney, k-anonymity: a model for protecting privacy, *Int. J. of Unc., Fuzz. and Knowledge Based Systems*. **10**(5), 557–570, (2002).

19. J. Nin, J. Herranz, and V. Torra, Attribute selection in multivariate microaggregation, *Post-Proc. of 11th ACM International Conference on Extending Database Technology.* pp. 51–60, (2008).

20. J. Nin, J. Herranz, and V. Torra, How to group attributes in multivariate microaggregation, *Int. J. of Unc., Fuzz. and Knowledge Based Systems*. **16**(1), 121–138, (2008).

21. A. Oganian and J. Domingo-Ferrer, On the complexity of optimal microaggregation for statistical disclosure control, *Statistical Journal of the United Nations Economic Commission for Europe*. **18**, 345 – 353, (2001).

22. R. Rojas, *Neural Networks: A Systematic Introduction*. (Springer, 1996).

23. J. A. Freeman and D. M. Skapura, *Neural Networks: Algorithms, Applications and Programming Techniques*. (Addison-Wesley Publishing Company, 1991).

24. G. Dahlquist and A. Björck, *Numerical Methods*. (Dover Publications, 2003).

25. U.S. Census Bureau, Data Extraction System. http://www.census.gov/, (1990).

26. J. Domingo-Ferrer, V. Torra, J. M. Mateo-Sanz, and F. Sebé. Systematic measures of re-identification risk based on the probabilistic links of the partially synthetic data back to the original microdata. Technical report, Cornell University, (2005).

27. U.S. Energy Information Authority. http://www.eia.doe.gov/, (2004).

28. D. Aha. UCI repository machine learning databases. http://archive.ics.uci.edu/ml/, (1994).

29. J. Nin, J. Herranz, and V. Torra, Rethinking rank swapping to decrease disclosure risk, *Data and Knowledge Engineering*. **64**, 346–364, (2007).

Chapter 6

Multi-Objective Evolutionary Optimization in Statistical Disclosure Control

Rinku Dewri, Indrajit Ray, Indrakshi Ray and Darrell Whitley

*Colorado State University, Department of Computer Science,
Fort Collins, CO 80523-1873, USA*
{rinku, indrajit, iray, whitley} @cs. colostate. edu

Statistical disclosure control involves the sanitization of personally identifying information in data sets prior to their dissemination. Such a process typically results in a loss in utility of the data. A data publisher is thus confronted with two requirements to fulfill – ensuring the safety of respondents and maintaining statistical utility in the anonymized data. Existing approaches model the first requirement as a constraint in an optimization framework directed towards maximizing data utility. An immediate consequence of this method is the requirement for exhaustive analysis if the much desired trade-off behavior between privacy levels and data utility has to be explored. In this chapter, we explore an alternative framework based on multi-objective optimization to cater to the data publisher's requirements. We show how the requirement of specifying parameter values of an anonymity model can be eliminated by formulating privacy as an explicit objective to maximize. Further, we discuss the application of evolutionary algorithms as a solution method with a focus on solution representation and operator requirements. We also present empirical results to demonstrate that the approach is a more practical optimization framework for a data publisher.

Contents

6.1. Introduction

Various scientific studies, business processes and legal procedures depend on quality data from large data sources. However, such data sources often contain sensitive personal information, dissemination of which is governed by various privacy requirements. Data in such cases need to be sanitized off personally identifying attributes before it can be shared. Anonymizing data is challenging because re-identifying the values in sanitized attributes is not impossible when other publicly available information or an adversary's background knowledge can be linked with the shared data.

Anonymization of data sets (tables) involve transforming the actual data into a form unrecognizable in terms of the exact values by using *generalization* and *suppression* techniques.[1] Generalization of data is performed by grouping together specific data attribute (*quasi-identifiers*) values into a more general one. An example of this is replacing a specific age by an age range. Quasi-identifier attributes typically correspond to publicly available information such as phone numbers, postal code, age, etc. Data suppression, on the other hand, removes entire tuples making them no longer existent in the data set. Performance of such data modification is gauged by their ability to satisfy one or more privacy constraint, typically enforced by models such as k–anonymity,[2,3] ℓ–diversity[4] and t–closeness.[5] These privacy models prevent the accurate re-identification of an individual or sensitive information pertaining to the individual.

An unavoidable consequence of performing anonymization is a loss in the quality of the data set. Researchers have therefore looked at different methods to obtain an anonymization that can satisfy the privacy constraint with minimal loss of information.

Several algorithms have been proposed to find effective k–anonymization. The μ-argus algorithm is based on the greedy generalization of infrequently occurring combinations of quasi-identifiers and suppresses outliers to meet the k–anonymity requirement.[6] Sweeney's Datafly approach used a heuristic method to generalize the attribute containing the most distinct sequence of values for a provided subset of quasi-identifiers.[2] Sequences occurring less than k times are suppressed. In the same work,

Sweeney proposed a theoretical algorithm that can exhaustively search all potential generalizations to find the one that minimally distorts the data during anonymization. Samarati proposed an algorithm[1] that identifies all generalizations satisfying k-anonymity. Choice of an optimal generalization can then be made based on certain preference information provided by the data recipient. Bayardo and Agrawal proposed a complete search method that iteratively constructs less generalized solutions starting from a completely generalized data set.[7]

A genetic algorithm based formulation to find optimal k-anonymous generalizations was first proposed by Iyengar.[8] Although the method can maintain a good solution quality, it has been criticized for being a slow iterative process. In this context, Lunacek et al. introduced a new crossover operator that can be used with a genetic algorithm for constrained attribute generalization and effectively showed that Iyengar's approach can be made faster.[9]

A major shortcoming in all these approaches is the single-objective treatment of privacy and utility. The focus has always been concentrated on maximizing the utility of an anonymization, given a privacy constraint specified by a pre-defined value(s) for the involved parameter(s). It is important to note that privacy in this framework receives no attention in terms of optimality. Instead, the requirement that a data publisher has strong understanding of the impact of choosing a parameter value in a privacy model is strictly enforced. In order to do so, a data publisher needs to answer questions of the following form.

- How does privacy/utility change with changes in utility/privacy?
- Given a particular choice of privacy and utility levels, is there a solution that can improve one aspect without affecting the other?
- Given a particular choice of privacy and utility levels, is there a solution that can improve one aspect with tolerable change in the other?

Answering these questions using existing techniques will require us to perform an exhaustive enumeration of parameter values in the privacy model to determine what is suitable. Nonetheless, it is imperative that the data publisher understands the implications. There is clearly a trade-off involved. Setting the parameter to a "very low" value impacts the privacy of individuals in the data set. Picking a "very high" value disrupts the inference of any significant statistical information from the anonymized data set. Such conflicting characteristics define the nature of a multi-objective optimization problem.

In this chapter, we shall explore multi-objective formulations incorporating a data publisher's requirements to maximize data privacy levels, and at the same time, maintain the data utility at a maximum. The chapter will demonstrate how a series of optimization problems can be formulated on a given anonymity and data utility model, depending on the requirements of the data publisher. Our approach is significantly different from the assumed norm in the sense that we no longer treat privacy as a constraint in the optimization framework. Rather, privacy is modeled explicitly as an objective to maximize along with the data utility. We shall show how a multi-objective evolutionary algorithm can be employed here to obtain a global picture of the mutual effects of privacy and utility.

The remainder of the chapter is organized as follows. A concise background on multi-objective optimization is presented in Section 6.2. Section 6.3 provides a preliminary background on statistical disclosure control. Section 6.4 provides a description of the multi-objective problems we can formulate on a privacy model. The specifics of the solution methodology as particular to solving the problems using an evolutionary algorithm is also given here. A brief discussion on the interpretation of results is presented in Section 6.5. Finally, Section 6.6 concludes the chapter.

6.2. Multi-objective Optimization

In real world scenarios, often a problem is formulated to cater to several criteria or design objectives and a decision choice to optimize these objectives is sought for. An optimum design problem must then be solved with multiple objectives and constraints taken into consideration. This type of decision making problems fall under the broad category of multi-objective or vector optimization problem. Multi-objective optimization differs from single-objective ones in the cardinality of the optimal set of solutions. Single-objective optimization techniques are used to find the global optima. There is no such concept of a single optimum solution in case of multi-objective optimization. This is due to the fact that a solution that optimizes one of the objectives may not have the desired effect on the others. As a result, it is not always possible to determine an optimum that corresponds in the same way to all the objectives under consideration. Decision making under such situations thus requires some domain expertise to choose from multiple trade-off solutions depending on the feasibility of implementation.

Formally we can state a multi-objective optimization problem (MOOP) in statistical disclosure control (SDC) as follows:

Definition 6.1 (SDC MOOP).
Let $f_1, \ldots, f_M$ denote M objective functions to maximize while performing a modification of a given table PT. *Find a generalized table* RT* *of* PT *which optimizes the M-dimensional vector function*

$$f(\text{RT}) = [f_1(\text{RT}), f_2(\text{RT}), \ldots, f_M(\text{RT})]$$

where RT *is a generalized version of* PT.

The objective functions in this case are either related to the privacy or utility level maintained in an anonymized table. Note that the privacy level can be inferred with respect to different privacy models. Hence the number of objectives can be more than two. In order to find an optimal solution to the SDC MOOP, we must be able to compare anonymizations with respect to all the objectives in hand. However, due to the conflicting nature of the objective functions, a simple objective value comparison between two anonymizations cannot be performed. Most multi-objective algorithms thus use the concept of dominance to compare feasible solutions.

Definition 6.2 (Dominance and Pareto-optimal set). *Given a table* PT *and M objectives to maximize, a generalized table* RT$_1$ *of* PT *is said to dominate another generalized table* RT$_2$ *of* PT *if*

1. $\forall i \in \{1, 2, \ldots, M\}$ $\quad f_i(\text{RT}_1) \geq f_i(\text{RT}_2)$ *and*
2. $\exists j \in \{1, 2, \ldots, M\}$ $\quad f_j(\text{RT}_1) > f_j(\text{RT}_2)$

RT$_2$ *is then said to be dominated by* RT$_1$, *denoted by* RT$_2 \preceq$ RT$_1$. *If the two conditions do not hold,* RT$_1$ *and* RT$_2$ *are said to be non-dominated w.r.t. each other, denoted by the $\npreceq$ symbol. Further, all generalized tables of* PT *which are not dominated by any possible generalized version of* PT *constitutes the Pareto-optimal set.*

In other words, a Pareto-optimal solution is as good as another solution in the Pareto-optimal set and better than other feasible solutions outside the set. The surface generated by these solutions in the objective space is called the *Pareto-front* or *Pareto-surface*. In the context of disclosure control, the Pareto-front for the two objectives – maximize privacy (as given by a parameter, say k) and minimize loss – provides the decision maker an understanding of the changes in the information loss when k is varied.

Consider two anonymized versions RT_1 and RT_2 of a data set, with corresponding k and $loss$ as $(k_1, loss_1)$ and $(k_2, loss_2)$ respectively. Let us assume that $k_1 < k_2$ and $loss_1 = loss_2$. A decision maker using RT_1, and unaware of RT_2, misses on the fact that a higher k value is possible without incurring any increase in the loss. A multi-objective algorithm using the dominance concept can expose this relationship between RT_1 and RT_2, namely $RT_1 \preceq RT_2$. As another example, consider the case with $loss_2 - loss_1 = \epsilon > 0$. RT_1 and RT_2 are then non-dominated solutions, meaning that one objective cannot be improved without degrading the other. However, if ϵ is a relatively small quantity acceptable to the decision maker, RT_2 might be preferable over RT_1. Such trade-off characteristics are not visible to the decision maker until a multi-objective analysis is carried out. Thus, the objective of the analysis is to find the Pareto-optimal set from the set of all possible anonymized versions of a given data set.

6.3. Statistical Disclosure Control

Public distribution of personal data is a requirement to facilitate various scientific studies. Statistical organizations collecting information for such purposes often face standard security issues when distributing the data, thereby forcing them to enforce disclosure controls to protect the identity of individuals represented in the collected information. However, the sole purpose of collecting the information would be lost if the controls prohibit any kind of statistical inference being made from the distributed data. Statistical disclosure control thus involves mediating the risk of publicly disseminated information with the statistical utility of the content.

Most models in statistical disclosure control employ data recoding using generalization and suppression schemes in their attempt to hide the information content of a data set in its exact form. A generalization scheme performs a one-way mapping of the data values to a form unrecognizable from the original values or to a form that induces uncertainty in recognizing them. More than often it may not be possible to enforce a chosen level of privacy due to the presence of outliers in the data set. In such a situation, a suppression scheme gets rid of the outliers by removing them from the data set altogether.

The resultant data set from a generalization, coupled with or without a suppression scheme, affects the utility of the data. Statistical inferences suffer as more and more diverse data are recoded to the same value, or records are deleted by a suppression scheme. One can argue that the privacy requirement ensures the non-inference of any individual information while the utility requirement enforces the inference of accurate aggregate information. A summary statistic relying on accurate individual information therefore deteriorates when stronger privacy is implemented. The harder problem is a quantification of this deterioration, in effect, the information lost in the process of data recoding.

6.3.1. *Preserving privacy*

A data set PT can be visualized as a tabular representation of a multi-set of tuples $r_1, r_2, \ldots, r_{n_{row}}$ where n_{row} is the number of rows in the table. Each tuple (row) r_i comprises of n_{col} values $\langle c_1, c_2, \ldots, c_{n_{col}} \rangle$ where n_{col} is the number of columns in the table. The values in column j correspond to an *attribute* a_j, the domain of which is represented by the ordered set $\Sigma_j = \{\sigma_1, \sigma_2, \ldots, \sigma_{n_j}\}$. The ordering of elements in the set can be implicit by nature of the data. For example, if the attribute is "age", the ordering can be done in increasing order of the values. For categorical data, obtaining an ordering requires the user to explicitly specify a hierarchy on the values. A hierarchy can be imposed based on how the values for the attribute can be grouped together. Fig. 6.1 shows an example hierarchy tree for the attribute "marital status". The leaf nodes in this example constitute the actual values that the attribute can take. The ordering for these values can be assigned based on the order in which the leaf nodes are reached in a preorder traversal of the hierarchy tree. The numbering on the leaf nodes specify this ordering. An internal node in the hierarchy tree specify valid groupings of child nodes.

Given such orderings on the attribute domains, a generalization specifies a valid grouping of the domain values for a particular attribute. Formally, a generalization G_j for an attribute a_j is a partitioning of the set Σ_j into ordered subsets $\langle \Sigma_{j_1}, \Sigma_{j_2}, \ldots, \Sigma_{j_K} \rangle$ which preserve the ordering in Σ_j, *i.e.* if σ_a appears before σ_b in Σ_j then, for $\sigma_a \in \Sigma_{j_l}$ and $\sigma_b \in \Sigma_{j_m}$, $l \leq m$. Further, every element in Σ_j must appear in exactly one subset. The elements in the subsets maintain the same ordering as in Σ_j. For the age attribute having values in the range of $[10, 90]$, a possible generalization can be $\langle [10, 30], [30, 50], [50, 70], (70, 90] \rangle$. A possible generalization for the marital status attribute can be $\langle$*Not Married, Spouse Absent, Civ-spouse, AF-spouse*$\rangle$. It is important to note that generalizations for categorical data is dependent on how the hierarchy is specified for it. Further, generalizations are restricted to only those which respect the hierarchy. The

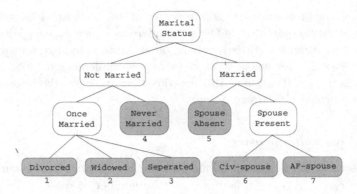

Fig. 6.1. Hierarchy tree for the *marital status* attribute. Numbering on the leaf nodes indicate their ordering in $\Sigma_{marital\ status}$.

generalization is said to be *constrained* in such a case. For example, the generalization $\langle \{Divorced,\ Widowed\},\ \{Separated,\ Never\ Married\},\ Married \rangle$ is not valid for marital status since the hierarchy tree specifies that the values $\{Divorced,\ Widowed,\ Separated\}$ can only be generalized as *Once Married*, if at all.

Given the generalizations $G_1, G_2, \ldots, G_{n_{col}}$, the data set PT can be transformed to the *anonymized* data set RT by replacing each value v_{ij} at row i and column j in PT by $G_j(v_{ij})$ where $G_j(v_{ij})$ gives the index of the subset to which v_{ij} belongs to in the generalization G_j. For the example generalization of the age attribute shown earlier, an age value of say 35 would thus be recoded by the range $(30, 50]$, or in other words, $G_{age}(35) = 2$. Note that, if a particular generalization G_j is equal to the domain of values Σ_j, say $G_{age} = \langle [10, 90] \rangle$ or $G_{marital\ status} = \langle Marital\ Status \rangle$, all values of the corresponding attribute will be transformed to the same subset index 1, in which case all information in that attribute is lost and the *cell is suppressed*.

Once the transformation is complete, equivalent tuples may appear in RT. Two tuples are equivalent if the recoded values for the quasi-identifiers are the same in both. Thus, the adopted generalization scheme maps the original values (which may be different) corresponding to a column in the two tuples to the same anonymized form. For example, both age values 35 and 45 will be mapped to $(30, 50]$ by the generalization shown earlier. Equivalent tuples can then be grouped together into equivalence classes. In other words, an equivalence class groups all tuples in PT that got transformed to the same tuple in RT under some generalization.

Although a generalization transforms the exact content of some or all data values, it is not impossible to re-establish the identity of a represented individual from the anonymized data set. Sweeney demonstrated this by using a *linking attack* on an anonymized medical insurance data set[3] of the Massachusetts state employees. The data set had been distributed for the purpose of research. Linking attacks can be launched by using information from other publicly available data sources to directly match shared attributes between the two data sources and arrive at a re-identification. For example, the governor of Massachusetts at that time, William Weld, was a state employee and hence his medical records were in the data set. Although the name was not revealed in the data, other pieces of information such as postal code, date of birth, gender etc. of the represented individuals were present. Governor Weld lived in Cambridge, Massachusetts. Sweeney managed to purchase a voter's registration list (containing information such as name, postal code, date of birth, gender etc.) for Cambridge. Sweeney observed from the voter's list that six people had Weld's particular birth date, three of which were men, and Governor Weld was the only one in his postal code, thereby revealing the exact way to identify his records on the medical data.

Matching shared attributes between different data sources can be made ambiguous by altering the released information to map to more number of individuals represented in the data set. In other words, the larger the size of the equivalence classes induced by a generalization, the more uncertainty there will be in identifying an individual. The k–anonymity model is thus proposed.[2,3]

Definition 6.3 (k–Anonymity problem). *Given a data set* PT, *find a set of generalizations for the quasi-identifiers in* PT *such that the equivalence classes induced by anonymizing* PT *using the generalizations are all of size at least* k.

The problem can also be explained as obtaining the generalizations under which every tuple in RT is same as at least $k - 1$ other tuples. A linking attack in this case can at best identify the equivalence class of an individual, but cannot certify which one of the k records in the equivalence class corresponds to the individual.

k–anonymity is conceptually a simple privacy model but has certain drawbacks when other forms of attacks are taken into consideration. To demonstrate such attacks, the set of attributes is first divided into *sen-*

sitive and *non-sensitive* classes. A sensitive attribute is one whose value must not be revealed (or get revealed) for any tuple in the data set. All other attributes are considered non-sensitive. Non-sensitive attributes usually constitute the quasi-identifiers. A *homogeneity attack* can result in unwanted disclosure of the sensitive attribute value for an individual if the equivalence classes in a k–anonymization have little or no diversity in the sensitive attribute values. An attacker, after successfully determining the equivalence class to which an individual's record belongs, knows the possible sensitive attribute values for the individual. If all sensitive attribute values in that equivalence class are the same, the attacker establishes an exact identification. Even for the case when the values are not all same, the attacker can apply existing *background knowledge* on the individual to eliminate possibilities. Such attacks exploit the non-existence of diversity in the sensitive attribute values in an equivalence class. Thus, the ℓ–diversity model enforces a diversity property on the classes.[4]

Let a_s be a sensitive attribute in a data set with the domain of values $\Sigma_s = \{\sigma_1, \sigma_2, \ldots, \sigma_{n_s}\}$. Further, let $Q_1, \ldots, Q_p$ be the equivalence classes induced by a generalization. If $c(\sigma)_j$, where $\sigma \in \Sigma_s$, denotes the count of the number of tuples with the sensitive attribute value σ in Q_j, then the ℓ–diversity problem can be stated as follows.

Definition 6.4 (ℓ–Diversity problem). *Given a data set* PT, *find a set of generalizations for the quasi-identifiers in* PT *such that for each equivalence class induced by anonymizing* PT *using the generalizations, the relation*

$$\frac{c(\sigma)_j}{|Q_j|} \leq \frac{1}{\ell} \tag{6.1}$$

holds for all $\sigma \in \Sigma_s$ and $j = 1, \ldots, p$.

In other words, the ℓ–diversity property guarantees that a sensitive attribute value cannot be associated with a particular tuple with a probability more than $1/\ell$. The higher the value of ℓ, the better is the privacy.

However, the ℓ–diversity model ignores the distribution of the sensitive attribute values. If it so happens that certain sensitive attribute values are not well represented in the original data set then achieving ℓ–diversity may not only become difficult but can also be impossible. The difficulty arises because there may not be many diverse values of the sensitive attribute that can help maintain the diversity property for a high value of ℓ. For example, if a sensitive attribute can take only 2 possible values, say tested *positive* or *negative* in a viral test, then one can never find a 3–diverse anonymization. Further, two different generalizations resulting in anonymizations with the same ℓ can be very different in terms of the statistical information they portray to an attacker. For example, if an equivalence class has equal number of records with positive and negative values – a 2–diverse class – then an attacker can infer that an individual tested positive (or negative) with 50% probability. On the other hand, consider the case when 90% records have positive and 10% records have negative in the sensitive attribute. This equivalence class is also 2–diverse, but with the difference that an attacker now knows that 90% of the individuals represented in the class tested positive. Such *skewness attacks* demonstrate that even if two equivalence classes are similarly diverse, the privacy risk present in them can be very different. Another attack possible on an ℓ–diverse equivalence class is the *similarity attack*. Similarity attacks exploit semantic relationships present between the sensitive attribute values of an equivalence class to deduce important information about an individual. For example, if an individual's record belongs to an equivalence class with the sensitive attribute (say disease) values "gastric ulcer", "gastritis" and "stomach cancer" then the attacker at least knows that the individual has some stomach related problem. The t–closeness model is thus proposed to avoid such forms of attacks.[5] The t–closeness model limits what an attacker can learn from an equivalence class on top of what it already knows from the entire anonymized data set.

Definition 6.5 (t–Closeness problem). *Given a data set* PT, *find a set of generalizations for the quasi-identifiers in* PT *such that for each equivalence class induced by anonymizing* PT *using the generalizations, the difference in distribution of a sensitive attribute in a class and the distribution of the attribute in the whole data set is no more than a threshold t.*

The question that comes to mind at this point is whether a privacy model can be applied to any data set given a particular value for its parameter. For k–anonymity, a data set is made anonymous by suppressing all tuples that belong to equivalence classes of size less than k. Similar suppression methods can be used to enforce the ℓ–diversity or t–closeness property. The case without suppression can be modeled into the scenario with suppression by assigning an infinite loss when suppression is performed.[7] However, it should be noted that the presence of outliers will always force the requirement for suppression, in which case the loss measurement will always become infinite. Furthermore, even though suppression is not allowed, such an approach enforces a privacy property by suppressing outliers. If all the data points in the data set have to stay in the anonymized data set as well, the desired privacy properties cannot be ascertained even after adopting such modeling.

As pointed out earlier, a fundamental outcome of applying these disclosure control mechanisms is a degradation in the quality of the data set for statistical studies. It is not trivial how decisions on a parameter of a privacy model affects the information content of a data set. In the next section, we shall see how the information lost as a result of a particular anonymization technique can be quantified to measure data utility.

6.3.2. *Estimating information loss*

An optimization algorithm requires a numeric representation of the information loss associated with a particular generalization. A quantified loss value enables the optimization algorithm to compare two generalizations for their relative effectiveness. Loss (cost) metrics assign some notion of penalty to each tuple whose data values get generalized or suppressed, thereby reflecting the total information lost in the anonymization process. However, cost quantification is a relatively harder and sparsely researched area. One should understand that the notion of information loss can vary from application to application. Hence, most of the proposed cost metrics are not rigorous enough to capture the data utility as would be perceived by a data publisher. They are rather estimates to compare different privacy models under a common test bed.

Early notion of utility is based on the number of generalization steps one has to take to achieve a given privacy requirement.[1] Such a method assumes that attribute domains can be progressively generalized and a partial order can be imposed on the domain of all generalizations for an attribute. For instance, postal codes can be generalized by dropping a digit from right to left at each generalization step. Postal addresses can be generalized to the street, then to the city, to the county, to the state, and so on. Given that such orderings can be imposed, a distance can be computed between two different generalizations for an attribute. The result is a distance vector with an entry for each attribute. Maximal utility is then said to be achieved if one can find generalizations for the attributes that satisfy the privacy requirement and results in a non-dominated distance vector computed from the origin (the case of no generalization). A non-dominated distance vector is one whose distance values are not higher than in another vector in all the attributes. In other words, utility is considered to be most when generalizations recode data values only to the extent necessary to achieve the privacy property.

Numerical estimations of information loss started with the *general loss metric* proposed by Iyengar.[8] The general loss metric computes a normalized information loss for each data value in an anonymized data set. The assumption here is that information in every column is potentially important and hence a flexible scheme to compute the loss for both numeric and categorical data is required.

Consider the data value v_{ij} at row i and column j in the data set PT. The general loss metric assigns a penalty to this data value based on the extent to which it gets generalized during anonymization. Let $g_{ij} = G_j(v_{ij})$ be the index of the subset to which v_{ij} belongs to in the generalization G_j, *i.e.* $v_{ij} \in \Sigma_{j_{g_{ij}}}$. The penalty for information loss associated with v_{ij} is then given as follows:

$$loss(v_{ij}) = \frac{|\Sigma_{j_{g_{ij}}}| - 1}{|\Sigma_j| - 1} \qquad (6.2)$$

For categorical data, the loss for a cell is proportional to the number of leaf nodes rooted at an internal node (the generalized node) of the hierarchy tree. The loss attains a maximum value of one when the cell is suppressed ($G_j = \langle \Sigma_j \rangle$), or in other words, when the root of the tree is the generalized node. Subtracting one ensures that a non-generalized value incurs zero loss since the cardinality of the subset to which it belongs would be one. The *generalization loss* is then obtained as the total loss over all the data values in the data set.

$$GL = \sum_{i=1}^{n_{row}} \sum_{j=1}^{n_{col}} loss(v_{ij}) \qquad (6.3)$$

Further, when a row is suppressed, all cells in the row are suppressed irrespective of the generalization. Each cell thereby incurs a loss of one. Let n_{sup} be the number of rows to be suppressed in the data set. The *suppression loss* for the data set is then given as,

$$SL = n_{col} \times n_{sup} \qquad (6.4)$$

A widely used cost metric, called the *discernibility metric*, assigns a penalty to each tuple based on the number of tuples in the transformed data set that are indistinguishable from it.[7] A tuple belonging to an equivalence class of size j is assigned a penalty of j. A suppressed tuple is assigned a penalty equal to the number of tuples in the data set. The idea behind using the size of the equivalence class as a measure of data utility is to penalize generalizations that result in equivalence classes bigger than what is required to enforce a given privacy requirement. A variant of this is to use the normalized average equivalence class size.[10]

Data utility is often measured in conjunction with privacy in an attempt to combine both objectives into a single metric. A metric of such nature favors generalizations that result in maximum gain in the information entropy for each unit of anonymity loss resulting from the generalization. Methods employing such a metric progressively increase the amount of generalization, called a *bottom up generalization* approach,[11] or decrease it, called a *top down specialization* approach,[12] with the objective of maximizing the metric without violating the anonymity requirement. Another metric, called *usefulness*, measures utility as the average diversity in the tuples belonging to an equivalence class.[13] This measurement is similar to the general loss metric, with differences being in the treatment of interval based attribute domains. For such domains, the loss is assigned as the normalized distance between the maximum and minimum values of the attribute in the equivalence class. Further, a complementary metric, called *protection*, uses the inverse of the tuple diversities as a measure of the privacy factor. By doing so, the two metrics inherently exhibit a reciprocal relationship, useful when a data publisher wants to modulate the anonymization process towards one objective or the other.

Researchers also argue that utility metrics should not only capture the information loss caused by the anonymization but also account for the importance of the different attributes. For example, given a disease analysis data set, an age attribute may be considered more critical than a zip code attribute. Generalizations that are able to maintain the age attribute more accurately should thus be favored. Based on this, the *weighted normalized certainty penalty* metric uses a weighted sum of the loss measurements in different attributes of the data set.[14] The loss measurement is similar as in the general loss metric and the usefulness metric. Introduction of such preference characteristics indicates that the measurement of utility can be a very subjective matter after all.

We want to re-emphasize that the notion of utility is still not understood well, probably much because of its subjective nature. Nonetheless, multiobjective formulations do not assume any inherent property in the cost metric used. The cost metric is only used in its functional form to evaluate the effectiveness of a generalization in maintaining the utility factor. The metric may be different for different purposes, however, the objective of the analysis remains the same.

6.4. Evolutionary Optimization

Any disclosure control mechanism has to cater to two primary objectives – maintaining a high privacy level and facilitating statistical inquiries by reducing the information loss. One should understand that both of these objectives are rather subjective in nature. The privacy level required in a shared data source is dictated by the sensitivity of the personal information contained in the source. This is often determined by the concern displayed by the individuals represented in the source about the extraction of certain pieces of information in its exact form. The requirement of data utility is determined by the nature of the analysis to be performed on the data set. It is therefore possible what evaluates as unusable for one statistical study is sufficient in another context. Such subjectivity compels a data publisher to reevaluate the control mechanisms under the light of the expressed relevance of the two objectives. Furthermore, the two objectives are conflicting in nature, meaning that a control mechanism cannot attain both at the same time. Thus, even if both objectives are specified as being equally important, a chosen control will always exhibit a bias towards one or the other. Given that such bias could be unavoidable, the data publisher must make a best attempt in understanding the deviations brought forth in the objectives by the selection of one control over another. This not only postpones the subjectivity of the two objectives to a post-analysis stage, but also aids the decision making process with a comprehensive overview of the effects of incremental modification in the expressed subjective relevance.

Classical approaches to solve multi-objective problems are mostly based on transformations of the problem into single objective instances. A typical method is the assignment of weights to objectives and then performing a single objective optimization of the scalarized objective function values. Other methods require the specification of preference orderings on the objective functions. Noticeably, these methods can only return a single solution from a single run and hence trade-off analysis shall require multiple runs to be performed. Recent advances in population-based evolutionary optimization have proved to be particularly effective in overcoming this bottleneck. The artificial intelligence community has seen a major flow of algorithms using dominance as the decisive factor for natural selection. These algorithms can not only identify non-dominated solutions, but also eliminate the need for repeated analysis by using population based approaches.

In the next few sections, we shall consider the k–anonymity model with the general loss metric as a working platform to describe the problem formulations. Nevertheless, formulations for other privacy models and utility metrics are not very dissimilar. We shall also see how specifics related to the application of an evolutionary algorithm to the problems are resolved.

6.4.1. *Multi-objective analysis*

A multi-objective analysis is not intended to provide the data publisher a "best" value for the parameter(s) involved in an anonymization technique. Rather, the methodology is meant to understand the implications of choosing a particular value for the parameter(s) in terms of the resulting privacy and the data utility. Hence, we shall often find that one or more solutions returned by the optimization process are trivially not acceptable either in terms of privacy or utility, or in some cases both. It is not our objective to consider such solutions as degenerate and prohibit them from appearing in the solution set. For example, an extreme solution will correspond to a situation where every tuple in the data set belongs to its own equivalence class, thereby resulting in no privacy and maximum utility. Another extremity is the case where all tuples are grouped together in a single equivalence class resulting in maximum privacy but no utility. One cannot deny the fact that in the case of privacy versus utility, both of these are possible solutions. The multi-objective optimization does not incorporate the required domain knowledge to identify these extremities (or other such solutions) as being impractical. Only the data publisher has the requisite knowledge to make such identification and disregard such solutions. This is often a post-optimization process.

Furthermore, the multi-objective analysis is not a direct means of protecting privacy. The problem formulations we present here shall show how privacy can be modeled as an objective to maximize rather than being treated as a constraint. By doing so, we can provide clues to the data publisher as to what levels of privacy can be obtained (for example by using k–anonymity) for a given amount of information loss. This trade-off analysis can be used by the data publisher to finally decide what privacy can it offer. More specifically, it offers the data publisher a method to understand the effects of setting a parameter in a privacy model on the utility of the data.

6.4.1.1. *In the absence of suppression*

The presence of outliers in a data set makes it difficult to find a suitable value of k when suppression of data is not allowed. In this formulation, we strictly adhere to the requirement that no tuple in the data set can be deleted. Intuitively, such a strict requirement makes the k–anonymity problem insensible to solve for a given k as the optimization algorithm will be forced to overly generalize the data set in its effort to ensure k–anonymity. The outliers usually belong to very small equivalence classes and the only way to merge them into a bigger one is by having more generalization. This results in more information loss which is often not acceptable to an user.

Although solving the k–anonymity problem is not possible in terms of its strict definition, it is worth noting that a generalization can still affect the distribution of the equivalence classes even when suppression is not allowed. An equivalence class E_k in this description groups all tuples that are similar to exactly $k-1$ other tuples in the anonymized data set. An ideal generalization would then maintain an acceptable level of loss by keeping the number of rows in smaller equivalence classes (small k) relatively lower than in the bigger equivalence classes. Although this does not guarantee complete k–anonymity, the issue of privacy breach can be solved to a limited extent by reducing the probability that a randomly chosen row would belong to a small equivalence class.

With this motivation we define the *weighted-k–anonymity* multi-objective problem to find generalizations that produce a high weighted-k value and low generalization loss. Each equivalence class E_k defines a k value, $k \leq n_{row}$, for its member tuples – every tuple in the equivalence class is same as exactly $k-1$ other tuples in the same class.

Note that this notion of an equivalence class is different from the one stated in the k–anonymity problem (Def. 6.3). Two rows in the original data set belong to the same equivalence class in the k–anonymity definition if the generalization transforms them into the same tuple. In this formulation, two rows belong to the same equivalence class E_i if a generalization makes them i–anonymous.

The weighted-k for a particular generalization inducing the equivalence classes $E_1, E_2, \ldots, E_{n_{row}}$ on the anonymized data set is then obtained as follows:

$$k_{weighted} = \frac{\sum_{i=1}^{n_{row}} (i \cdot |E_i|)}{\sum_{i=1}^{n_{row}} |E_i|} \qquad (6.5)$$

The problems introduced by the presence of outliers can also be addressed by using the concept of local recoding.[15] A local recoding scheme produces a k–anonymization by using an individual generalization function (instead of a global one) for each tuple in the data set. This is a more powerful scheme compared to having a single generalization function since outliers can be easily suppressed without the drawbacks of an over generalization, hence data utility can be maintained. The weighted-k–anonymity based generalization is orthogonal to this concept in certain ways. Local recoding explores the domain of generalization functions and uses multiple points in this domain to recode different subsets of the data set differently. This puts outliers in their own subset(s), thereby making it easy to enforce a given minimum equivalence class size (k). Weighted-k–anonymity, on the other hand, works with a single generalization function and instead of trying to enforce a fixed minimum equivalence class size, flexibly creates equivalence classes of different sizes with no minimum size constraint. The outliers then must lie on smaller equivalence classes in order to maximize data utility. The common criteria in both the methods is that the outliers gets treated differently than the rest of the data set.

In most cases, not all equivalence classes with all possible k values will be generated. The weighted-k value provides a sufficiently good estimate of the distribution of the equivalence classes. A high weighted-k value implies that the size of the equivalence classes with higher k is relatively more than the size of the lower k ones. The multi-objective problem is then formulated as finding the generalizations that maximize the weighted-k and minimize the generalization loss.

6.4.1.2. *With pre-specified suppression tolerance*

In this problem, we enable suppression and allow the user to specify an acceptable fraction, denoted by η, of the maximum suppression loss possible ($n_{row} \cdot n_{col}$). Such an approach imposes a hard limit on the number of suppressions allowed.[7] However, by allowing the user to specify a suppression loss limit independent of k, the optimization procedure can be made to explore the trade-off properties of k and generalization loss within the constraint of the imposed suppression loss limitation.

When suppression is allowed within an user specified limit, all tuples belonging to the equivalence classes $E_1, \ldots, E_d$ can be suppressed, such that d satisfies the relation

$$\sum_{i=1}^{d}(|E_i| \cdot n_{col}) \leq \eta \cdot n_{row} \cdot n_{col} < \sum_{i=1}^{d+1}(|E_i| \cdot n_{col}) \qquad (6.6)$$

Satisfying the relationship results in the suppression of tuples beginning from the ones which has the least number of duplicates (smaller equivalence class) and ending when further suppression will violate the specified tolerance. Thus, the k value induced by the generalization is equal to $d+1$, which also satisfies the suppression loss constraint. We can now define our optimization problem as finding the generalizations that maximize d and minimize the generalization loss. The problem can also be viewed as the maximization of k and minimization of GL satisfying the constraint $SL \leq \eta \cdot n_{row} \cdot n_{col}$.

6.4.1.3. *For comprehensive overview*

The third problem is formulated as an extension of the second one where the user does not provide a maximum limit on the suppression loss. The challenge here is the computation of k, GL and SL for a generalization without having a baseline to start with. Since the three quantities are dependent on each other for their computation, it is important that we have some base k value to proceed. The weighted-k value is adopted at this point. Although not very precise, the weighted-k value provides a good estimate of the distribution of the equivalence classes. If a very high weighted-k value is obtained for a generalization then the number of tuples with low k's is sufficiently small, in which case we can suppress them. If the weighted-k value is low then most of the tuples belong to equivalence classes with low k. In this case, a higher amount of suppression is required to achieve an acceptable k for the anonymized data set. Also, high weighted-k generally implies a high generalization loss. Such trade-off characteristics are the point of analysis in this problem.

To start with, a particular generalization's weighted-k value is first computed. Thereafter, all tuples belonging to an equivalence class of $k < k_{weighted}$ are suppressed, enabling the computation of SL. This makes the k for the anonymized data set equal to at least $k_{weighted}$. The generalization loss GL is then computed from the remaining data set. The multi-objective problem is defined as finding the generalizations that maximize $k_{weighted}$ and minimize the generalization and suppression losses.

6.4.2. *Solution encoding*

Before applying an evolutionary algorithm to obtain solutions to the fore mentioned problems, a viable representation of the generalizations has to be designed for the algorithm to work with. Consider the numeric attribute

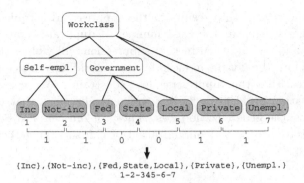

Fig. 6.2.   Example generalization encoding for the *workclass* constrained attribute. i^{th} bit is 0 if i^{th} and $(i+1)^{th}$ intervals are combined, otherwise 1.

age with values in the domain $[10, 90]$. Since this domain can have infinite values, the first task is to granularize the domain into a finite number of intervals. For example, a granularity level of 5 shall discretize the domain to $\{[10, 15], (15, 20], \ldots, (85, 90]\}$. Note that this is not the generalization used to anonymize the dataset. The discretized domain can then be numbered as $1 : [10, 15], 2 : (15, 20], \ldots, 16 : (85, 90]$. The discretized domain still maintains the same ordering as in the continuous domain. A binary string of 15 bits can now be used to represent all possible generalizations for the attribute. The ith bit in this string is 0 if the ith and $(i+1)^{th}$ intervals are supposed to be combined, otherwise 1. For attributes with a small domain size and a defined ordering of the values, the granularization step can be skipped. For categorical data, a similar encoding can be obtained once an ordering on the domain values is imposed as discussed in Section 6.3. Fig. 6.2 shows an example generalization encoding for a "workclass" attribute. The individual encodings for each attribute are concatenated to create the overall encoding for the generalizations for all attributes.

6.4.3. *Non-dominated Sorting Genetic Algorithm-II*

The Non-dominated Sorting Genetic Algorithm-II (NSGA-II)[16] is a popular evolutionary algorithm to perform multi-objective optimization. It employs the concept of dominance, as discussed in Section 6.2, to find Pareto-optimal solutions in the space of all possible generalizations of a given data set. Note that NSGA-II is just an algorithm of choice in this study. Other evolutionary algorithms do exist that can help perform a similar analysis.[17] However, the primary objective in this chapter is not to focus on performance analysis of multi-objective optimization but to demonstrate the usage of pre-existing techniques in the artificial intelligence community to resolve the problems in disclosure control. The extensive usage of NSGA-II in solving real world problems has motivated us to choose NSGA-II over others. Having said so, these algorithms are typically very generic. Any application of the algorithm thus requires appropriate problem and operator representations. We have already discussed how a solution in SDC can be represented for NSGA-II. Other components are discussed in subsequent sections.

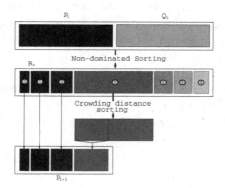

Fig. 6.3.   One generation of NSGA-II.

The algorithm starts with a population P_0 of N random generalizations. A generation index $t = 0, 1, \ldots, Gen_{MAX}$ keeps track of the number of iterations of the algorithm. Each trial generalization is used to create the anonymized dataset and the corresponding values of the quantities to be optimized are calculated. Each generation of NSGA-II then proceeds as follows. An offspring population Q_t is first created from the parent population P_t by applying the usual genetic operations of selection, crossover and mutation.[18] This is done by first forming a mating pool of best solutions, next recombining solutions from this pool to generate offspring, and finally mutating the offspring to get a new solution. For constrained attributes, a special crossover operator is used as discussed in the next subsection. The offspring population also gets evaluated. The parent and offspring populations are then combined to form a population $R_t = P_t \cup Q_t$ of size $2N$. A non-dominated sorting is applied to R_t to rank each solution based on the number of solutions that dominate it. Rank 1 solutions are all non-dominated solutions in the population. A rank r solution is only dominated by solutions of lower ranks.

The population P_{t+1} is generated by selecting N solutions from R_t. The preference of a solution is decided based on its rank; lower the rank, higher the preference. By combining the parent and offspring populations, and selecting from them using a non-dominance ranking, NSGA-II implements an elite-preservation strategy where the best solutions obtained are always passed on to the next generation. However, since not all solutions from R_t can be accommodated in P_{t+1}, a choice is likely to be made when the number of solutions of the currently considered rank is more than the remaining positions in P_{t+1}. Instead of making an arbitrary choice, NSGA-II uses an explicit diversity-preservation mechanism. The mechanism, based on a *crowding distance metric*,[16] gives more preference to a solution with a lesser density of solutions surrounding it, thereby enforcing diversity in the population. The NSGA-II crowding distance metric for a solution is the sum of the average side-lengths of the cuboid generated by its neighboring solutions. Fig. 6.3 depicts a single generation of the algorithm. For a problem with M objectives, the overall complexity of NSGA-II is $O(MN^2)$.

6.4.4. *Crossover for constrained attributes*

The usual single point crossover operator in a genetic algorithm randomly chooses a crossover point. It then creates an offspring by combining the bit string before the crossover point from one parent and the bit string after the crossover point from the other. As shown in Fig. 6.4 (left), such an operation can result in an invalid generalization for constrained attributes. Iyengar proposed modifying such invalid generalizations to the nearest valid generalization.[8] However, finding the nearest valid generalization can be time consuming, besides destroying the properties on which the crossover operator is based on. In this regard, Lunacek et al. proposed a special crossover operator that always create valid offspring for constrained attributes.[9] Instead of randomly choosing a crossover point, their operator forces the crossover point to be chosen at a location where the bit value is one for both parents. By doing so, both parts (before and after the crossover point) of both parents can be guaranteed to be valid generalizations individually, which can then be combined without destroying the hierarchy requirement. Fig. 6.4 (right) shows an instance of this operator.

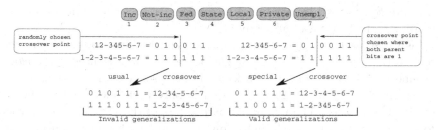

Fig. 6.4. Usual single point crossover (left) and special crossover for constrained attributes (right). Usual operator may generate invalid offspring generalizations. Special operator always creates valid offspring generalizations.

6.4.5. *Population initialization*

In order to be able to use the special crossover operator, the validity of the parent solutions must be guaranteed. This implies that the initial random population that NSGA-II starts with must contain trial solutions with valid generalizations for the constrained attributes. For a given hierarchy tree, the following algorithm can generate valid generalizations for the constrained attributes in the initial population.

Starting from the root node, a node randomly decides if it would allow its subtrees to be distinguishable. If it decides not to then all nodes in its subtrees are assigned the same identifier. Otherwise the root of each subtree receives an unique identifier. The decision is then translated to the root nodes of its subtrees and the process is repeated recursively. Once all leaf nodes are assigned an identifier, two adjacent leaf nodes in the imposed ordering are combined only if they have the same identifier. Since a parent node always make the decision if child nodes will be combined or not, all generalizations so produced will always be valid.

6.5. Some Empirical Results

We show here some results obtained by applying the NSGA-II algorithm to a standard "adult census" test data set[a]. The data was extracted from a census bureau database and has been extensively used in studies related to k–anonymization. All rows with missing values are removed from the dataset to finally have a total of 30162 rows. The attributes "age", "education", "race", "gender" and "salary class" are kept unconstrained, while the attributes "workclass", "marital status", "occupation" and "native coun-

---

[a]ftp://ftp.ics.uci.edu/pub/machine-learning-databases/adult/

try" are constrained by defining a hierarchy tree on them. The remaining
attributes in the dataset are ignored.

For NSGA-II, we set the population size as 200. The maximum number
of iterations is set as 250. A single point crossover is used for unconstrained attributes while Lunacek et al.'s crossover operator is used for
constrained attributes. Also, mutation is only performed on the unconstrained attributes. The remaining parameters of the algorithm are set as
follow: crossover rate = 0.9, mutation rate = 0.1 with binary tournament
selection. We ran the algorithm with different initial populations but did
not notice any significant difference in the solutions obtained. The results
here are from one such run.

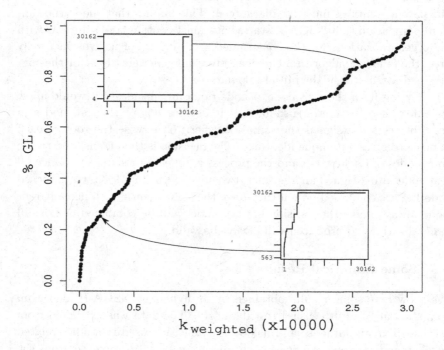

Fig. 6.5. Solutions found by NSGA-II when suppression is not allowed. Each point
corresponds to a generalization with a particular value of $k_{weighted}$ and GL, thereby
demonstrating the trade-off behavior. Generalization loss increases as bigger equivalence
classes are generated. Inset figures show cumulative distribution of $|E_k|$ as k increases.
Distribution of equivalence class sizes can be very different for two solutions.

Fig. 6.5 shows the different trade-off solutions obtained by NSGA-II when no suppression is allowed on the data set. A point in the plot corresponds to a solution that induces a particular distribution of equivalence class sizes (k values) on the anonymized data set. As expected, the generalization loss increases as the distribution of equivalence classes gets more inclined towards higher k values. In the absence of suppression, a single k value is often hard to enforce for all tuples in the data set. Thus, a solution here results in different k values for different tuples. A higher weighted-k value signifies that most tuples have a high k value associated with them, in which case, the generalization loss is higher. A solution with low weighted-k value results in a generalization with low k values for its tuples.

The inset figures in the plot depict the cumulative distribution of the number of tuples belonging to equivalence classes (y-axis) with different k values (x-axis). Note that the distributions for the two example solutions are not complementary in nature. For the solution with lower generalization loss, the distribution has a continuously increasing trend, implying that equivalence classes of different k values exist for the solution. The other solution shows an abrupt increase signifying that the tuples either belong to equivalence classes with very small k or ones with very large k. The sought balance in the distribution can therefore exist with an acceptable level of generalization loss.

Fig. 6.6 shows the trade-off between k and $loss = GL + SL$ when a maximum of 10% suppression loss is allowed. The top-leftmost plot shows all the solutions obtained for the problem. Each subsequent plot (follow arrows) is a magnification of the steepest part in the previous plot. Each plot shows the presence of locally flat regions where a substantial increase in the k value does not have a comparatively high increase in the *loss*. These regions can be of interest to a data publisher since it allows one to provide higher levels of data privacy without compromising much on the information content.

Interestingly, the trend of the solutions is similar in each plot. The existence of such repeated characteristics on the non-dominated front suggests that a data publisher's choice of a specific k, no matter how big or small, can have avenues for improvement, specially when the choice falls in the locally flat regions. A choice of k made on the rising parts of the front is seemingly not a good choice since the publisher would then be paying a high cost in degraded data quality without getting much improvement on the privacy factor. The rational decision choice in such a case would be to lower the value of k to a flat region of the front.

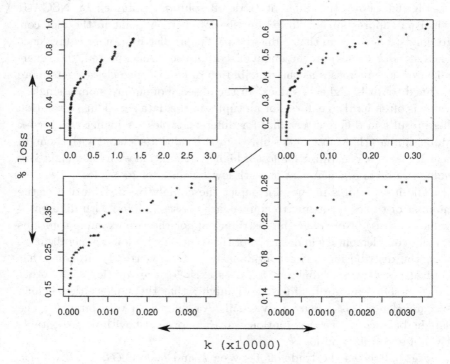

Fig. 6.6. Solutions found by NSGA-II with suppression tolerance $\eta = 10\%$. Top-leftmost plot shows all obtained solutions. Each point corresponds to a generalization with a particular value of k and *loss*, and with a maximum of 10% suppression loss. Each subsequent plot (follow arrows) is a magnification of a region of the previous plot. Solution set depicts flat regions in the non-dominated front, implying that one objective can be substantially improved with negligible changes in the other. Such trends are visible in all parts of the front.

6.6. Summary

We presented the method of multi-objective analysis to demonstrate that the choice of a parameter in a privacy model can be made in a much informed manner rather than arbitrarily. The multi-objective problems are formulated to cater to differing requirements of a decision maker, primarily focused on the maximization of the privacy parameter and minimization of the losses. For generalizations without suppression, an unique value for the parameter may not be available. However, generalizations may be possible that provide a higher level of privacy for a higher fraction of the dataset without compromising much on its information content. When suppression is allowed up to a hard limit, the nature of the non-dominated solution set can provide invaluable information on whether an anonymization exists to improve a particular value of the model parameter without much degradation in quality of the data. First-level explorations in this context can begin with gaining an overall understanding of the trade-off characteristics in the search space. The formulations presented in this chapter also address the data publisher's dilemma. They provide a methodology to analyze the problem of data anonymization in manners that appeal to the actual entity that disseminates the data. We believe that such an analysis not only reinstates the data publisher's confidence in its choice of a particular privacy model parameter, but also identifies ways of examining if the level of privacy requested by a human subject is achievable within the acceptable limits of perturbing data quality.

Future work in this direction can start with examination of the framework with other models of privacy preservation. Hybrid models catering to different forms of attacks are also required. Work on this can begin with an exploration on what trade-offs are generated when looking for the existence of two or more privacy properties simultaneously.

Acknowledgment

This work was partially supported by the United States Air Force Office of Scientific Research under contracts FA9550-07-1-0042 and FA9550-07-1-0403. The views and conclusions contained in this document are those of the authors and should not be interpreted as representing official policies of the U.S. Air Force or other federal government agencies.

References

1. P. Samarati, Protecting Respondents' Identities in Microdata Release, *IEEE Transactions on Knowledge and Data Engineering*. **13**(6), 1010–1027, (2001).
2. L. Sweeney, Achieving k–Anonymity Privacy Protection Using Generalization and Suppression, *International Journal on Uncertainity, Fuzziness and Knowledge-based Systems*. **10**(5), 571–588, (2002).
3. L. Sweeney, k–Anonymity: A Model for Protecting Privacy, *International Journal on Uncertainity, Fuzziness and Knowledge-based Systems*. **10**(5), 557–570, (2002).
4. A. Machanavajjhala, J. Gehrke, D. Kifer, and M. Venkitasubramaniam. ℓ–Diversity: Privacy Beyond *k*–Anonymity. In *Proceedings of the 22nd International Conference on Data Engineering*, p. 24, Atlanta, GA, USA, (2006).

5. N. Li, T. Li, and S. Venkatasubramanian. *t*–Closeness: Privacy Beyond *k*–Anonymity and *ℓ*–Diversity. In *Proceedings of the 23rd International Conference on Data Engineering*, pp. 106–115, Istanbul, Turkey, (2007).
6. A. Hundepool and L. Willenborg. Mu and Tau Argus: Software for Statistical Disclosure Control. In *Proceedings of the Third International Seminar on Statistical Confidentiality*, (1996).
7. R. J. Bayardo and R. Agrawal. Data Privacy Through Optimal k-Anonymization. In *Proceedings of the 21st International Conference on Data Engineering*, pp. 217–228, Tokyo, Japan, (2005).
8. V. S. Iyengar. Transforming Data to Satisfy Privacy Constraints. In *Proceedings of the 8th ACM SIGKDD International Conference on Knowledge Discovery and Data Mining*, pp. 279–288, Alberta, Canada, (2002).
9. M. Lunacek, D. Whitley, and I. Ray. A Crossover Operator for the k-Anonymity Problem. In *Proceedings of the 8th Annual Conference on Genetic and Evolutionary Computation*, pp. 1713–1720, Seattle, Washington, USA, (2006).
10. K. LeFevre, D. J. DeWitt, and R. Ramakrishnan. Mondrian Multidimensional K-Anonymity. In *Proceedings of the 22nd International Conference on Data Engineering*, p. 25, Atlanta, GA, USA, (2006).
11. K. Wang, P. Yu, and S. Chakraborty. Bottom-Up Generalization: A Data Mining Solution to Privacy Protection. In *Proceedings of the 4th IEEE International Conference on Data Mining*, pp. 249–256, Brighton, UK, (2004).
12. B. C. M. Fung, K. Wang, and P. S. Yu. Top-Down Specialization for Information and Privacy Preservation. In *Proceedings of the 21st International Conference on Data Engineering*, pp. 205–216, Tokyo, Japan, (2005).
13. G. Loukides and J. Shao. Capturing Data Usefulness and Privacy Protection in K-Anonymisation. In *Proceedings of the 2007 ACM Symposium on Applied Computing*, pp. 370–374, Seoul, Korea, (2007).
14. J. Xu, W. Wang, J. Pei, X. Wang, B. Shi, and A. Fu. Utility-Based Anonymization Using Local Recodings. In *Proceedings of the 12th Annual SIGKDD International Conference on Knowledge Discovery and Data Mining*, pp. 785–790, Philadelphia, PA, USA, (2006).
15. A. Takemura. Local Recoding by Maximum Weight Matching for Disclosure Control of Microdata Sets. CIRJE F-Series CIRJE-F-40, CIRJE, Faculty of Economics, University of Tokyo, (1999).
16. K. Deb, A. Pratap, S. Agarwal, and T. Meyarivan, A Fast and Elitist Multiobjective Genetic Algorithm: NSGA–II, *IEEE Transactions on Evolutionary Computation.* **6**(2), 182–197, (2002).
17. K. Deb, *Multi-objective Optimization Using Evolutionary Algorithms.* (John Wiley & Sons Inc., 2001).
18. D. E. Goldberg, *Genetic Algorithms in Search, Optimization, and Machine Learning.* (Addison-Wesley, 1989).

Chapter 7

On the Definition of Cluster-Specific Information Loss Measures

Vicenç Torra

IIIA, Institut d'Investigació en Intel.ligència Artificial
CSIC, Consejo Superior de Investigaciones Científicas
Campus UAB, E-08193 Bellaterra, Catalonia, Spain
vtorra@iiia.csic.es

The main difficulty when defining protection methods is to find a good trade-off between information loss and disclosure risk. As maximum protection is achieved when the data is completely distorted and, thus, usually useless, utility and risk are in a contradiction.

In this paper we consider the problem of evaluating information loss when users intend to use data for clustering. We will consider information loss in this context. We will review some cluster-specific information loss measures and show some results about their comparison with generic ones.

Contents

7.1. Introduction

Statistical offices and companies need to transfer their data to third parties for their analysis. Nevertheless, transferred data should not allow the disclosure of personal and/or confidential information. Privacy Preserving

Data Mining[1,2] (PPDM) is the area of research that studies methods that permit data owners such data transfer avoiding disclosure. This area also studies methods that permit data owners to perform data analysis without disclosing information to the people that will analyses the data. Statistical Disclosure Control (SDC) is an area with similar interests, focused on the data from National Statistical Offices.

Two main approaches can be distinguished in PPDM, the cryptographic approach and the perturbative approach. The cryptographic approach[3] is based on secure multiparty computation.[4] The typical scenario in this approach consists of several parties that want to compute a function f from their data, but without disclosing their own data to the other parties. The perturbative approach[5-7] consists of modifying the original data (e.g. adding some noise) and then publishing them, or transferring them to third parties, for their subsequent analysis. Such protection is based on the fact that the disclosure of sensitive information is not possible when data have been perturbated with an adequate level of noise.

In this paper we focus on the perturbative approach. The difficulties of this approach are that in order to ensure a complete protection (to avoid, at any rate, disclosure risk) the degree of distortion (the *quantity* of noise to be added) might be very large, and this makes data useless for analysis. In fact, the more distortion data suffers the less data utility.

Therefore, in the perturbative approach, data protection and data utility are in contradiction, and, in practice, a good trade-off between the two terms has to be found. In this way, good protection mechanisms are those that ensure a reasonable level of privacy while permitting, at the same time, the user to obtain the same result from the protected data as the one he would obtain from the original data.

As a good trade-off between data protection and data quality is sought, two families of measures[8] have been defined. They measure these two qualities of the data: disclosure risk and information loss.

Information loss measures will be reviewed in Section 7.2.2. However, an important question arises with respect to these measures. Formally, information loss measures are defined to evaluate the extent in which the perturbated data is useful for performing the same analysis and inferences as the ones performed with the original data.

Nevertheless, such data utility depends on the analysis and inferences to be performed. So, an important aspect to be taken into account is the intended use of the data by the third party. However, as such use is usually not known, and it might be rather diverse for a single file (see, e.g., the case of the data published in the web that can be used by different researchers for completely different purposes), *generic* information loss measures have been developed. They are measures for a non specific use. They are formally defined as the divergence of a few statistics between the original data file and the protected data file. The probabilistic information loss measure[9] is an example of such measures. See[8,10,11] for details on such measures.

Due to the difficulty of knowing the intended data use, generic measures play an important role on the evaluation of protection methods. See *e.g.*[8,10] Nevertheless, due to the possible divergence between such measures and the results of concrete analysis of the data, it is also important to develop analyses of the influence of the protection methods on particular tools for data analysis.

In this paper we consider this problem in the particular case that the user applies clustering to the protected data. Formally, we will define *specific* information loss measures, in contrast to *generic* ones. More specifically, we will define cluster-specific information loss measures, as the final goal is to evaluate the divergence between the results applying clustering in the original data and the protected data.

Besides of information loss, another aspect to be considered when evaluating protection methods is disclosure risk. Disclosure risk measures[8] are to determine to what extent a protected file ensures privacy. There are a few approaches for measuring the risk. Our approach is based on record linkage algorithm. Formally, a subset of the original data (the one we presume the intruder has) is linked against the protected data (the one published). The proportion of correct links corresponds to a measure of the risk. As such measures do not depend on the data use, we will not discuss such measures in detail.

The structure of the paper is as follows. In Section 7.2 we review some preliminaries that are needed latter on. In particular, we review information loss measures and some aspects related with fuzzy clustering. Then, in Section 7.3 we consider the definition of cluster-specific information loss measures. The paper finishes with some conclusions.

7.2. Preliminaries

This section starts with a review on protection methods and generic information loss measures, and then moves to fuzzy clustering and related topics. We will review fuzzy c-means and a few other algorithms for fuzzy clustering. Such algorithms will be used latter when defining the cluster-specific information measures.

7.2.1. *Protection methods*

In this section we review a few perturbative protection methods (masking methods) for numerical data. They were discussed and compared in[8] with respect to their trade-off between information loss and disclosure risk. The description uses the following notation: X is the original data file, and X' is the new masked one. $x_{i,V}$ corresponds to the value in the i-th record for variable V. The description is based on.[6,12]

Additive noise. Data is perturbated adding noise into the original file. In order to have a low information loss, the random noise has the same correlation structure as the original data.[13]

Data distortion by probability distribution. This   protection method is defined by three steps. The steps are applied to each variable separately. First, we need to identify an underlying density function and determine its parameters (using *e.g.* a fitting algorithm). Second, generate distorted series using the estimated density function. Third, the distorted series are put in place of the original ones.

Resampling. This method, that is applied to each variable separately, consists on applying three steps. Their description assumes that V is the variable and that the database contains n records. The steps are as follows. First, obtain t independent samples for variable V obtained from the original file with replacement. Let $X_1, \ldots, X_t$ be such samples. Second, order the samples (using the same ordering criteria in all cases). Let X'_i be the samples once ordered. Third, define the value for variable V of the new j-th record (for $j = 1, \ldots n$) as the average of the j-th values in samples X'_i (*i.e.*, $x'_{j,V} = \sum_{i=1}^{t} X'_{ij}/t$ for $j = 1, \ldots, n$).

Microaggregation. Records in the original file X are grouped in small clusters. For a fixed k, all clusters should contain at least k records and at most $2k$ records. Thus, their size is small. Then, for each record x in X define the masked version x' as the value of the centroid of its corresponding cluster.

In the case of considering data files with several variables, univariate and multivariate approaches can be distinguished. Univariate methods consider each variable at a time. That is, when m variables are considered, m sets of clusters are built. An optimal method for the univariate case is given in.[14] Multivariate methods apply microaggregation considering sets of variables. It is proved that the optimal microaggregation is NP-hard[15] in the multivariate case, due to this, heuristic methods are applied.

Lossy compression. The approach consists on taking a numerical data file as an image. Then, a lossy compression method is applied to the *image*, obtaining a *compressed image*. Such *compressed image* corresponds to the masked file. JPEG has been used for such purpose.

Rank swapping. Rank swapping is applied to each variable V in a n-record file X following the next steps. First, the values for V in X are ordered (in ascending order). Let Y be such values. Then, for each Y_i select Y_i' as any of the values in Y (random selection) occupying positions $[i - p*n, i + p*n]$. Here, p is a fixed percentage. Then, undo the ordering on Y' obtaining X'.

7.2.2. *Generic information loss measures*

As we have stated in the introduction, information loss measures are to evaluate in what extent the analysis on the original data and the analysis on the protected data diverge. Generic information loss measures are defined to measure general aspects of the data so that they are useful in different contexts. In this section we review briefly some of these measures. This description is based on our previous work.[12]

First steps on the definition of this family of information loss measures were presented in[10] and.[8] There, information loss was defined as the discrepancy between a few matrices obtained on the original data and the masked one. Covariance matrices, correlation matrices and a few other matrices (as well as the original file X and the masked file X') were used. Mean square error, mean absolute error and mean variation were used to compute matrix discrepancy. *e.g.*, mean square error of the difference between the original data and the protected one is defined as $(\sum_{i=1}^{n} \sum_{i=1}^{p} (x_{ij} - x_{ij}')^2)/np$ (here p is the number of variables and n is the number of records).

Nevertheless, these information loss measures are unbounded, and problems appear *e.g.* when the original values are close to zero. To solve these problems,[11] proposed to replace the mean variation of X and X' by a measure more stable when the original values are close to zero.

Trottini[16] detected that using such information loss measures together with disclosure risk measures for comparing protection methods was not well defined because information loss measures where unbounded. That is, when an overall score is computed for a method (see[10] and[11]) as *e.g.* the average of information loss and disclosure risk, both measures should be defined in the same commensurable range. To solve this problem, Trottini proposed to settle a predefined maximum value of error. More recently, in,[9] probabilistic information loss measures were introduced to solve the same problem avoiding the need of such predefined values.

Here we review such measures introduced in.[9] Let us start considering the discrepancy between a population parameter θ on X and a sample statistic Θ on X'. Let $\hat{\Theta}$ be the value of that statistic for a specific sample. Then, the standardized sample discrepancy corresponds to

$$Z = \frac{\hat{\Theta} - \theta}{\sqrt{Var(\hat{\Theta})}}$$

where $Var(\Theta)$ is the variance of Θ (defined below).

This discrepancy can be assumed to follow a $N(0,1)$ (see[9] for details). Then, we define the probabilistic information loss measure, pil, for $\hat{\Theta}$ as follows:

$$pil(\hat{\Theta}) = 2 \cdot P\left(0 \leq Z \leq \frac{\hat{\theta} - \theta}{\sqrt{Var(\hat{\Theta})}}\right) \tag{7.1}$$

Five particular measures based on this approach are described below. They are the same five measures previously used in,[8,9] and,[10] among others. The measures are based on the following statistics:

- Mean for variable V ($Mean(V)$):

$$\sum_{i=1}^{n} x_{i,V}/n$$

- Variance for variable V ($Var(V)$):

$$\sum_{i=1}^{n} (x_{i,V} - Mean(V))^2/n$$

- Covariance for variables V and V' ($Cov(V'V')$):

$$\frac{\sum_{i=1}^{n'} (x_{i,V} - Mean(V))(x_{i,V'} - Mean(V'))}{n'}$$

- Correlation coefficient for V and V' ($\rho(V, V')$):

$$\frac{\sum_{i=1}^{n} \left(x_{i,V} - Mean(V)\right)\left(x_{i,V'} - Mean(V')\right)}{\sum_{i=1}^{n} \left(x_{i,V'} - Mean(V')\right)^2 \sum_{i=1}^{n} \left(x_{i,V} - Mean(V)\right)}$$

- Quantiles, Q, for variable V: That is, the values that divide the distribution in such a way that a given proportion of the observations are below the quantile. The quantiles for i from 5% to 95% with increments of 5% have been considered.

$pil(Mean)$, $pil(Var)$, $pil(Cov)$, $pil(\rho)$ and $pil(Q)$ are computed using Expression 7.1 above. In fact, for a given data file with several variables V_i, these measures are computed for each V_i (or pair V_i, V_j) and then the corresponding pil averaged. In the particular case of the quantile, $pil(Q(V))$ is first defined as the average of the set of measures $pil(Q_i(V))$ for $i = 5\%$ to 95% with increments of 5%.

In order to have a single value, the average of these measures is used. Such average is denoted by $aPil$. That is,

$$aPil := (pil(Mean) + pil(Var) + pil(Cov) + pil(\rho) + pil(Q))/5.$$

7.2.3. *Fuzzy sets, fuzzy partitions, and fuzzy clustering*

Fuzzy clustering algorithms are based on the concept of fuzzy partition, which is based on the concept of fuzzy sets. Formally, a fuzzy set is a generalization of crisp sets where objects can belong to a set with a partial membership. In this section we review the concepts of fuzzy sets, fuzzy partitions and some of the algorithms for fuzzy clustering.

Definition 7.1. Let X be a reference set. Then $\mu : X \to [0, 1]$ is a membership function.

Definition 7.2. Let X be a reference set. Then, a set of membership functions $\mathcal{M} = \{\mu_1, \ldots, \mu_m\}$ is a fuzzy partition of X if for all $x \in X$ it holds

$$\sum_{i=1}^{m} \mu_i(x) = 1$$

Typically, clustering methods are to partition a set of data into disjoint sets. In the case of fuzzy clustering, a fuzzy partition is built instead of a crisp one. In this paper we will mainly focus on fuzzy c-means, although other algorithms for fuzzy clustering will also be considered. See *e.g.*[17-19] for details on fuzzy clustering. Fuzzy *c*-means, that was first proposed in[20] (see also[21]), is described in most books on fuzzy sets and fuzzy clustering. See, *e.g.*, the above mentioned references.

We describe below the fuzzy *c*-means in some detail. We will use in the description the following notation. We will use X as the set of objects to be clustered, that in our case corresponds to the records in the original file. x_k denotes the kth object, as it is common in fuzy clustering. Then, we want to build c clusters from this data set. In this way, the method builds a fuzzy partition of X. The fuzzy partition (the clusters) are represented by membership functions μ_{ik}, where μ_{ik} is the membership of the kth object to the ith cluster. Naturally, $i = 1, \ldots, c$ and $k = 1, \ldots, n = |X|$.

Fuzzy *c*-means needs an additional value m that should satisfy $m \geq 1$. When m is near to 1, solutions tend to be crisp (with the particular case that $m = 1$ corresponds to the crisp *c*-means, or *k*-means). In contrast, when m is *large*, solutions tend to be clusters with large fuzziness in their boundaries.[21]

Formally, fuzzy *c*-means constructs the fuzzy partition μ from X solving the minimization problem stated below. In the formulation of the problem, V denotes the cluster centers and v_i is used to represent the cluster center, or centroid, of the i-th cluster.

Minimize

$$J_{FCM}(\mu, V) = \{\sum_{i=1}^{c} \sum_{k=1}^{n} (\mu_{ik})^m \|x_k - v_i\|^2\} \qquad (7.2)$$

subject to the constraints $\mu_{ik} \in [0, 1]$ and $\sum_{i=1}^{c} \mu_{ik} = 1$ for all k.

A (local) optimal solution of this problem is obtained using an iterative process that interleaves two steps. One that estimates the optimal membership functions of elements to clusters (when centroids are fixed) and another that estimates the centroids for each cluster (when membership functions are fixed). This iterative process is described in the following algorithm:

Noise clustering (NC), possibilistic *c*-means (PCM) and fuzzy possibilistic *c*-means (FPCM) are some of the variations of fuzzy *c*-means. We have used them on our analyses. Noise clustering was introduced in[22] to reduce the effects of noisy data (noisy data might distort the position of cluster centers). To do so, the method introduces a special noise cluster. Possibilistic *c*-means also includes some noise clusters but in this case there is a noise cluster for each regular cluster. This method was introduced in.[23] Fuzzy possibilistic *c*-means is a variation of PCM, introduced in,[24] to avoid co-

---

Algorithm 7.1 Fuzzy c-means

Step 1:   Generate initial μ and V

Step 2:   Solve $min_{\mu \in M} J_{FCM}(\mu, V)$ computing:

$$\mu_{ik} = \Big(\sum_{j=1}^{c} \Big(\frac{||x_k - v_i||^2}{||x_k - v_j||^2} \Big)^{\frac{1}{m-1}} \Big)^{-1}$$

Step 3:   Solve $min_V J_{FCM}(\mu, V)$ computing:

$$v_i = \frac{\sum_{k=1}^{n} (\mu_{ik})^m x_k}{\sum_{k=1}^{n} (\mu_{ik})^m}$$

Step 4:   If the solution does not converge, go to step 2; otherwise, stop

---

incident clusters (*i.e.*, different cluster centers converge to the same point) and to make the final clusters less sensitive to initializations.

7.3. Information loss measures for clustering

Given an original file X and the corresponding protected file X', information loss measures are based on the comparison of the results of a few statistics (or data analyses) on both X and X'. For example, we can compare the mean of X and X' for the different variables in the files. Then, the larger is the difference, the larger the information loss.

Similar approaches can be applied to any other data analysis tool. This is also the case for clustering. Let us consider a given clustering algorithm *clust* with parameters *par*, and let denote its application to the data file X by $clust_{par}(X)$. Then, we can define the information loss of $clust_{par}$ applied to the data file X and its protected data file X' as the divergence or distance between $clust_{par}(X)$ and $clust_{par}(X')$. That is,

$$IL(X, X') = distance(clust_{par}(X), clust_{par}(X')).$$

Naturally, it holds that the larger the divergence, the larger the loss. In the remaining part of this section we discuss this problem with some detail. In particular, we discuss on how to measure the distance between clusters.

7.3.1. *Comparison of crisp clusters*

In the case of partitive crisp clustering (that is, a method that returns a partition of the objects), there are a few tools for comparing the clusters (see *e.g.*[25,26]). To name a few, there exist the Rand[27] and the Adjusted Rand index, the Jaccard index, and the Mántaras distance.[28] We can define the loss as proportional to the distance, or inversely proportional to the above mentioned indices.

We review these definitions below. To do so, we consider that $\Pi = \{\pi_1, \ldots, \pi_m\}$ and $\Pi' = \{\pi'_1, \ldots, \pi'_n\}$ are two crisp partitions, and, therefore, each of them is a set of clusters. Then, we consider r, s, t and u as follows: r is the number of pairs (a, b) where a and b are in the same cluster in Π and in Π'; s is the number of pairs where a and b are in the same cluster in Π but not in Π'; t is the number of pairs where a and b are in the same cluster in Π' but not in Π; u is the number of pairs where a and b are in different clusters in both partitions. Then, we denote $np(\Pi)$ as the number of pairs within clusters in the partition Π.

Rand index:

$$RI(\Pi, \Pi') = (r + u)/(r + s + t + u)$$

Jaccard Index:

$$JI(\Pi, \Pi') = r/(r + s + t)$$

Adjusted Rand Index: This is a correction of the Rand index so that the expectation of the index for partitions with equal number of objects is 0. This adjustment was done assuming generalized hypergeometric distribution as the model of randomness. That is,

$$ARI(\Pi, \Pi') = \frac{r - exp}{max - exp}$$

where $exp = (np(\Pi)np(\Pi'))/(n(n-1)/2)$ and where $max = 0.5(np(\Pi) + np(\Pi'))$.

Wallace Index:

$$WI(\Pi, \Pi') = r/\sqrt{np(\Pi)np(\Pi')}$$

Mántaras distance :[28]

$$MD(\Pi, \Pi') = \frac{I(\Pi/\Pi') + I(\Pi'/\Pi)}{I(\Pi' \cap \Pi)}$$

where

$$I(\Pi/\Pi') = -\sum_{i=1}^{n} P(\pi'_i) \sum_{j=1}^{m} P(\pi_j/\pi'_i) \log P(\pi_j/\pi'_i)$$

Table 7.1.   (a) Columns 2-6 give the distance and indexes computed for several microaggregated files when the clustering algorithm selected is the c-means; (b) last column includes the averaged probabilistic information loss measure (aPIL); (c) last row corresponds to the correlation of the measures and distance with respect to the aPIL.

k	Rand	Jaccard	Adjusted Rand	Wallace	Mantaras	aPIL
3	0.943	0.454	0.594	0.625	0.416	15.189
4	0.943	0.464	0.602	0.633	0.425	19.325
5	0.936	0.406	0.542	0.577	0.472	22.724
6	0.936	0.408	0.545	0.580	0.473	25.760
7	0.929	0.367	0.499	0.537	0.500	28.750
8	0.933	0.402	0.538	0.574	0.479	31.185
9	0.925	0.359	0.488	0.528	0.513	33.883
Correlation	-0.930	-0.882	-0.887	-0.882	0.931	1.000

$$I(\Pi' \cap \Pi) = -\sum_{i=1}^{n}\sum_{j=1}^{m} P(\pi_i' \cap \pi_j) \log P(\pi_i' \cap \pi_j)$$

Example 7.1. For illustration, we give in Table 7.1 the results obtained for a few microaggregated files (multivariate with 3 variables at a time, and $k = 3, 4, \ldots, 9$. Such table gives, for each of the files, the cluster-specific information loss measures (indices or distances) and the generic information loss measure. Such measures correspond to the index or distance that compares the clusters obtained from the original file and the masked file. The results corresponds to the case of applying c-means, the crisp clustering method. The table includes also the correlation coefficient for each of the clustering method and the cluster-specific measure. The correlation coefficient shows that there is a high correlation between the generic information loss measure (aPil) and the cluster-specific ones. Note that the correlation is negative when the indexes are compared against the measure, and positive when the comparison is with a distance.

7.3.2.   *Comparison of fuzzy clusters*

In the case of fuzzy clusters, there is no such variety of methods. In the rest of this section we describe a few approaches we have introduced for tackling this problem.

A first approach[12] was to consider the transformation of the fuzzy partition into crisp sets applying α-cuts. Recall that the α-cut of a fuzzy set for a given $\alpha \in [0, 1]$ is a standard subset (the set of elements with a membership function larger than α). However, this approach presents a problem as an α-cut of a fuzzy partition does need to be a partition. Therefore, we cannot

Table 7.2.   (a) Columns 2-5 give the α-cut based
distance computed for several microaggregated
files when the clustering algorithm selected is one
of the fuzzy clustering methods; (b) the last column includes the averaged probabilistic information loss measure (aPIL); (c) last row corresponds
to the correlation of the cluster-specific measures
with respect to the aPIL.

k	FCM	Noise	PCM	FPCM	aPIL
3	0.026	0.030	0.033	0.035	15.189
4	0.034	0.027	0.041	0.038	19.325
5	0.037	0.029	0.046	0.050	22.724
6	0.038	0.033	0.049	0.064	25.760
7	0.100	0.076	0.052	0.105	28.750
8	0.103	0.078	0.058	0.119	31.185
9	0.072	0.057	0.057	0.053	33.883
	0.797	0.764	0.979	0.653	1.000

apply directly the indices and distances for fuzzy partitions. So, we need to
apply an ad-hoc approach. In our experiments we used three α-cuts (with
$\alpha_1 = 0.9$, $\alpha_2 = 0.5$ and $\alpha_1 = 0.1$) and then we used the distance between
the resulting crisp clusters.

Example 7.2. The results given in Table 7.2 follow this approach. They
follow Example 7.1 but using fuzzy clustering methods. As before, the table
includes the measures as well as the correlation coefficient for each of the
clustering method and the cluster-specific measure.

In addition, Table 7.3 presents the results of such distances computed
on the results of different fuzzy clustering algorithms for a data file with
1,080 records and 13 variables. Each row corresponds to a different level of
protection (protection using noise addition with a parameter $p = 0.1, 0.2$,
..., 2.0 – the first column indicates the degree of protection). The data
file (named **census**), which is public and is described in detail in,[29] has
been used by several researchers in several experiments.[8,11] The Table also
includes the correlation of such measures with respect to the average PIL,[9]
a generic information loss. It can be observed that there is also correlation
between the cluster-specific measures and the generic ones, although in this
case is not as large as in the case of crisp clustering.

Later on, in order to overcome the difficulties of the previous approach
(α-cuts do not necessarily lead to a partition) and, at the same time, avoiding the transformation from a fuzzy partition to a set of crisps sets, we
proposed two different distances for fuzzy partitions. This result, presented

Table 7.3. (a) Columns 2-5 give the α-cut based distance computed for several files (protected with noise addition with different values of noise, first column) when the clustering algorithm selected is one of the fuzzy clustering methods; (b) the last column includes the averaged probabilistic information loss measure (aPIL); (c) last row corresponds to the correlation of the cluster-specific measures with respect to the aPIL.

p	FCM	NC	PCM	PFCM	aPIL
0.1	0.0037	0.0030	0.0036	0.0029	4.1310
0.2	0.0084	0.0049	0.0072	0.0063	6.4298
0.4	0.0153	0.0092	0.0136	0.0192	9.2348
0.6	0.0209	0.0141	0.0197	0.0188	12.6145
0.8	0.0310	0.0165	0.0261	0.0270	16.6538
1.0	0.0229	0.0322	0.0318	0.0245	18.5534
1.2	0.0943	0.0796	0.0393	0.0840	24.5021
1.4	0.0314	0.0257	0.0414	0.0560	28.6009
1.6	0.0356	0.0448	0.0491	0.0603	33.7005
1.8	0.0969	0.0735	0.0585	0.0934	35.6461
2.0	0.1622	0.0367	0.0737	0.0654	37.5090
	0.7679	0.7403	0.9780	0.8923	1.0000

in,[30] permitted us to compare two fuzzy clustering methods: fuzzy c-means and fuzzy c-means with tolerance.[31]

The two distances proposed were based, respectively, on the cluster centers and the membership functions. We define them below.

- **Distance based on cluster centers.** The distance is solely based on the cluster representatives of each cluster. That is, their centroids. First, a mapping between the clusters is obtained so that the clusters of each clustering result are *aligned* (the *nearest* cluster center is assigned in the alignment). Then, the Euclidean distance between a center and its associated one is computed. The overall distance is the summation of the distances between the pairs of clusters. We will denote this distance by d_1.

- **Distance based on membership functions.** The distance is based on the membership functions. The computation uses the mapping established before, and then computes for each record, the distance between its membership values to the clusters obtained for the original file and the membership values to the clusters obtained for the protected file. We will denote this distance by d_2.

The ranges of the two distances are rather different. The maximum values we have obtained for d_1 and d_2 after all our experiments using different clustering algorithms, parameterizations and noisy data, is 130 for d_1 and 5500 for d_2.

The application of these distances to real data presents an additional problem. Clustering algorithms ensure convergence to local optima, but not to a global one. Due to this, different executions of the method might result into different clusters.

Local convergence of clustering algorithms is not a big problem in some applications of unsupervised machine learning. The different fuzzy partitions obtained in different executions can represent different knowledge, and might correspond to different points of view. Nevertheless, in our case, when we are interested in measuring the information loss, this is a big problem.

Note that due to the local optima, different executions of the same algorithm with the same data might result into different clusters. Therefore, we might have that $clust_{par}(X) \neq clust_{par}(X)$ for different executions of $clust$ with parameter par on the same data set X. Moreover, we might have that the difference between $clust_{par}(X)$ and $clust_{par}(X')$ is very large not because X and X' are different but because we are just in rather different local optima.

In,[30] for each data file X, each cluster algorithm $clust$ and each parameterization par, we have considered several executions of $clust_{par}(X)$ computing for each of them its objective function. Then, we have selected the fuzzy partition with the lowest membership function. Such fuzzy partition is the one used latter for comparison.

Up to 20 executions have been done in[30] for each $< X, clust, p >$. Nevertheless, we still got several local optima as we got a few results with $clust_{par}(X) \neq clust_{par}(X')$ when $X' = X + noise$ with $noise = 0$.

Table 7.4 shows the results of the distance between the original file and the protected one when data is clustered using fuzzy c-means on the whole file (all 13 variables) and the number of clusters is 10 (i.e., $c = 10$). The two distances defined above d_1 and d_2 are used. Nevertheless, the results show that the distance is not monotonic with respect to the noise added. This is due to the different local minima found.

In Table 7.5 we present similar results, but in this case only 2 of the variables are considered in the clustering. As in this case we get a better convergence, we have monotonicity of the distance with respect to the noise. Two cases are presented, one with the number of clusters equal to 10 (i.e., $c = 10$) and the other with the number of clusters equal to 20 (i.e., $c = 20$).

Table 7.4. Distances d_1 and d_2 between the clusters originated from the original and the protected file for different values of noise and using the fuzzy c-means (FCM) as the clustering algorithm. Executions with the number of clusters set to 10 (*i.e.*, $c = 10$). The values achieved for the objective function (*O.F.*) are also included for each protected file (last column). The optimal value found for the original file was 2851. The last row corresponds to the correlation with aPIL.

p	d_1	d_2	*O.F.*
0.0	3.21	40.73	2826.0
0.1	3.21	40.67	2827.0
0.2	3.17	40.86	2829.0
0.4	0.32	0.92	2859.0
0.6	3.28	42.09	2844.0
0.8	3.48	43.48	2862.0
1.0	3.55	48.87	2886.0
1.2	2.24	55.56	2908.0
1.4	1.44	18.35	2935.0
1.6	2.27	36.83	2978.0
1.8	2.71	45.59	3006.0
2.0	4.24	96.87	3028.0
	0.0125	0.4073	

7.3.3. *Extensions using intuitionistic fuzzy sets*

To solve the difficulties of local optima, we have considered the use of intuitionistic fuzzy sets for expressing the results of the execution of fuzzy clustering. Intuitionistic fuzzy sets are used when there is some uncertainty on the membership function.

Formally, this uncertainty is represented with a pair of functions μ and ν. μ corresponds to the membership function and ν permits to express the uncertainty.

Then, using intuitionistic fuzzy sets, we might consider the definition of an intuitionistic fuzzy partition, which permits us to summarize the 10 or 20 fuzzy partitions obtained from the different executions of the fuzzy clustering algorithm. Initial steps on the definition of intuitionistic fuzzy partitions have been presented in.[32,33] Our definition for an intuitionistic fuzzy partition is in such a way that there is convergence to a standard fuzzy partition when the number of executions increases. That is, the larger the number of executions, the more similar is the intuitionistic fuzzy partition to a fuzzy one.

Convergence results have been proven for a few fuzzy clustering methods. *e.g.*, fuzzy c-means and fuzzy c-means with entropy.[34]

Table 7.5. Distances d_1 and d_2 between the clusters originated from the original and the protected file for different
values of noise and using the fuzzy c-means (FCM) as the
clustering algorithm; and values for the objective function
($O.F.$). Results correspond to the best result after 20 executions. Clustering was based on the first 2 variables of the
file and 10 clusters (left) and 20 clusters (right). The optimal
value found for the original file was 225.26 for the case of 10
clusters (left) and 107.06 for the case of 20 clusters (right).
The last row corresponds to the correlation with aPIL.

	$c = 10$			$c = 20$		
p	d_1	d_2	$O.F.$	d_1	d_2	$O.F.$
0.0	5E-9	1E-15	225.26	2.86	208.90	107.19
0.1	0.10	0.92	225.67	3.03	157.10	107.20
0.2	0.08	1.74	225.02	0.69	13.46	107.21
0.4	0.21	8.45	224.63	1.80	113.00	106.97
0.6	0.49	25.27	225.45	2.15	73.73	106.67
0.8	3.16	217.38	224.85	3.22	214.29	108.47
1.0	1.29	73.13	226.53	2.80	224.25	108.66
1.2	3.80	252.37	225.21	3.96	259.46	109.11
1.4	0.66	80.99	227.00	4.45	318.17	109.61
1.6	3.13	257.35	228.43	2.92	337.55	112.14
1.8	3.20	315.55	230.97	5.11	454.07	111.77
2.0	3.25	313.78	231.82	5.31	510.52	110.00
	0.78	0.87		0.75	0.85	

7.4. Conclusions and future work

In this paper we have studied cluster-specific information loss measures.
We have reviewed a few approaches for computing the differences between
clusters and we have shown the difficulties such methods pose. In particular, we have explained that fuzzy clustering algorithms converge into an
optimum that might be a local optimum. This causes some inconveniences
when comparing the results of the same clustering algorithm on both the
original and the protected file.

As a future work, we plan to use our approach based on intuitionistic
fuzzy partitions to evaluate protection methods and, then, compare the
corresponding cluster-specific measures with the generic ones. This will
extend our current results for fuzzy clustering reported in[12] and.[35]

Acknowledgments

Partial support by the Spanish MEC (projects ARES – CONSOLIDER
INGENIO 2010 CSD2007-00004 – and eAEGIS – TSI2007-65406-C03-02)

is acknowledged. Part of the experiments reported in this paper were performed by Susana Ladra.

References

1. R. Agrawal and R. Srikant. Privacy Preserving Data Mining. In *Proc. of the ACM SIGMOD Conference on Management of Data*, pp. 439–450, (2000).
2. V. S. Verykios, E. Bertino, I. N. Fovino, L. P. aand Y. Saygin, and Y. Heodoridis, State-of-the-art in Privacy Preserving Data Mining, *SIGMOD Record.* **33**(1), 50–57, (2004).
3. J. Vaidya, C. W. Clifton, and Y. M. Zhu, *Privacy Preserving Data Mining.* (Springer, 2006).
4. A. Yao. Protocols for Secure Computations. In *Proc. of 23rd IEEE Symposium on Foundations of Computer Science*, pp. 160–164, Chicago, Illinois, (1982).
5. S. Mukherjee, Z. Chen, and A. Gangopadhyay, A privacy-preserving technique for euclidean distance-based mining algorithms using fourier-related transforms, *The VLDB Journal.* **15**(2), 293–315, (2006).
6. J. Domingo-Ferrer and V. Torra. Disclosure Control Methods and Information Loss for Microdata, Confidentiality, Disclosure, and Data Access. In *Theory and Practical Applications for Statistical Agencies*, pp. 91–110. Elsevier Science, (2001).
7. L. Willenborg and T. de Waal, *Elements of Statistical Disclosure Control.* Lecture Notes in Statistics, (Springer-Verlag, 2006).
8. J. Domingo-Ferrer and V. Torra. A Quantitative Comparison of Disclosure Control Methods for Microdata. In *Theory and Practical Applications for Statistical Agencies*, pp. 111–133. Elsevier Science, (2001).
9. J. M. Mateo-Sanz, J. Domingo-Ferrer, and F. Sebé, Probabilistic information loss measures in confidentiality protection of continuous microdata, Data Mining and Knowledge Discovery, *Data Mining and Knowledge Discovery.* **11**(2), 181–193, (2005).
10. J. Domingo-Ferrer, J. M. Mateo-Sanz, and V. Torra. Comparing SDC methods for microdata on the basis of information loss and disclosure risk. In *Preproceedings of ETK-NTTS'2001*, vol. 2, pp. 807–826, Creta, Greece, (2001). Eurostat, ISBN 92-894-1176-5.
11. W. E. Yancey, W. E. Winkler, and R. H. Creecy, Disclosure risk assessment in perturbative microdata protection, inference control in statistical databases, *Lecture Notes in Computer Science.* **2316**(1), 135–152, (2002).
12. S. Ladra and S. Torra, On the comparison of generic information loss measures and cluster-specific ones, *International Journal of Uncertainty, Fuzziness and Knowledge-Based Systems.* **16**(1), 107–120, (2008).
13. G. Sullivan and W. A. Fuller. Construction of masking error for categorical variables. In *Proc. of the ASA Section on Survey Research Methodology*, pp. 435–439, (1990).
14. S. Hansen and S.Mukherjee, A Polynomial Algorithm for Optimal Univariate

Microaggregation, *Transactions on Knowledge and Data Engineering.* **15**(4), 1043–1044, (2003).

15. A. Oganian and J. Domingo-Ferrer, On the complexity of optimal microaggregation for statistical disclosure control, *Statistical J. United Nations Economic Commission for Europe.* **18**(4), 345–354, (2000).

16. M. Trottini. *Decision models for data disclosure limitation, PhD Dissertation.* Phd dissertation, Carnegie Mellon University, (2003).

17. F. Höppner, F. Klawonn, R. Kruse, and T. Runkler, *Fuzzy cluster analysis.* (Wiley, 1999).

18. S. Miyamoto, *Introduction to fuzzy clustering.* (Ed. Morikita, Tokyo, 1999). in Japanese.

19. S. Miyamoto and K. Umayahara, *Methods in Hard and Fuzzy Clustering,* In *Soft Computing and Human-Centered Machines,* pp. 85–129. Springer, Tokyo, (2000). Z. Q. Liu and S. Miyamoto (Eds.).

20. J. C. Dunn, A Fuzzy Relative of the ISODATA Process and Its Use in Detecting Compact Well-Separated Clusters, *Journal of Cybernetics.* **3**, 32–57, (1973).

21. J. C. Bezdek, *Pattern Recognition with Fuzzy Objective Function Algorithms.* (Plenum Press, New York, 1981).

22. R. N. Davé, Characterization and detection of noise in clustering, *Pattern Recognition Letters.* **12**, 657–664, (1991).

23. R. Krishnapuram and J. M. Keller, A possibilistic approach to clustering, *IEEE Trans. on Fuzzy Systems.* **1**, 98–110, (1993).

24. N. R. Pal, K. Pal, and J. C. Bezdek. A Mixed c-Means Clustering Model. In *Proc. of the 6th IEEE Int. Conf. on Fuzzy Systems,* pp. 11–21, Barcelona, Spain, (1997).

25. L. Hubert and P. Arabie, Comparing partitions, *Journal of Classification.* **2** (1), 193–218, (1985).

26. V. V. Raghavan and M. Y. L. Ip. Techniques for measuring the stability of clustering: a comparative study. In *Proc. of the 5th annual ACM conference on Research and development in information retrieval,* pp. 209–237, (1982).

27. W. M. Rand, Objective criteria for the evaluation of clustering methods, *J. of the American Statistical Association.* **66**, 846–850, (1971).

28. R. Lopez de Mantaras, A Distance-Based Attribute Selection Measure for Decision Tree Induction, *Machine Learning.* **6**, 81–92, (1991).

29. E. Project. CASC: Computational Aspects of Statistical Confidentiality. http://neon.vb.cbs.nl/casc/.

30. V. Torra, Y. Endo, and S. Miyamoto. On the comparison of some fuzzy clustering methods for privacy preserving data mining: towards the development of specific information loss measures. In press.

31. Y. Hasegawa, Y. Endo, Y. Hamasuna, and S. Miyamoto. Fuzzy c-means for data with tolerance defined as hyper-rectangle. In *Proc. MDAI 2007, Lecture Notes in Artificial Intelligence,* vol. 4617, pp. 237–248, (2007).

32. V. Torra and S. Miyamoto. Intuitionistic fuzzy partitions for the comparison of fuzzy clusters. submitted.

33. V. Torra, S. Miyamoto, Y. Endo, and J. Domingo-Ferrer. On intuitionistic

fuzzy clustering for its application to privacy. In *Proc. FUZZ-IEEE 2008 (ISBN 978-1-4244-1818-3)*, pp. 1042–1048, Hong Kong, China, (2008).

34. S. Miyamoto and M. Mukaidono. Fuzzy c - means as a regularization and maximum entropy approach. In *Proc. of the 7th IFSA Conference*, vol. 2, pp. 86–92, (1997).

35. S. Ladra and S. Torra, Information loss for synthetic data through fuzzy clustering, *International Journal of Uncertainty, Fuzziness and Knowledge-Based Systems*. (2007). Submitted.

Chapter 8

Privacy Preserving and Use of Medical Information in a Multiagent System

Karina Gibert[1], Aida Valls[2], Lenka Lhotska[3], Petr Aubrecht[3]

[1] *Universitat Politècnica de Catalunya, Dep. Statistics and Operations Research, Knowledge Engineering and Machine Learning group, Barcelona, Spain*
karina.gibert@upc.edu

[2] *Universitat Rovira i Virgili, Dep. Computer Science and Mathematics, Intelligent Technologies for Advanced Knowledge Acquisition group, Tarragona, Spain*
aida.valls@urv.cat

[3] *Czech Technical University in Prague, Dep. of Cybernetics, Faculty of Electrical Engineering Prague, Czech Republic*
{lhotska, aubrech}@labe.felk.cvut.cz

Health-Care applications involve complex structures of interacting processes and professionals that need to exchange information to provide the care services. In this kind of systems many different professional competencies, ethical and sensibility requirements as well as legal frameworks coexist and because of that the information managed inside the system should not be freely accessed, on the contrary it must be subject to very complex privacy restrictions. This is particularly critical in distributed systems, where additionally, security in remote transmissions must be ensured. In this chapter the contribution of artificial intelligence techniques to deal with privacy preserving in distributed medical applications is addressed. The particular case of the HomeCare will be explained since it is especially interesting because of its inherent complexity. Finally, the result of the K4Care project will be briefly analysed.

Contents

8.1. Introduction

Medical environments use to involve high complex structures of interacting processes and professionals where a high quantity of information is managed and exchanged.

However, not all information is equal and it may require different degree of protection. Common information may be of the following types:

- *Public*: information that is already a matter of public record or knowledge, for example names and sex of politicians or artists.
- *Personal*: it belongs to a private individual. It depends on his/her decision to share this information with others, for example, address, phone number and email address.
- *Private*: information associated with an individual and whose disclosure may not be in the individual's interest, for example credit card number or bank account number.
- *Sensitive*: Some types of private information are considered sensitive and may be protected by privacy laws. This concerns person's health record, ethnic origin, religion, political attitude.
- *Confidential*: information whose disclosure may harm business or personal integrity. In HomeCare this concerns information, for example, about psychic state of a person, about oncological diagnosis, or HIV.

Protection methods differ according to the place of information where security is addressed (during data transitions, storage, or even during data processing in the system environment).

In medical environments, most pieces of information are usually very sensitive, private or even confidential and special care is required when dealing with them. An important aspect of information security and risk management is recognizing the value of information and defining appropriate procedures and protection requirements for the information.

In this chapter, some elements to guarantee security and privacy preserving in information technology distributed applications which provide some kind of support to complex medical domains are addressed. In this kind of systems many different professional competencies, ethical and sensibility requirements as well as legal frameworks coexist and, because of that, the information managed inside the system should not be freely accessed, on the contrary it must be subject to very complex privacy restrictions. This is particularly critical in distributed systems, where additional security in remote transmissions must be ensured.

In a medical system, design has to solve all levels of determining user rights - identification, authentication and authorization. The particular case of the medical domain of HomeCare assistance will be presented as a real application, owing to two reasons. First, it is especially interesting because of its inherent complexity. Indeed, HomeCare involves professionals from different institutions (hospital, social work organizations, etc.) structurally independent, which must interact around any particular patient, and which usually are located in different physical places having their own and independent information systems. Second, long research on building a distributed platform to support integral management of the care of chronic disabled patients staying at home has been done in the K4Care European project[1] and the results of the project are a clear example of how artificial intelligence techniques can contribute to privacy preserving in this kind of systems.

The chapter has the following structure: it starts presenting the privacy preserving and security aspects to be taken into account when developing a distributed system for a medical domain. Specific sections are devoted to each of these aspects. Ontologies and multiagent systems are presented as a good solution for this kind of complex and distributed environments, where different organisational and legal norms must be strictly followed. The particular case of HomeCare is analysed. The last section gives some details of the particular solutions used in the K4Care European project. The chapter ends with a discussion synthesizing the most important issues.

8.2. Privacy preserving and security in a distributed platform for medical domains

Privacy preserving and data security is a complex field, which deals with many different problems and provides different solutions, as privacy and security can be threatened in many ways. Solutions usually lead to obstructions in normal use. Here, the most important problems are described and methods to reach the desired level of privacy and security are provided in next sections. Advantages and drawbacks are discussed.

A global privacy preserving and security solution has to start with a definition of a set of internal privacy and security rules, security guidelines. These rules specify how the sensitive data has to be treated, where it can appear. The rules must exactly define physical places of data in each of its life cycle. At the end, users have to be educated, they should know how the security protection work and how to resist against (often social) attacks, including safe habits regarding password.

To build a platform that supports a complex medical model, as for example the HomeCare assistance, is not a trivial task and requires a careful design. One of the most critical aspects to be regarded is the one related with security and privacy preserving, which includes, for those kind of complex systems, the following issues:

- The system must be protected against external attacks and non-authorized accesses. This is a common problem of almost all private systems and the most popular way to control that is to implement *identification, authentication* and *user's failure mechanisms*, as well as to use well-known and proven tools to prevent non-authorized breaks into the system. Section 8.3 provides details about these issues.
- In many information systems, different users play different roles and, thus, they must have different access rights. Generally in medical domains professional liabilities use to have legal implications (for example, in the particular case of HomeCare assistance, a continuous care giver cannot directly ask for a blood analysis of the patient to the laboratory). Thus the system must guarantee, from a technical point of view, that every user is allowed to do the activities for which he/she is competent. One of the most suitable solutions to face the activities distribution is to implement an *authorization* mechanism based on the definition of *user profiles* (see section 8.4). A knowledge based approach is the most suitable option here.

- The previous point concerned the constraints on the kind of activities allowed to a certain user. But there is also another issue to be taken into account, which is related to the kind of information that is accessible to every user when different types of professionals with different types of competences coexist. In this case, information access rights must be different for each one. So, the system must guarantee that every user can only access to the information which is permitted to her/him (*e.g.* a radiotherapist is not allowed to read a psychological assessment scale result). This is faced by defining personal *information access rights*. If user profiles are defined in the system, as it is the case presented here, this point can be addressed in a single model which takes into account both aspects.
- One of the most important characteristics required to a platform supporting a complex medical domain is to work in a distributed environment. Two different levels can be distinguished:

  (a) The users involved in the process should be able to work from different physical points and they may have to interact without spatio-temporal coincidence. A very flexible paradigm to support this kind of systems where different users, with different liabilities and permissions need to interact from different physical places without requiring instantaneous communication is to use a *multiagent system* accessible through the Web. Section 8.5 introduces this paradigm.

  (b) The information is usually stored in different physical places under different formats. Management of distributed information is easily improved when a *multilayer architecture* is used including an intermediate intelligent layer, which manages the communication between the multiagent platform and the information system (see section 8.6).

- When a system is distributed and works using the Web, the security problems inherent to transaction in public networks arise. Since most of the transactions in this kind of medical systems will involve private medical information, it is critical to implement mechanisms to guarantee privacy preserving. Therefore, security infrastructure is required for the exchange of medical data from point of origin to point of destination in a communication process and also on the side of data storage. *Cryptography* also plays an important role in this case (see section 8.7).
- Finally, one of the biggest problems in all computer system is *internal security leak*. Technical staff has physical access to data storage (to hard disks, to backup tapes and so on) and the possibility to steal such

data together with high price and with anonymity of such act can be too tempting. As more confidential information is stored in the system, bigger is the risk. Cryptography is also offering interesting solutions for that problem.

8.3. Identification and authentication

Access to protected information must be restricted to people who are authorized to access it. The computer programs, and in many cases the computers that process the information without human intervention, must also be authorized. This requires mechanisms to control the access to protected information. The sophistication of the access control mechanisms should be in parity with the value of the information being protected - the more sensitive or valuable the information the stronger the control mechanisms need to be.[2] The foundation, on which access controlmechanisms are built, starts with identification and authentication. *Identification* is an assertion of who someone is or what something is. *Authentication* is the act of verifying a claim of identity.[3]

Methods for authentication are based on one of the following:

- what user *knows* (usually password)
- what user *is* (biometrics[4] - fingerprint, eye scan, hand geometry, voice, vein pattern, etc.)
- what user *has* (*e.g.* private key on a smartcard or memory stick, RFID card, real key unlocking particular device)

Of course, security levels are different upon the method:

- Password is known to be the cheapest but a weak protection. In fact, one of the security holes which is hard to tighten is *user's failure* (*e.g.* password written on a paper and glued on top of monitor).
- Biometrics is very secure, because it is hard to enter the right measurements by unauthorized people, but either with high false-negative ratio (fingerprint) or inconvenient (eye scan). Of course, it also requires specific hardware on the user side - fingerprint readers, scanners.
- Smartcards are frequently used, but as a physical thing, it can be stolen. The system must react quickly and reject usage of the card soon after its loss announcement. Smartcards can be used in two modes - as data holder of private keys and as a cryptographic machine. The later mode is far more secure, the key never leaves the card and cannot be stolen without

the physical card. A successful method is a combination of a variety of approaches, *e.g.* smartcard with a short password (user will remember it), which will block after three bad password attempts (protection against password cracking).

In Europe, patient identification in medical systems could be technically provided by the European Health Insurance Card[5] at the same time electronically implementing the E-111 form. Extending such card's functions according to the German health card project, this card could also store patient-related data, such as an emergency data set, immunization information but also secure pointers to patient information stored at patients' residences. This challenge is directly related to the need for a common procedure for patient identifiers. Alternatively, patient identification can also be provided according to the Scandinavian approach of using citizen cards.[6]

The identification and authentication of health professionals will be provided by health professional cards enabling strong authentication, encoding/decoding and digital signature mechanisms, see section 8.7.

The aforementioned security services are provided on the basis of a Public Key Infrastructure (PKI).

Finally, for the protection of external non-authorized attacks it is expected a site protected by network specialists, who use some well-known and proven tools, like firewall (for unauthorized access to services), traffic analysis (for protecting against port scan, checks for known patterns during attacks), intrusion detection systems and honeypots (for automated discover of attacks, attacker accesses a server/service, which is not normally used and which initiate alarm), client's and server's private and public keys (*e.g.* for bidirectionally secure SSL connection). Those measures make very hard to illegally break into the system from outside.

On top of authentication, the system determines a set of actions, which can be performed by the user. This process is called authorisation and it is described in detail in section 8.4.

8.4. Authorization and information access rights

Once a user has been identified and authenticated, the system must know exactly what resources and actions he/she is able to access to. This is called authorization. That process guarantees that the behaviour of the users is constrained according to his/her permissions. As said before, this point is critical in general in any complex organization and particularly crucial in medical applications. Healthcare organisations must follow national and international legal rules. Among others, the distribution of patients' information must always preserve privacy constraints, and the professional liabilities are strictly defined.

In this kind of domains, it is required to define a model that describes the set of actors and their associated user profiles. This is one of the basic pillars to design a distributed multiagent system, in charge of managing the system performance. In this section, it will be illustrated how real user profiles can be transferred to a computer system to properly manage competencies, as well as, to define constraints on the actors' behaviour.

To have a semantic description of the actors' profiles, it is particularly interesting to use a high-level knowledge data representation structure. Ontologies are a formalism widely used in Knowledge Engineering, Artificial Intelligence and Computer Science, which provide a very suitable formal frame to represent the knowledge related to a complex domain, as a qualitative model of the system. Ontologies can be used to represent the structure of a domain by means of defining concepts and properties that interrelate them.

In the following subsections ontologies are defined, the use of ontologies for user profiling is described.

8.4.1. *Ontologies*

"From the ancient Greeks, learned people were concerned about what things are. But currently, the new science codifies the features of things and tries to extract the essence of things. The more the essence of things is captured the more possible the ontology can be shared".[7]

Following this statement, ontologies facilitate the possibility of reusing and sharing knowledge. Ontologies are designed for being used in applications that need to process the content of information instead of just presenting information to humans. They permit greater machine interpretability of Web content than that supported by XML, RDF, and RDF Schema (RDF-S), by providing additional vocabulary along with a formal semantics.

In Studer[8] an ontology is defined as a formal, explicit specification of a shared conceptualization, providing an abstract model of some phenomenon by identifying the relevant concepts of that phenomenon. Ontology captures consensued knowledge, that is, not a personal view of the target phenomenon of some particular individual, but one accepted by a group.

The main components of an ontology are:

- *Classes*: they represent concepts taken in a broad sense.
- *Relations*: they represent a type of association between concepts of the domain. Binary relations are sometimes used to express concept properties.
- *Instances*: they are used to represent elements or individuals in the ontology.

Ontologies help to build better and more interoperable information systems.[9] In particular, the correct use of complex concepts, as medical ones, is a crucial feature in medical information systems. These systems must include a medical terminology with a clear and non-confusing meaning. Ontologies are widely used in medicine.[10,11] The ontology represents medical terminology, modelling healthcare entities with its relations, and collecting semantic categories of those medical concepts. It is convenient that a group of medical experts develops one or several ontologies about the target domain in order to reach an efficient way to store and communicate general medical knowledge and patient-related information. If there is also an ontology defining user profiles, the behaviour of the system can be also described. In the case of medical systems, the definition of profiles involving roles and data access permissions concerns privacy preserving and security issues, as it will be described in detail in this section.

To build the ontology of a very complex medical domain, as HomeCare for example, is a huge and a very complex task, because of the great number of people and institutions involved in such a system. So it is very difficult to find a formal representation to express all the interactions among the components of the system. This is not a particular problem of medical domains, but concerning any complex field. Knowledge Engineering is an area of Artificial Intelligence that provides different ontology construction techniques to support this task,[7] like Methontology or On-To-Knowledge,[12] and semiautomatic techniques as TextToOnto[13] for ontology learning from text or to automatically learn domain ontologies from the Web.[14] In addition, tools that facilitate the codification of ontologies are available, as Protégé.[15]

Standard languages for codifying ontologies have also been defined by the World Wide Web Consortium (W3C). The most used are OWL (Web Ontology Language) and RDF (Resource Description Framework).[16]

8.4.2. *Actor Profile Ontologies*

An Actor Profile Ontology (APO) is characterized in Gibert et al.[17] as an ontology which stores the information that defines the behaviour of every kind of actor involved in a certain system.

In general, the purpose of an APO is to facilitate the integration and coordination of the different actors that are needed to provide the medical services, since the APO clearly defines what and how care will be provided.

The structure of an APO requires a previous conceptual model of the domain, which clearly identifies:

- which medical *Services* are provided by the system. A Service will be defined for each function provided to the user in order to support the provision of medical care.
- which *Actors* participate in the provision of those services. An Actor will be associated with every sort of human figure included in the structure of the medical system.
- how they interact among them to provide those *Services*.

    (a) *Professional Actions* have to be defined, associated to every individual action that an actor can perform to contribute to the accomplishment of a *Service*.

    (b) *Actions* are combined into *Procedures* to provide the desired Services. So one or several Procedures will be linked to every *Service*.

- which information is required and produced when performing the *Service*. Using *Documents* as the basic unit of information storage and exchange inside such a model provides high flexibility.
- how the *Actors* interact with the stored information to provide the *Services*. This means to define *Actors* access rights to the *Documents* and the role of *Documents* in *Procedures* and *Actions*.

Correspondingly, the APO has to include a class for every concept identified in the domain. Regarding to the implantation of the system in different contexts (*i.e.* countries with different organizational structure or different laws), it is recommendable to define a nuclear structure (NS) which comprises the minimum number of common elements needed to support the domain. Then, this nuclear structure can be extended with an optional number of *care units* that provide accessory services (AS), which can be modularly added to the system depending on the particular context (or country) where the system is implanted. For example, some specialized care services (like rehabilitation or oncology) cannot be found in all the medical centres. In addition, this modular model facilitates the extension of the system capabilities produced by the evolution of the domain itself along time. In summary, the distinction between *Nuclear* and *Accessory* services provides flexibility, adaptability and compatibility of the model with either current legal frames of different countries or regions and future medical legislations. In Figure 8.1 the structure of an Actor Profile Ontology for a medical domain is proposed. The *Entity* concept refers to

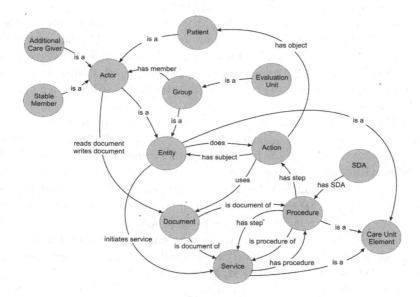

Fig. 8.1.   Actor Profile Ontology general structure

all the people or groups involved in the domain. Entity is subdivided into two main classes: (1) Group: representing teams with healthcare liabilities (*e.g.* an *evaluation unit* formed by different professional actors that work together to make a comprehensive assessment of the patient); and, (2) Actor: representing individual participants (patient, nurse, physician in charge of the patient, head nurse, family doctor). Those two type of entities appear in almost any medical system. Other specific domain classes may be considered depending on the particular domain, as social worker or additional care giver (*e.g.* family members, volunteers). Entities store information about the services they can initiate and the actions they can perform. Actors usually also have a set of reading or writing rights over Documents.

When modelling the domain, a *Service* has to be defined as a medical activity that involves the work of one or more actors in a coordinated way. They can be classified into Access Services (management services), Medical Services, and Information Services. The Service class is linked to the Entities that are able to activate the service, according to their capabilities and liabilities. It is also linked to the Procedures that can be applied (*i.e.* there may be one or more alternative ways of performing a certain service). Finally, each Service is bind to the set of documents that may be required for the achievement of that service. Actions represent the single steps that should be done to perform a service. The ontology can distinguish many subtypes of actions. Actions have an object that receives the action (usually a patient in medical systems), and a subject that is the entity able to perform that action. Actions can also work over one or several documents.

A *Procedure* represents the way a Service is provided in terms of the available actions or other services. It stores information about the service being provided, the steps of the procedure or actions and services involved in the provision of the service and a formal State-Decision-Action algorithm (SDA) indicating which are the relations between the actions in the procedure. The concept SDA is also included in the ontology because different Units can have different SDAs for the same procedure.

The *Documents* class models the communication between Entities all along Service performance. They can be used in different Procedures, by different Actors with different read/write access rights.

To model the distinction between Nuclear Services and Additional Services in an ontology, the *Care Unit Element* has been defined, representing each additional care unit of a particular medical centre (*e.g.* oncology department). Every leaf class of the hierarchies of concepts Entity, Service, Procedure and SDA inherits from the Care Unit Element hierarchy. This permits to indicate which Care Unit they refer to. For every new pack of accessory services used to extend the capabilities of the medical Model, the APO must have a new subclass of CareUnitElement (for example, in the HomeCare case, it makes sense to include to the general HomeCare model, the sets of services offered by rehabilitation units).

As it has been said, actor profile ontologies define the behaviour of each type of actor inside a complex system. However, sometimes it is convenient to have the possibility of personalizing the interaction of a particular user in certain situations. Personalization techniques can be applied to an ontology in order to customize the profile to a particular user.[18] In the case of healthcare assistance, the possibility of personalizing the system, together with usability and security aspects, can play a crucial role in the acceptance and socialisation of this kind of software tools.

8.5. Multiagent system

Multiagent systems appeared in the 1980s and since the very beginning the international interest of the Artificial Intelligence and Computer Science communities have grown enormously. This is due to the fact that intelligent agents are an appropriate software paradigm for complex open distributed systems. Healthcare applications have some characteristics that make multiagent systems a particularly appropriate model:[19]

- Knowledge is distributed in different locations.
- The provision of services involves the coordination of the effort of different individuals with different skills and functions.
- Finding standard software engineering solutions for healthcare problems is not straightforward. Interaction of different software applications is sometimes required.
- In the last years, there has been a shift towards health care promotion, shared patient provider decision making and managed care. Shared decisions and actions need to be coordinated to make sure that the care is efficient and effective.
- There is an increasing demand for information and online systems providing access to the medical knowledge available on the Internet.

A multiagent system can be defined as a collection of autonomous agents that communicate among themselves to coordinate their activities in order to be able to solve collectively a problem that could not be tackled by any agent individually. An agent is a computer system that is situated in some environment and that is capable of autonomous action in this environment in order to meet its design objectives.[20]

As it has been argued, when a domain implies different kind of actors with different functionalities interacting among themselves from different physical places and accessing to information distributed in different hosts, the use of multiagent systems is particularly suitable to support the system. The medical domain is one of those complex systems, and HomeCare is one of the domains which has a higher degree of physical distribution either from the actor point of view as from the information storage point of view. In those cases, implementing the system with a multiagent system facilitates the interaction between different types of wireless devices, the communication between different components and the distribution of tasks according to the actors' roles. Figure 8.2 shows the architecture of such a distributed system. In the proposed architecture, the agent-based

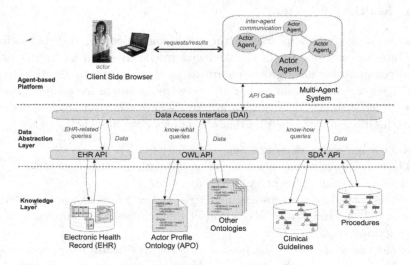

Fig. 8.2. Medical distributed system architecture

platform provides services to the users. Services may invoke other services or actions, defining a distributed service-oriented architecture. Service petitions are solved through agents' communication and cooperation. This cooperation is based on the procedures associated to each service and clinical guidelines that define how care must be delivered for each disease (both of them can be described using some sort of SDA scheme).[21]

In section 8.4 the Actor Profile Ontology has been presented. It stores the profiles of the users of the system. Since the advantage of the ontological representation over other data representation structures is the machine readibility of its contents, the contents of the APO ontology is a perfect source of knowledge to automate the implementation and deployment of personal agents.[22]

In the model proposed, every user is represented by an agent in the system. Each particular user has its own agent. When the user is logged in for the first time, the code generator creates one agent class corresponding to the actor type of the user. So, the knowledge stored in the APO is used to determine the capabilities and permitted behaviours of all the agents created into the system in such a way that the actions declared for the actor type profile in the APO are the only allowed to the corresponding user.

With this approach, the APO makes the system scalable and adaptable not only to the particularities of any instanciation of the system, but also to the evolutions of healthcare management policies that the APO captures or may capture in the future. The advantage of this approach is that the APO represents all the structural domain knowledge. This knowledge can be continuously updated and the system will result on an automatic seamless adaptation to the new laws, norms, or ways of doing with a null reprogramming effort.

8.6. Intermediate layer for knowledge-interface communications

As said before, the multiagent system uses the knowledge contained into the APO to associate different types of agents with different roles and rights to real users. In this kind of complex systems, there are also other important information sources playing an important role in the global performance of the system. The set of knowledge sources described below can be considered as a representative sample of the kind of knowledge that must be taken into account in most complex medical systems:

- The *Actor Profile Ontology* (APO) contains information about all the type of actors involved into.[23] It stores data about the services, actions, documents, and permissions of the different kinds of actors.
- *Other Medical Ontologies*: many ontologies to describe concepts in the medical domain are being developed. They are very important to achieve a real integration of the medical systems. For example, GALEN, UMLS and ON9 are representative ontologies in medicine.[9]
- *Clinical Guidelines* are general descriptions, usually defined by international care organisations, of the way in which a particular pathology should be dealt with. Clinical Guidelines contain a set of directions or principles to assist the health care practitioner with patient care decisions about appropriate diagnostic, therapeutic, or other clinical procedures for specific clinical circumstances.[24]
- The *Electronic Health Record* (EHR) and the administrative data. This data is usually stored in databases following some standard Electronic Health Record model.[25,26] This EHR contains anamnesis, medical vis-

its and ongoing treatments in form of personal documents and general document schemas that health professionals manage during the patient assistance. It may also contains Individual Intervention Plans (IIP). An IIP is a Clinical Guideline adapted to the health particularities of a single patient. In addition, the database contains administrative information about the users (*e.g.* name, address, phone, login name),

• A repository of the *procedures* that implement the services provided in the system. They store the steps needed and define the control flow that must be followed to complete the service successfully according to the different possible paths of execution.

In such a complex application, where many different types of knowledge are distributed into different knowledge sources and encoded in different formats, special attention on how this information is accessed to guarantee the correct use is needed. Moreover, the spatial distribution of the knowledge sources (which can even be in different computers from different buildings) makes more difficult to find the data required in a certain task, mainly when the agents make complex queries where information from different data sources has to be simultaneously retrieved or even combined. In addition, if the information is stored in different representation languages, the access to each particular source implies that the agents must know all the languages required to retrieve the data. Providing direct access to the knowledge sources to the agents is an inefficient solution. The information format and location should be transparent for the multiagent system.

A three layer architecture is a good solution to allow agents to work independently on the organization of the knowledge. The architecture, as previously shown in Figure 8.2, is divided in three main modules:[27] the *Knowledge Layer*, the *Data Abstraction Layer* and the *agent-based platform*. The agent-based platform contains the multiagent system together with the web interface with the real user. This upper level layer is separated from a *knowledge layer* (which includes all the data and knowledge sources as described before) by introducing an intermediate layer which contains the intelligence required to:

• retrieve any information required by the multiagent system from the correct data source.

• know the correct format of every data source to send queries to it in the proper way verify the correct access to the information according to the type of user.

This intermediate layer, called *Data Abstraction Layer* (DAL), provides high-level functions that allow the *agent-based platform* entities to retrieve the data and knowledge they need to perform their tasks. This layer offers a wide set of high-level queries that provide transparency between the data (knowledge) and its use (platform). The DAL implicitly understands the different languages used to represent the data and knows where the knowledge is located. Therefore, it is able to manage the communication requirements between the proper knowledge sources and the multiagent system.[27]

The DAL is composed by different Application Programming Interfaces (APIs) and a new element called Data Access Interface (DAI). The APIs are a set of Java methods that work as a bridge between the knowledge stored in a particular place and the rest of the system while the DAI contains all the intelligence to manage the communication with APIs and with agents and to composes the proper answers to the agent's queries.

8.7. Private data protection

As said before, one of the biggest problems in data protection is *internal security leak*. Currently available technologies offer few ways of how to improve security in this area. As an example, Oracle database offers technology called Oracle Database Vault, which hides sensitive data from unauthorized users, even database administrators.

Cryptography is also used in information security to transform usable information into a form that renders it unusable by anyone other than an authorized user. This process is called encryption. Information that has been encrypted (rendered unusable) can be transformed back into its original usable form by an authorized user, who possesses the cryptographic key, through the process of *decryption*.[3,28] Cryptography is used in information security to protect information from unauthorized or accidental discloser while the information is in transit (either electronically or physically) and while information is in storage. It can be used in different ways.

A simple protection against machine data processing of stolen data is splitting *administrative* and *medical information* into two independent parts, which are linked in a nontrivial way, done by a cryptography algorithm, in such a way that identity of the data owner cannot be easily discovered, without knowledge of the algorithm. The algorithm can be changed for a particular installation and thus make it harder to merge the two parts together. The algorithm itself is fast and has no impact on system performance. This can be implemented in the system to prevent unauthorized accesses to confidential data.

Even splitting administrative data in a separate structure, the information is still readable and potentially subject of global information mining. A complete hiding of information can be achieved using *cryptography*. The encrypted content can be opened using patient's private key, stored on his/her smartcard, but in case of losing the card, the data is further inaccessible. So there must be more private keys able to unlock the content. Another reason is statistical processing, which needs to read the data as well. Although it is possible to append multiple signs to one document, encryption can be done only by one key, so using multiple keys mean multiple copies. Unfortunately, this has real impact on both complexity and performance of the system, but it is convenient to pay this price to ensure security. A solution can be a long password, which is used to encrypt the content of the protected message. This password is then encrypted by multiple public keys of authorized actors.

Signature issues are also a major concern, particularly in medical applications, because many healthcare actions rely on an order being signed. Documentary evidence of action depends on the authenticity of the signature. EHRs make authentication easier because entries can be stamped automatically with date, time, and user identification. This would be considered as an electronic signature if encryption and non-repudiation are also included. However, controls must ensure that the electronic signature elements are not altered or deleted. The possible solutions are either electronic or digital signatures:[3]

- Electronic signature is often used for signing transcribed dictation or orders in a computer physician order entry system. In its simplest form, only scanned handwritten sign is attached to a message, it is possible to attach various biometric measurements. Biometrics is very appropriate here, because it ensures real presence of the signer. Only in case, when the sign is securely bound to the document, the non-repudation can be achieved.
- Digital (as the signature is a long list of digits) signature or Cryptographic (as it always involve cryptography) signature authenticates the user (only appropriate certificate can be used to verify the sign), provides non-repudiation, and ensures message integrity.

As said before, this chapter concerns distributed medical complex systems, where private medical data is transmitted through the network. Besides encryption, the security of data transmission can be reinforced using a *defense-in-depth strategy*. The idea behind the defense-in-depth approach is to defend a system against any particular attack using several, varying methods. It is a layering tactic, conceived by the National Security Agency (NSA) as a comprehensive approach to information and electronic security. This can be implemented in different ways. Here, a suitable possibility is described. First, the two communicating systems must authenticate each other, which is accomplished with the standard SSL handshake with dual authentication option. Authentication is done using X.509 certificates that are preinstalled on the communicating systems. Both the Honest Broker and the external system must identify, authenticate and authorize the other system before transmission will begin. The data transmission is protected using the battle-tested SSL protocol with a few changes to the default configuration. Instead of the typical single server authentication, in K4Care both sides of the connection are authenticated.

In addition to the above controls, traffic will be restricted to specific Internet Protocol (IP) addresses and data formats. No direct login to the Honest Broker system will occur during normal data transfer. All interaction is accomplished using the Web Services API that is hardened for exposure to the network.

Another concern is *physical security*. It is expected that in full operation the servers are housed in a dedicated machine room with electronic locks, environmental controls, backup processes, and restricted personnel access. Off-site backups will be stored in a physically secured, patrolled location.

8.8. A real case: the K4Care project

The K4Care European project (Knowledge based HomeCare eServices for an Ageing Europe) is a Specific Targeted Research of Innovation Project funded within the Sixth Framework Program of the European Commission that brings together 13 academic and industrial institutions from 7 countries for a period of 3 years starting March 2006.

The elderly population needing full time care is increasing due to the increasing longevity and increasing survival to acute accidents and diseases. The care of chronic and disabled patients involves life long treatment under continuous expert supervision. Moreover, healthcare professionals and patients agree that institutionalisation in hospitals or residentials facilities may be unnecessary and even counterproductive. For this reason, Home-

Care is considered fundamental.

The care of HomeCare patients is particularly complex because of the growing number of people in such circumstances, because of the great amount of resources required to guarantee a good longterm assistance, and because the typical patient is a person with comorbid conditions and diseases, cognitive and/or physical impairment, functional loss from multiple disabilities and impaired self-dependence. All this complexity is studied in the K4Care project.

The main goal of the project is to build a system that captures and integrates the information, skills and experiences of specialized HomeCare centres and professionals of several old and new EU countries, and to incorporate them into an intelligent platform based on a multiagent system accessible via web, in order to provide e-services to health professionals, patients and citizens in general.

Particular results of the project are presented here as a concrete example of the concepts presented in this chapter. The experience of the K4Care project is an excellent illustration of a real application of the problems and solutions explained along this chapter.

8.8.1. *The K4Care model*

In the K4Care project, a model of HomeCare (HC) has been proposed. It takes into account the expert knowledge of a wide set of medical and social experts in HomeCare from different European countries, including Eastern ones.[29] The K4Care model aims to be an initial step towards the definition of an European standard that respects the different norms and lows of each country.

The K4Care model defines a nuclear structure of Services (HCNS) with the minimum number of common elements needed to provide a basic HC. The main components, presented in section 8.4, have been also identified in the K4Care model:[1] actors, services, actions, procedures and documents. With respect to *Actors*, the K4Care model proposes to classify the Actors of HomeCare assistance in three main groups: patients, stable members and additional care givers. Part of the stable members can participate in *Evaluation Units* (composed by a physician in charge, a head nurse, a family doctor and a social worker), which are temporal groups of actors that are in charge of assessing and evaluating a particular patient (see Figure 8.3).

In the K4Care APO, there are 49 HCNS *Services*, which are classified into Access Services (management services), Patient Care Services, and In-

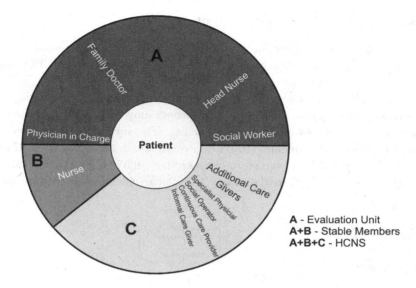

Fig. 8.3. K4care HCNS Actors Structure

formation Services. For every service, a decomposition in particular Actions is provided. For every action, the interaction between Actors is defined in the *Procedures*, as well as, which *Documents* are needed and the access permissions of every actor to each kind of document.

A HomeCare Accessory Service (HCAS) have been also considered in this project: Rehabilitation. The rehabilitation care unit is implemented including 21 Services, from which 2 services are not defined in the HCNS. Some of those services have a different procedure, which uses different actions. In fact, 16 new rehabilitative actions have been added to the ontology. The use of the hierarchy of Care Unit Elements (as proposed in 8.4) allows the correct identification of the appropriate action for each particular Accessory Service module.

In this project, the distinction between the HCNS and HCASs is particularly useful to get compatibility with both the current situation of Home-Care in the European countries, where the international, national, and regional laws define different HC systems for different countries, as well as, with the forthcoming expected situation in Europe.

8.8.2. *The knowledge management*

The K4Care system is structured in three layers, as proposed in section 8.6. The Knowledge Layer is composed by: the EHR, the APO, the CPO, the FIPs and the Procedures.

In the EHR, administrative and medical information has been split in two independent parts, linked by a cryptography algorithm to prevent unauthorized accesses to confidential data. The medical information is stored in form of documents, stored in a relational database as XML documents,[30] encrypted and signed to be safely transmitted. Figure 8.4 shows the structure of the K4Care database. To reach an efficient way to store and

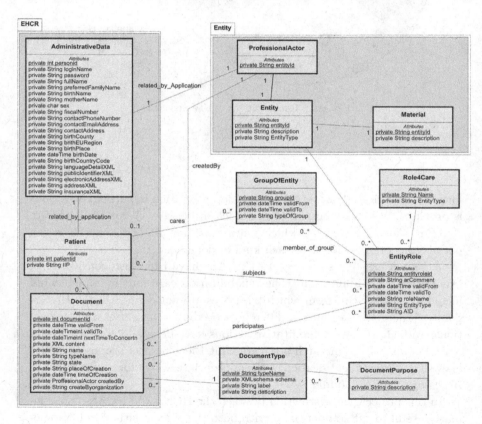

Fig. 8.4. K4Care Database Architecture

communicate general medical knowledge and patient-related information, a group of medical experts, assisted by the knowledge engineers, developed two separate ontologies. One devoted to the user profiles and information accesses (the Actor Profile Ontology, APO) and another describing diseases and symptoms to be considered in HomeCare assistance (Case Profile Ontology).

Following what has been explained in section 8.4, the APO is the basis for the user profiling of the system and contains a class for every concept identified in the K4Care model. The structure on the K4Care APO is, in fact, the one shown in Figure 8.1. In K4Care, it has also been studied how to taylor the APO to a particular Care Unit, so getting the whole set of services, actors, procedures, actions, SDAs and documents of a given HCAS, as well as, how to personalize the particular actor APOs with some additional action usually performed by other type of actors, when properly justified.[18]

The CPO is devoted to represent in a formal way all the health care knowledge required for the treatment of HomeCare patients. It has been designed to integrate concepts related to syndromes, diseases, signs, symptoms, social issues, problem assessment and intervention.[31]

Finally, a database of Formal Intervention Plans (FIP) is also included. FIPs represent procedural knowledge about treatments of syndromes and diseases. They store the guidelines to assist patients who suffer from particular ailments or diseases. Differently from clinical guidelines, FIPs can be instanciated to a particular patient in a personal Individual Intervention Plan (IIP). When a patient is diagnosed and assessed, an individual intervention plan (IIP) is defined. The IIP indicates which care actions must be done on this particular patient. The execution of this IIP is based on an SDA scheme.

Security and privacy protection is managed by means of the Data Abstraction Layer (see section 8.6), which controls the access to the different knowledge sources and provides high-level communication functionalities.

8.8.3. *The K4Care system architecture*

The K4Care system is a web-based application implemented according to the 3-layer architecture presented in section 8.6 (see figure 8.5). On the top of the architecture, a multiagent system is in charge of providing the services to the users. Service petitions are solved through agents' communication and cooperation. Services may invoke other services or actions, defining a distributed service-oriented architecture.

To provide the medical services, agents use the procedure associated to each service (represented using SDA* schemes).[21] In addition, when a patient is diagnosed and assessed, an individual intervention plan (IIP) is defined. The IIP indicates which care actions must be done on this patient. IIPs are also represented in an SDA* scheme. Therefore, an SDA* Engine Agent has been designed, which is able to interpret SDA* descriptions (FIPs or IIPs) and coordinate the other agents properly during its execution (see Figure 8.5).

Every user is represented by an agent in the system. Each particular user has its own agent. When the user is logged in for the first time, the code generator creates one agent class corresponding to the actor type of the user. So, the knowledge stored in the APO is used to determine the capabilities and permitted behaviours of all the agents created into the system in such a way that the actions declared for the actor type profile in the APO are the only allowed to the corresponding user. In this approach, the APO is the

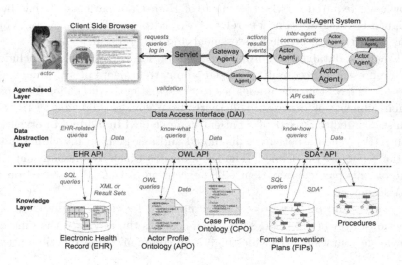

Fig. 8.5.   K4Care system

first source of information to generate the code of an agent automatically. However, other elements are needed: elementary capabilities (actions) of actors that must be programmed by IT experts, Electronic Health Care Record schemes represented in an international standards (XML Schema Definition Language), the procedures logic (from SDA* diagrams) must implemented by SDA* experts, and finally, the application knowledge that formalizes agent technology (MAS ontology) is introduced by agent experts.[22]

The deployment of the architecture then means the assignment of agent types to real people in the real organization. Actors can initiate certain procedures, create new IIPs at runtime that are performed by SDA* Engine Agents. This solution guarantees the flexibility of the system. In this manner, when static knowledge changes, the implementation can be easily recreated in an automatic way. In the case of new dynamic knowledge, it is applied immediately without any other intervention on the platform.

Regarding the security of the transmissions between agents, the considerations explained in section 8.7 have been taken into account. In fact, the data exchanged is transformed into XML messages, using HL7 standards when appropriate. The XML message is then wrapped into a Simple Object Access Protocol (SOAP) message and transmitted to the second system. After the second system received the message, the data is extracted in reverse order of the above encapsulation. The encrypted content can be opened using patient's private key.

8.9. Discussion

In this chapter, it can be seen how different methodologies of Artificial Intelligence, such as multiagent systems, knowledge reasoning techniques and knowledge representation frames as ontologies, can be integrated to strictly guarantee security and privacy preserving in a system supporting a very complex domain. The particular case of health care applications has been analysed. Medical contexts are especially interesting because of the legal constraints related to privacy preserving and security.

One of the contributions of this work has been to clearly identify which are the security and privacy preserving issues related with the development of a multiagent system for medical complex domains. It can be said that a medical system must be protected against external or internal attacks, and that those attacks mainly consist of:

- illegal attempt to access to some protected information stored into the system.
- illegal attempt to perform some action from inside the system.

In this chapter, security and privacy preserving has been described from a technical point of view. The different problems have been addressed by means of appropriate Artificial Intelligence and computer science techniques.

Using a multiagent system paradigm facilitates the communication and coordination among the different users following some organizational rules, even if they are in different physical places. So, it is specially suitable for distributed systems, either at the level of users location or at the level of information location.

Using an ontology to define user profiles and information access rights guarantees that all the actions and information accesses are performed according to the user' liabilities and competencies and guarantees privacy preserving and security.

Including an intermediate layer into the system architecture to manage the communication between the agents and the knowledge sources provides the possibility to store the knowledge in different places and formats with transparency for the multiagent system.

Combining a multiagent system with an ontology which defines the user profiles is the key to guarantee adaptability of the system to future structural modifications of the model, either in short, mid or long term.

Protection of sensitive data with cryptography is a key requirement valid especially for medical application. Data must be protected during all stages of its life cycle and in every place it can appear, including server disks, transport lines, backup storage, etc. A database design for this purpose has been proposed.

Finally, the access must be done with the proper authentication and identification mechanisms than prevent external attackers to come into the system.

HomeCare has been used in this chapter to illustrate the kind of security and privacy preserving problems to be addressed when developing real multiagent systems, as it involves most of the security issues to be regarded in complex medical systems in general. In the last section, the K4Care project has been revised to illustrate a real case study. From this experience, it seems clear that security and privacy preserving requires special attention to guarantee the deployment of such kind of sensible systems.

Finally, this chapter is a vast illustration of how the application of some Artificial Intelligence techniques can provide powerful and flexible approaches to support privacy preserving and security issues in distributed complex medical domains.

Acknowledgements

This research has been partially financed by the EU Project K4Care (IST-2004-026968), the Spanish HYGIA project (TIN2006-15453-C04), the Spanish ARES CONSOLIDER-2010 project (CSD2007-00004), the Spanish e-AEGIS project (TSI-2007-65406-C03) and the research program MSM 6840770012 of the CTU in Prague, Czech Republic. The medical and social experts in the field of geriatrics and HC participating in the panel of experts were F. Campana, R. Annicchiarico, S. Ercolani, A. Federici, T. Caseri, E. Balint, L. Spiru, D. Amici, R. Jones and P. Mecocci. Authors want to thank D. Sánchez and D. Isern for his help in the camera ready preparation, M. Batet and J. Doležal for their collaboration in the K4Care implementation.

References

1. F. Campana, A. Moreno, D. Riaño and L. Varga. K4care: Knowledge-based homecare e-services for an ageing europe. In *Agent Technology and e-Health*, Whitestein Series in Software Agent Technology and Autonomic Computing, pp. 95–116. Birkhauser Verlag, (2008).
2. L. Lhotska, P. Aubrecht, A. Valls, and K.Gibert. Security recommendations for implementation in distributed healthcare systems. In *In Proc. of the 42nd Annual 2008 IEEE Int'l Carnahan Conf. on Security Technology*, pp. 76–83, Prague, (2008).
3. M. Stamp, *Information Security: principles and practice*. (John Wiley & Sons, 2006).
4. G. Davida, Y. Frankel, and B. Matt. On enabling secure applications through off-line biometric identification. In *IEEE Symposium on Security and Privacy*, pp. 148–157, (1998).
5. Wikipedia. European health insurance card. http://en.wikipedia.org/wiki/European_Health_Insurance_Card.
6. B. Blobel, Comparing approaches for advanced e-health security infrastructures, *International Journal of Medical Informatics*. **76(5-6)**, 454–459, (2007).
7. A. Gómez-Pérez, M. Fernández-López, and O. Corcho, *Ontological Engineering*. (Springer Verlag, 2004), 2nd printing edition.
8. R. Studer, R. Benjamins, and D. Fensel. Knowledge engineering: Principles and methods. In *IEEE Trans. On Data and Knowledge Eng.*, vol. 25, pp. 161–197, (1998).
9. D. Pisanelli, Ed., *Ontologies in Medicine*. vol. 102, *Studies in Health Technology and Informatics*, (IOS Press, 2004).
10. D. Pisanelli and A. Gangemi, *If ontology is the solution, what is the problem?*,

In *Ontologies in Medicine*, vol. 102, *Series in Studies in Health Technology and Informatics,* pp. 1–19. IOS Press, (2004).

11. The National Center for Biomedical Ontology. Bioportal: Open Biomedical Ontologies. http://www.bioontology.org/tools/portal/bioportal.html.

12. S. Staab, H. P. Schnurr, R. Studer, and Y. Sure, Knowledge processes and ontologies, *IEEE Intelligent Systems.* **16(1)**, 26–34, (2001).

13. A. Maedche and S. Staab. Ontology learning for the semantic web. In *IEEE Intelligent Systems, Special Issue on Semantic Web*, vol. 16(2), pp. 72–79, (2001).

14. D. Sánchez and A. Moreno, Learning non-taxonomic relationships from web documents for domain ontology construction, *Data Knowledge Engineering.* **63(3)**, 600–623, (2008).

15. N. Noy, R. Fergerson, and M. Musen. The knowledge model of Protégé-2000: Combining interoperability. in: R. Dieng and O. Corby. In *12th International Conference in Knowledge Engineering and Knowledge Management (EKAW'00). (Lecture Notes in Artificial Intelligence LNAI 1937)*, pp. 17–32, Germany, (2000). Springer-Verlag.

16. D. Fensel, The semantic web and its languages, *IEEE Intelligent Systems.* **15(6)**, 67–73, (2000).

17. K. Gibert, A. Valls, and D. Riaño, Knowledge engineering as a support for building an actor profile ontology for integrating homecare systems, *Technology and Informatics.* **136**, 95–100, (2008).

18. M. Batet, A. Valls, K. Gibert, S. Martínez, and E. Morales. Tailoring of the actor profile ontology in the k4care project. In ed. D. Riaño, *ECAI Workshop on Knowledge Management for Healthcare Processes (ECAI)*, pp. 40–44, (2008).

19. A. Moreno and J. Nealon, Eds., *Applications of Software Agent Technology in the Health Care Domain*. Whitestein Series in Software Agent Technologies, (Birkhäuser Verlag, Switzerland, 2003).

20. M. Wooldridge, Ed., *An Introduction to MultiAgent Systems.* Whitestein Series in Software Agent Technologies, (John Wiley & Sons, England, 2002).

21. D. R. no. The sda* model: A set theory approach. In *Machine Learning and Management of Health-Care Procedural Knowledge*, Maribor, Slovenia, (2007). 20th IEEE Int. Workshop on CBMS 2007.

22. A. Hajnal, A. Moreno, G. Pedone, D. R. no, and L. Varga, *Formalizing and leveraging domain knowledge in the K4CARE home care platform.* (Idea Group publisher, IRM Press, CyberTech Publishing, 2008). to appear.

23. K. Gibert, A. Valls, and J. Casals, Enlarging a medical actor profile ontology with new care units, *Lecture Notes on Artificial Intelligence: K4CARE 2007.* **4924**, 101–116, (2008).

24. D. Isern and A. Moreno. Computer-based management of clinical guidelines: A survey. In *In Proc. of Fourth Workshop on Agents applied in Healthcare in conjunction with the 17th European Conference on Artificial Intelligence (ECAI 06)*, pp. 71–80, Italy, (2006).

25. I. Iakovidis, Towards personal health records. current situation, obstacles and trends in implementation of electronic healthcare records in europe, *Int. J.*

Medical Informatics. **52(1)**, 105–115, (1998).

26. M. Batet, A. Valls, and K. Gibert. Survey of electronic health records standards. Technical Report Research Report DEIM-RR-06-004, Department of Computer Engineering and Mathematics, Universitat Rovira i Virgili, (2006).

27. M. Batet, K. Gibert, and A. Valls, The data abstraction layer as knowledge provider for a medical multi-agent system, *Lecture Notes on Artificial Intelligence: K4CARE 2007.* **4249**, 86–100, (2008).

28. G. Kessler, *Handbook of Local Area Networks.* (Auerbach, J. Sloan (ed.), Boston, 1999). W3C Recommendation http://www.w3.org/xml.

29. F. Campana et al. Knowledge-based homecare eservices for an ageing europe. k4care deliverable d01, eu, (2007). http://www.k4care.net/fileadmin/k4care/public_website/downloads/K4C_Model_D01.rar.

30. T. Bray, J. Paoli, C. Sperberg-McQueen, E. Maler, and F. Yergeau, Eds., *Extensible Markup Language (XML) 1.0 (Fourth Edition).* Whitestein Series in Software Agent Technologies, (John Wiley & Sons, 2006). W3C Recommendation http://www.w3.org/xml.

31. D. Riaño, F. Real, F. Campana, S. Ercolani, and R. Annicchiarico. An ontology for the care of the elder at home. In *AMIA 2008 Annual Symposium: Biomedical and Health Informatics*, (2008).

PART 3
Security by means of Artificial Intelligence

Chapter 9

Perimeter Security on Noise-Robust Vehicle Detection Using Nonlinear Hebbian Learning

Bing Lu, Alireza Dibazar, Sageev George, and Theodore W. Berger

University of Southern California, Department of Biomedical Engineering, Los Angeles, CA 90089, USA

{blu, dibazar, sageev}@usc.edu, berger@bmsr.usc.edu

The acoustic signature recognition of approaching vehicles is intended for integration into a perimeter security context. The recognizer can be used to detect vehicles that may be loaded with explosives approaching a restricted area. We propose using a new approach, a nonlinear Hebbian learning method, to implement the task of vehicle detection. The proposed learning rule processes both time and frequency components of input data. The spectral analysis is realized by using auditory gammatone filterbanks. The gammatone-filtered feature vectors are then assembled over multiple temporal frames to establish a high-dimensional spectro-temporal representation (STR). With the exact acoustic signature of running vehicles being unknown, a nonlinear Hebbian learning (NHL) rule is employed to extract representative independent features from the spectro-temporal ones and to reduce the dimensionality of the feature space. During the learning, weight vectors are obtained to transform the input features into the representative space. Comparing with linear Hebbian learning (LHL) which explores the second-order moment of data, the applied NHL involves all-order statistics of data, thus leading to a more optimal learning.

Simulation and real-time field testing results show that the whole proposed system can more accurately recognize vehicle sound and identify vehicle type than its counterparts in severely noisy circumstances. For recognizing vehicle sound, at low SNR= 0 dB, the proposed system dramatically decreases the error rate by 16%, 25%, and 68%, over normally used feature extraction method, MFCC (mel frequency cepstral computation), when vehicle data is corrupted by AWGN, human vowel utterances, and bird chirps, respectively; moreover, the proposed system decreases the error rate by 15.3%, 20%, and 2%, over LHL. For identifying vehicle type, when gasoline heavy wheeled car is mixed with AWGN at SNR= 5 dB, NHL improves the performance by 40% over LHL.

Contents

9.1. Introduction

Using artificial intelligence to design smart sensors or machines for perimeter security has attracted increased attention recently, such as an acoustic recognizer of running vehicles. This acoustic recognizer is intended for integration into a larger security context. It is normally assumed that there exists a fixed asset to protect and a perimeter that defines the vicinity around that asset for surveillance, while providing security by human is dangerous or expensive. The sound recognizer of incoming vehicles is developed for perimeter protection in national, agricultural, airport, prison, military sites, and residential areas. For example, the recognizer can be used to detect approaching vehicles that may be loaded with explosives or suicide bombers to a military asset.

The acoustic sound of interest from a running vehicle is complicated and affected by multiple factors, such as vehicle type, gearing, number of cylinders, muffler choice, state of maintenance, running speed, distance from the microphone, tires, and the road on which the vehicle travels. Moreover, the problem is complicated because of the presence of uncontrolled interference emitted by surrounding background, such as human voice, bird chip, and wind. Real-world acoustic recognition of running vehicles thus is very challenging.

Recently, some studies[1-7] have been done for acoustic recognition of running vehicles. It is not easy to give a unified comparison among these studies as their databases and testing environments are significantly different. Generally in acoustic signal processing, extracting representative

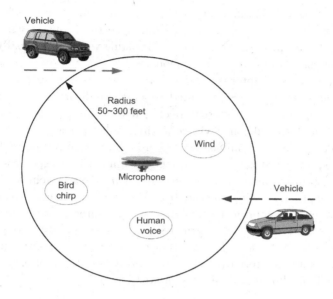

Fig. 9.1.   An illustration of vehicle recognition environment.

features is the most important element to characterize the *unknown signatures* of running vehicles. Choe et al.,[1] Maciejewski et al.,[2] and Averbuch et al.[6] applied wavelet-based analysis for feature extraction of the incoming waveforms. Wu et al.[4] and Munich[5] used the short-term Fourier transform (STFT) to provide a precise representation of the acoustic data, and then used linear principal component analysis (PCA) to convert the high-dimensional features to low-dimensional ones. Besides, Munich[5] proposed a reliable probabilistic recognizer based on both principal subspace and complementary subspace, and compared his method with the baseline method Mel frequency cepstral computation (MFCC). In addition, STFT, then PCA and one independent component analysis (ICA) method used in[8] were compared, and it was stated that PCA method is better.[7] In this chapter, our proposed method is compared with PCA (or equivalently LHL), and with MFCC (as MFCC is a normally used feature extraction technique in acoustic signal recognition, and it decreases the dimensionality of STFT while maintaining much original spectral information).

The purpose of the designed recognizer is to detect approaching vehicle and identify its type with minimum error rates. The proposed technologies pursued in this chapter are motivated by biological studies. In addition, the acoustic data of running vehicles is recorded from one microphone. The purpose of using one microphone is to analyze the acoustic signatures of running vehicles, instead of tracking or localizing vehicles (normally accomplished by using an array of microphones).

The rest of this chapter is organized as follows. In Sect. 9.2, an overview description of the system is presented, in which, auditory gammatone filterbanks are applied to characterize spectral features, and a spectro-temporal representation is established via collecting multiple such spectral feature vectors along time. A nonlinear Hebbian learning rule is analyzed in Sect. 9.3, which plays a critical role in reducing the dimension of spectro-temporal features and in learning *unknown acoustic signatures* of vehicles. Concurrent to this process, weight vectors from input to output neurons are adaptively learned, which projects the data onto the representative feature space of vehicle sound. With these learned signatures and synaptic weights, simulation results in Sect. 9.5 show that the proposed system significantly outperforms its counterparts, especially more robust to noise. Then some highlighted conclusion and discussion are given in Sect. 9.6.

9.2. Description of the Proposed System

In real-world applications, there may co-exist many environmental noises. They can be highly time-varying and unknown to the recognizer. Without the knowledge of noise sources, the goal of designing a recognizer is to make it capable of extracting representative features which are not affected by unknown noises. With this goal in mind, the whole recognizer is proposed in Fig. 9.2, which includes an artificial intelligent ear (auditory signal processing) and a brain-like neural network (nonlinear neural learning). A Hamming window is used to divide signals into frames with duration on the order of tens of milliseconds, such that the signal within the window could be assumed to be quasi-stationary and thus suitable for the following frequency analysis.

In order to extract spectral features, a series of bandpass auditory gammatone filters (GTF) are applied to process hamming-windowed frames. The gammatone auditory function was first introduced by Johanesma,[9] which characterizes the physiological impulse response of cat's primary auditory fibers. The impulse response of gammatone filter is

$$f(t) = t^{n-1}\exp(-2\pi bt)\cos(2\pi f_c t + \phi), \tag{9.1}$$

where n is the filter order, b represents the filter bandwidth, f_c denotes the

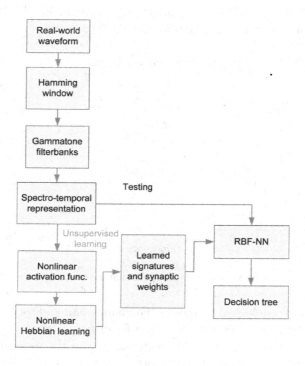

Fig. 9.2. Description of the proposed system.

center frequency, and ϕ is the tone phase. The primary parameters of the filter are n and b. When the order of the filter is 4, the magnitude shape is very similar to that of human auditory filter.[10,11] A gammatone filter well represents the cochlear impulse responses of auditory system.[10,12–14] The bandwidth of the filter depends on the center frequency and is described by an equivalent rectangular bandwidth (ERB)

$$b(f_c) = 1.019 \times 24.7(1 + \frac{4.37 f_c}{1000}), \qquad (9.2)$$

where 1.019 is the correction factor.[13]   In order to derive the transfer function of analog gammatone filter, impulse invariant transformation (IIT)[15][pp. 443–449] is applied, which is shown to have a smaller digital implementation error than other transformation methods.[16] As gammatone filters can extract more features at various levels of nonlinearities than other conventional feature extraction approaches, such as MFCC, it can thus achieve better performance under noisy environments.[17] An example of gammatone filterbanks is illustrated in Fig. 9.3.

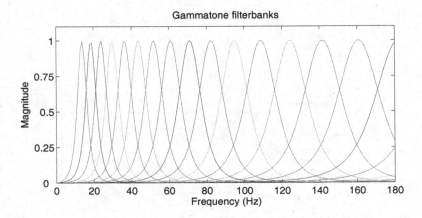

Fig. 9.3.   An example of gammatone filterbanks.

Based on physiological studies of the mammalian auditory cortex, neurons in the brain process both time and frequency components of signals, and the temporal receptive field is extended up to the order of hundreds of milliseconds.[18-20] A spectro-temporal representation (STR) is thus established by collecting multiple frames of gammatone-filtered vectors. Integrating acoustic information along time can greatly attenuate the drawback of spectral features, which is the sensitiveness to changes in the acoustic environments such as background noise or channel distortion. Hence, the performance of the STR recognizer is expected to be better than that of the single spectral recognizer, since incorporation of features in both domains maintains more intrinsic properties of input data.

Next, a nonlinear Hebbian learning (NHL) for extracting *unknown acoustic signatures* of running vehicles is described, which is motivated by neural learning functions in the brain. Concurrent to this process, synaptic weights connecting input and output neurons are adaptively learned. Then, at the testing stage, the learned synaptic weights and signatures (patterns) are favorable to be used as inputs to a supervised associative network, radial basis function neural network (RBF-NN). The proposed recognizer is able to make two level decisions, as shown in Fig. 9.4. Firstly, decide urban vehicle or non-vehicle (human voice, bird chirps, and wind); secondly, decide which type the vehicle is (gasoline light wheeled car, gasoline heavy wheeled car, diesel truck, and motorcycle).

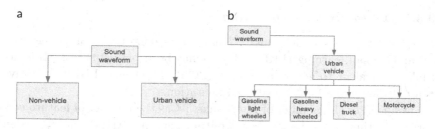

Fig. 9.4.   (a) Vehicle vs. non-vehicle recognition., (b) Four type vehicle identification.

9.3. Unsupervised Nonlinear Hebbian Learning

When testing conditions are different from the conditions where the training signals are recorded, which is almost always the case in reality, the proposed system is designed to be capable of eliminating or attenuating unexpected noises in the real, untrained environments. Moreover, there exist many unknown noise sources in surrounding backgrounds, and generally they are time varying. It is not feasible to track and model every noise source, and then to remove its effect. We are thus motivated to work on extracting representative features that are robust enough against noise variation.

How does the brain form a useful representation of signals of interest even if there are many uncontrolled noises in surrounding environments? It has been suggested that neurons employing Hebbian learning rule can learn to code a set of patterns in such a way that important components are strengthened while unimportant components are weakened.[21-28] There is strong physiological evidence for Hebbian learning in the area of the brain called the hippocampus. The hippocampus plays an important role in certain aspects of learning or memory. This physiological evidence makes Hebbian learning all the more appealing. Hebb's postulate of learning is the oldest and most famous of all learning rules. Quoting from Hebb's book[29][p.62], a statement is made in a neurobiological context, "When an axon of cell A is near enough to excite a cell B and repeatedly or persistently takes part in firing it, some growth process or metabolic changes take place in one or both cells such that A's efficiency as one of the cells firing B, is increased." According to Palm,[30] a Hebbian synapse increases its strength with positively correlated presynaptic and postsynaptic signals, and decreases its strength when these signals are negatively correlated.

9.3.1. *Linear Hebbian Learning*

Many studies and applications[21-24] have been done based on generalized linear Hebbian learning (LHL) rules. It has been proved that LHL is actually equivalent to generalized linear PCA, except that LHL is adaptive computation while PCA is batch computation.

Define Q as the number of filterbanks, M as the number of feature vectors along time, L as the number of output neurons. And define x_{qm} as an input feature element at the $\{q\}_{q=1}^{Q}$th spectral filter and at the $\{m\}_{m=1}^{M}$th temporal frame. An Q-by-M spectro-temporal representation is an input to the learning. $\{y_l\}_{l=1}^{L}$ denotes an output. w_{qml} is the synaptic weight connecting input neuron x_{qm} and output neuron y_l. A generalized LHL is realized by iteratively computing

$$y_l = \sum_{q=1}^{Q} \sum_{m=1}^{M} w_{qml} x_{qm}, \ l \in [1, L];$$

$$\Delta w_{qml} = \eta y_l \left(x_{qm} - \sum_{i=1}^{l-1} w_{qmi} y_i - w_{qml} y_l \right), \qquad (9.3)$$

$$q \in [1, Q], m \in [1, M], l \in [1, L],$$

where η is the learning rate. It has been proved that this LHL maximizes variance $E\{y^2\}$, (where $E\{\cdot\}$ is expectation computation). Upon convergence, the output patterns y_ls are the largest eigenvalues of data correlation matrix. And the synaptic weight vectors are corresponding eigenvectors, which project data into LHL-learned feature space.[21-24]

Example A: One example is given here to illustrate the limitation of LHL. The only given information to the system is the observation data $\mathbf{x}$ in x_1-x_2 space in Fig. 9.5(a). It is composed of two independent components. One s_1 is uniform-distributed within the range $[-2, 2]$, the other s_2 is Gaussian-distributed with mean 0 and variance 1. Two components are composed, $\mathbf{x} = \mathbf{As}$, $\mathbf{A} = [0.9397 \ -0.7660; -0.3420 \ 0.6428]$. Both component distributions and composing matrix are randomly selected. The system does *NOT* know component distributions *NOR* their composing property. In order to find the principal feature space, LHL maximizes the variance of data, and extracts components approximately along two diagonal lines of the observation data. The synaptic weight matrix is calculated, $\mathbf{W}_L = [-0.8785 \ 0.4807; 0.4778 \ 0.8727]$. Via $\mathbf{W}_L$ to project data, the re-

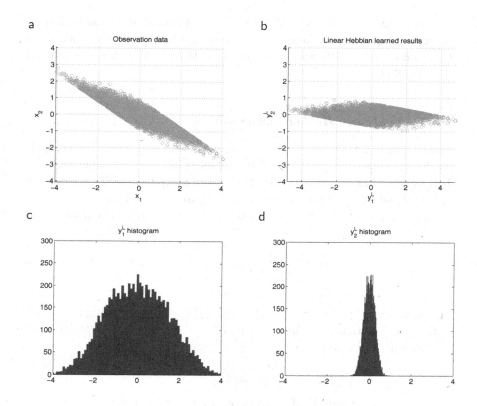

Fig. 9.5.   (a) The observation is a mixture of two components.   One is uniform-distributed within the range $[-2, 2]$, and the other is Gaussian-distributed with mean 0 and variance 1. These two components are composed with matrix $\mathbf{A}$. The system does *NOT* assume any knowledge of the components *NOR* their composing property. The only given information is the observation data in x_1-x_2 space. (b) In order to find the representative feature space, LHL optimizes the variance of data, and finds the components approximately along two diagonal lines. The observation data is projected to LHL-learned feature space. (c) The histogram of LHL-learned y_1^L is not equal to the distribution of either real component. (d) The histogram of LHL-learned y_2^L is not equal to the distribution of either real component.

sult is illustrated in Fig. 9.5(b). The LHL-components do not appear like $[-2, 2]$ uniform nor $(0, 1)$ Gaussian, as illustrated in Figs. 9.5(c)-(d). This indicates that LHL is not able to correctly extract two components (one uniform, one Gaussian), as it is not able to find their real feature space. When the decomposing synaptic weight matrix multiplies the composing one, $\mathbf{W}_L\mathbf{A} = [-1.1915 \; -0.2168; 0.6076 \; 0.3966] \neq \mathbf{I}$, where $\mathbf{I}$ is identity matrix. Then, $\mathbf{y} = \mathbf{W}_L \mathbf{x} = \mathbf{W}_L \mathbf{A} \mathbf{s} \neq \mathbf{s}$. The potential reason is that the inherent properties of independent components involve higher-order statistics, and thereby LHL which only explores the second-order moment fails to extract them.

9.3.2. *Nonlinear Hebbian Learning*

In an information-theoretic context, the second-order moment is inadequate to describe data property, as data property involves all-order statistics. LHL has been extended to nonlinear Hebbian learning with several different sets of equations[25-28] for explore all-order statistics of data.

The output y_l, produced in response to a set of inputs, is given by

$$y_l = \sum_{q=1}^{Q} \sum_{m=1}^{M} w_{qml} x_{qm}, \quad l \in [1, L]. \tag{9.4}$$

Define nonlinear neuron outputs $\{z_l = g(y_l)\}_{l=1}^{L}$ with $g(\cdot)$ being a nonlinear activation function, as illustrated in Fig. 9.6. The NHL optimizes the variance of nonlinear neurons,

$$\begin{aligned}
\text{maximize } J &= \mathrm{E}\{g^2(y_l)\}, \\
\text{subject to } \mathbf{w}_{l_1}^T \mathbf{w}_{l_2} &= \delta_{l_1, l_2}, \quad l, l_1, l_2 \in [1, L],
\end{aligned} \tag{9.5}$$

where $\mathbf{w}_l = [w_{11l}, w_{12l}, \ldots, w_{1Ml}, \ldots, w_{Q1l}, w_{Q2l}, \ldots, w_{QMl}]^T$ is an interleaved vector of spectro-temporal synaptic weights for output neuron l. The inner-product of synaptic weight vectors from different output neurons satisfies the constrained condition, Kronecker function $\delta_{l_1, l_2} = 1$, if $l_1 = l_2$, otherwise, $\delta_{l_1, l_2} = 0$, where $(\cdot)^T$ is transposition computation. This condition prevents extensive growth of synaptic weights, and guarantees that the learned weight vectors are orthonormal. Specially, a proper nonlinear activation function $g(y)$ can be Taylor expanded and then have all-order moments of y. Thus this variance of nonlinear activation function is able to catch higher-order moments of data rather than just the second-order moment. With more statistical characteristics involved, NHL can extract components that are more representative than LHL can.

Using Lagrange function in eq. (9.5), and differentiating it with respect to w_{qml}, the update of synaptic weight can be derived in accordance with

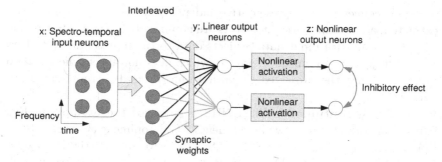

Fig. 9.6.   An illustration of nonlinear neural learning. Synaptic weights connecting input and output neurons are adaptively learned. The linear output neurons denote extracted representative independent components. And the nonlinear output neurons with an activation function play a crucial role in statistical optimization of NHL procedure.

a stochastic approximation approach

$$\Delta w_{qml} = \eta g(y_l) g'(y_l) \left(x_{qm} - \sum_{i=1}^{l-1} w_{qmi} y_i - w_{qml} y_l \right),$$

$$q \in [1, Q], m \in [1, M], l \in [1, L] \tag{9.6}$$

where $g'(y_l)$ denotes the derivative of $g(y_l)$.

The w_{qml} learning is derived from the NHL method.[27] In the present study the difference is two fold. First, the real extracted output (signature) here is y rather than z in the method.[27] We care about acoustic signal recognition of one-class data, while the method[27] cares about multi-class clustering. Neuron z clusters data into 1 or -1 end point in a bounded range $[-1, 1]$,[27] which is excellent for multi-class data clustering, but not good for one-class pattern recognition that needs extracting real representative features. Secondly, the nonlinear activation function is chosen based on implicit acoustic signal distribution in the present study. But the method[27] considers the big-gap boundary issue in clustering problem, and outliers may be closely centered with signals of interest.

To summarize, NHL iteratively updates neuron outputs and synaptic weights via the following two steps.

Step I) Neuron output computation:
$y_l = \sum_{q=1}^{Q} \sum_{m=1}^{M} w_{qml} x_{qm}$, $l \in [1, L]$;

Step II) Synaptic weight update:
$\Delta w_{qml} = \eta g(y_l) g'(y_l) \left(x_{qm} - \sum_{i=1}^{l-1} w_{qmi} y_i - w_{qml} y_l \right)$, $q \in [1, Q], m \in [1, M], l \in [1, L]$.

Upon convergence, representative independent signatures $\{y_l\}_{l=1}^{L}$ are extracted, and synaptic weight vectors are nonlinearly learned. Multiplying weight vectors with input data projects data to the representative feature space. Projection is a linear operation, which does not affect inherent data property. Thus the projected signatures can be used to represent input data.

Example A continued: When NHL is used for the example in Fig. 9.5, it can correctly find two components. The nonlinear activation function is defined as in Sect. 9.3.3. Synaptic weight matrix is $\mathbf{W}_N = [1.6613\ 1.9878; 0.9487\ 2.6608]$. Via $\mathbf{W}_N$ to project data, the result is illustrated in Fig. 9.7(b). As in Figs. 9.7(c)-(d), the extracted component y_1^N is uniform-distributed within $[-2, 2]$, corresponding to s_1; and y_2^N is Gaussian-distributed with mean 0 and variance 1, corresponding to s_2. When the decomposing synaptic weight matrix multiplies the composing one, $\mathbf{W}_N \mathbf{A} = [0.8813\ -0.0052; -0.0185\ 0.9837] \cong \mathbf{I}$. Then, $\mathbf{y} = \mathbf{W}_N \mathbf{x} = \mathbf{W}_N \mathbf{A}\mathbf{s} \cong \mathbf{s}$. Hence, NHL which involves higher-order statistical characteristics of data can extract real independent components.

From the perspective of pattern recognition, the practical value of NHL is to provide an effective technique of *dimensionality reduction*. As in Fig. 9.6, the dimension of STR feature input can be very high, *e.g.* 600 if $Q = 30$ frequency bins and $M = 20$ temporal frames, (Reasons of these choices are in Sect. 9.5). Such high dimensionality may cause very complex computation at the testing stage if they are used as patterns. Besides, high-dimensional features may be less useful than real representative features as high-dimensional ones may be easily mixed with unrelated noises. To tackle the curse of dimensionality, NHL projects this messy high-dimensional representation $\mathbb{R}^{Q \times M}$ to a low-dimensional space $\mathbb{R}^L$ ($L \ll Q \times M$). During the learning, useful features that are related to signals of interest are extracted while unrelated ones are removed.

In addition, the proposed algorithm is sped up by including a *sphering* step prior to NHL. In the present study we use LHL as a sphering step. This computation works on the first and the second-order statistics of data. And the full representation of synaptic weights is thus the product of the sphering result and the NHL result, $\mathbf{W} = \mathbf{W}_L \mathbf{W}_N$.

9.3.3. Nonlinear Activation Function

The nonlinear activation function $g(\cdot)$ is critical for NHL. Generally a smooth, monotonic increasing, invertible, bounded, and differentiable func-

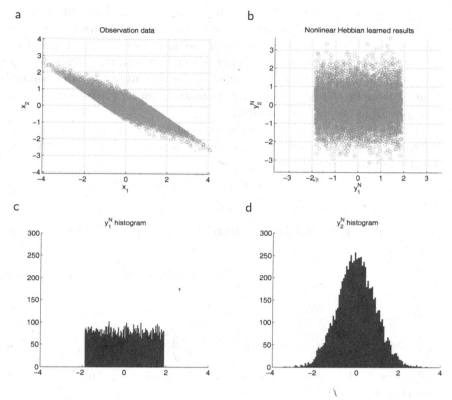

Fig. 9.7.   (a) The given mixture. (b) The result is obtained by projecting the observation data using synaptic weight matrix $\mathbf{W}_N$. (c) The histogram of y_1^N is a uniform distribution within $[-2, 2]$, corresponding to s_1. (d) The histogram of y_2^N is a Gaussian distribution with mean 0 and variance 1, corresponding to s_2.

tion[26,27,31] can be used. On the other hand, which representative components are picked up depends not only on the activation function but also on the implicit signal distribution. NHL is unsupervised learning, which does not assume any knowledge of component distribution or composing property. Nevertheless, some prior knowledge about acoustic data distribution is helpful. It is hypothesized that general acoustic sound is approximately super-Gaussian distributed, with higher peak and longer tail than Gaussian distribution.[32,33] Similar to the method[33] that computes histogram of speech signals, it can be shown that vehicle sound is super-Gaussian distributed. The kurtosis of vehicle sound is 1.09, which is greater than Gaussian kurtosis 0. In order to provide a more stable learning, it is better to choose an activation function that considers some inherent property of data distribution. When the slope of the activation function can be aligned with the high density portion of the input distribution, the mutual information of input and output is optimized.[32,34] And this alignment can transform input data to a range which raises sensitivity for the adaptation of synaptic weights. Such transformation can help escaping of early trapping from pre-matured saturation.

Considering the general requirements for an activation function, and regarding the implicit statistics of acoustic data, we format an activation function in the range $[-1, 1]$,

$$
g(y) = \begin{cases} h(y), & y \geq 0 \\ -h(|y|), & y \leq 0 \end{cases}, \tag{9.7}
$$

where $h(y)$ is cumulative gamma distribution, which belongs to the super-Gaussian class

$$
h(y) = \frac{\gamma(\alpha, \beta y)}{\Gamma(\alpha)}, \ y > 0, \ \text{where}
$$

$$
\gamma(\alpha, \beta y) = \int_0^y \tau^{\alpha-1} e^{-\tau} d\tau, \ \text{and} \tag{9.8}
$$

$$
\Gamma(\alpha) = \int_0^\infty \tau^{\alpha-1} e^{-\tau} d\tau.
$$

α denotes the shape, $1/\beta$ represents the scale and slope.[35] And its derivative function is

$$
h'(y) = y^{\alpha-1} \frac{\beta^\alpha \exp(-\beta y)}{\Gamma(\alpha)}. \tag{9.9}
$$

Around $y = 0$ this activation function is continuously differentiable. Specially, the incomplete gamma function $\gamma(\alpha, \beta y)$ in $h(y)$ can be Taylor expanded in terms of all-order polynomials of y^{36} (*Taylor expansion of nonlinear activation function* in Sect. 9.6). As a result, the nonlinear activation function involves all-order moments of data and lead to a statistical optimization.

9.4. Real-time Field Testing Results

We have applied the proposed algorithms together with appropriate hardware for real-time field testing, as illustrated in Fig. 9.8. The system makes use of the CZM microphone to convert acoustic sound waveforms in outdoor environment into electrical signals. The pre-amplifier is used to amplify the microphone-recorded signals. The gain of the pre-amplifier is adjustable. Between hardware and software interface, there is equipped with the micro-controller A/D. The output of the pre-amplifier is sampled at rate 22,050 Hz. The acoustic signature recognizer of running vehicles is an efficient processor, whose processing time around 80 ms is much less than the one-time data acquiring length 200 ms. Hence, no delay for online data processing and no buffer is needed. When there is a vehicle approaching, the positive detection results are sent to the command center, which slews the camera toward the detected range and takes the picture.

We have tested the proposed system in Panama City (Florida, USA), Joshua Tree (California, USA), and non-busy streets in Los Angeles (California, USA). We have tested the system under various conditions, such as on paved or sandy desert roads, or various vehicle running speeds. In all, we have achieved good recognition results 98 ~ 100%. Especially for the field testing in Panama City airport in 2007, we demonstrated our real-time system in front of Transportation Security Administration (TSA). All approaching vehicles were successfully recognized and all background sounds (such as human voice, bird chirps, wind, footstep, explosive sound) were rejected. The recognition distance was 50 ~ 300 feet from microphone, which can provide an early alarm. The system could send the on-site recognition results to the camera which was located on command center. Positive result activated the camera and slewed it to the detected area, as illustrated in Fig. 9.9. In the middle of Fig. 9.9 is the taken picture of detected vehicle. In the marked bar of 'vehicle icon' in the lower part of Fig. 9.9, there are continuous dots to denote the period of time when vehicle is detected.

9.5. Simulation Results

We recorded four types of vehicle sounds, gasoline light wheeled car, gasoline heavy wheeled car, diesel truck, and motorcycle. The road conditions were paved and sandy. The microphone was set 3 ~ 7 meters away from the road. Height of the microphone was 0 ~ 3 meters. 10 min data of each vehicle type is used for training. Other 6 min data of each vehicle type is for testing. In non-vehicle class, 5 min human sentences and 5 min wind were recorded using the same microphone; 5 min bird chirps are from a dataset of north American bird sounds.[37] These three sounds are used to test whether the proposed system can correctly reject them. The window size is 20 ms with 10 ms overlapping, the sampling rate is 22,050 Hz, the gammatone spectral range is 50 ~ 11,025 Hz. The number of filterbanks

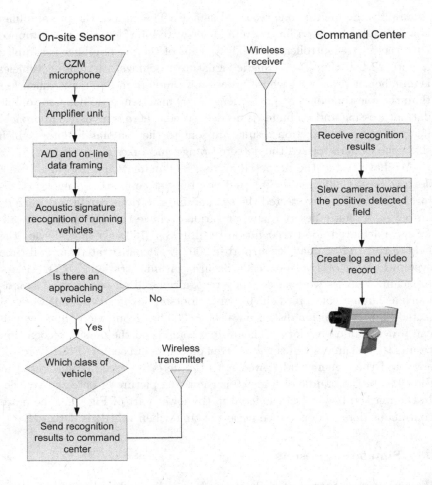

Fig. 9.8.   The practical system includes several hardware devices and real-time software.

$Q = 30$ is selected in order to cover enough high-frequency subbands within this spectral range. The number of consecutive feature vectors $M = 20$ indicates 200 ms $((20 - 10) \times 20 = 200)$ temporal duration. $L = 15$ is chosen based on a coarse estimation of the number of dominant signatures.

Using LHL for sphering, input features are shifted by the mean and normalized by the variance. To provide a stable NHL, the learning rate is set at 0.01 for the first 10 iterations. It is then decreased by multiplying a factor 0.7 every 10 iterations. Convergence is decided when the synaptic

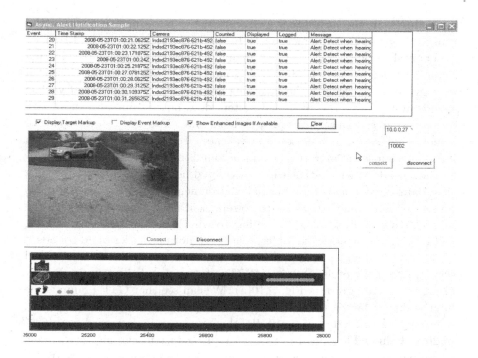

Fig. 9.9. In the middle part, the camera has been slewed to the detected area and taken a picture of the vehicle. In the marked bar of "vehicle icon" in the lower part, there are continuous dots meaning the alerts sent by on-site vehicle detector.

weight vectors are orthonormal and the synaptic weight change is less than 10^{-4} over two consecutive iterations. NHL is implemented for 5 trials, with each trial using one set of different initial values of synaptic weights. The trial that provides maximal variance of nonlinear output $E\{g^2(y)\}$ is chosen as a desirable result.

9.5.1. *Decision I: Vehicle vs. Non-vehicle Recognition*

The recognizer is able to make two level decisions. Firstly, as illustrated in Fig 9.4(a), recognize urban vehicle (patterns from different types of vehicles are generalized) and reject non-vehicle (human voice, bird chirps, and wind) in city environments. The comparing metric is error rate, which is the summation of false alarm rate and false negative rate. As mentioned in Sect. 9.1, MFCC has been viewed as a baseline spectral feature extraction technology. We compare the performance between the proposed system and MFCC. In the meantime, we compare the performance between the proposed system and the method,[4,5] linear PCA (or equivalently LHL).

For real-world testing, there are many unexpected noises emitted by surrounding backgrounds. Both vehicle sounds and noises may be co-sensed by a microphone. Hence, the incoming data would be mixtures of vehicle sounds and noises. The proposed system does not assume any knowledge of noise sources. But it can project noisy data into the feature space of vehicle sounds, in which noises are weakened. To mimic the situation when incoming signals are mixtures of vehicle sounds and other noises, clear vehicle data is added with either white or colored noises at various SNRs. The clear data we recorded under normal environments has SNR 20 ∼ 30 dB. So we select SNR range −10 ∼ 20 dB to represent noisy environments. In the present study, we use AWGN (similar to wind), human vowel utterances, and bird chirps as noise examples, which are normal background sounds.

Firstly, without the knowledge of noise source, we test how the proposed system is capable of attenuating AWGN effects on vehicle sounds. Recognition results are given in Fig. 9.10(a). We can see that GTF (gammatone filterbanks) is better than MFCC (mel frequency cepstral computation), especially when SNR= −5 ∼ 10 dB, the error rate is decreased from 62% to 20%. Using STR (spectro-temporal representation) can improve system performance further, such as at SNR= 12 dB, the improvement is 16.5%. Next, using LHL (linear Hebbian learning, or equivalently, PCA) can improve the performance, while NHL (nonlinear Hebbian learning) can more significantly improve it. At very low SNR= −10 dB, LHL has error rate 58%, while NHL decreases it down to 42% with 16% improvement; at low SNR= 0 dB, LHL has error rate 17%, while NHL decreases it down to 1.7% with 15.3% improvement. In all, at low SNR range from −10 to 0 dB, the error rate of the proposed system is decreased from 42% to 1.7% when the error rate of normally used MFCC is 62%. Then, the error rate of the proposed system stays low at 0.7 ∼ 1.5% until SNR= 20 dB. This nearly plateau indicates NHL has effectively separated vehicle signals from noises.

Secondly, we test the robustness against unknown colored noise, human vowel voice. Different vowels with various spectrums are mixed with vehicle sounds along time. In Fig. 9.10(b), the compared results indicate that GTF is a little better than MFCC, for example, when SNR> 5 dB the improvement is 5%. Using STR can improve system performance further. The averaged improvement is 3 ∼ 5% at SNR −10 ∼ 20 dB. Next, using LHL can improve the performance, while NHL can more significantly improve it. At very low SNR= −10 dB, LHL has error rate 24%, while

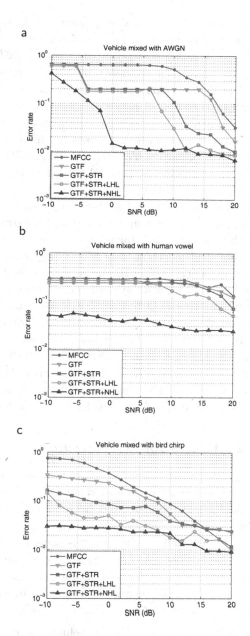

Fig. 9.10. Recognition results when vehicle data mixed with (a) White Gaussian noise (b) Colored human vowel noise (c) Colored bird chirp noise.

NHL decreases it down to 5% with 19% improvement. In all, when SNR = $-10 \sim 15$ dB, the proposed system has low error rate $2.5 \sim 5\%$, with a total improvement $25 \sim 27.5\%$ when compared with MFCC. Again this low error rate plateau implies the efficiency of NHL to eliminate human voice effects on vehicle signals. Comparing with Fig. 9.10(a), NHL shows more robustness within a lower SNR range in noisy human voice test than in AWGN test. The implicit reason could be that human voice and vehicle may have some different frequency components, so human voice can be attenuated in the feature space of vehicle signals. But AWGN occupies all frequency subbands, and thereby there is AWGN effect on any frequency subband that vehicle data dominates.

Next the proposed system is tested against unknown bird chirp noise, another colored noise often existing in surrounding backgrounds. Various bird chirps out of the dataset[37] are mixed with vehicle sounds. In Fig. 9.10(c), we can see that GTF is better than MFCC, especially when SNR< 15 dB. For example, at SNR= -10 dB, the error rate is decreased from 74% to 35%. Using STR can improve system performance further, such as at SNR= -10 dB, the improvement is 18%. Next, using LHL can improve the performance, while NHL can more significantly improve it. At very low SNR= -10 dB, LHL has error rate 17%, while NHL decreases it down to 3% with 14% improvement. In all, when SNR -10 to 10 dB, the proposed system has the error rate staying low at $2 \sim 3\%$, while MFCC has high error rate from 74% to 9%. This low error rate plateau again indicates that NHL has efficiently separated vehicle signals from bird chirps.

9.5.2. *Decision II: Vehicle Type Identification*

As illustrated in Fig. 9.4(b), if the coming waveform is recognized as vehicle, then we need to decide what type of vehicle it is. The sounds from various types of vehicles may be generated by some common factors and thus highly correlated with each other, which makes vehicle identification difficult. In this section, vehicle identification is analyzed when vehicle data is corrupted by unknown noises. During learning procedure, one representative feature space and one projection synaptic weight matrix are learned for each type of vehicles. Then four feature spaces and four weight matrixes are learned to represent patterns of four types. During testing, identification results are listed in Tables 9.1-9.3 when vehicle data is corrupted by unknown AWGN, human vowel utterances, and bird chirps, respectively. The performance of LHL and NHL is compared. From these tables, we can see that in general NHL can achieve better performance than LHL can. For example, when gasoline heavy wheeled car is mixed with AWGN at SNR= 5 dB, NHL decreases the error rate by 40% over LHL; when diesel truck is mixed with human vowel utterances at SNR= 0 dB, NHL decreases the error rate by 25% over LHL. In all, the proposed system can offer very robust identification results, such as at SNR= 5, 10 dB, the error rates of diesel truck and motorcycle are $0 \sim 5\%$. At very low SNR= $-5, 0$ dB, the performance degrades, whereas the system is still at a workable status.

Table 9.1.   Identification results when vehicle mixed w/ AWGN

	Gasoline light wheeled		Gasoline heavy wheeled		Diesel truck		Motorcycle	
	LHL	NHL	LHL	NHL	LHL	NHL	LHL	NHL
SNR=-5 dB	65%	55%	55%	50%	45%	35%	40%	35%
0 dB	60%	40%	50%	30%	30%	15%	25%	15%
5 dB	60%	20%	50%	10%	25%	5%	20%	5%
10 dB	50%	15%	45%	5%	20%	5%	20%	0%

Table 9.2.   Identification results when vehicle mixed w/ human vowel utterances

	Gasoline light wheeled		Gasoline heavy wheeled		Diesel truck		Motorcycle	
	LHL	NHL	LHL	NHL	LHL	NHL	LHL	NHL
SNR= -5 dB	65%	55%	55%	60%	55%	50%	55%	50%
0 dB	50%	40%	50%	35%	45%	20%	40%	20%
5 dB	40%	15%	30%	10%	25%	5%	20%	5%
10 dB	30%	10%	25%	5%	15%	5%	15%	0%

Table 9.3.   Identification results when vehicle mixed w/ bird chirps

	Gasoline light wheeled		Gasoline heavy wheeled		Diesel truck		Motorcycle	
	LHL	NHL	LHL	NHL	LHL	NHL	LHL	NHL
SNR= -5 dB	50%	40%	50%	30%	40%	20%	35%	20%
0 dB	35%	20%	30%	10%	25%	10%	25%	10%
5 dB	15%	15%	15%	10%	10%	5%	10%	5%
10 dB	10%	15%	5%	5%	5%	0%	0%	0%

9.6. Conclusion and Discussion

The intelligent neural learning in the mammalian cortex provides us with some heuristics to explore the vehicle sound recognition and identification tasks. We contribute original work to use a nonlinear Hebbian learning for acoustic signature recognition of running vehicles under noisy environments. The proposed system can selectively extract representative independent components from high-dimensional input data. We have demonstrated the designed real-time recognizer in front of Transportation Security Administration and achieved good detection results. The compared simulation results show that the proposed system can more accurately recognize approaching vehicles with a lower error rate than its counterparts, even if the recorded sound is severely corrupted by white noise or colored noise (human vowel utterances, bird chirps) at SNR= $-10 \sim 0$ dB. When a coming sound is recognized as urban vehicle, its type can be identified against noises. For example, when gasoline heavy wheeled car is mixed with AWGN at SNR= 5 dB, the proposed system improves the performance by 40% over LHL.

Influence of AWGN, human vowel utterances, and bird chirps

Comparing results in Fig. 9.10, the noisy influence of AWGN, human vowel utterances, and bird chirps is different. When vehicle data is mixed with human vowel utterances or bird chirps, NHL can dramatically decreases the error rate, even at very low SNRs. The underlying reason can be, vowel voice or bird chirps may have some different frequency components that vehicle sound may not have in its learned feature space. Hence, NHL which involves all-order statistics of data can independently separate vehicle components from noisy ones, and has low error rates. On the other hand, other algorithms including LHL could not reveal the properties of independent components, and have much higher error rates.

The error rate tendency appears different when vehicle data is mixed with AWGN. Spectral components of AWGN are spread over all frequency subbands. Hence, AWGN effects are in every frequency subband that vehicle data dominates. It is reasonable that recognition results are worse in this test. The error rate curve of NHL is more like a decreasing slope rather than a plateau along increasing SNRs. But when SNR> 0 dB, NHL still offers a very robust performance with error rates $0.7 \sim 1.5\%$. This implies that NHL has effectively functioned on noise elimination since SNR> 0 dB.

LHL vs. NHL

Super-Gaussian-like statistics of acoustic sounds indicates why LHL is inadequate to extract its principal components. Gaussian-distributed data is described with mean and variance, so LHL, which optimizes the second-order moment of data, is a good tool for its principal component extraction. However, in real-world environments, other non-Gaussian data generally exists. They cannot be described with just mean and variance. Hence, an approach such as NHL that explores higher-order moments of data is necessary.

Taylor expansion of nonlinear activation function

To show that the used nonlinear activation function involves all-order statistics of data, Taylor series can be used to expand it in terms of polynomials of y,[36]

$$h(y) = (\beta y)^{\alpha} e^{-\beta y} \sum_{n=0}^{\infty} \frac{\beta^n y^n}{\Gamma(\alpha + n + 1)}, \qquad (9.10)$$

where the lower incomplete gamma function $\gamma(\alpha, \beta y)$ is the primary function. Otherwise, Taylor series can be used to expand the upper incomplete gamma function $\Gamma(\alpha, \beta y) = \int_y^{\infty} \tau^{\alpha-1} e^{-\tau} d\tau$ in terms of polynomials of y. And then we can obtain the Taylor-expanded function with the relation

$$h(y) = 1 - \frac{\Gamma(\alpha, \beta y)}{\Gamma(\alpha)}. \qquad (9.11)$$

Acknowledgment

This project was supported in part by grants from ONR, NAVY, and DARPA. Authors of this chapter would also like to thank Safety Dynamics Inc. for their support and all members of Neural Dynamics Laboratory for their invaluable help.

References

1. H. C. Choe, R. E. Karlsen, G. R. Gerhert, and T. Meitzler, Wavelet-based ground vehicle recognition using acoustic signal, *Wavelet Applications III.* **2762**, 434–445, (1996).
2. H. Maciejewski, J. Mazurkiewicz, K. Skowron, and T. Walkowiak. Neural networks for vehicle recognition. In eds. U. Ramacher, H.Klar, and A. Koenig, *Proc. of the 6th International Conf. on Microelectronics for Neural Networks, Evolutionary, and Fuzzy Systems*, pp. 292–296, (1997).
3. L. Liu. Ground vehicle acoustic signal processing based on biological hearing models. Master's thesis, University of Maryland, College Park, USA, (1999).
4. H. Wu, M. Siegel, and P. Khosla, Vehicle sound signature recognition by frequency vector principal component analysis, *IEEE Trans. on Instrumentation and Measurement.* **48**, 1005–1009, (1999).

5. M. E. Munich. Bayesian subspace methods for acoustic signature recognition of vehicles. In *Proc. of the 12th European Signal Processing Conf.*, (2004).

6. A. Averbuch, V. Zheludev, N. Rabin, , and A. Schclar, *Wavelet-based acoustic detection of moving vehicles.* (Springer Netherlands, 2007). http://www.cs. tau.ac.il/amir1/PS/Acoustics2.pdf.

7. H. Xiao, C. Cai1, Q. Yuan, X. Liu, and Y. Wen. Advanced intelligent computing theories and applications. In eds. D. S. Huang, L. Heutte, and M. Loog, *A comparative study of feature extraction and classification methods for military vehicle type recognition using acoustic and seismic signals*, pp. 810–819. Springer Berlin, (2007).

8. Y. Zhang and W. H. Abdulla. Eigenanalysis applied to speaker identification using gammatone auditory filterbank and independent component analysis. In *ISSPA*, (2007).

9. P. I. M. Johanesma. The pre-response stimulus ensemble of neurons in the cochlear nucleus. In *Proc. Symposium on Hearing Theory*, pp. 58–69, Eindhoven, Netherlands, (1972).

10. E. de Boer, Synthetic whole-nerve action potentials for the cat, *The Journal of the Acoustical Society of America.* **58**, 1030–1045, (1975).

11. R. D. Patterson and B. C. J. Moore. Frequency selectivity in hearing. In ed. B. C. J. Moore, *Auditory filters and excitation patterns as representations of frequency resolution*, pp. 123–177. Academic Press Limited, London, (1986).

12. B. R. Glasberg and B. C. J. Moore, Derivation of auditory filter shapes from notched-noise data, *Hear Res.* **93**, 401–417, (1990).

13. R. D. Patterson, K. Robinson, J. Holdsworth, D. MeKeown, C. Zhang, and M. H. Allerhand. Auditory physiology and perception. In eds. Y. Cazals, L. Demany, K. Horner, and Pergamon, *Complex sounds and auditory images*, pp. 429–446. Oxford, (1992).

14. M. Slaney. An efficient implementation of the Patterson-Holdsworth auditory filter bank. Apple computer technical report #35, Apple Computer Inc., (1993).

15. A. V. Oppenheim, R. W. Schafer, and J. R. Buck, *Discrete-time Signal Processing.* (Prentice Hall, Englewood Cliffs, 1999).

16. L. V. Immerseel and S. Peeters, Digital implementation of linear gammatone filters: comparison of design methods, *Acoustics Research Letters Online.* **4** (3), 59–64, (2003).

17. O. Cheng, W. Abdulla, and Z. Salcic, Performance evaluation of front-end algorithms for robust speech recognition, *Proceedings of the Eighth International Symposium on Signal Processing and its Applications.* **2**, 711–714, (2005).

18. S. Shamma, H. Versnel, and N. Kowalski. Ripple analysis in ferret primary auditory cortex: 1. response characteristics of single units to sinusoidally rippled spectra. Technical report, Maryland Univ. College Park Inst. for Systems Research, (1995).

19. J. Z. Simon, D. A. Depireux, and S. A. Shamma. Representation of complex dynamic spectra in auditory cortex. Technical report, Institute for Systems Research & Electrical Engineering Department, University of Mary-

land, College Park, MD 20742, U.S.A., (1998). http://www.isr.umd.edu/
CAAR/posters/ISH11.pdf.
20. D. Klein, D. Depireux, J. Simon, and S. Shamma, Robust spectro-temporal
reverse correlation for the auditory system: optimizing stimulus design, *J.
Comput. Neurosci.* **9**(1), 85–111, (2000).
21. E. Oja, A simplified neuron model as a principal component analyzer, *Journal
of Mathematical Biology.* **15**(3), 267–273, (1982).
22. T. D. Sanger. Advances in neural information processing systems. In *An optimality principle for unsupervised learning*, vol. 1, pp. 11–19. Morgan Kaufmann, San Mateo, CA, (1989).
23. T. D. Sanger, Optimal unsupervised learning in a single-layer linear feedfor-
ward neural network, *Neural Networks.* **12**, 459–473, (1989).
24. T. D. Sanger, Analysis of the two-dimensional receptive fields learned by the
hebbian algorithm in response to random input, *Biological Cybernetics.* **63**,
221–228, (1990).
25. E. Oja, H. Ogawa, and J. Wangviwattana, Learning in non-linear constrained
hebbian networks, *ICANN.* pp. 385–390, (1991).
26. E. Oja, PCA, ICA, and nonlinear Hebbian learning, *In Proc. Int. Conf. on
Artificial NeuralNetworks ICANN-95.* pp. 89–94, (1995).
27. A. Sudjianto and M. H. Hassoun, Statistical basis of nonlinear hebbian learning and application to clustering, *Neural Networks.* **8**(5), 707–715, (1995).
28. A. Hyvärinen and E. Oja, Independent component analysis by general nonlinear hebbian-like learning rules, *Signal Processing.* **64**, 301–313, (1998).
29. D. O. Hebb, *The Organization of Behavior: A Neuropsychological Theory.*
(Wiley, New York, 1949).
30. G. Palm, *Neural Assemblies, an Alternative Approach to Artificial Intelligence.* (Springer-Verlag, New York, 1982).
31. A. Hyvärinen, One-unit contrast functions for independent component analysis: a statistical analysis, *Neural Networks for Signal Processing VII.* pp.
388–397, (1997).
32. A. J. Bell and T. J. Sejnowski, An information-maximization approach to
blind separation and blind deconvolution, *Neural Computation.* **7**(6), 1129–
1159, (1995).
33. T. Lotter and P. Vary, Speech enhancement by MAP spectral amplitude estimation using a super-Gaussian speech model, *EURASIP Journal on Applied
Signal Processing.* **7**, 1110–1126, (2005).
34. T.-W. Lee, M. Girolami, , and T. J. Sejnowski, Independent component
analysis using an extended infomax algorithm for mixed sub-Gaussian and
super-Gaussian sources, *Neural Computation.* **11**(2), 417–441, (1999).
35. S. C. Choi and R. Wette, Maximum likelihood estimation of the parameters
of the gamma distribution and their bias, *Technometrics.* **11**(4), 683–669,
(1969).
36. W. Gautschi, A computational procedure for incomplete gamma functions,
ACM Trans. on Mathematical Software. **5**, 466–481, (1979).
37. Naturesongs.com and D. V. Gausig. North american bird sounds. http://
www.naturesongs.com/birds.html.

Chapter 10

Texture-Based Approach for Computer Vision Systems in Autonomous Vehicles

Domenec Puig[1], Jaime Melendez[1] and Miguel Angel Garcia[2]

[1]*Intelligent Robotics and Computer Vision Group*
Department of Computer Science and Mathematics
Rovira i Virgili University.
Av. Pasos Catalans 26, 43007 Tarragona, Spain.
{domenec.puig,jaime.melendez}@urv.cat
[2]*Department of Informatics Engineering*
Autonomous University of Madrid.
Francisco Tomas y Valiente 11, 28049 Madrid, Spain.
miguelangel.garcia@uam.es

Autonomous surveillance vehicles operating in outdoor scenarios are expected to have sufficient local processing capabilities for being able to analyze images of their environment gathered in real time in order to perform mission-related tasks, such as secure navigation or intelligent scene monitoring. In this scope, computer vision systems must be able to deal with images captured in a wide range of operational conditions, from daylight using conventional video camerasto night light using image intensifiers or thermal imaging devices. The images acquired in such diverse conditions and the inherent complexity of outdoor images make texture the most appropriate visual cue to be analyzed, well beyond color and shape. Hence, new efficient texture-based image classifiers and segmenters are to be developed. This chapter compares different state-of-the-art texture classifiers and proposes an efficient solution to the problem of per-pixel classification of textured images with multichannel Gabor wavelet filters. Results with complex real images obtained from both land-based and aerial vehicles are presented and discussed.

Contents

10.1. Introduction

Currently, the visual capabilities of autonomous surveillance vehicles are still far from those of human vision. Therefore, those vehicles are mostly teleoperated in practice. Thus, they are controlled by human operators from remote locations via communication links. Most cognitive processes are performed by those operators based on sensory feedback from remote input devices mounted on those vehicles, such as conventional video cameras, image intensifiers or thermal imaging devices. Those vehicles are unmanned and either manually or semiatutomatically controlled from a distance according to their observed performance. In some simpler cases, autonomous surveillance vehicles follow preplanned routes through previously known environments. This chapter contributes to the development of new visual capabilities for autonomous surveillance vehicles whose vision systems must be able to deal with images captured in a wide range of operational conditions. The own nature of the images acquired in such conditions and the inherent complexity of outdoor images make texture the most appropriate visual cue to be analyzed.

In this context, the proposed chapter describes a new efficient nonparametric distance-based classifier as a solution to the per-pixel texture classification problem. Within this problem, every image pixel must be characterized by a feature vector in a local neighborhood, thus potentially generating an enormous number of prototypes to compare with during the classification stage. Therefore, current pixel-based texture classifiers suffer from an expensive computational cost, which, in practice, makes those classifiers unsuitable for real-time tasks, such as the ones potentially performed by autonomous surveillance vehicles. Experiments with both real outdoor images obtained by Unmanned Ground Vehicles (UGV) and aerial images from Unmanned Aerial Vehicles (UAV), and comparisons with alternative classification techniques show that the developed classification scheme is effective in terms of classification rates and computation time.

The organization of this chapter is as follows. Section 10.2 reviews previous work in autonomous surveillance vehicles. Section 10.3 presents the

Fig. 10.1. Some examples of different types of autonomous survelliance vehicles. (a) Examples of UGV: NASA Mars Exploration Rover, (b) ActivMedia Robotics Pioneer2AT endowed with a 3-D video camera, (c) Example of UAV: AAI Corporation Fixed-wing; (d) Example of UUV: Bluefin-12 by Bluefin Robotics Corporation.

proposed pixel-based texture classifier for dealing with images captured by those vehicles. Section 10.4 describes a new technique for automatic parameter selection oriented to model the different texture classes present in those images with a reasonable computational time. Section 10.5 shows experimental results after applying the proposed technique, as well as comparisons with well-known texture classifiers. Finally, conclusions and further improvements are given in Section 10.6.

10.2. Background

Over the last years, considerable effort has been devoted to the development of autonomous surveillance vehicles for a great variety of applications, such as search and rescue operations, obstacle discovery, intruder detection, building or terrain mapping, explosives neutralization, reconnaissance and surveillance.

Autonomous surveillance vehicles with the above capabilities are based on mobile robotic platforms that can be mainly classified into Unmanned Ground Vehicles (UGV), Unmanned Aerial Vehicles (UAV) and Unmanned Undersea Vehicles (UUV) (see Fig. 10.1 a-d). Mobile robotic platforms with those capabilities enhance the ability to counter threats , limit risks to personnel, and reduce manpower requirements in hazardous environments. Those platforms offer a tremendous potential as intelligence, surveillance and reconnaissance facilities for early detection of security threats and for acquisition and maintenance of situation awareness in crisis conditions.

A number of initiatives to develop autonomous surveillance vehicles have been carried out in recent years, the wide majority for military purposes.

In this line, Sandia National Laboratories developed a teleoperated UGV[1] for the US Army to improve robotic ground vehicle tactics. Similar teleoperated battlefield mobile robot research was reported.[2,3] Some of these robots included multiprocessor computing, differential GPS, and laser radar for autonomous navigation.

Further surveillance UGV include vehicles for developing autonomous off-road applications,[4] and vehicles designed around the MDARS-E project,[5] which aims to provide an automated intrusion detection and inventory assessment capability. Each is capable of some degree of autonomous navigation via DGPS and other sensors, and can convey position and environmental information to a ground station.

In fact, the development of UAV started in the middle of the twentieth century for military surveillance. UAV have the potential to dramatically increase the availability and usefulness of aircrafts as information-gathering platforms. UAV have unmatched qualities that often make them cost effective means of carrying out tasks that may be either highly risky to pilots or where their presence is not necessary. Recent innovations in UAV hardware and software technologies, as well as economies of scale, make UAV feasible for increasingly diverse surveillance purposes.[6–8]

A significant UAV platform developed in the last years is the Autonomous Rotorcraft Project,[9] an Army/NASA effort to develop high-level autonomy for airborne observation missions of interest to both organizations. The vehicle selected for the project was a helicopter that can fly at low speed or remain in a hover for approximately one hour. Alternatively, recent research by the British Antarctic Survey and the Technical University of Braunschweig[10] has led to the first ever series of flights by UAV in Antarctica. Besides take-off and landing, those UAV are completely autonomous, flying on their own according to a pre-programmed flight plan. Each flight lasts for forty minutes, covering around forty-five kilometers and taking a hundred measurements per second. This is the first time that unpiloted UAV have been successfuly used in the Antarctic, opening a major new approach for gathering scientific data in harsh environments.

Besides the development of ground and aerial vehicles, some of the first UUV were developed at the Massachusetts Institute of Technology in the 1970s. Scientists use UUV to study the ocean and the ocean floor.[11,12] One of the main motivations for the development of UUV was the execution of surveillance tasks for military missions, such as submarine detection or mine search. Although not currently operational, there are several designs of UUV that are capable of subsea intervention and not only of fly-by data collection. The development of subsea processing in deep and ultra deep offshore oilfields and their cost of maintenance will be the most likely motivation to encourage the development of these vehicles. In this line, the oil and gas industries use UUV to make detailed maps of the seafloor before they start building subsea infrastructure. Those maps allow oil companies to install subsea infrastructures with an effective cost reduction and minimum disruption to the environment.[13]

Notwithstanding, UGV, UAV and UUV still have many limitations. Hence, it is necessary to address a range of practical and theoretical problems in order to develop their potential capabilities to a full extent. Thus, in practice, current autonomous surveillance vehicles are based on standalone platforms endowed with rather limited autonomous capabilities through the use of costly and power-intensive sensors (*e.g.*, laser range imaging sensors), high-bandwidth communication links and sophisticated remote control stations. The path-planning algorithms used by those vehicles often require a priori knowledge of free paths and obstacles in the environment. This can be sufficient for some applications, but for others, higher levels of autonomy can be advantageous.

Therefore, reducing the intervention of human operators is a key goal. In this way, it is necessary to take advantage of computer systems embedded in autonomous surveillance vehicles with the goal of exploiting the enormous potential of those vehicles in a great number of scopes, such as exploration, surveillance and, in general, intelligence-related tasks. Thus, a number of initiatives have been developed to address the problem of increasing the degree of autonomy of surveillance vehicles for tackling some particular tasks.[14–16]

In this line, some key issues for increasing the autonomy of those vehicles are related to the use of multiple platforms, as well as to the coordination between teams of autonomous vehicles. This has led to ongoing research in the area of multi-agent and swarm systems[17,18]), which are non-centralized collections of relatively autonomous entities interacting with each other in dynamic environments. A distributed multi-agent approach offers several advantages. First, a larger number of sensors can be deployed over a greater area. Intelligent cooperation may thus allow the use of less expensive sensors. Second, task robustness is increased, since even if some agents fail, others remain to complete the task. Finally, task performance is more flexible, since groups of agents can perform different tasks at various locations. For example, the likelihood of finding an object or target increases if multiple sensors from different locations are utilized.

In addition, recent research has been addressed in order to exploit computer vision for provinding autonomous surveillance vehicles with relevant information about the environment and, therefore, to contribute to improve their autonomy and performance. Hence, a remarkable trend consists of endowing all-purpose exploration vehicles with 2D and 3D camerascontrolled by embedded computers (see Fig. 10.1 b). In this line, it was proposed new strategies that allow a team of mobile robots to deploy collaboratively in order to obtain processable three-dimensional models of wide-area, unknown environments.[17,19] Every robot maps its surroundings and simultaneously determines its position and orientation in space by processing visual information obtained by means of an off-the-shelf stereo camera.

In this framework, texture is an important visual cue necessary for extracting low-level features useful for many common visual tasks.[20,21] It may allow a system to distinguish among different objects or surfaces that have similar shape or color. Unfortunately, texture is the visual cue most difficult to model, as it is intrinsically noisy by nature and affected by various external factors, such as illumination, rotation and scale, which alter its perception. For this reason, many research efforts have been devoted to texture analysis. In this way, a wide variety of texture feature extraction methods have been proposed in the literature.[20,22-27] They can be divided into four major categories: statistical, signal processing, structural and model-based methods.

Statistical methods are one of the early approaches proposed for texture feature extraction in the literature. They are based on the spatial distribution of gray values inside a textured image. Usually, those methods are based on the computation of local features parallelly at each pixel in a texture image. A local feature is defined by the combination of intensities at specified positions relative to each pixel in the image. According to the number of points which define the local feature, three broad families of statistical methods have been proposed: first-order statistics, second-order statistics and higher-order statistics. Signal processing methods analyze the frequency content of the textures present in an image. They are supported by some psychophysical evidence that shows that the human brain does a similar analysis. Most signal processing techniques try to compute certain features from filtered images.

Structural methods regard texture as being composed of texture elements or primitives. A primitive is a connected set of resolution cells characterized by a list of attributes. There exists a number of neighborhood operators to extract primitives, such as those utilized in edge detection, adaptive region extraction, and mathematical morphology. Once the primitives and information about them have been identified, there are two major approaches to analyzing texture: computing statistical properties from the primitives and use these measures as features, in a kind of statistical approaches based on structure, or trying to determine the placement rule that describes texture, yielding pure structural methods.

Finally, model-based methods construct a parametric generative model of the observed intensity distribution, which is considered to be a combination of a function representing the known structural information on the image and a random noise sequence. The key problem is how to estimate this function and how to choose an appropriate model. Once the model is complete, it can also be used to syntethize texture.

Hence, this chapter proposes an efficient solution to the problem of per-pixel classification of textured images suitable for real time tasks, such as the ones potentially performed by autonomous surveillance vehicles.

10.3. Per-Pixel Texture Classifier

The texture classification methodology proposed in this work is schematized in the flowchart shown in Fig. 10.2. During an initial training stage, a set of prototypes is extracted from every texture pattern that must be recognized. The training image/s associated with each pattern are first filtered by applying a multichannel Gabor filter bank, obtaining a cloud of texture feature vectors for every pattern. A set of prototypes is then extracted in order to represent that cloud.

During the evaluation stage of the classifier, a given test image is processed with the purpose of identifying the texture pattern corresponding to each of its pixels. This is done by first applying the multichannel Gabor filter bank to the test image. A feature vector is thus obtained for every pixel. Each vector is classified into one of the given texture patterns by a K-NN classifier fed with the prototypes extracted during the training stage. The final classified image is obtained after post-processing that result. The stages involved in this scheme are detailed below.

10.3.1. *Feature Extraction*

Among the large amount of texture feature extraction methods summarized in Section 10.2, multichannel filtering techniques based on Gabor filters have received considerable attention due to some specific properties, such

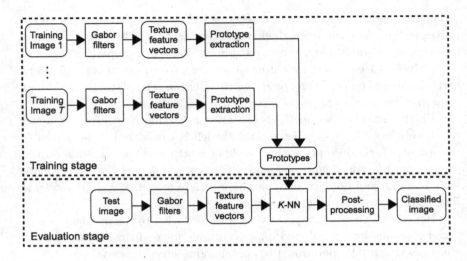

Fig. 10.2. Flowchart of the proposed classification methodology.

as optimal joint localization in both the spatial and frequency domains,[28] and the physiological fact that 2-D Gabor filters can approximate the simple cells in the visual cortex of some mammals.[29]

A two dimensional Gabor function $g(x, y)$ and its Fourier transform $G(u, v)$ can be written as:

$$g(x, y) = \left(\frac{1}{2\pi\sigma_x\sigma_y} \right) exp \left[-\frac{1}{2} \left(\frac{x^2}{\sigma_x^2} + \frac{y^2}{\sigma_y^2} \right) + 2\pi j\Omega x \right] \qquad (10.1)$$

$$G(u, v) = exp \left[-\frac{1}{2} \left(\frac{(u - \Omega)^2}{\sigma_u^2} + \frac{v^2}{\sigma_v^2} \right) \right] \qquad (10.2)$$

where σ_x and σ_y are the Gaussian standard deviations, $\sigma_u = 1/2\pi\sigma_x$, $\sigma_v = 1/2\pi\sigma_y$, and Ω is the modulation frequency. Gabor functions form a complete but non-orthogonal basis set.[30] Expanding a signal using this basis provides a localized frequency description.

In a multichannel filtering scheme, an input image is typically decomposed into a number of filtered images, each containing intensity variations over a narrow range of frequencies and orientations.[31] Measures computed from these filtered images can be used as features for either classification or segmentation.[32]

In this sense, a class of self-similar functions, referred to as *Gabor wavelets*, is now considered. Let $g(x, y)$ be the mother Gabor wavelet. A self-similar filter dictionary can then be obtained by appropriate dilations and rotations of $g(x, y)$ through the generating function:

$$g_{mn}(x, y) = a^{-m} g(x', y') \tag{10.3}$$

where m and n specify the scale and orientation of the wavelet respectively, with $m = 0, 1, \ldots, S - 1$, $n = 0, 1, \ldots, K - 1$, S being the total number of scales and K the total number of orientations. In addition, $x' = a^{-m}(x \cos\theta + y \sin\theta)$ and $y' = a^{-m}(-x \sin\theta + y \cos\theta)$, where $\theta = n\pi/K$ and a^{-m}, $a > 1$, is a scale factor, which is meant to ensure that the wavelets' energy is independent of m.

Given an image $I(x, y)$, its Gabor wavelet transform is then defined as follows (in this work, only grey level images have been considered, $I(x, y) \in [0, 255]$):

$$W_{mn}(x, y) = \int I(x, y) g_{mn}^*(x - x_1, y - y_1) dx_1 dy_1 \tag{10.4}$$

where * indicates the complex conjugate.

A multichannel Gabor wavelet filtering approach has been used for the texture feature extraction stage of this work. In particular, the original design of those Gabor filters,[25] which has been widely utilized for texture classification and segmentation tasks,[33-35] and more recently adopted by the MPEG-7 standard,[36] is followed.

The non-orthogonality of Gabor wavelets implies that there is redundant information in the filtered images. Thus, this design strategy is used to reduce such redundancy by ensuring that the half-peak magnitude support of the filter responses in the frequency spectrum touch each other (see Fig. 10.3), resulting in the following definitions of the filter parameters:

$$a = (U_h/U_l)^{\frac{1}{S-1}} \tag{10.5}$$

$$\sigma_u = \frac{(a - 1)U_h}{(a + 1)\sqrt{2\ln 2}} \tag{10.6}$$

$$\sigma_v = \tan\left(\frac{\pi}{2k}\right) \left[U_h - 2\ln\left(\frac{2\sigma_u^2}{U_h}\right)\right] \left[2\ln 2 - \frac{(2\ln 2)^2 \sigma_u^2}{U_h^2}\right]^{-\frac{1}{2}} \tag{10.7}$$

where U_l and U_h denote the lower and upper frequencies of interest.

For the task at hand, the filter bank parameters are set based on the values proposed by Manjunath[25] and Chen:[37] Low frequency 0.05, high

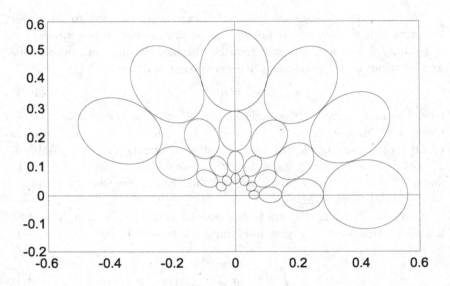

Fig. 10.3. Example of design strategy for the Gabor filter bank (the contours indicate the half-peak magnitude of the filter responses) with parameters: $U_l = 0.05$, $U_h = 0.4$, $S = 4$, $K = 6$. The center of each ellipse is related to the modulation frequency W of each filter.

frequency 0.4, six scales and four orientations. After filtering an input image, the texture features that will characterize every pixel and its surrounding neighborhood (window) are the mean μ_{mn} and standard deviation σ_{mn} of the magnitude of the Gabor wavelet coefficients:

$$\mu_{mn} = \int \int |W_{mn}(x, y)| dx dy \qquad (10.8)$$

$$\sigma_{mn} = \sqrt{\int \int (|W_{mn}(x, y)| - \mu_{mn})^2 dx dy} \qquad (10.9)$$

A feature vector f is now defined using μ_{mn} and σ_{mn} as feature components:

$$f = (\mu_{00}, \mu_{01}, \ldots, \mu_{S-1,K-1}, \sigma_{00}, \sigma_{01}, \ldots, \sigma_{S-1,K-1}) \qquad (10.10)$$

Therefore, every feature vector will have a total of $6 \times 4 \times 2 = 48$ dimensions. All dimensions are normalized between 0 and 1.

In order to take advantage of the output produced by the filter bank, the texture features mentioned above are computed for W different window sizes (W is set to 6 in this case): 3×3, 5×5, 9×9, 17×17, 33×33 and 65×65. This means that, given a set of T texture patterns to be recognized, there will be $T \times W$ sets of feature vectors at the training stage. Only W sets will be used for testing as there is only one input test image. In this way, it is expected to have a better characterization of each of the texture patterns.

For the setup to be complete, there is still one parameter to be configured: the kernel size, which is the grid used to sample the Gabor filter. The study conducted by Chen[37] in the context of image retrieval concludes that a kernel size of 13×13 is the best choice.However, as previously stated, in this work, six different window sizes are used. Therefore, the kernel size has been set to coincide with each of those window sizes. This is due to the fact that every texture feature is computed from the pixels contained in the window in process. In addition, independent experiments conducted while developing this work have shown that the texture features obtained in this way lead to better classification results than those obtained with a fixed kernel size.

10.3.2. *Texture Model Reduction*

After the feature extraction stage, a 48-dimensional feature vector per image pixel is obtained. Taking into account the size of the training images associated with the various texture patterns, it is clear that the number of vectors that will model each texture pattern given a window size is enormous. While this is a requirement for a test image, in which every individual pixel has to be classified, it is not necessary nor desirable for modeling the texture patterns of interest, since the core of the classifier is a K-NN algorithm and, hence, the classification cost is quadratic in the number of prototypes.

In order to reduce the number of necessary texture prototypes, a variation of the k-means clustering algorithm is applied, in such a way that the process is not directed by the number of clusters (this value is unknown *a priori*), but by a resolution parameter R that determines the size of the clusters.

K-means[38] is one of the simplest and most popular unsupervised learning algorithms that solves the well known clustering problem. The procedure follows a simple strategy to classify a given data set constituted by n observations of a random d-dimensional variable into a certain number of clusters. It is assumed that the desired number of clusters is known *a pri-*

ori. Basically, k centroids are defined, one for each cluster. These centroids must be placed in a subtle way since different locations lead to different results. Hence, the best choice is to place them as far away from each other as possible. The next step is to take each observation belonging to the data set and associate it with its nearest centroid. When all observations have been assigned to a centroid, it is necessary to recalculate k new centroids as the means of the clusters resulting from the previous step. After the new centroids have been computed, a new assignment must be carried out between the data set points and their nearest new centroids. By iterating this process, the k centroids change their locations step by step.

The k-means algorithm aims at minimizing an objective function, sometimes called a *distortion measure*, given by:

$$J = \sum_{i=1}^{n} \sum_{j=1}^{k} \|x_i^{(j)} - c_j\|^2 \tag{10.11}$$

which represents the sum of squares of the distances between each data point $x_i^{(j)}$ and its assigned centroid c_j.

The two phases of reassigning data points to clusters and recomputing the cluster means, which respectively correspond to the E (expectation) and M (maximization) steps of the EM algorithm, are repeated until there is no further change in the assignments or until some maximum number of iterations is exceeded. Since each phase reduces the value of the objective function J, the convergence of the algorithm is assured. However, it may converge to a local rather than to a global minimum of J. In addition, k-means is also significantly sensitive to the initial cluster centers, which are usually selected randomly, although the algorithm may be run multiple times to reduce this effect.

The proposed variation of k-means described in this chapter has also two main stages: splitting and refinement. For the splitting stage, suppose there are already C clusters, with their respective centroids modeling the feature space. The hypercube that delimits the volume of each cluster is found and the length of its longest diagonal computed. If this value is greater than a resolution parameter R, which is defined as a fraction of the longest diagonal of the hypercube that bounds the whole feature space, then that cluster is split in two. The value of R is computed as described in Section 10.4. Therefore, after a single pass of the algorithm, there will be between C (if no clusters are split) and $2C$ (in case all previous clusters are split) new clusters.

The splitting of a cluster is deterministically done by dividing the bounding box of the original cluster by its longest dimension. New centroids are set at the centers of the two resulting bounding boxes. Once the splitting is complete, the refinement stage follows. It simply consists of applying the traditional k-means, but using all the available centroids as initial seeds for the algorithm. The k-means algorithm iterates until convergence.

Both the splitting and refinement stages are repeated until all clusters meet the resolution criterion R. The algorithm is always initialized with a single cluster, whose centroid is the average of all the available feature vectors. Fig. 10.4 shows a 2-D example of the clustering process described above.

This algorithm resembles previously proposed wrapper methods based on the classical k-means, such as the X-means[39] and G-means[40] clustering algorithms, in the sense that it is able to determine an appropriate number of clusters by continuously splitting the existing ones until a certain criterion is satisfied. However, it differs from them in the way the search of the space for cluster locations is conducted. While the X-means algorithm tries to optimize either the Bayesian Information Criterion (BIC) or the Akaike Information Criterion (AIC), and the G-means algorithm is based on the Anderson-Darling statistical test for the hypothesis that a subset of data follows a Gaussian distribution, the proposed algorithm, as mentioned above, drives the search based on the clusters' size.

Although both X-means and G-means have proven to be good alternatives for data clustering, the proposed resolution-guided clustering approach is more suitable for the classification scheme developed in this work. In particular, a group of independent experiments have shown that the number of prototypes necessary for the classification task found by the proposed resolution-guided clustering approach is considerably smaller than the ones obtained with G-means and specially smaller than the number of prototypes determined with X-means, since the latter tends to overestimate the number of clusters as was previously shown.[40] The reason is that R does not have to be too small (or alternatively there is no need for having a very large number of prototypes) in order to distinguish among the given textures, at least for the texture features and classification methodology used in this work. In addition, the proposed clustering scheme does not make any assumptions about the data distribution, in contrast to G-means.

Furthermore, the proposed algorithm (as well as X-means and G-means) has at least three advantages over the traditional K-means. First, as stated earlier, there is no need for setting the desired number k of clusters *a priori*.

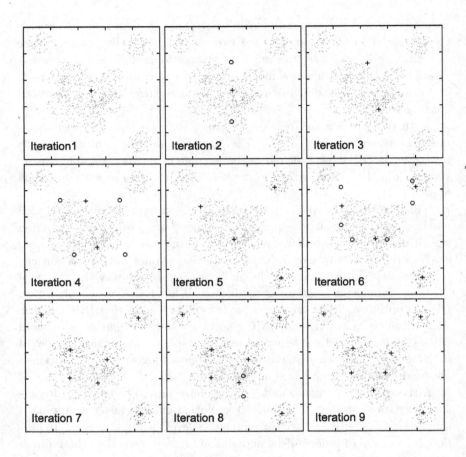

Fig. 10.4. A 2-D example of the splitting and refinement procedure described in Section 10.3.2. Circles indicate the new initial centroids after splitting, while crosses indicate the new centroids after refinement ($R = 0.3$).

In turn, the desired resolution R is introduced and the algorithm finds out the number of clusters that satisfy it. However, a resolution parameter R is more intuitive than a number of clusters K when dealing with high-dimensional spaces. Notwithstanding, the proposed resolution R will be automatically determined by the selection algorithm explained in Section 10.4. Second, the algorithm always behaves in the same way given the same input points. Therefore, due to its deterministic nature, there is no need to run it multiple times and keep the best set of centroids according to some measure, as is the case when the initialization stage of K-means has a random component. Third, it can handle a variable number of prototypes per texture class given a fixed resolution, a property that makes it more flexible when modeling a complex feature space.

A disadvantage of this kind of algorithms, however, is the time necessary to converge when the size of the sought clusters is too small (*e.g.*, $R < 0.3$), especially when having lots of high-dimensional vectors. However, since this procedure is run during the training stage, classification times are not affected. Moreover, as mentioned above and as will be shown later, there is no need for R being too small in order to achieve good classification rates in practice.

10.3.3. *K-Nearest Neighbors Classification*

Consider the case of m classes $\{c_i\}$, $i = 1, \ldots, m$, and a set of n samples $\{p_j\}$, $j = 1, \ldots, n$, whose classification is known *a priori*. Let s denote an incoming pattern. The *nearest neighbor* rule for classifying s consists of assigning it to the pattern class to which the sample nearest to s belongs, *i.e.* if

$$\|s - p_j\| = \min_{1 \leq k \leq n} \|s - p_k\| \tag{10.12}$$

then $s \in class(p_j)$.

This minimum distance classification scheme can be modified by considering the K *nearest neighbors* to s, resulting in s being assigned the label most frequently represented among the K nearest samples.

Although the K-NN rule is a suboptimal procedure as it will usually lead to an error rate greater than the Bayes Rate, which is the minimum possible error, it is a good choice in case of arbitrary distributions whose underlying densities are unknown. Furthermore, even with this knowledge, a high-dimensional distribution (recall from Section 10.3.1 that feature vectors are 48-dimensional) might be difficult to be accurately estimated due to the nature of data. Hence, the applicability of this type of classifier is well justified.

In this work, The K-NN classifier is implemented without changes. It proceeds by comparing a vector that characterizes a pixel in the test image given a certain window size with all the vectors (prototypes) that constitute each of the T texture models for the same window size. Once all window sizes have been evaluated, a list with the K best distances among all $T \times W$ sets of possible values is obtained. Then, the most repeated texture among the candidates is chosen to be the texture to which the analyzed pixel belongs. If there is a tie, the winning texture will be the one with the smallest distance. The value of K is computed as described in Section 10.4.

10.3.4. *Post-Processing*

This last stage aims at removing the noisy regions that usually appear after following a classification scheme such as the one described above. It consists of two steps. First, a small window of 5×5 pixels is displaced along the entire image pixel by pixel. The enclosed region is then filled with its dominant texture, but only if the number of pixels for that texture is greater than a threshold. This process is repeated until the amount of changed pixels is not significant. This amount of pixels and the previous threshold have been determined experimentally. The second step ensures that there will be no regions of uniform texture with less than a certain number of pixels by assigning them to the adjacent region with the largest number of neighboring pixels.

10.4. Automatic Parameter Selection

The classifier described in Section 10.3 depends on two parameters: the resolution R that limits the clusters' size, and the number of neighbors K of K-NN. The performance of the classifier greatly depends on the choice of those parameters. A simple parameter selection algorithm entirely based on the training set is also applied during the training stage.

The selection algorithm applies the proposed classifier in order to compute classification rates for the training images corresponding to the T texture patterns of interest. The classifier is run with different combinations of R and K. Since an exhaustive search for R and K is prohibitive, a sampled search is performed with R varying from 1.0 to 0.3 with decrements of 0.1 (8 different values), and K being 2^n, where n varies from 0 to 8 with increments of 1 (9 different values). However, some of the 8×9 combinations of those parameters are unfeasible, since some values of K are not valid depending on the value of R as discussed below.

Given a certain value of R, let p be the number of prototypes of the texture pattern with the minimum number of clusters according to the prototype extraction algorithm described in Section 10.3.2. In order to guarantee that all texture patterns can be identified, K has been forced to be lower than or equal to p. Without this constraint, some texture patterns could not be identified, such as in the example shown in Fig. 10.5, in which the given feature vector is wrongly classified. In the experiments conducted in this work, 53 different combinations of R and K have been considered.

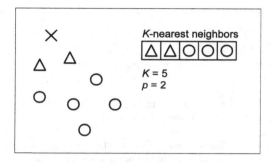

Fig. 10.5. Misclassification of a feature vector (represented by "X") into the second pattern (prototypes represented by circles) due to an invalid value of K. The feature vector should have been classified as belonging to the first pattern (prototypes represented by triangles).

Next, the average of all classification rates for each combination of R and K by considering all the given texture patterns is computed. For instance, Fig. 10.6 shows the average classification rates for the texture patterns belonging to the first test image in Fig. 10.7. The best combination of R and K is marked with a circle. In general, the finer the resolution R, the larger the number of neighbors K necessary to achieve good classification results.

In the end, the combination of R and K that yields the maximum classification rate is selected to provide the configuration parameters of the classifier described in Section 10.3. A group of independent experiments (not included in this chapter due to space limitations) have shown that the classification rates obtained in unknown test images, when using parameters R and K determined as described in this section, are similar to the ones achieved with optimal values of R and K computed by costly optimization techniques.

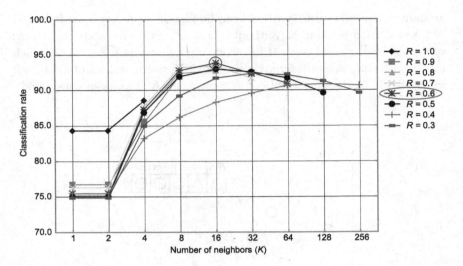

Fig. 10.6.   Average classification rate curves for the patterns belonging to the first test image in Fig. 10.7 by considering different combinations of R and K. The best combination is marked with a circle.

10.5. Experimental Results

The proposed technique has been evaluated on complex real images obtained from both ground and aerial vehicles. Fig. 10.7 shows these input test images (images from 1 to 8 were acquired by UGV, while images from 9 to 12 were acquired by UAV).

Fig. 10.7.   Experimental test images.

In order to validate the proposed methodology for per-pixel texture classification, a comparison with other supervised texture classification techniques in terms of classification rates and computation time has been performed. These alternative techniques are: (a) the extreme alternative that naturally fits in the approach of the proposed classifier, which stores all the available feature vectors as prototypes for the given training texture patterns. In order to yield a comprehensive computation time, only the window size that leads to the best classification rate has been considered. (b) The texture classifier based on integration of multiple methods and windows.[21] (c) The K-NN ($K = 5$) and multivariate Gaussian classifiers utilized in the MeasTex suite.[41] In order to achieve per-pixel classification with MeasTex, which is a framework oriented to the classification of whole images instead of individual pixels, the classifiers of MeasTex have been run to classify every pixel of the test images given a subimage of 32×32 pixels quasi-centered at that pixel (32×32 pixels is the minimum subimage size accepted by MeasTex). Both MeasTex classifiers have been independently evaluated with features derived from classical Gabor filters, the fractal dimension, gray level co-occurrence matrices and Markov random fields. One tenth of the available samples has been used as classification patterns. (d) A straightforward extension to per-pixel classification of the LBP-based classifier,[27] with its same *local binary pattern* (LBP) operators as feature extractors and the G statistic as dissimilarity measure. This extension has been performed in a similar way as the one described for MeasTex, but with subimages of 16×16.[27]

Results for this comparison are presented in Table 10.1. They have been computed considering 25% of the input test pixels (*i.e.*, one out of four pixels). This percentage is thought to suffice to recognize the different explored areas that make up the input images captured by the autonomous vehicles. Only the best classification result is reported for the MeasTex and LBP-based classifiers. Fig. 10.8 and Fig. 10.9 display the classification maps produced by the five approaches. The first column shows the ground-truth for each test image. Black areas represent image regions that do not correspond to any of the sought texture patterns. Pixels that belong to these "unknown" texture patterns have not been taken into account when computing the classification rates. On the other hand, black borders appearing in the classification maps correspond to those pixels that could not be classified because of the minimum used window size. Again, these pixels have been discarded for the reported classification rates.

From Table 10.1, it is clear that the proposed technique is a good ap-

Table 10.1.   Classification rates (%) and computation time in seconds (Pentium 4 at 3.0 GHz) for the proposed classifier and alternative approaches.

	Proposed		"All-proto."		Integration		MeasTex		LBP	
Im.	Clas. rate	CPU time	Clas. rate	CPU time	Clas. rate	CPU time	Clas. rate	CPU time	Clas. rate	CPU time
1	92.8	5	92.2	317	87.8	64	73.3	39	82.1	213
2	91.8	5	91.0	317	87.4	64	70.2	68	76.9	213
3	91.8	5	90.8	317	85.8	64	67.7	67	69.1	1019
4	76.7	6	81.3	342	74.6	76	70.3	35	74.4	266
5	77.4	6	80.8	396	81.8	76	55.1	67	55.1	266
6	94.9	6	94.6	342	91.1	76	69.3	33	57.5	266
7	81.0	6	81.6	140	86.1	76	78.3	67	42.1	615
8	84.2	6	79.2	200	76.3	76	68.6	68	45.0	615
9	98.4	6	99.0	528	95.0	100	73.6	9	78.4	1278
10	91.3	6	90.8	528	83.2	100	72.2	67	73.2	1278
11	97.6	6	97.7	528	90.5	100	79.4	67	81.2	1278
12	93.5	6	96.0	528	26.4	100	88.4	28	39.1	588

proximation of the classifier that stores all the available feature vectors as prototypes, since the classification rates obtained by the former are comparable and, in many cases, better than those obtained by the latter. In terms of computational time, however, the proposed classifier is clearly superior as, on average, it classifies an input image more than sixty times faster. The comparison with the remaining approaches is also favorable to the proposed technique since the classification rate is higher in almost all cases and the execution time is, on average, around fourteen times lower than the one achieved by the fastest alternative classifier, which is the algorithm based on integration of methods. In this sense, since per-pixel texture classification is always a complicated and time demanding task, the performance of the proposed classifier is closer to real-time than those of the other techniques.

10.6. Conclusions and Future Work

This chapter presents a new distance-based, per-pixel texture classifier based on clustering techniques and multichannel Gabor wavelet filters that achieves higher classification rates and lower computational times than other well-known classifiers. This means that the proposed technique is more suitable for real-time tasks than other recent and traditional supervised texture classifiers. Such tasks being those potentially performed by

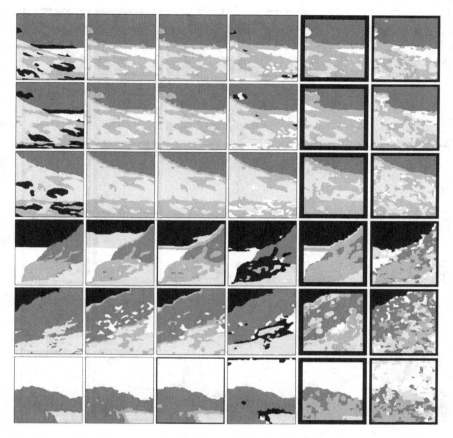

Fig. 10.8. Classification maps for test images 1 to 6 produced by the proposed classifier (*second column*), the classifier that stores all feature vectors as texture models (*third column*), the integration-based classifier (*fourth column*), the best MeasTex classifier (*fifth column*) and the best LBP-based classifier (*sixth column*). Corresponding ground-truth (*first column*).

autonomous surveillance vehicles.

A technique to automatically select the configuration parameters corresponding to k-means (the resolution R, which limits the size of the clusters and, therefore, the maximum number K of prototypes) and the number of neighbors of K-NN has also been developed. It has been shown that this selection algorithm determines appropriate configuration parameters that yield a good performance.

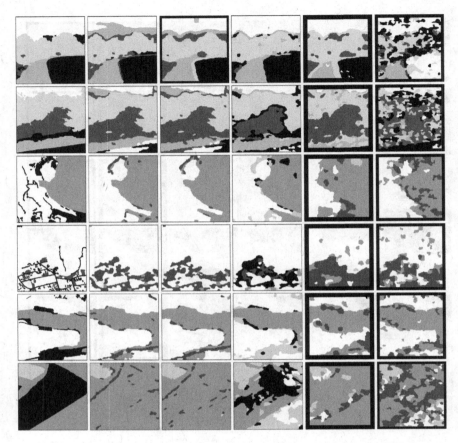

Fig. 10.9. Classification maps for test images 7 to 12 produced by the proposed classifier (*second column*), the classifier that stores all feature vectors as texture models (*third column*), the integration-based classifier (*fourth column*), the best MeasTex classifier (*fifth column*) and the best LBP-based classifier (*sixth column*). Corresponding ground-truth (*first column*).

Classification results for real images acquired by ground-based and aerial autonomous surveillance vehicles have been presented and comparisons with other recent and traditional supervised classification schemes have also been performed. In almost all cases, the proposed classifier yielded the best classification rates with a significantly lower computation time.

Future work will consist of studying better schemes for integration of different window sizes in order to reduce the information sources when classifying a given feature vector, and thus, improving the accuracy and computation time of the algorithm. Additionally, as the proposed methodology is thought to be valid for any texture method or group of texture methods provided they produce feature vectors as output, this technique is expected to be extended in order to integrate different feature extraction methods in a coherent way.

Finally, the proposed methodology will be adapted to unsupervised per-pixel texture segmentation. The goal in this case is to automatically determine sets of prototypes that characterize the different regions of homogeneous texture within a given image.

Acknowledgements

This work has been partially supported by the Spanish Ministry of Education and Science under project DPI2007-66556-C03-03.

References

1. J. Pletta and J. Sackos, *An advanced unmanned vehicle for remote applications.* (Sandia National Laboratories Report, 1998).
2. W. Aviles and et al. Issues in mobile robotics: The unmanned ground vehicle program teleoperated vehicle. In *Proceedings of SPIE*, vol. 1388, pp. 587–597, (1990).
3. C. Metz, H. Everett, and S. Myers. Recent developments. Technical report, Associaton for Unmanned Vehicle Systems, Huntsville, AL, (1992).
4. T. S. et al. A small scaled autonomous test vehicle for developing autonomous off-road applications. In *Proceedings of the Internatonal Conference on Machine Automation*, (1994).
5. J. Kurtur, *Robotic Rover.* (Systems Technology, MD, 1993).
6. E. Bone and C. Bolkcom. Unmaned aerial vehicles: Background and issues for congress. Technical report, Report for Congress, (2003).
7. J. Roos, Organic air vehicle, *The ISR Journal.* (2002).
8. O. of the Secretary of Defense. Unmanned aerial vehicle roadmap 2002-2027. Technical report, Pentagon Reports, (2002).
9. M. Whalley, M. Freed, M. Takahashi, D. Christian, A. Patterson-Hine, G. Schulein, and R. Harris. The nasa/army autonomous rotorcraft project. In *Proceedings of the American Helicopter Society 59th Annual Forum*, Phoenix, Arizona, (2003).
10. T. Spiess, J. Bange, M. Buschmann, and P. Vrsmann, First application of the meteorological mini-uav 'm2av', *Meteorologische Zeitschrift.* **16**(2), 159–169, (2007).
11. H. Robinson and A. Keary. Remote control of unmanned undersea vehicles.

In *International Unmanned Undersea Vehicle Symposium*, Newport (24-28 April, 2000).

12. K. Kim, A. Kostrzewski, and D. Erwin. Intelligent obstacle avoidance system for unmanned undersea vehicles in shallow water, unattended/unmanned ground, ocean, and air sensor technologies and applications vi. In *Proceedings of the SPIE*, vol. 5417, pp. 162–169, (2004).

13. D. Bingham, T. Drake, A. Hill, and R. Lott. The application of autonomous underwater vehicle (auv) technology in the oil industry - vision and experiences. In *FIG XXII International Congress*, (2002).

14. C. Diehl, M. Saptharishi, J. Hampshire, and P. Khosla. Collaborative surveillance using both fixed and mobile unattended ground sensor platforms. In *Proceedings of SPIE Unattended Ground Sensor Technologies and Applications*, vol. 3713, pp. 178–185, (1999).

15. M. Saptharishi, C. S. Oliver, C. Diehl, K. Bhat, J. Dolan, A. Trebi-Ollennu, and P. Khosla, Distributed surveillance and reconnaissance using multiple autonomous atvs: Cyberscout, *IEEE Trans. Robot. Autom.* **18**(5), (2002).

16. C. Piciarelli, C. Micheloni, and G. Foresti, An autonomous surveillance vehicle for people tracking, *Lect. Notes Comput. Sci.* **3617**, (2005).

17. A. Solanas and M. Garcia. Coordinated multi-robot exploration through unsupervised clustering of unknown space. In *International Conference on Intelligent Robots and Systems*, vol. 1, pp. 717–721, (2004).

18. P. Stone. Learning and multiagent reasoning for autonomous agents. In *20th International Joint Conference on Artificial Intelligence*, p. 1330 (January, 2007).

19. M. Garcia and A. Solanas. 3D simultaneous localization and modeling from stereo vision. In *IEEE Internatonal Conference on Robotics and Automation*, pp. 847–853, (2004).

20. T. Randen and J. H. Husoy, Filtering for texture classification: A comparative study, *IEEE Trans. Pattern Anal. Mach. Intell.* **21**(4), 291–310, (1999).

21. M. A. Garcia and D. Puig, Supervised texture classification by integration of multiple texture methods and evaluation windows, *Image Vis. Comput.* **25** (7), 1091–1106, (2007).

22. R. Haralick, K. Shanmugan, and I. Dinstein, Textural features for image classification, *IEEE Trans. Syst. Man Cybern.* **6**(3), 610–622, (1973).

23. K. Laws. *Textured Image Segmentation*. PhD thesis, USC ISG-TRI-IPI-940, (1980). Ph.D. thesis.

24. T. R. Reed and J. M. H. du Buf, A review of recent texture segmentation and feature extraction techniques, *Comput. Vis. Image Understand.* **57**(3), 359–372, (1993).

25. B. S. Manjunath and W. Y. Ma, Texture features for browsing and image retrieval, *IEEE Trans. Pattern Anal. Mach. Intell.* **18**(8), 837–842, (1996).

26. J. Malik and et al., Contour and texture analysis for image segmentation, *Int. J. Comput. Vis.* **43**(1), 7–27, (2001).

27. T. Ojala, M. Pietikinen, and T. Menp, Multiresolution gray-scale and rotation invariant texture classification with local binary patterns, *IEEE Trans. Pattern Anal. Mach. Intell.* **24**(7), 971–987, (2002).

28. J. G. Daugman, Uncertainty relation for resolution in space, spatial frequency, and orientation optimized by two-dimensional visual cortical filters, *J. Opt. Soc. Am. A.* **2**(7), 1160–1167, (2002).

29. J. G. Daugman, Two-dimensional spectral analysis of cortical receptive field profiles, *Vis. Res.* **20**, 847–856, (1980).

30. T. Acharya and A. K. Ray, *Image Processing.* (John Wiley and Sons, 2005).

31. A. K. Jain and S. K. Bhattacharjee, Address block location on envelopes using gabor filters, *Pattern Recogn.* **25**(12), 1459–1477, (1992).

32. S. E. Grigorescu, N. Petkov, and P. Kruizinga, Comparison of texture features based on gabor filters, *IEEE Trans. Image Process.* **11**(10), 1160–1167, (2002).

33. W. Y. Ma and B. S. Manjunath, A texture thesaurus for browsing large aerial photographs, *J. Am. Soc. Inform. Sci.* **49**(7), 633–648, (1998).

34. W. Y. Ma and B. S. Manjunath, Netra: A toolbox for navigating large image databases, *Multimed. Syst.* **27**, 184–198, (1999).

35. W. Y. Ma and B. S. Manjunath, Edgeflow: A technique for boundary detection and image segmentation, *IEEE Trans. Image Process.* **9**(8), 1375–1388, (2000).

36. B. S. Manjunath and et al., Color and texture descriptors, *IEEE Trans. Circ. Syst. Video Tech.* **11**, 703–715, (2001).

37. L. Chen, G. Lu, and D. Zhang. Effects of different gabor filter parameters on image retrieval by texture. In *Proceedings of the 10th International Multimedia Modelling Conference*, pp. 273–278, (2004).

38. S. P. Lloyd, Least squares quantization in pcm, *IEEE Trans. Inform. Theor.* **28**(2), 129–137, (1982).

39. D. Pelleg and A. Moore. X-means: Extending k-means with efficient estimation of the number of clusters. In *Proceedings of the 17th International Conference on Machine Learning*, pp. 727–734, (2000).

40. G. Hamerly and C. Elkan. Learning the k in k-means. In *Proceedings of the 17th Annual Conference on Advances in Neural Information Processing Systems*, pp. 281–288, (2003).

41. G. Smith and I. Burns, Measuring texture classification algorithms, *Pattern Recogn. Lett.* **18**(14), 1495–1501, (1997).

Chapter 11

An Aggression Detection System for the Train Compartment

Zhenke Yang, Siska Fitrianie, Dragos Datcu, and Leon Rothkrantz

Delft University of Technology,
Man-Machine-Interaction Group, Faculty of Electrical Engineering,
Mathematics and Computer Science,
Mekelweg 4 2628CD Delft, The Netherlands
{Z.Yang, S.Fitrianie, D.Datcu, L.J.M.Rothkrantz}@tudelft.nl

This chapter describes an integrating system that combines different aggression detection systems to make the overall system become more effective. Our contribution consists of an automated system for detecting unusual events without being an invasion of individual privacy. Secondly, an icon-language based reporting application for smart phones enables the best aggression detectors (human beings) to anonymously supply input to the detection system. Finally, an underlying framework allows for the fusion of information and delivers the infrastructure to transparently integrate all the systems. To evaluate the system, several hours of audio and video recordings were taken of aggressive and common scenarios in a real Dutch international train compartment. Ongoing work is on creating an experiment setup for on-line testing of the system that complies with the privacy regulations for public transport in the Netherlands. We expect that our system will contribute to public safety by increasing the chance of detection and thus helping to prevent all forms of aggression and terrorism.

Contents

11.1. Introduction

The safety of train travelers is a subject that increasingly concerns the
Dutch railway (NS). As a result, investments to ensure the safety and security of train passengers (and personnel) increased from 45 million to 50
million euros in 2006. Among the efforts are measures to actively confront
passengers that exhibit aggressive behavior whenever possible, installing
more camerasand microphones in the train compartments and joining the
national alerting system for terrorism prevention.

   In recent years, numerous attempts have been made to build automated
aggression/unusual event recognition systems. Despite advances in pattern
recognition, human beings still outperform machines in detecting aggression
by far. As a result, to date, human operators are still the only reliable
resource when it comes to monitoring camera images. To take advantage of
humans as aggression detectors, services have been made available in trains
that allow passengers to alert security personnel of dangerous situations.
Research indicates that people can become extremely cooperative, in these
situations *e.g.* massive surges of volunteerism, as we could see on 9/11.
Against this backdrop, we foresee a transition phase in which human and
computer based detection systems will work side by side to uphold the safety
of public transport. In the long run, computer based systems will gradually
become more prominent as the reliability, robustness, and precision of these
systems increase.

   For now, this chapter describes an integrating system that uses AI techniques to combine automated detection systems with human powered aggression reporting facilities while maintaining the privacy of the passengers
in the train compartment. The system consists of an automated component

for detecting unusual events that makes monitoring surveillance cameras-more effective without being an invasion of individual privacy. Secondly, an icon-language based reporting application for smart phones enables the travellers to supply input to the detection system. Finally, an underlying integrating framework allows for multimodal fusion of information and delivers the infrastructure to transparently integrate all the components.

The system was tested with several hours of audio and video recordings taken of aggressive and common scenarios in a real Dutch international train compartment. The recordings were manually annotated afterwards to establish the ground truths necessary to measure the performance of the detection systems. An ontology for describing aggression was created to form the basis of the grammar for annotation. Furthermore, the ontology served as a formalized way to describe and reason with (aggressive) scenarios in a train. Results show that the system is able to detect potential unusual situations given the video streams and user inputs. Our target users were able to communicate their reports appropriately using the provided reporting software. Due to privacy issues real online testing has yet to be conducted. Ongoing work is on creating an experiment setup for on-line testing of the system that complies with the privacy regulations for public transport in the Netherlands. We expect that our system will contribute to public safety by increasing the chance of detection and thus helping to prevent all forms of aggression and terrorism.

The remainder of this chapter is structures as follows: first we give an overview of related research divided into an automated aggression detection part and an event reporting part. Next we present our system starting with an overview of the system, after which we will gradually delve into the inner workings of the system. Finally we present the evaluation of the system and end up with conclusions and an outlook for the future.

11.2. Related work

The use of surveillance technology to increase the safety in public areas has major privacy implications that point to a tension between security and privacy of individuals. An individual may not want his location to be tracked. In some countries, this issue is solved with legislation: the privacy right is explicitly dispensed when the situation is considered as an emergency. As a result, an increase of security as a result of the employment of surveillance systems is commonly associated with a decrease in privacy. That this is not always the case will be illustrated by the system we present in this chapter. But first we discuss some related research in this field. Since our contribution is twofold, we have divided this section into two subsections: automated aggression detection and an event reporting.

11.2.1. *Automated aggression detection*

The bulk of existing work on automated aggression detection systems have largely depended on video analysis. As a result, video based surveillance related algorithms have been extensively investigated.[1] The underlying algorithms consist of methods ranging from simple background extraction to more complex methods such as dynamic layer representations[2] and optical flow methods.[3]

Audio based surveillance algorithms are usually sound event detectors or recognizers. These algorithms use various features extracted from training sound signals to obtain characteristic acoustic signatures of the different types of events.[4-6] Sound based algorithms are most effective when used in combination with sensors from different (in particular the visual) modalities. Audio can be used complimentary to help resolve situations where video based trackers loose track of people due to occlusion by other objects or other people. The combined approach yields better and more robust results as demonstrated by different researchers using decentralized Kalman filters,[7] particle filters[8] and importance particle filters.[9] Other techniques used in higher-level fusion are Bayesian networks[10-12] rule based systems[13] and agent-based systems.

At a higher level, automated surveillance is focused on semantic interpretation of the events in their spatial and temporal relationships. Ivanov et. al.[14] discuss an automatic surveillance system that performs labeling of events and interactions in an outdoor environment. Generally, high level approaches are heavily dependent on the context in which the system is applied. In the PRISMATICA project[12] a surveillance system for railway stations is designed to integrate different intelligent detection devices. In the PRISMATICA system, detection of events is done in geographically distributed visual, audio and other types of devices and using different algorithms. Bayesian networks are used for presenting and fusing the data by these devices. In the ADVISOR project,[13] a surveillance system was developed for detecting specific behavior (such as fighting or vandalism) in metro stations. Different methods have been defined to compute specific types of behaviors under different configurations. And at the higher level these methods are integrated in a coherent framework.

11.2.2. *Human based event reporting*

Recent world-wide crisis events have drawn attention to the role that the public, equipped with communication technology such as mobile phones, can play in warning and response activities.[15,16] The emergency response system, WHISPER[17] includes a text-based web interface for emergency responders to share information during emergency response activities. The system integrates data repository of all emergency services to support their decision making process. The CAMAS system in the RESCUE[18] project allows not only for the emergency responders but also the general public to send text-reports via their web interface. This system parses and analyzes text-input, classifies crisis events and creates situation awareness. The web interface of VCMC model[19] allows for the general public to share information and discuss problem situations in real-time.

Visual icon-based languages provide an alternative to text and writing as a mode of comprehension and expression.[20] Icons can be used to communicate about topics that are difficult to speak about, or to support people that do not sharing a common language[21,22] or for the speech impaired.[23,24] In icon-based languages a message is composed using an arrangement of icons or using combinations of symbols to compose new symbols with new meanings.[25,26] The arrangement can be realized in a rigid sequence order[27-29] or in a two-dimensional order.[26,30] Conversion to natural language text or speech can be done by interpreting the icon messages using Linguistics theory like the Conceptual Dependency Theory[a] or Basic English[b].

Fitrianie et al.[29,30] developed an icon-based communication interfaces for reporting observations for PDAs and smart-phones. The system utilizes a wireless ad-hoc architecture to connect the mobile devices without the need for a central base station. A blackboard structure is used for distributing information to support people who must work collaboratively (*e.g.* rescue teams, crisis center operators, victims and witnesses). A dedicated Natural Language Processing-based grammar has been used to interpret the visual messages. The interface was later extended with adaptive features such as prediction[33] and an n-grams language model[34] for a faster and more efficient icon-selection.

Dymon[35] reviewed the use of existing icons for hazard and emergency maps, including those of US military and NATO (APP-6a - 1999). The

---

[a]The Conceptual Dependency Theory[31] introduces the notions of conceptualizations and concepts which are units of meaning loosely corresponding to the grammatical units of clauses and words (*e.g.* noun, verb, and adjective) in a sentence construction.
[b]The Basic English is an attempted core subset of the English language.[32]

resulting symbols are claimed to be scalable and flexible across both discipline and cultural differences. These standard map icons are promoted for emergency response applications by the U.S. Government[c] and tested on a national basis. The set of icons is also used by the governments of Australia and New Zealand. Tatomir and Rothkrantz[36] developed a set of icons for sharing and merging topological maps in damaged buildings using observations from individuals present in an infrastructure-less network. The knowledge was used for reasoning about the state of the building and providing guidance to given locations.

11.3. System overview

The aggression detection system presented in this chapter combines two related (but autonomous) aggression detection components. The first component consists of an automated system for detecting unusual events that makes monitoring surveillance camerasmore effective by pointing out the train compartments with a high possibility of aggression. The second component depends on humans equipped with a smart phone running a reporting application to supply the input to the detection system. An underlying framework allows for the fusion of information and delivers the infrastructure to transparently integrate all the systems. An overview of the system and its components is shown in Fig. 11.1: an automatic detection system, which is a computer inside the train compartment, continuously analyses data from microphones and camerasin the compartment to automatically detect aggression. The system uses well known algorithms to detect and classify activities and events in the train compartment. At a higher level, the possible scenario is inferred based on knowledge of the characteristics of similar scenarios. At the same time, travelers can use there mobile phones to report aggressive situations. Reports are automatically analyzed and presented to human operators in a central operator room, where they can decide to investigate the situation further.

For the automatic recognition of aggressive situations, we installed four camerasand microphones in the train compartment. The microphones are positioned in a zig-zag fashion, while the camerasare places along the corridor of the train. All sensors are attached to the roof of the train compartment. Since half of the camerasare opposed to each other and strategically placed along the corridor (see Fig. 11.2), the probability of detecting a face facing the camera maximized. Considering the confined space of the train

---

[c]Homeland Security Working Group Symbology Reference. http://www.fgdc.gov/hswg

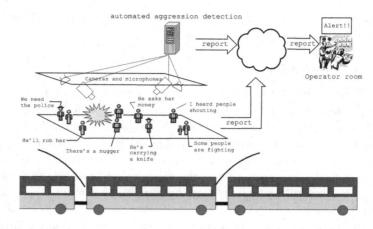

Fig. 11.1. A schematic overview of the aggression detection system.

compartment, the resolution of the faces is generally large enough for the detection algorithm.

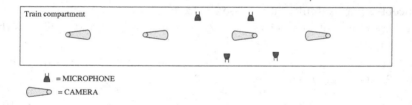

Fig. 11.2. The locations of the sensors seen from a topview of the train compartment.

11.4. Knowledge representation

In order for a computerized system to communicate with humans about what it is witnessing, it needs to share with humans a common (and consistent) means for communication and knowledge representation. For our system we used an ontology to conceptualize knowledge in the aggression domain. The ontology was created in W3C-OWL[d]. This section explores

[d]Ontology Web Language: http://www.w3.org/TR/owlguide/

the reasons for that choice, and the advantages of an ontology-based knowledge representation.

11.4.1. *Motivation*

One issue in the choice of representation is expressiveness. Interviews with experts, not surprisingly, reveal that experts communicate with each other with all the expressiveness of natural language. This, though, goes beyond what we need and wish in our system. The main issue with natural language is ambiguity. This matters greatly, since we are representing the knowledge for a purpose: we want to use the represented knowledge in reasoning. Reasoning means, at least in part, figuring out what must be true, given what is known.

An ontology consists of a set of concepts, a set of relationships and a set of axioms that describe a domain of interest. Complimented with two partial orders defining the concept hierarchy and relation hierarchy respectively. With an ontology we can precisely define the concepts we use. This allows us to place the appropriate rules on their respective concepts. First, we identify the common concepts for example, the relation "x caused y". Then, we use logical relationships to formulate rules about those common concepts. For example, "if x caused y, then x temporally precedes y". An ontology representation, gives us enough expressiveness, and facilitates the reasoning as well.

11.4.2. *Ontology overview*

The ontology is built for two purposes; the first is to assist annotators of train data in the annotation process. Using a standardized annotation language derived from the ontology results in more consistent annotations. Second the ontology will be used by the aggression detection system for semantic interpretation of complex situations (as both automated aggression detection as the reporting tool use the knowledge in the ontology to infer the context of observed events). We start the conceptualization with a definition of the core ontology. The core ontology Fig. 11.3 captures the basic dynamic concepts of situations and their dynamics over time and space. Next, this core ontology is extended with two domain specific extension: (a) the train compartment and all the objects of relevance for aggression in it (static context) and (b) a specification of aggressive scenarios represented by the essential actors and the chain of events that take place when the scenario occurs (dynamic context). The knowledge of both contexts is stored in ontology represented in W3C-OWL. Each of the extensions is discussed in more detail below.

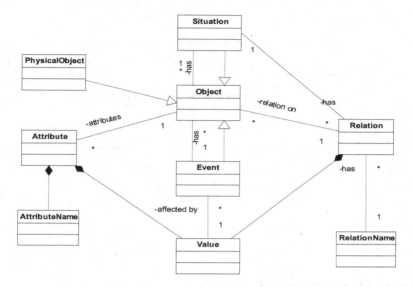

Fig. 11.3. Core aggression ontology.

11.4.3. *The static context*

The static context (Fig. 11.4) discusses the objects of relevance to aggression in the train compartment and presents the formal definition of these objects in the ontology. We will focus on a single train compartment, but this can easily be extended to the entire train.

The TrainCompartment encompasses all of the objects that are in a train compartment. PhysicalObject are special kinds of Objects that exist somewhere, so they necessarily have a position and an orientation attribute (StaticObject). Furthermore, special physical objects can sometimes move, in which case they may have a velocity (DynamicObject). We modeled TrainObjects which we limited to some static objects in the train compartment, for example seats and tables. These TrainObjects are included because they can also be the victim of damage due to paint, fire, etc. HumanObject are physical objects which can trigger events and cause a situation in the train.

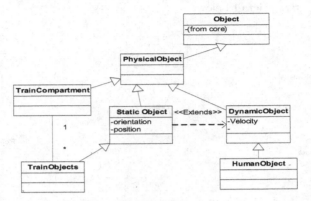

Fig. 11.4. Overview of the static context.

11.4.4. *Dynamic context*

The dynamic context describes how objects can interact within the train environment. The central classes are situation and event. The relation between situation and event is given in the sub ontology diagram in Fig. 11.5. According to the ontology, a situation includes some objects and relationships among them (in the form of Relation tuples). As Situation is a subclass of Object, every instance of Situation can have attributes like any other Object. The same holds for Event. Events are objects that contain information about events in the real world observed at a specific time that affects the value of Attributes and Relations. Relations define the relations between ordered sets of objects *e.g.* inRange(x, y). Values have two attributes, one is the actual value and the other is the certainty.

Scenarios describe situations in the train, more specifically it summarizes the events and actions that are usually observed and their order of occurrence when such a situation takes place. According to our ontology, a scenario consists of a sequence of situations and a sequence of events. An event that leads to a transition of one situation into another is represented by a situation switch (Fig. 11.5). An important entity in the dynamic context is the HumanObject. The HumanObject is capable of manipulating (generating events in) the dynamic context (by actions and behaviors). Ag-

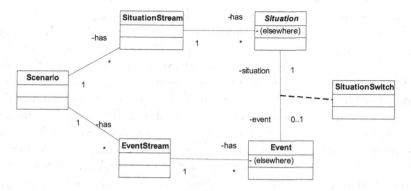

Fig. 11.5. Overview of the scenario sub ontology.

gressive behavior involves a human aggressor and one or more human or non-human victims. A chain of situations that occurs by a combination of an aggressor and possibly one or more Object will be a scenario. An action or event caused by a humanObjects and possibly using other humanObjects could result in another situation being triggered and possible switching the scenario to maybe an even more dangerous one. Below is a list of the types of Scenarios in the ontology:

- Annoyances: This is a combination of irritation perceived by other passengers. For example loud shouting, talking too loud on a mobile phone etc.
- Danger: This indicates that a serious situation occurred. For example fighting, terrorist attack etc.
- Damages: This indicates for example the presence of hooligans damaging the train property.
- Sickness: This scenario indicates that an actor in the train compartment is not feeling well. For example vomiting or fainting.
- Neutral: This is just when everything is quiet in the train compartment and no strange event is taking place. This is mostly the scenario that railways want in their trains.

11.5. Automated aggression detection

Currently there is a surveillance platform consisting of security camerasinstalled in compartments of Dutch international trains. However, the system is based on the supervision of human operators. This is a major drawback given that there is not enough manpower to monitor all these camerascontinuously. Operators have to make a selection of train compartments to watch. This selection is often driven by tips from outside, by experience (*e.g.* hooligans in train before or after important soccer matches) or (and most often) by co-incidence. This section discusses the theoretical model of our automated aggression detection system and identifies the features and techniques to automatically distinguish aggression from normal situations. We present a system that automatically scans video images and audio data for unusual situations and generates a list of the train compartments with the highest potentially dangerous situations. The results of this analysis can then be used to provide suggestions of compartments to be monitored. In this way, the detection is based less on co-incidence.

11.5.1. *Approach*

As indicated previously we use video as well as audio data as input for the automated detection system. The raw data goes through a process of feature extraction, classification and recognition (see Fig. 11.6 to become a quantitative conclusion about the aggression level in the train compartment. The process consists of two phases: a fusion and classification phase in which features from different modalities are extracted and combined into high level concepts and a reasoning phase in which a high level reasoning system infers scenarios from the high level concepts.

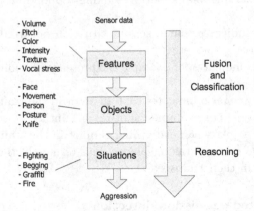

Fig. 11.6. Overview of the automated aggression detection process.

11.5.2. *Fusion and classification*

The detection of aggression in train compartments is based on using a set of relevant high-level features which thoroughly describe the body gestures of a person. A specific type of features relates to the emotional state of the passengers. The system processes the raw data from microphones and video camerasin train compartments and automatically extracts the audio and video features for each passenger. The most important characteristic of the automatic system is that the detection of aggressive behavior is done without taking into account features regarding the identity of the persons. Indeed we do not incorporate any identity recognition system in our framework. More specifically, only the features we extract and that are related to gestures and emotion of the subjects are used to track and to analyze the behavior of one person. In this way, the algorithm we propose fully complies with the privacy issues in public spaces.

The emotion recognition algorithm works with the prototypic emotions[37] and is based on semantic fusion of audio and video data. In the case of video data processing, we have developed automatic systems for the recognition of facial expressions for video sequences. The recognition was done by using Viola&Jones features and boosting techniques for face detection,[38] Active Appearance Model[39] (AAM) for the extraction of face shape and Support Vector Machines[40,41] (SVM) for the classification of feature patterns in one of the prototypic facial expressions. For training and testing the systems we have used Cohn-Kanade database[42] by creating a subset of relevant data for each facial expression.

The features we compute for the recognition of facial expressions relate to the shapes of face and facial features (eyes, eyebrows and mouth). Subsequently we identify some characteristic points on the face and track them in time. The assessment of the facial expressions is realized as a classification of temporal patterns of face shape deformations. Fig. 11.7 illustrates an example of face shape deformation for each of the six basic facial expressions.

In order to extract the emotion of one person we determine the emotion from speech and from facial expressions. Finally the algorithm semantically combines the two types of information so as to get a more accurate estimation of the emotion. In order to do that, we distinguish two processing contexts (Fig. 11.8). The first is the case of non-speaking passengers and allows for computing the facial expressions by using the full features set of face shape deformations. The second is the case of speaking passengers.

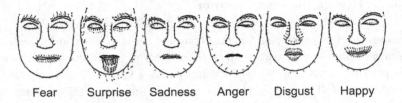

| Fear | Surprise | Sadness | Anger | Disgust | Happy |

Fig. 11.7. The emotion facial shape deformation patterns for the six prototypic emotion classes.

The estimation of facial expressions involves the use of a smaller set of facial deformation features. We remove the features determined based on mouth shape deformation so as to remove the influence of speech over facial features deformation. More exactly, we consider speech influence as noise and we want to filter it out during the estimation of facial expressions.

Fig. 11.8. Silence/non-silence detection using multimodal data. Sample taken from eNTERFACE 2005 database: "Oh my god, there is someone in the house!".

The results of different types of emotion assessment for speech and non-speech multimodal data segments are combined for obtaining smooth transitions (Fig. 11.9).

Our algorithm for the recognition of emotions in videos implies initial processing of the multimodal data. Firstly, the audio-video input data is rescaled by conversion to a specific frame-rate (Fig. 11.10). This process may imply downscaling by skipping some video and audio frames. Secondly, the audio data is processed in order to determine the silence and non-silence segments. The resulting segments are correlated to the correspondent audio data and constitute the major data for the analysis. The identification of silence and non-silence segments is realized by using both acoustic and video information. Apart from running acoustic analysis of the data, speech can be detected by tracking features from a simple facial characteristic points-

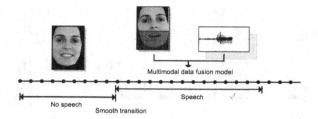

Fig. 11.9. Emotion recognition regarding the transition between two adjacent segments.

based model that includes data from the mouth area.

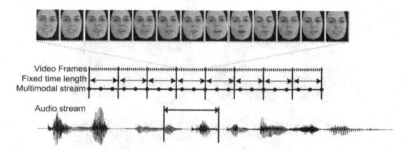

Fig. 11.10. Multimodal frame rescaling algorithm.

The bi-modal data fusion model aims at determining the most probable emotion of the subject given the emotions determined previously. We realize the semantic fusion of features using Dynamic Bayesian Network[43] (DBN). Fig. 11.11 shows an example of the multimodal emotion recognition algorithm. High-level data fusion works only during the analyses of speech-enhanced multimodal segments.

11.5.2.1. *Facial expression recognition*

AAM makes sure the shapes of the face and of the facial features are correctly extracted from each detected face (Fig. 11.12). Starting with the samples we have collected from the Cohn-Kanade database, we have determined the average face shape and texture.

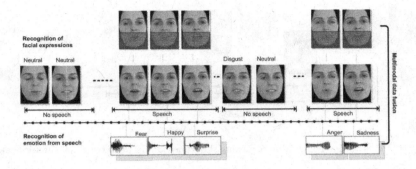

Fig. 11.11.   The sequential recognition of human emotions from audio and video data.

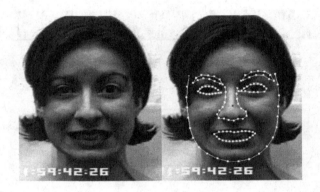

Fig. 11.12.   The use of Active Appearance Models for the extraction of facial features.

Based on the AAM face shape, the facial expression recognition algorithm generates a set of features to be used further on during the emotion classification stage. The features stand for geometric parameters as distances computed between specific Facial Characteristic Points (FCPs) (Fig. 11.13). For the recognition of expressions in still pictures, the distances determined from one face form a representative set of features to reflect the emotion at a certain moment of time. In the case of recognition of facial expressions in video sequences, the features are determined as the variation of the same distances between FCPs as observed during several consecutive frames.

The recognition of emotions is realized differently for silence segments

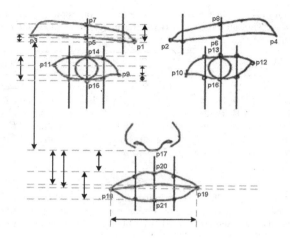

Fig. 11.13.   The Facial Characteristic Point FCP model.

and non-silence segments. For silence segments, the emotion is represented by the facial expression as determined by the facial expression classification algorithm. For the non-silence segments, the emotion recognition is based on the multimodal semantic fusion of the results of the emotion classification on single modalities. Additionally, the facial expression classification algorithm for non-silence segments determines the most probable facial expression by considering a different set of geometric features. The input features in this case relate to only FCPs from the upper part of the face. The reason for not considering the FCPs of the mouth is explained by the natural influence of the phoneme generation on the mouth shape during the process of speaking. The geometric features used for the recognition of facial expressions are illustrated in Table 11.1 for silence data segments and in Table 11.2 for non-silence data segments.

All the FCPs are adjusted for correcting against the head rotation prior to computing the values of the geometric features used for the facial expression classification.

Moreover, another adjustment of the FCPs applies a correction against the variance of the distance between the subject and the camera. This is realized by scaling all the distance-oriented feature values by the distance between the inner corners of the eyes. The models that use the feature sets in Table 11.1 and Table 11.2 allow for the independent consideration

Table 11.1. The geometric feature set for facial expression recognition for silence data segments (LEB=Left eyebrow, REB=Right eyebrow, LE=Left eye, RE=Right eye, M=Mouth).

	Feature			Feature			Feature	
v_1	$(P_1, P_7)_y$	LEB	v_7	$(P_{14}, P_{15})_y$	LE	v_{13}	$(P_{17}, P_{20})_y$	M
v_2	$(P_1, P_3)_y$	LEB	v_8	$(P_9, P_{11})_y$	LE	v_{14}	$(P_{20}, P_{21})_y$	M
v_3	$(P_2, P_8)_y$	REB	v_9	$(P_9, P_{15})_y$	LE	v_{15}	$(P_{18}, P_{19})_y$	M
v_4	$(P_2, P_4)_y$	REB	v_{10}	$(P_{13}, P_{16})_y$	RE	v_{16}	$(P_{17}, P_{18})_y$	M
v_5	$(P_1, P_{17})_y$	LEB	v_{11}	$(P_{10}, P_{12})_y$	RE	v_{17}	$(P_{17}, P_{19})_y$	M
v_6	$(P_2, P_{17})_y$	REB	v_{12}	$(P_{10}, P_{16})_y$	RE			

Table 11.2. The geometric feature set for facial expression recognition for speech-containing enhanced data segments (LEB=Left eyebrow, REB=Right eyebrow, LE=Left eye, RE=Right eye).

	Feature			Feature	
v_1	$(P_1, P_7)_y$	LEB	v_7	$(P_{14}, P_{15})_y$	LE
v_2	$(P_1, P_3)_y$	LEB	v_8	$(P_9, P_{11})_y$	LE
v_3	$(P_2, P_8)_y$	REB	v_9	$(P_9, P_{15})_y$	LE
v_4	$(P_2, P_4)_y$	REB	v_{10}	$(P_{13}, P_{16})_y$	RE
v_5	$(P_1, P_9)_y$	LEB	v_{11}	$(P_{10}, P_{12})_y$	RE
v_6	$(P_2, P_{10})_y$	REB	v_{12}	$(P_{10}, P_{16})_y$	RE

of features from both sides of the face. The advantage of a facial expression recognition system that makes use of such a set of features is the ability to still offer good results for limited degrees of occlusion. For such cases, the features computed from the side that is not occluded can be mirrored to the features from the occluded side of the face.

11.5.2.2. *Emotion recognition from speech*

In the case of emotion recognition from speech, the analysis is handled separately for different number of frames per speech segment.[44] In the current approach there are five types of split methods applied on the initial audio data. Each type of split produces a number of data sets, according to all the frame combinations in one segment. The data set used for emotion analysis from speech is Berlin[45] a database of German emotional speech. The database contains utterances of both male and female speakers, two sentences per speaker. The emotions were simulated by ten native German actors (five female and five male). The result consists of ten utterances (five short and five long sentences). The length of the utterance samples ranges from 1.2255 seconds to 8.9782 seconds. The recording frequency is 16kHz.

The Praat[e] tool was used for extracting the features from each sample from all generated data sets. According to each data set frame configuration, the parameters mean, standard deviation, minimum and maximum of the following acoustic features were computed: Fundamental frequency (pitch), Intensity, F1, F2, F3, F4 and Bandwidth. All these parameters form the input for separate GentleBoost classifiers according to data sets with distinct segmentation characteristics. The GentleBoost strong classifier is trained for a maximum number of 200 stages. Separate data sets containing male, female and both male and female utterances are considered for training and testing the classifier models.

11.5.2.3. *Results for the extraction of emotion-related features*

For the classification of facial expressions, different models have been taken into account. In our experiments we have used 2-fold Cross Validation method for testing the performance of the models. For training, we have used Cohn-Kanade database for experiments on facial expression recognition and Berlin database for emotion extraction from speech.

We have partly used the eNTERFACE05 audio-visual emotion database[46] for testing our multimodal algorithms for emotion recognition. The results show the performance achieved by our algorithms for facial expression recognition in processing silence (Table 11.3) and speech segments (Table 11.4). Additionally we show the results in the case of emotion recognition from speech (Table 11.5). The terms ac means the accuracy, tpr is the true positive rate and fpr is the false positive rate obtained by the model on the testing database. Ongoing work is set to test the multimodal fusion model by using eNTERFACE05 data set. The results of the facial expression recognition clearly show that a higher performance is obtained by the models that make use of features computed from the entire face shape in comparison to the model that uses information regarding only the eyes and eyebrows.

---

[e]Praat: doing phonetics by computer: http://www.fon.hum.uva.nl/praat/

Table 11.3. The results for facial expression recognition using SVM (polynomial kernel of degree 3) for sequence of frames.

%	Fear	Surprise	Sadness	Anger	Disgust	Happy
Fear	**88.09**	2.38	4.76	3.57	1.19	0
Surprise	0	**88.67**	2.83	8.49	0	0
Sadness	5.43	2.17	**85.86**	2.17	1.08	3.26
Anger	10.71	0	3.57	**85.71**	0	0
Disgust	5.35	5.35	3.57	1.78	**82.14**	1.78
Happy	4.62	0	7.40	2.77	5.55	**79.62**

Table 11.4. The results for facial expression recognition using SVM (polynomial kernel of degree 3) for sequence of frames using only the eyes and eyebrows information.

%	Fear	Surprise	Sadness	Anger	Disgust	Happy
Fear	**70.59**	0	0	0	29.41	0
Surprise	15.00	**70.00**	15.00	0	0	0
Sadness	15.79	15.79	**63.16**	0	5.26	0
Anger	16.67	16.66	0	**66.67**	0	0
Disgust	0	21.22	2	11.11	**65.67**	0
Happy	0	36.36	0	0	0	**63.64**

Table 11.5. The optimal classifier for each emotion class, Berlin data set.

(%)	ac (%)	tpr (%)	fpr (%)
Anger	0.83±0.03	0.72±0.16	0.13±0.06
Boredom	0.84±0.07	0.49±0.18	0.09±0.09
Disgust	0.92±0.05	0.24±0.43	0.00±0.00
Fear	0.87±0.03	0.38±0.15	0.05±0.04
Happy	0.81±0.06	0.54±0.41	0.14±0.13
Sadness	0.91±0.05	0.83±0.06	0.08±0.06

11.5.2.4. *Event and activity recognition*

For activity recognition we compare the characteristics of the trajectory of people with known trajectories. We apply greedy nearest-neighbor matching to construct most probable tracks from the coordinates of detected faces. To limit the number of false positives, we apply a mask focused on the areas around the corridor and the seats; the idea being that people always enter the compartment through one of the two doors. To account for the low detection rate, we search over a maximum of 10 frames increasing the search area by 5 pixels after every frame without a face found. The trajectories thus obtained are compared to some predefined trajectory templates of actions such as entering the compartment and sitting, walking through the corridor, begging etc. The resulting measurement vector is compared to the template. The sum of the Euclidean distances between the current trajectory coordinates and each template trajectory coordinates is calculated and the action template with the smallest cumulative difference is selected. Since this approach produces satisfactory (*e.g.* Fig. 11.14) results we did not try alternative prediction methods, such as linear- and Kalman-filtering are widely used.[47,48] However, in our training data for activity recognition, we selected fragments containing little or no occlusion of actors. Different methods might work better under circumstances where more occlusion takes place.

Fig. 11.14. The paths obtained from face recognition are combined into tracks.

11.5.3. *Reasoning model*

In the recognition phase algorithms detect emotions, motions and event based on the movement and sounds of people in the train. In the reasoning phase, the results are compared to the usual behavior of passengers given the current time and under the current situation. If the behavior differs too much from the expected behavior or if the behavior is similar to known unusual behavior, the situation in that compartment is classified as unusual.

The theoretical model behind the reasoning part is based on the work of Schank and Abelson[49] who state that, in the human mind, practical knowledge is stored as scripts. Triggered by the key events being perceived by the senses, a script is recognized without having perceived all the events that constitute the script.[33] Following this theory, scenarios in our reasoning model are also represented as scripts. Events in a script are distinguished by some concepts in the ontology being observed by the recognition algorithms. A weight value is assigned to each event to show how important that event is for the scenario. This reasoning model is designed to detect a particular type of aggressive situations known in psychology as instrumental aggression.[50] Instrumental aggression can be conceived as aggression committed with a goal.

A rule based approach is adopted here to match incoming events with scenario scripts for the purpose of calculating scenario plausibility (Fig. 11.15). Events arriving at the classification phase are compared for matches of concepts in the scenarios. All scenarios that comply with the received event receive an increment in their score. Initially, each scenario has an initial credibility value of zero, and varies dynamically as fusion of live data streams proceed in time. As more concepts are perceived, the evidence in favor of the correct scenario increases. On the other hand, evidence might contradict a condition in the script; in this case another script becomes more plausible. Based on knowledge in ontology, certain concepts can be inferred from the existence of other concepts, *e.g.* if (someone) asks money using a knife there is a robbery, even though that is not specifically reported by a user or observed by the system. As concepts in ontology have direct links to concepts in scripts, derived concepts can influence the plausibility of a script.

Other techniques to detect unusual behavior could be considered, but some of these approaches such as speech identification or face identification (to identify known troublemakers) may cause unacceptable invasion of individual privacy. Our approach is based on the recognition of general aggressive patterns and thus does not rely on identification of individuals nor a database of usual suspects.

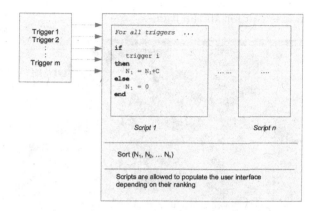

Fig. 11.15.   Schematic overview of the reasoning model.

11.5.4. *Implementation*

Fig. 11.16 shows a snap shot of our software implementation[51] for the bimodal human emotion recognition system. Our system runs on Windows machines. For the detection of faces we have mainly used the implementation of Viola&Jones method from Intels Open Source Computer Vision Library (OpenCV). We have used AAM-API libraries[52] for the implementation of Active Appearance Models. For the speech processing part we have built Tcl/Tk scripts in combination with Snack Sound Toolkit, a public domain toolkit developed at KTH Swedish Royal Institute of Technology. Finally, we have built our facial feature extraction routines, the facial expression recognition system and the emotion extraction from speech in C++ programming language. For the classification component, we have used LIBSVM[f]. On an Intel Core 2 CPU @2.00 GHz, 2.00 GB of RAM our software implementation works at speed of about 5 fps.

The AAM module of our initial facial expression recognition system requires the detection of faces for each frame in the incoming video sequence. We have obtained a considerable improvement in terms of speed by nearly doubling the frame rate with an algorithm that uses information regarding the face shape of one subject at the current frame as initial location for the AAM fitting procedure at the next frame in the video sequence. In this way the face detection is run only at certain time intervals comparing to

---

[f]LIBSVM: http://www.csie.ntu.edu.tw/~cjlin/libsvm

the case when it is run for all the frames.

Fig. 11.16. A snapshot during a working session; experimental setup with our software implementation of the emotion recognition system.

11.6. Icon-based reporting tool on smart phones

The idea behind the reporting tool is to use people to supply input to detection system. Currently, NS has reporting devices at fixed locations in the train. These are not effective: people have to go to the device and press a button to speak into it. If they are threatened or already surrounded by hostile people that is a problem. Furthermore, people might not dare to repost because of fear of revenge. In our solution, passengers can use a smart device with an icon language to reporting hostile situations without being noticed. To distribute the tool, it can be for example supplied with NS timetable software for mobile phones. Key to the solution is that we use the existing communication infrastructure and a convenient icon language for reporting. By using an icon language, reports can be made quicker and easier. An ontology of concepts and their relation is used at the server side, to construct the general situation of what is going on from all incoming messages. At the server side, a probabilistic approach is adopted to generate hypothesis that are supported by the given inputs. A top-down verification process is employed by checking the security camerasto verify the situation.

11.6.1. *The icon interface*

Fig. 11.17(a) shows the developed icon-language based interface for reporting observation in aggressive situations on a smart phone. The interface provides a drawing area where users can attach and re-arrange icons on. The users can group related icons by drawing an ellipse around them or placing them relatively near to each other but far from other icons. Icons (or groups of icons) can be linked using a line to represent a direct link or an arrow to represent a causality link (an icon generates/results another icon). The interface supports the users with mechanisms to draw and delete ellipse and links. An icon can be selected by three options: (a) the icon menu in which the icons are grouped based on their concepts, (b) the next icon prediction results, which are calculated by adapting an n-gram word prediction technique, and (c) the search engine, which finds icons based on a keyword.

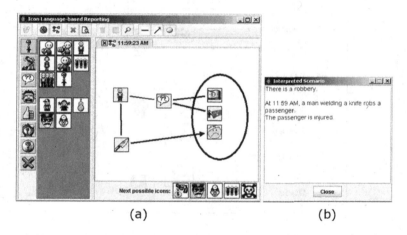

(a)   (b)

Fig. 11.17. Icon language-based interface: an example message on the drawing area (a) and the resulting interpretation (b).

As messages are constructed, the system will continuously analyze, create or adapt its internal representation of the state of the world and try to find the scenario that matches the messages.

11.6.2. *System knowledge representation*

The system uses two knowledge representations: (1) the world model and
(2) scripts. The world model is a symbolic representation of real world
environment. It has a structured record of relevant entities, processes and
events that have been depicted on the communicated information. The
world model is based on the ontology described in section 11.4. The icons on
the user interface have direct links to concepts in the ontology. Fig. 11.18(a)
shows the class PhysicalObject, which refers to an entity involved in an
aggression event. The icons are the instances of the subclasses of this class.
For example, the icon "man" is a HumanObject with the property gender
is "male".

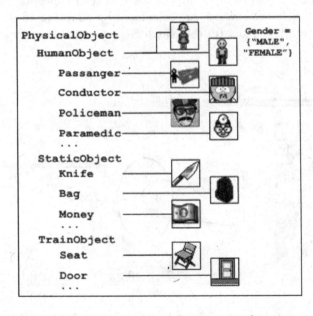

Fig. 11.18.   A schematic overview of the aggression detection system.

The geospatial knowledge of aggression situations is represented using
graphs for data modeling. The graph connects its nodes based on their
approximated spatial coordinates in the world. The lower nodes represent
objects, actions or events in the world. They do not only contain specific information of events and objects, but also their current status (*e.g.*

living condition, dynamic spatial state), their temporal information (*e.g.* frequency, time point), and their spatial information (*e.g.* current location, origin, destination, path). The arcs represent the hierarchy of groups of individuals or show the relations among concepts (*e.g.* result, cause, contain). At the root, a node describes the perspective location of the crisis event.

A script represents the chain of events that identify a possible scenario (see section 11.5.3).

11.7. Communication framework

The functional components of the aggression detection system are transparently integrated by an underlying multimodal framework.[53] One of the most important characteristics of the framework is the ability to automatically fuse data coming from various surveillance video camerasand microphones in the train compartments.

The multimodal framework being described in this paper is centered on the shared memory paradigm. It introduces a novel technique in the way data is handled by different purpose data consumers. Comparing with the traditional way implying direct connections between the system components each connection having its own data format, the new approach suggests a more human-modeled alternative to store, retrieve and process the data.

The shared memory in the current design of the multimodal framework takes the form of XML data spaces. The data is conferred an underlying structure that complies with eXtended Markup Language (XML). XML Schema is used to validate each existing XML document prior to extracting the meaningful information.

In addition, the framework also consists of a set of software tools to monitor the state of registered processing components, to log different type of events and to debug the flow of data given any running application context.

11.8. The operator room

In the operator room, conclusions from automatic aggression detection systems in all train compartments are gathered. A overview of the situation on the rail is made and shown to the human operator. The human operator can add or remove the kind of scenario he wants to monitor. He can

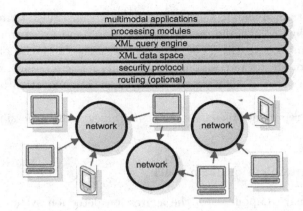

Fig. 11.19.   The diagram showing the functional layers of the multimodal framework.

also set a threshold for a sound alarm for each scenario. When a scenario reaches the threshold, the operator can get more information about the compartment in which the scenario is taking place. The operator can then request video and audio data from that particular compartment. He has to decide what actions to take upon inspection of the data. Unlike automated aggression detection, evaluation of user reports takes place inside the operator room. A icon message interpreter is responsible for making a coherent and context dependent interpretation of incoming icon language messages.

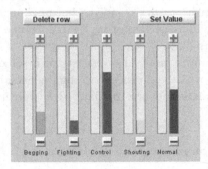

Fig. 11.20.   A bars displaying the possibilty of the each scenario.

11.8.1. *Icon language message interpreter*

Awareness about the situations can emerge as adaptations to the outcomes of interactions with properties of reported concepts (defined by the ontology) and inferred scenarios (defined by the scripts). Inspired by the work of Dor,[54] the construction process is accomplished by an agent-based architecture (Fig. 11.21).

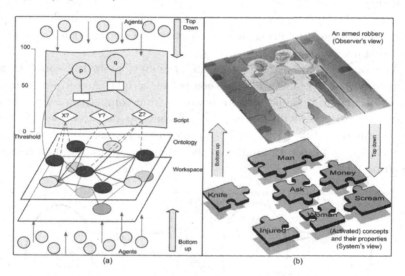

Fig. 11.21. Agent-based approach for icon language message interpretation(a) and Concept-based puzzle arrangement metaphor(b).

On the 'workspace' perceptual structures are built on top of the drawing area (user input). It contains all instances of concepts that are represented by icons (or groups of icons) and the relations between icons and groups of icons (*i.e.*, which are represented by links).

The ontology holds predefined concepts in the form of graph of concepts and properties. Each concept can be viewed as a puzzle piece (Fig. 11.21). Each piece can have properties to be filled in by other concepts. This creates relations between them. A relation or some relations may generate a new active concept. By relating all or some important pieces, we can see the actual picture, *i.e.* the observers view. This view is used to define a script (based on a scenario). The selection of the right script is the goal of this interpretation process.

Agents are created to continually look for interesting properties and dynamically build relationships among the concepts and message structures on the workspace. When a concept in the ontology is activated, it will try to assign as many properties as possible by launching more agents to search for more values. As a result an active concept will spread some activation to other relevant concepts. The activation levels of concepts decay at predefined intervals when agents fail to fill in their properties. By this mechanism, the system processes concepts which were dynamically deemed relevant, while still allowing new concepts to be perceived by constantly launching agents.

As more concepts are active in the Ontology, more key concepts are represented most common to some competing scripts. As a result, certain scripts become impossible and are removed from competition. This entire construction process will be stopped if all concepts on the workspace have been evaluated. Fig. 11.22 shows an example of a user input, proposed new concept and links resulted from the construction process, and resulted scenario.

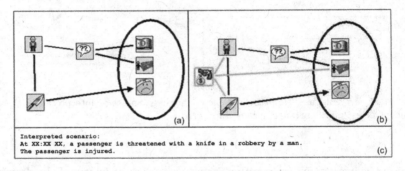

Interpreted scenario:
At XX:XX XX, a passenger is threatened with a knife in a robbery by a man.
The passenger is injured.

(c)

Fig. 11.22. An example of (a) user input, (b) proposed new concept and links resulted from the interpretation process, and resulted scenario.

Based on the interpretation results, the interface displays an associated scenario as feedback to a users icon-based message. The user can check the resulted scenario and use it to fine tune her/his icon arrangement on the drawing area if necessary. The scenario generator works by simple concept-name recognition and substitution of the property-names by their values controlled by XML format. A category provides some possible scenarios that can be selected depending on the concept-name. A concept can have many categories, but different set of properties values to fill in. Fig. 11.23 shows an example of a scenario template for "Robbery".

```
<scenario>
   <category>
      <concept name="Robbery"/>
      <properties>
         <property name="agent"/>
         <property name="patient"/>
         <property name="instrument"/>
         <property name="beginTime"/>
      </properties>
      <template><random>
         <li> At <get name="beginTime" type="DateTime"/>, <get name="agent" type="Human"/>
              wielding <get name="instrument" type="AgentProperty"/> robs
              <get name="patient" type="Human"/>.
         </li>
         <li> At <get name="beginTime" type="DateTime"/>, <get name="patient" type="Human"/>
              is threatened with <get name="instrument" type="AgentProperty"/> in a robbery
              by <get name="agent" type="Human"/>.
         </li>
      </random></template>
   </category>
</scenario>
```

Fig. 11.23. An example unit in the scenario-template database.

11.8.1.1. *Multiple messages processor*

The interface allows users to create multiple pages of icon-based messages. Later when these messages are submitted, an aggregated view about the state of the world can be formed based on observations of multiple users. In both situations, overlay operation is utilized.[55] It is a formal operation based on unification of typed feature structures. Overlay operates on two typed feature structures called covering and background. This operation can be seen as putting structures on top of each other (Fig. 11.24). We can view the background as the old state of the world, while the covering is a new incoming message

We defined the score (Eq. 11.1) of an overlay operation that reflects how well the covering fits the background in terms of non-conflicting features (*i.e.* property values) based on Pfleger et al.:[56]

$$score(co, bg, tc, cv) = \frac{co + bg - (tc + cv)}{co + bg + tc + cv} \in [-1...1] \qquad (11.1)$$

where co is the total number of non-conflicting or absent features and values in the covering; bg is the total number of non-conflicting or absent features and values in the background; tc is the total number of not-identical

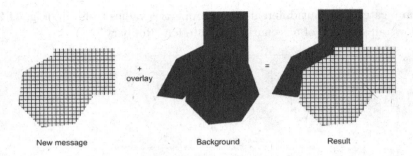

Fig. 11.24.   Schematic view of overlay operation: "putting shapes on each other".

types of both the covering and the background; and cv is the total number of
conflicting values (if the value of a feature of the background is overwritten).
The score(co, bg, tc, cv) = 1 indicates the feature structure are unifiable;
score(co, bg, tc, cv) = -1 indicates all information from the background
has been overwritten. The current implementation processes all incoming
messages that have overlay score bigger than 0. Those messages whose
overlay score less and equal to 0 are stored in a stack until there are some
evidences (other new messages) that support these messages.

We also defined an activation level of concepts in the aggregated world-
model. The level will grow if new incoming messages include these concepts.
Their activation level decays at predefined intervals, otherwise. By this
mechanism, only up-to-date concepts are active in the aggregated world-
model.

The entire interpretation process and the resulted world model do not
include any private information of the users, except information about location. Each individual that is involved in an aggression situation, is treated
as an (anonymous) actor doing a certain action in a certain location in
the world. The information about these actors, combining with information about specific objects and events appeared in the world, builds up a
scenario of a certain aggression event. Using the proposed interpretation
method, the built interpretation about the state of the world is expected
based on reliable messages from trusted users; while those un-reliable messages (or those from distrusted users) by the mechanism eventually will be
discarded.

11.9. Evaluation

The automatic aggression detection system can be divided into two steps. A first step to detect the features and events in the incoming sensor data and a second step to combine these events (over time) into activities and scenarios. For surveillance/activity recognition in relatively controllable environments (*e.g.* rooms, offices) data can be collected quite easily. Thanks to the controlled environment, feature extraction and event recognition can also be robustly performed. In the train compartment however, we have to cope with more challenging circumstances. These include the varying (and unpredictable) light conditions throughout the course of the day, occlusion and echos as a result of the confined space of the compartment etc.

In order to evaluate the system, a data collection experiment was conducted to gather data that can be used to test the aggression detection algorithms. Due to the scarcity of this kind of recordings and the privacy issues involved, we hired semi-professional actors to perform the scenarios described above in a real train (Fig. 11.25). We used multiple microphones and camerasto record the actions. Most scenarios were performed in the middle of the train, where the two camerasin the middle have the largest overlap. The resulting dataset consists of recordings of aggressive as well as non-aggressive scenarios with multiple camerasand multiple microphones.

The recordings were manually annotated afterwards to establish the ground truths necessary to measure the performance of the detection systems. Overall results show that the system is able to detect potential unusual situations given the video streams and user inputs. The quantitative results of the individual algorithms have been included in the respective sections as much as possible.

We have tested the reporting tool in simulated scenarios with participants playing certain roles and reporting back to the center. The participants were divided into some groups of roles, such as normal passengers, conductors, policemen. The scenario presented to respondents in the form of photographs and a map of the environment with explicitly information on what direction they are looking at. During the experiments, the respondents were asked to report what they might see, hear, or even feel and experience.

Our target users were able to communicate their concepts appropriately using the provided reporting tool. Due to privacy issues real online testing has yet to be conducted yet. In the experiments we only focused on the integration of the HCI system using the developed framework. In particular

Fig. 11.25. The scenarios were performed by semi professional actors and captured on multiple cameras and multiple microphones.

to the output module, preliminary results show that the module is able to receive abstract representation of the world and dialog actions and generate appropriate multimodal responses based on available modalities and user contexts. However, some issues emerge during experiments, which can be classified in two categories:

- Users wanted to report about events, which were out of the systems domain.
- Not all functions of the module were tested. The combination of the unrealistic experiment setup and the respondents not being experienced reporters may have caused them to miss important events and showing only controlled emotions.

11.10. Conclusions and future work

An increase of security as a result of the employment of surveillance systems is commonly associated with a decrease in privacy. Key issues of concern by the general public are that the system might be abused once installed or that the system might be used in covert ways. Futhermore there is a general unease at 'being watched' and a fear that there may be a gradual erosion of civil liberties.

The system we presented in this chapter does not modify the way the surveillance process is conducted today. Human operators are still neccesary to make the decisions. The system only allows for a more efficient way to detect (possible) aggressive situations in train compartments. Train travellers can report about aggressive situations without having there identity directly exposed to other travellers or the surveillance system. As such, our system does not lead to a decrease in privacy, however it also does not lead to an increase in privacy.

Ongoing work is on creating an experiment setup for on-line testing of the system that complies with the privacy regulations for public transport in the Netherlands. We expect that our system will contribute to public safety by increasing the chance of detection and thus helping to prevent all forms of aggression and terrorism.

References

1. G. L. Foresti, C. Micheloni, L. Snidaro, P. Remagnino, and T. Ellis, Active video-based surveillance system: the low-level image and video processing techniques needed for implementation, *IEEE Signal Processing Magazine.* **22**(2), 25–37, (2005).
2. H. Tao, H. S. Sawhney, and R. Kumar, Object tracking with Bayesian estimation of dynamic layer representations, *IEEE Transactions on Pattern Analysis and Machine Intelligence.* **24**(1), 75–89, (2002).
3. J. Shin, S. Kim, S. Kang, S. Lee, J. Paik, B. Abidi, and M. Abidi, Optical flow-based real-time object tracking using non-prior training active feature mode, *ELSEVIER Real-Time Imaging.* **11**(3), 204–218, (2005).
4. C. Clavel, T. Ehrette, and G. Richard. Events Detection for an Audio-Based Surveillance System. In *Proc. IEEE Int. Conf. on Multimedia and Expo*, pp. 1306–1309, (2005).
5. R. S. Goldhor. Recognition of Environmental Sounds. In *Proc. of IEEE Int. Conf. on Acoustics, Speech and Signal Processing*, vol. 1, pp. 149–152, (1993).
6. A. Härmä, M. F. McKinney, and J. Skowronek. Automatic surveillance of the acoustic activity in our living environment. In *Proc. of the IEEE Int. Conf. on Multimedia and Expo (ICME 2005)*, (2005).
7. S. Spors, R. Rabenstein, and N. Strobel. Joint Audio-video Object Tracking. In *IEEE International Conference on Image Processing (ICIP)*, vol. 1, pp. 393–396, Thessaloniki, Greece, (2001).
8. D. N. Zotkin, R. Duraiswami, and L. S. Davis, Joint Audio-Visual Tracking using Particle Filters, *EURASIP Journal on Applied Signal Processing.* **1**, 1154–1164, (2002).
9. D. Gatica-Perez, G. Lathoud, I. McCowan, J. M. Odobez, and D. Moore. Audio-visual speaker tracking with importance particle filters. In *Proc. of the Int. Conf. on Image Processing (ICIP 2003)*, vol. 3, pp. 25–28, (2003).

10. S. Hongeng, F. Bremond, and R. Nevatia. Bayesian Framework for Video Surveillance Application. In *Proc. Int. Conf. on Pattern Recognition (ICPR'00)*, vol. 1, pp. 164–170, (2000).

11. O. Javed, Z. Rasheed, O. Alatas, and M. Shah. Knight: A Real-time Surveillance System for Multiple Overlapping and Nonoverlapping Cameras. In *Proc. Int. Conf. on Multimedia and Expo (ICME 2003)*, vol. 1, pp. 649–652, (2003).

12. S. A. Velastin, M. Vicencio-Silva, B. Lo, and L. Khoudou, A distributed surveillance system for improving security in public transport networks, *Meas Control, Special Issue on Remote Surveillance Measurement and Control.* **35** (8), 209–213, (2002).

13. F. Cupillard, A. Avanzi, F. Bremond, and M. Thonnat. Video Understanding For Metro Surveillance. In *Proc. of the IEEE Int. Conf. on Networking, Sensing and Control*, vol. 1, pp. 186–191, Taipei, Taiwan, (2004).

14. Y. Ivanov, C. Stauffer, A. Bobick, and W. E. L. Grimson. Video Surveillance of Interactions. In *Proceedings of the Second IEEE Workshop on Visual Surveillance*, (1999).

15. D. Gillmor, We the Media: The Rise of Citizen Journalists, *National Civic Review.* **93**(3), 58–63, (2004). doi: 10.1002/ncr.62.

16. L. Palen and S. B. L. Citizen. Citizen communications in crisis: anticipating a future of ICT-supported public participation. In *Proc. of the SIGCHI Conf. on Human Factors in Computing Systems (CHI '07)*, pp. 727–736, ACM, New York, NY, (2007).

17. S. Ramaswamy, M. Rogers, A. D. Crockett, D. Feaker, and M.Carter, WHISPER - Service Integrated Incident Management System,, *Int. Journal of Intelligent Control and Systems.* **11**(2), 114–123, (2006).

18. S. Mehrotra, C. Butts, D. Kalashnikov, N. Venkatasubramanian, K. Altintas, P. Hariharan, H. Lee, Y. Ma, A. Myers, J. Wickramasuriya, R. Eguchi, and C. Huyck. CAMAS: a Citizen Awareness System for Crisis Mitigation. In *Proc. of ACM SIGMOD'04, Int. Conf. Management of Data*, pp. 955–956, USA, (2004).

19. J. Otten, B. van Heijningen, and J. F. Lafortune. The Virtual Crisis Management Center - An ICT implementation to canalize Information. In *Proc. of ISCRAM'04*, Belgium, (2004).

20. A. Singhal and E. Rattine-Flaherty, Pencils and Photos as Tools of Communicative Research and Praxis, *International Communication Gazette.* **68**(4), 313–330, (2006).

21. M. Yazdani and S. Mealing. Communicating through Pictures. In *Artificial Intelligent Review*, vol. 2-3, *9*, pp. 205–213. Springer Netherlands, (1995).

22. S. Fitrianie. An Icon-based Communication Tool on a PDA. Postgraduate thesis, Eindhoven University of Technology, (2004).

23. P. L. Albacete, S. Chang, G. Polese, and B. Baker. Iconic language design for people with significant speech and multiple impairments. In *Proceedings of the first annual ACM conference on Assistive technologies'94*, vol. 1458, pp. 23–30, Marina Del Rey, California, United States, (1994). ACM New York.

24. A. Basu, S. Sarkar, K. Chakraborty, S. Bhattarcharya, M. Choudhury, and

R. Patel. Vernacular Education and Communication Tool for the People with Multiple Disabilities. In *Development by Design Conference*, Bangalore, (2002).

25. C. K. Bliss, *The Blissymbols Picture Book*. (Semantography Press, Sidney, 1984).

26. T. I. Housz. The Elephant's Memory. http://www.khm.de/~timot, (1994-1996).

27. C. Beardon, CD-Icon: an Iconic Language-Based on Conceptual Dependency, *Intelligent Tutoring Media*. **3**(4), 111–116, (1992).

28. N. E. M. P. Leemans. VIL: A Visual Inter Lingua, Doctoral Dissertation, Worcester Polytechnic Institute, USA, (2002).

29. S. Fitrianie and L. J. M. Rothkrantz. Communication in Crisis Situations using Icon Language. In *Proc. of IEEE ICME '05*, pp. 1370–1373, Netherlands, (2005).

30. S. Fitrianie, D. Datcu, and L. J. M. Rothkrantz. Constructing Knowledge of the World in Crisis Situations using Visual Language. In *Proc. of IEEE SMC'06*, vol. 1, pp. 121–126, Taiwan, (2006).

31. R. Schank, Conceptual Dependency - a Theory of Natural Language Understanding, *Cognitive Psychology*. **3**(4), 552–631, (1972).

32. C. K. Ogden. Basic English - A General Introduction with Rules and Grammar, (1930).

33. Z. Yang and L. J. M. Rothkrantz. Dynamic Scripting in Crisis Environments. In *HCI International'07*, vol. LNCS 4560, pp. 554–563, China, (2007). Springer Berlin/Heidelberg.

34. S. Fitrianie, D. Datcu, and L. J. M. Rothkrantz. Human Communication based on Icons in Crisis Environments. In *HCI International '07*, vol. LNCS 4560, pp. 57–66, China, (2007). Springer Berlin/Heidelberg.

35. U. J. Dymon, An Analysis of Emergency Map Symbology, *Int. Journal of Emergency Management*. **1**(3), 227–237, (2003).

36. B. Tatomir and L. J. M. Rothkrantz. Crisis Management Using Mobile Ad-Hoc Wireless Networks. In *Proc. of ISCRAM'05*, Belgium, (2005).

37. P. Ekman and W. Friesen, *Facial Action Coding System*. (Consulting Psychologists Press, Inc., Palo Alto California, USA, 1978).

38. Viola and M. Jones, Robust Real-time Object Detection, *International Journal of Computer Vision*. (2001).

39. T. F. Cootes, G. J. Edwards, and C. J. Taylor. Active appearance models. In *European Conference on Computer Vision*, vol. LNCS 1407, pp. 484–498, Germany, (1998). Springer.

40. V. Vapnik, *The Nature of Statistical Learning Theory*. (Springer-Verlag, New York, 1995).

41. V. Vapnik, *Statistical Learning Theory*. (John Wiley and Sons, Inc., New York, 1998).

42. T. Kanade, J. F. Cohn, and Y. Tian. Comprehensive database for facial expression analysis. In *Proc. of the 4th IEEE Int. Conf. On Automatic Face and Gestures Recognition*, pp. 46–53, France, (2000).

43. D. Datcu and L. J. M. Rothkrantz. Semantic Audio-Visual Data Fusion for

Automatic Emotion Recognition. In *Proc. of Euromedia 2008*, pp. 58–65, Eurosis, Portugal, (2008).

44. D. Datcu and L. J. M. Rothkrantz. The recognition of emotions from speech using GentleBoost Classifier. In *Proc. of CompSysTech'06*, Bulgaria, (2006).
45. F. Burkhardt, A. Paeschke, M. Rolfes, W. Sendlmeier, and B. Weiss. A Database of German Emotional Speech. In *Proc. Interspeech*, pp. 1517–1520, Lissabon, Portugal, (2005).
46. O. Martin, I. Kotsia, B. Macq, and I. Pitas. The eNTERFACE'05 Audio-Visual Emotion Database. In *Proc. of the 22nd Int. Conf. on Data Engineering Workshops (ICDEW'06)*, p. 8. IEEE Computer Society, (2006).
47. L. Wang, W. Hu, and T. Tan, Recent Developments in Human Motion Analysis, *Pattern Recognition.* **36**(3), 585–601, (2003).
48. B. Hese va. Real-Time Localization and Tracking of Multiple People in a Closed Environment with Facial Detection Using a Multi-Camera Setup. Master's thesis, Delft University of Technology, Delft, Netherlands, (2008).
49. R. Schank and R. Abelson, *Scripts, Plans, Goals and Understanding.* (Hillsdale, NJ: Erlbaum, 1977).
50. A. Bandura, *Social Foundations of Thought and Action: A Social-Cognitive Theory.* (Prentice-Hall, Englewood Cliffs, NJ, 1986).
51. D. Datcu and L. J. M. Rothkrantz. Multimodal workbench for human emotion recognition. In *Multimodal workbench for human emotion recognition, Software Demo at IEEE Computer Society Conference on Computer Vision and Pattern Recognition (CVPR'07)*, Minneapolis, Minnesota, USA, (2007).
52. M. B. Stegmann. The AAM-API: An Open Source Active Appearance Model Implementation. In *Medical Image Computing and Computer-Assisted Intervention - MICCAI 2003, 6th Int. Conference*, pp. 951–952, Montréal, Canada (nov, 2003). Springer.
53. D. Datcu, Z. Yang, and L. Rothkrantz. Multimodal workbench for automatic surveillance applications. In *Multimodal Surveillance: Sensors, Algorithms, and Systems*, pp. 311–338. Artech House Publishers (July, 2007). ISBN 1596931841.
54. R. Dor and L. J. M. Rothkrantz, The Ears Mind, An emergent self-organising model of auditory perception, *Journal of experimental and theoretical artificial intelligence.* (2008). Accepted for publication.
55. J. Alexandersson and T. Becker. The Formal Foundations Underlying Overlay. In *Proc. of International Workshop on Computational Semantics (IWCS-5)*, pp. 22–36, Netherlands, (2003).
56. N. Pfleger, J. Alexandersson, and T. Becker. Scoring Functions for Overlay and their Application in Discourse Processing. In *Proc. of KONVENS 2002*, pp. 139–146, Germany, (2002).

Chapter 12

K-Means Clustering for Content-Based Document Management in Intelligence

Sergio Decherchi, Paolo Gastaldo, Rodolfo Zunino

University of Genoa, Dept. Biophysical and Electronic Engineering
Via Opera Pia 11a, 16145, Genova (Italy)
{sergio.decherchi, paolo.gastaldo, rodolfo.zunino}@unige.it

Text-mining methods have become a key feature for homeland-security technologies, as they can help explore effectively increasing masses of digital documents in the search for relevant information. This chapter presents a model for document clustering that arranges unstructured documents into content-based homogeneous groups. The overall paradigm is hybrid because it combines pattern-recognition grouping algorithms with semantic-driven processing. First, a semantic-based metric measures distances between documents, by combining a content-based with a behavioral analysis; the metric considers both lexical properties and the structure and styles that characterize the processed documents. Secondly, the model relies on a Radial Basis Function (RBF) kernel-based mapping for clustering. As a result, the major novelty aspect of the proposed approach is to exploit the implicit mapping of RBF kernel functions to tackle the crucial task of normalizing similarities while embedding semantic information in the whole mechanism. In addition, the present work exploits a real-world benchmark to compare the performance of the conventional k-means algorithm and recent k-means clustering schemes, which apply Johnson-Lindenstrauss-type random projections for a reduction in dimensionality before clustering. Experimental results show that the document clustering framework based on kernel k-means provide an effective tool to generate consistent structures for information access and retrieval.

Contents

12.1. Introduction

The automated surveillance of information sources is of strategic importance to effective homeland security.[1-3] The increased availability of data-
intensive heterogeneous sources provides a valuable asset for the intelligence
task, but such a situation poses the major issue of sifting security-relevant
information from clutter. Data-mining methods have therefore become a
key feature for security-related technologies,[3,4] as they can help explore
effectively increasing masses of digital data in the search for relevant information. In fact, the pristine view of using mining methods for pinpoint-
ing critical situations is progressively fading away due to the unattainable
classification accuracy;[5] by contrast, the use of data-mining tools for the
discovery and acquisition of strategic information is more and more widely
accepted.[1,4,6]

   Text mining techniques provide a powerful tool to deal with the large
amounts of text data[7-11] (both structured and unstructured) that are gathered from/any multimedia source (e.g., from Optical Character Recognition,
from audio via speech transcription, from web-crawling agents, etc.). The
general area of text-mining methods comprises various approaches:[11] de-
tection/tracking tools continuously monitor specific topics over time; document classifiers label individual files and build up models for possible
subjects of interest; clustering tools process documents for detecting relevant relations among those subjects. As a result, text mining can profitably
support intelligence and security activities in identifying, tracking, extracting, classifying and discovering patterns, so that the outcomes can generate
alerts notifications accordingly.[12-15]

   This work addresses document clustering and presents a dynamic, adaptive clustering model to arrange unstructured documents into content-based
homogeneous groups. Clustering tools can support security applications in

the development of predictive models of the observed phenomenon that automatically derive the thematic categories from the data. Hence, intelligence analysis can exploit the unsupervised nature of document clustering to tackle 1) scenarios that cannot rely on a set of predefined topics or 2) scenarios that cannot be properly modeled by a classifier because of the non-stationary nature of the underlying phenomenon, which requires continuous updating for incorporating unseen patterns.

The present framework implements a hybrid paradigm, which combines a content-driven similarity processing with pattern-recognition grouping algorithms. Distances between documents are worked out by a semantic-based hypermetric. The specific approach integrates a content-based with a user-behavioral analysis, as it takes into account both lexical and style-related features of the documents at hand. The clustering engine builds up a structured representation of the document space in a hierarchical fashion; a top-down hierarchical strategy supports the clustering model.[16] The core clustering strategy exploits a kernel-based version of the conventional k-means algorithm[17,18] to group similar documents; the present implementation relies on a Radial Basis Function (RBF) kernel-based mapping.[19] The advantage of using such a kernel consists in supporting normalization implicitly; normalization is a critical issue in most text-mining applications, and prevents that extensive properties of documents (such as length, lexicon, etc) may distort representation and affect performance.

The crucial novelty aspect of the proposed approach consists indeed in using the implicit normalization of RBF kernel functions while embedding semantic information in the whole mechanism. A kernel-based formulation can effectively support the critical normalization process by reducing all inner products within a limited range, thus avoiding that extensive properties of documents (length, lexicon, etc) may distort representation and ultimately affect clustering performance. The hybrid method is compared with the classical text-mining approach based on a vector-space representation of documents. Advanced approaches in the vector-space paradigm are also considered, which apply Johnson-Lindenstrauss-type random projections for a reduction in dimensionality before clustering.[20] The analysis tackles in particular the critical aspect concerning the trade off between clustering accuracy and computational complexity, which is a general issue in all text-mining applications, and can be particularly relevant when using k-means for document clustering.

Two real-world benchmarks provide the experimental domains for the present framework. The first experimental session exploits a standard benchmark for content-based document management, the Reuters database,[21] to show that the document clustering framework based on kernel k-means provide an effective tool to generate consistent structures for information access and retrieval. Indeed, the second experimental session exploits the largest real email corpus in the public domain, the Enron mail dataset,[22] to evaluate the ability of the proposed framework to deal with a scenario that resembles the kind of data collected as part of counterterrorism efforts.[23]

The rest of the chapter is organized as follows. Section 12.2 outlines the general document-clustering model and discusses the crucial aspects to be addressed when designing such model. Section 12.3 introduces the two fundamental parts of the proposed clustering methodology: the document similarity measure, which integrates a content-based with a user-behavioral analysis, and the kernel-based k-means clustering. Section 12.4 outlines the overall document-clustering model and describes the use of Johnson-Lindenstrauss-type random projections for a reduction in dimensionality before clustering. The experimental results are presented in Section 12.5, and, finally, some concluding remarks are drawn in Section 12.6.

12.2. Document Clustering in Text Mining for Security Applications

Huge quantities of valuable knowledge are embedded in unstructured texts that are gathered from heterogeneous multimedia sources, ranging from hardcopy documents via Optical Character Recognition, to audio via speech transcription, to link analysis mining via web-crawling agents, etc. The resulting mass of data gives law-enforcement and intelligence agencies a valuable asset, but also poses the major issue of extracting and analyzing structured knowledge from unstructured texts.

Text-mining technologies in security applications[6,12-15] can automate, improve and speed up the analysis of existing datasets, with the goal of preventing criminal acts by the cataloguing of various threads and pieces of information, which would remain unnoticed when using traditional means of investigation. In general, the text-mining process may involve different sub-goals,[11,14] such as information extraction, topic tracking, summarization, categorization, clustering, concept linkage, information visualization, and question answering. For prevention, text mining techniques can help identify novel "information trends" revealing new scenarios and threats to be monitored; for investigation, these technologies can help distil relevant information about known scenarios whose actors, situations and relations must be completed, structuring them in patterns really usable for end-users in conjunction with the instruments and methods they daily use.

Within the text mining framework, the present work addresses document clustering, which represents one of the most effective techniques to organize documents in an unsupervised manner. Clustering tools can support the development of predictive models of the observed phenomena, and derive automatically the thematic categories embedded in the data. Therefore, such an unsupervised framework makes document clustering a promising solution for those intelligence tasks that either lack a set of predefined topics, or cannot rely on an exhaustive training set. Clustering can be used to refine and continuously maintain a model of a known distribution of documents, and therefore supports investigation activities by a tracking action. At the same time, clustering can pinpoint emerging, unknown patterns by identifying people, objects, or actions that deserve resource commitment or attention, and thereby support prevention by a novelty-detection capability.

When dealing with text documents, clustering techniques exploits machine learning, natural language processing (NLP), information retrieval (IR), information extraction (IE) and knowledge management to discover new, previously unknown information by automatically extracting information from different written resources.[24] In the following, Section 12.2.1 outlines the document retrieval model, which in a generic process framework for a text-mining application is designed to define how a document should be represented. Then, Section 12.2.2 addresses the specific document clustering problem.

12.2.1. *Document indexing*

A text mining framework should always be supported by an information extraction (IE) model,[25–27] which is designed to pre-process digital text documents and to organize the information according to a given structure that can be directly interpreted by a machine learning system; in this regard, Figure 12.1 sketches a generic process model for a document-clustering application. Actually, IE defines how a document and a query are represented and how the relevance of a document to a query is computed.

Document retrieval models typically describe a document D as a set of representative tokens called *index terms*, which result from a series of operations performed on the original text. Stop-words removal and stemming typically are among those operations: the former takes out frequent and semantically non-selective expressions from text; stemming simplifies inflectional forms (sometimes derivationally related forms) of a word down to a common radix form (*e.g.*, by simplifying plurals or verb persons).

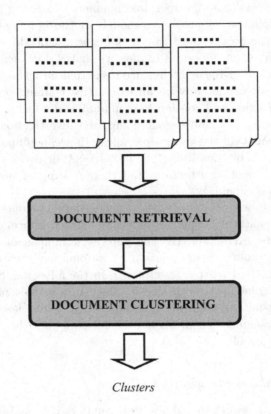

Clusters

Fig. 12.1.   A generic process model for a document-clustering application

Thus, a document D is eventually reduced to a sequence of terms and is represented as a vector, which lies in a space spanned by the *dictionary* (or vocabulary) $\mathcal{T} = \{t_j;\ j = 1,..,n_T\}$. The dictionary collects all terms used to represent any document D, and can be assembled empirically by gathering the terms that occurs at least once in a document collection $\mathcal{D} = \{D_1, \ldots, D_n\}$. As a consequence, by this representation one loses the original relative ordering of terms within each document. Different models[25,27] can be used to retrieve index terms and to generate the vector that represents a document, D. The classical Boolean model involves a binary-valued vector, $\mathbf{v} = \{b_j; \ j=1,..,n_T\}$, in which each bit component, $b_j \in \{0,1\}$, just indicates the presence (absence) of term t_j in the document. This approach is most effective for fast searching but proves inaccurate when content-based analysis is required, because it does not render the actual distributions of terms within the considered documents.

The *vector space* model[28] is the most widely used method for text mining and, in particular, for document clustering. Given a collection of documents $\mathcal{D}$, the vector space model represents each document D as a vector of real-valued weight terms $\mathbf{v} = \{w_j; \ j=1,..,n_T\}$. Each component of the n_T-dimensional vector is a non-negative *term weight*, w_j, that characterizes the j-th term and denotes the relevance of the term itself within the document D.

Several approaches have been proposed to compute term weights.[29] The popular *tf-idf* weighting scheme[30,31] relies on two basic assumptions: 1) the number of occurrences of a term t in a document D is proportional to the importance of t within D (term frequency, *tf*); 2) the number of occurrences of t across different documents is *inversely* proportional to the discriminating power of t, *i.e.*, a term that appears frequently throughout a set of documents is not effective in localizing a specific document in the set (inverse document frequency, *idf*). Weights computed by tf-idf techniques are often normalized so as to contrast the tendency of tf-idf to emphasize lengthy documents.

Document indexing is a necessary and critical component of any text mining tool, especially because it allows a system to filter out irrelevant information and attain an efficient and cogent representation of content. Such results may be used for document retrieval, as is the case for typical search engines;[32] in the security-related applications that are the scope of this chapter, however, the index-based representation constitutes an intermediate step for comparing documents and arranging them into homogeneous groups, which is the ultimate purpose of the clustering engine.

12.2.2. *Document clustering*

Clustering is conventionally ascribed to the realm of pattern recognition and machine learning.[33] When applied to text mining, clustering algorithms are designed to discover groups in the set of documents such that the documents within a group are more similar to one another than to documents of other groups. As opposed to text categorization,[11] in which predefined categories enter the learning procedure, document clustering follows an unsupervised approach to search, retrieve, and organize key topics when a proper set of categories cannot be defined *a-priori*. The unsupervised paradigm can address challenging scenarios, in which local episodes of interest can fade away in the clutter of very large datasets, where events or profiles are ambiguous, unknown, or possibly changing with respect to the original models.

The document clustering problem can be defined as follows. One should first define a set of documents $\mathcal{D} = \{D_1, \ldots, D_n\}$, a similarity measure (or distance metric), and a partitioning criterion, which is usually implemented by a cost function. *Flat* clustering[25] creates a set of clusters without any a-priori assumption about the structure among clusters; it typically requires that the number of clusters to be specified in advance, although adaptive methods exist for determining the cluster cardinality adaptively.[34] Hence, one sets the desired number of clusters, K, and the goal is to compute a membership function $\phi : \mathcal{D} \to \{1, \ldots, K\}$ such that ϕ minimizes the partitioning cost with respect to the similarities among documents. On the other hand, *hierarchical* clustering[25] arranges groups in a structural, multilevel fashion and does not require a pre-specified number of clusters; these advantages often come at the cost of a lower computational efficiency. Hierarchical clustering need not define the cardinality, K, because it applies a series of nested partitioning tasks, which eventually yield a hierarchy of groups. In addition to that choice between a flat or a hierarchical scheme, three main issues should be addressed when designing the overall clustering framework.

The first issue is the curse of dimensionality. When using a vector-space approach, documents lie in a space whose dimensionality typically ranges from several thousands to tens of thousands. Nonetheless, most documents normally contain a very limited fraction (1%–5%) of the total number of admissible terms in the entire vocabulary, hence the vectors representing documents are very sparse. This can make learning extremely difficult in such a high-dimensional space, especially due to so-called the curse of dimensionality.[35] It is typically desirable to project documents preliminarily into a lower-dimensional subspace, which preserves the semantic structure of the document space but facilitates the use of traditional clustering algorithms. Several methods for low-dimensional document projections have been proposed,[36] such as spectral clustering,[37] clustering using the Latent

Semantic Index (LSI),[38,39] clustering using the Locality Preserving Indexing (LPI),[40] and clustering based on nonnegative matrix factorization.[41] Those methods are quite popular but also exhibit theoretical and practical drawbacks. Both the LSI and the LPI model rely on Singular Value Decomposition (SVD),[42] which optimizes a least-square criterion and best performs when data are characterized by a normal distribution. In fact, the latter assumption does not hold in the general case of term-indexed document matrixes. Besides, LSI, LPI and spectral clustering all require the computation of eigenvalues; as such, these methods often prove both heavy from a computational viewpoint and quite sensitive to outliers. Spectral clustering has also been proved to be a special case of a weighted form of the kernel k-means.[43] Nonnegative matrix factorization (NMF) differs from other rank reduction methods for vector spaces, especially because of specific constraints that produce nonnegative basis vectors. However, the iterative update method for solving NMF problem is computationally expensive and produces a non-unique factorization.

The second issue in setting up an effective clustering process is the definition of the similarity measure. Since the partitioning criterion often relates strictly to the similarity measure, the choice of the underlying metrics is critical for getting meaningful clusters. For documents, it is normal to address some content-based similarity, and most clustering tools adopt the vector-space model because such a framework easily supports the popular cosine similarity:

$$sim(D_i, D_j) = \frac{\mathbf{v}_i \cdot \mathbf{v}_j}{|\mathbf{v}_i| \, |\mathbf{v}_j|} \tag{12.1}$$

where $\mathbf{v}_i$ is the vector representation of the document D_i and the operator $(\cdot)$ denotes the conventional inner product in the vector space. The normalization implied by the denominator in (12.1) prevents that two documents having similar distributions of terms appear distant from each other just because one is much longer than the other. In fact, the cosine similarity seems to not outperform the conventional Euclidean distance when high dimensional spaces are concerned.[44]

The third issue in clustering for text mining concerns the specific algorithm to be implemented. Although the literature offers a wide variety of clustering algorithms, the majority of research in text mining involves three approaches, namely, *k-means* clustering, Self Organizing Maps (SOMs), and the Expectation-Maximization (EM) algorithm.[27,45–47] Alternative approaches include models based on fuzzy clustering techniques.[48,49]

Furthermore, on a slightly different perspective, the works of Hammouda et al.[50] and Chim et al.[51] proposed document-clustering schemes exploiting a phrase-based document similarity. The former scheme[50] exploits the Document Index Graph (DIG), which indexes the documents while maintaining the sentence structure in the original documents; the latter scheme[51] is based on the Suffix Tree Document (STD) model.[52]

12.3. Hybrid Approach to k-Means Clustering

The hybrid approach described in this Section combines the specific advantages of content-driven processing with the effectiveness of an established pattern-recognition grouping algorithm. The ultimate goal of the clustering process is to group a set of documents into a (possibly adaptive) structure of clusters, which contain documents that are affine for both contents and structural features. The presentation of the method will mostly address the three main issues discussed in the previous section.

With respect to the dimensionality problem, the method extends a conventional vector-space representation, mostly because that approach was shown to suffer from curse-of-dimensionality problems even in the presence of sparse matrixes. Even though a document is represented by the set of composing terms annotated with frequency and positional information, the subsequent processing steps do not involve any matrix-intensive computation such as SVD-related methods. This is intentionally done to reduce sensitivity to outliers; moreover, the dimensionality problem is strictly related to the effectiveness of the actual clustering strategy adopted, and the proposed approach facilitates kernel-based implementations as will be clarified in the following.

Document similarity is defined by a content-based distance, which combines a classical distribution-based measure with a behavioural analysis of the style features of the compared documents. The involved metric thus considers lexical properties, the structures, and some style features that characterize the processed documents. The method intentionally does not consider semantic-based information (such as the use of ontologies and deductive methods)[53] mostly to keep the computational cost within reasonable limits, although the overall approach preserves a general validity and is therefore open to future expansions toward that direction.

The core engine relies on a kernel-based version of the classical k-means partitioning algorithm[17,18] and groups similar documents by a top-down hierarchical process. In the kernel-based approach, every document is mapped into an infinite-dimensional Hilbert space, where only inner products among elements are meaningful and computable. The kernel trick applies to any clustering method, and in the present case the kernel-based version of k-means[54] provides a major advantage over the standard k-means formulation.

In the following, $\mathcal{D} = \{D_u; u= 1,..,n_D\}$ will denote the *corpus*, holding the collection of documents to be clustered. The set $\mathcal{T} = \{t_j; j= 1,..,n_T\}$ will denote the *vocabulary*, which is the collection of terms that occur at least one time in $\mathcal{D}$ after the pre-processing steps of each document $D \in \mathcal{D}$ (*e.g.*, stop-words removal, stemming). Accordingly, $\mathbf{d}$ will represent the document D as a sequence of indexes; thus $\mathbf{d}_u = \left\{ d_q^{(u)}; q = 1,.., n_E^{(u)} \right\}$, where $d_q^{(u)}$ is the index in $\mathcal{T}$ of the q-th term in D_u and $n_E^{(u)}$ is the number of terms in document D_u. Obviously, the order of the indexes in $\mathbf{d}_u$ matches the relative ordering of the terms in the document. Figure 12.2 gives an example of how vector $\mathbf{d}$ is generated. The vector includes the indexes of the terms that appear in the text. Thus, the term "analyst" is represented by its index in the vocabulary (in the example, number 21); analogously, the verb "said" is represented by the index of the corresponding radix form "say" (in the example, number 105). The same procedure applies to the following words included in the text.

12.3.1. *Document distance measure*

A novel aspect of the method described here is the use of a document-distance that takes into account both a conventional content-based similarity metric and a behavioral similarity criterion. The latter term aims to improve the overall performance of the clustering framework by including the structure and style of the documents in the process of similarity evaluation. To support the proposed document distance measure, a document D is here represented by a pair of vectors, $\mathbf{v}\prime$ and $\mathbf{v}\prime\prime$.

Vector $\mathbf{v}\prime(D)$ actually addresses the content description of a document D; it can be viewed as the conventional n_T-dimensional vector that associates each term $t \in \mathcal{T}$ with the normalized frequency, *tf*, of that term in the document D. Therefore, the k-th element of the vector $\mathbf{v}\prime(D_u)$ is defined as:

$$v'_{k,u} = \frac{tf_{k,u}}{\sum\limits_{l=1}^{n_T} tf_{l,u}} \tag{12.2}$$

where $tf_{k,u}$ is the frequency of the k-th term in document D_u. Thus $\mathbf{v}'$
represents a document by a classical vector model, and uses term frequencies
to set the weights associated to each element. Thanks to its local descriptive
nature, $\mathbf{v}'$ can be worked out without using global properties of the corpus
$\mathcal{D}$ such as the idf measure.

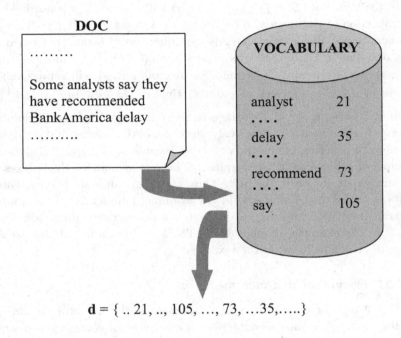

$$\mathbf{d} = \{ \ .. \ 21, .., \ 105, \ ..., \ 73, \ ...35,.....\}$$

Fig. 12.2.   Vector $\mathbf{d}$ represents the document as a sequence of indexes

From a different perspective, the structural properties of a document,
D, are represented by a set of probability distributions associated with the
terms in the vocabulary. Each term $t \in \mathcal{T}$. that occurs in D_u is associated with a distribution function that gives the spatial probability density
function (pdf) of t in D_u. Such a distribution, $p_{t,u}(s)$, is generated under the hypothesis that, when detecting the k-th occurrence of a term t
at the normalized position $s_k \in [0,1]$ in the text, the spatial pdf of the
term can be approximated by a Gaussian distribution centered around s_k.
In other words, the proposed behavioral similarity criterion supposes that
if the term t_j is found at position s_k within a document, another document with a similar structure is expected to include the same term at the

same position or in a neighborhood thereof, with a probability defined by a Gaussian pdf. Although empirical, the (practically reasonable) assumption is that the spatial probability density function of a term t in a document can characterize the document itself. In fact, one must be aware that such an assumption may not hold for heavily unstructured text data. In this respect, the eventual distance value, $\Delta(D_u, D_v)$ between two documents should properly mix the relative contribution of the two similarity criterions according to the applicative scenario; such aspect will be addressed later in this section. Actually, the ultimate validation of the document-distance measure will only stem from testing the empirical performance of the clustering framework on the experimental domain.

To derive a formal expression of the pdf, assume that the u-th document, D_u, holds n_O occurrences of terms after simplifications; if a term occurs more than once, each occurrence is counted individually when computing n_O, which can be viewed as a measure of the length of the document. The spatial pdf can be defined as:

$$p_{t,u}(s) = \frac{1}{A} \sum_{k=1}^{n_O} G(s_k, \lambda) = \frac{1}{A} \sum_{k=1}^{n_O} \frac{1}{\sqrt{2\pi}\lambda} \exp\left[-\frac{(s-s_k)^2}{\lambda^2}\right] \tag{12.3}$$

where A is a normalization term.

In practice, one uses a discrete approximation of (12.3) first by segmenting evenly the document D into S sections. Then, an S-dimensional vector is generated for each term $t \in \mathcal{T}$, and each element estimates the probability that the term t occurs in the corresponding section of the document. The following algorithm sketches the exact procedure to work out $\mathbf{v}''(D)$.

12.3.1.1. *Algorithm for generating* $\mathbf{v}''(D)$

Input: the vector $\mathbf{d}_i$ generated from the original document D_i
  the vector $\boldsymbol{\gamma} = \{\gamma_k; k = 1, ..., n_\gamma\}$ that approximates a discrete Gaussian distribution

(1) *Segmentation*
  Evenly segment D_i into S parts:
  $$\mathbf{d}_i = \mathbf{d}_i^{(1)} \cup \mathbf{d}_i^{(2)} \cup ... \cup \mathbf{d}_i^{(S)}$$
  where

$$\mathbf{d}_i^{(s)} = \left\{ d_i^{(i)} \middle| (s-1)\frac{n_E}{S} + 1 \leq q \leq s\frac{n_E}{S} \right\}$$

(2) *Term frequency*
For each $t_j \in T$, build up the vector $\boldsymbol{f}_j = \{f_{s,j}; s = 1, .., S\}$ as follows:

$$f_{s,j} = tf_{j,s}.$$

where $tf_{j,s}$ is the term frequency of the term t_j in the segment $\mathbf{d}_i^{(s)}$.

(3) *Probability distribution*
For each $t_j \in T$, build up the vector $\boldsymbol{\pi}_j = \{\pi_{s,j}; s=1,..,S\}$, which represents the discrete approximation of (12.3), as follows:

For $s=1$ to S
For $l = -\frac{n_\gamma - 1}{2}$ to $\frac{n_\gamma - 1}{2}$

$$\bar{\gamma}\left(s + l + \frac{n_\gamma - 1}{2}\right) = \gamma\left(l + \frac{n_\gamma + 1}{2}\right) \cdot f_{s,j}$$

For $m=1$ to S

$$\pi(m) = \pi(m) + \bar{\gamma}(m)$$

(4) *Build vector*
Work out $\mathbf{v}''(D)$ as follows:

$$\mathbf{v}''(D) = \{\boldsymbol{\pi}_1, .., \boldsymbol{\pi}_{n_T}\}$$

As a result, $\mathbf{v}''(D)$ is an array of n_T vectors having dimension S. Figure 12.3 sketches the procedure that supports the computation of $\mathbf{v}''$ for a term t_j. First, the document is evenly segmented into S parts; then, the term frequency for each segment $\mathbf{d}_i^{(s)}$ is worked out. Finally, the vector $\mathbf{v}''$ is built up as a superposition of Gaussian distributions.

The behavioral component, ascribed to term t, of the style-related distance between a pair of documents can therefore be computed as the distance between the two corresponding pdf's:

$$\Delta_t^{(b)}(D_u, D_v) = \int_0^1 [p_{t,u}(z) - p_{t,v}(z)]^2 \, dz \qquad (12.4)$$

Vector $\mathbf{v}'$ and vector $\mathbf{v}''$ support the computations of the frequency-based distance, $\Delta^{(f)}$, and the behavioral distance, $\Delta^{(b)}$, respectively. The former term is usually measured according to a standard Minkowski distance, hence the content distance between a pair of documents (D_u, D_v) is defined by:

$$\Delta^{(f)}(D_u, D_v) = \left[\sum_{k=1}^{n_T} |\mathbf{v}'_{k,u} - \mathbf{v}'_{k,v}|^p\right]^{1/p} \qquad (12.5)$$

The present approach adopts the value $p = 1$ and therefore actually implements a Manhattan distance metric. The term computing behavioral distance, $\Delta^{(b)}$, applies an Euclidean metric to compute the distance between probability vectors $\mathbf{v}$. Thus:

$$\Delta^{(b)}(D_u, D_v) = \sum_{k=1}^{n_T} \Delta_{t_k}^{(b)}(D_u, D_v) \tag{12.6}$$

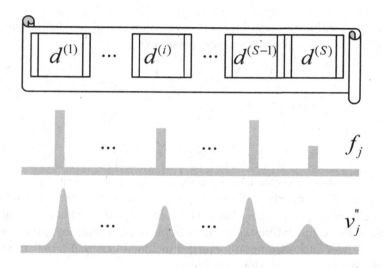

Fig. 12.3. Vector $\mathbf{v}''(D)$ is built up as a superposition of Gaussian distributions

Both terms (12.2) and (12.3) contribute to the computation of the eventual distance value, $\Delta(D_u, D_v)$, which is defined as follows:

$$\Delta(D_u, D_v) = \alpha \cdot \Delta^{(f)}(D_u, D_v) + (1 - \alpha) \cdot \Delta^{(b)}(D_u, D_v) \tag{12.7}$$

where the mixing coefficient $\alpha \in [0, 1]$ weights the relative contribution of $\Delta^{(f)}$ and $\Delta^{(b)}$. It is worth noting that the distance expression (12.7) obeys the basic properties of non-negative values and symmetry that characterize general metrics, but does not necessarily satisfy the triangular property.

12.3.2. *Kernel k-means*

The conventional k-means paradigm supports an unsupervised grouping process,[17,18] which partitions the set of samples, $\mathcal{D} = \{D_u; u = 1, .., n_D\}$, into a set of K clusters, C_j $(j = 1,\ldots, K)$. In practice, one defines a "membership vector" $\mathbf{m} \in \{1,\ldots,K\}^{n_D}$, which indexes the partitioning of input patterns over the K clusters as: $m_u = j \Leftrightarrow D_u \in C_j$, otherwise $m_u = 0$; $u = 1,\ldots,n_D$. It is also useful to define a "membership function" $\delta_{uj}(D_u, C_j)$, that defines the membership of the u-th document to the j-th cluster: $\delta_{uj}=1$ if $m_u = j$, and 0 otherwise. The result of the clustering strategy is twofold: the method assigns the input samples to any of the K clusters uniquely, and, therefore, the cluster centroids (often also called prototypes) can be computed explicitly, and are the average positions of the samples within the respective clusters. With the above definitions, the number of members of a cluster is expressed as

$$N_j = \sum_{u=1}^{n_D} \delta_{uj}; \quad j = 1,\ldots,K \qquad (12.8)$$

and the cluster centroid is given by:

$$\mathbf{w}_j = \frac{1}{N_j} \sum_{u=1}^{n_D} \mathbf{x}_u \delta_{uj}; \quad j = 1,\ldots,K \qquad (12.9)$$

where $\mathbf{x}_u$ is any vector-based representation of document D_u.

The key idea underlying kernel-based k-means clustering is indeed that the actual coordinates of the cluster centroids may *not* be known explicitly, as long as one is just interested in the memberships of samples to the various groups. Under such assumption, one can include the kernel-based approach into the k-means formulation as follows.

First, one assumes that a function, Φ, can map any element, D, of the input space into a corresponding position, $\Phi(D)$, in a possibly infinite dimensional Hilbert space. The mapping function defines the actual 'Kernel', which is formulated as the expression to compute the inner product:

$$K(D_u, D_v) = \Phi(D_u) \cdot \Phi(D_v) \overset{def}{=} \Phi_u \cdot \Phi_v \qquad (12.10)$$

The Hilbert space spanning vectors Φ has an arbitrary dimension (even infinite) and just requires that an inner product be defined, under some basic constraints called Mercer conditions.[55] Several formulations of admissible kernels have been proposed in the literature;[56] the approach presented here adopts the Radial Basis Function (RBF) model of kernel computation, hence a kernel expression (12.10) is computed as

$$K(D_u, D_v) = \exp\left[-\frac{\Delta(D_u, D_v)}{\sigma^2}\right] \qquad (12.11)$$

It is worth stressing here an additional, crucial advantage of using a kernel-based formulation in the text-mining context: the approach (12.11) can effectively support the critical normalization process by reducing all inner products within a limited range, thereby preventing that extensive properties of documents (length, lexicon, etc) may distort representation and ultimately affect clustering performance. Such an advantage is clearly paid at the price of an additional (hyper)parameter, σ^2, which should be tuned in order to balance the tendency of RBF kernels to amplify discrepancies between close elements.

The kernel-based version of the k-means algorithm, according to the method proposed by Girolami,[54] replicates the basic partitioning schema (12.8)-(12.9) in the Hilbert space, where the centroid positions, Ψ, are given by the averages of the mapping images, Φ_u:

$$\Psi_j = \frac{1}{N_j} \sum_{u=1}^{n_D} \Phi_u \delta_{uj}; \quad j = 1, \ldots, K \tag{12.12}$$

The ultimate result of the clustering process is the membership vector, **m**, which determines prototype positions (12.9) even though they cannot be stated explicitly. As a consequence, for a document, D_u, the distance in the Hilbert space from the mapped image, Φ_u, to the cluster Ψ_j as per (12.9) can be worked out as:

$$d\left(\Phi_u, \Psi_j\right) = \left\| \Phi_u - \frac{1}{N_j} \sum_{v=1}^{n_D} \Phi_v \delta_{vj} \right\|^2 = \tag{12.13}$$

$$= \left(\frac{1}{N_j} \sum_{v=1}^{n_D} \Phi_v \delta_{vj} \right) \cdot \left(\frac{1}{N_j} \sum_{v=1}^{n_D} \Phi_v \delta_{vj} \right) + \Phi_u \cdot \Phi_u - \frac{2}{N_j} \sum_{v=1}^{n_D} \delta_{vj} \left(\Phi_u \cdot \Phi_v\right) =$$

$$= \frac{1}{(N_j)^2} \sum_{m,v=1}^{n_D} \delta_{mj} \delta_{vj} K\left(D_m, D_v\right) + K\left(D_u, D_u\right) - \frac{2}{N_j} \sum_{v=1}^{n_D} \delta_{vj} K\left(D_u, D_v\right) =$$

$$= 1 + \frac{1}{(N_j)^2} \sum_{m,v=1}^{n_D} \delta_{mj} \delta_{vj} K\left(D_m, D_v\right) - \frac{2}{N_j} \sum_{v=1}^{n_D} \delta_{vj} K\left(D_u, D_v\right)$$

By using this expression, which includes only kernel computations, one can identify the closest prototype to the image of each input pattern, and assign sample memberships accordingly. The overall feature-space k-means algorithm can be outlined as follows:

12.3.2.1. *The feature-space version of k-means clustering*

(1) *Initialize* **m** with random memberships $\mathbf{m}_u \in \{1, \ldots, K\}$; mark **m** as 'modified'
(2) *while* (**m** is modified):
   (a) Compute distances as per (12.13):
      $d(\Phi_u, \Psi_j)$; $j = 1, \ldots, K$; $u = 1, \ldots, n_D$;
   (b) Update **m** such that :
      $m_u = \arg\min_j d(\Phi_u, \Psi_j)$; $u = 1, \ldots, n_D$

The crucial advantage in moving to a Hilbert space is that a representation that might be contorted in the original space may turn out to be straightforward in the mapping space. Thus, even though individual points are no longer identifiable explicitly, one is interested in structures among points (documents). In classification applications[57] kernel methods can solve, in a linear fashion manner, problems that are non-linearly separable in input space; in clustering domains, k-means clustering can notably help separate groups and discover clusters that would have been difficult to identify in the base space. From this viewpoint one might even conclude that a kernel-based method might represent a viable approach to tackle the dimensionality issue.

12.4. The Document-Clustering Framework

Section 12.3 has introduced the two fundamental parts of the document clustering scheme proposed in this work: the similarity measure and the clustering technique. In the following, a comprehensive overview of the eventual document-clustering framework will be presented. Furthermore, the issue of curse of dimensionality will be addressed by proposing a dimensionality reduction model based on Random Projections.[20] Finally, the computational complexity of the proposed framework will be analyzed.

12.4.1. *The document-clustering algorithm*

The proposed framework for document clustering combines a semantic-driven processing with pattern-recognition grouping algorithms. First, a semantic-based metric measures distances between documents, by combining a content-based with a behavioural analysis; then, the core clustering engine exploits a kernel-based version of the classical k-means algorithm to group similar documents, either adopting a flat paradigm or a hierarchical paradigm. The following pseudocode outlines the complete framework.

12.4.1.1. *The document-clustering procedure*

Input: a corpus $\mathcal{D} = \{D_u; u = 1,..,n_D\}$

(1) *Document pre-processing*

For every $D_i \in \mathcal{D}$, generate the corresponding document $\bar{D}_i$ as follows

(a) Apply stop-words removal
(b) Apply stemming

Thus $\bar{D}_i$ is a sequence of terms (*i.e.* the stemmed words).
In the following, $\mathcal{D}^* = \{\bar{D}_u; u = 1,..,n_D\}$ denotes the collection of processed documents.

(2) *Build vocabulary*

Generate the vocabulary $\mathcal{T} = \{t_j; j = 1,..,n_T\}$ as the set of terms that occurs at least one time in the corpus D^*.

(3) *Vector representation*

For every $\bar{D}_i \in \mathcal{D}^*$:

(a) work out vector $\mathbf{v}\prime(\bar{D}_i)$ as per (12.2)
(b) work out vector $\mathbf{v}\prime\prime(\bar{D}_i)$ as per (12.3)

(4) *Build distance matrix*

Compute the distance matrix Δ as follows

$$\Delta = \begin{bmatrix} \Delta_{11} & \cdots\cdots & \Delta_{1n_D} \\ \vdots & \ddots & \vdots \\ \vdots & & \ddots & \vdots \\ \Delta_{n_D1} & \cdots\cdots & \Delta_{n_Dn_D} \end{bmatrix}$$

where $\Delta_{mn} = \Delta(\bar{D}_m, \bar{D}_n)$ is the document distance (12.7) between document $\bar{D}_m$ and document $\bar{D}_n$.

(5) *Build dot matrix*

Compute the dot matrix Θ as follows:

$$\Theta = \begin{bmatrix} K_{11} & \cdots\cdots & K_{1n_D} \\ \vdots & \ddots & \vdots \\ \vdots & & \ddots & \vdots \\ K_{n_D1} & \cdots\cdots & K_{n_Dn_D} \end{bmatrix}$$

where $K_{mn} = K(\bar{D}_m, \bar{D}_n)$ is computed as per (12.10).
(6) *Clustering*

Use the k-means algorithm and the dot matrix Θ to cluster the documents in $\mathcal{D}$.

If flat clustering: generate K partitions.

If hierachical clustering: generate cluster hierarchy.

The framework can support both flat clustering and hierarchical clustering. When flat clustering is addressed, the algorithm partitions the set of documents $\mathcal{D}$ into K clusters, where K is an input parameter; however, no explicit structure is produced that would relate clusters to each other. Conversely, the hierarchical clustering model applies a top-down paradigm to generate a cluster hierarchy. Hence, the procedure starts with all the documents in single cluster. Then, the cluster is split using the flat clustering technique; this procedure is applied recursively until some stopping criterion is met. In the present work, the desired number of levels in the eventual hierarchy drives the clustering procedure. Figure 12.4 proposes an example of the outputs of flat clustering and hierarchical clustering with a corpus including 12 documents.

12.4.2. *Dimension reduction for document clustering by using random projections*

As anticipated in Section 12.2, the curse of dimensionality represents a crucial issue when dealing with document clustering. By adopting the vector space model, the total number of unique terms in a text data set represents the number of dimensions, which is usually in the thousands. Nonetheless, sparsity is an accompanying phenomenon of such data representation model. Therefore, in the recent years several works have addressed the problem of dimensionality reduction for document clustering tools.[36-41]

The present research tackles this significant aspect by comparing the performance of the conventional k-means algorithm with that of a k-means clustering scheme recently proposed by Biau et al.,[20] which exploits random projections for a reduction in dimensionality before clustering. In that work, a notable theoretical discussion led to the conclusion that Johnson-Lindenstrauss-type random projections to lower-dimensional subspaces are particularly well suited for clustering purposes, as they can outperform other dimension reduction schemes based on factorial methods (*e.g.* Principal Component Analysis).

$$\mathcal{D} = \{D_1, D_2, D_3, D_4, D_5, D_6, D_7, D_8, D_9, D_{10}, D_{11}, D_{12}\}$$

(a) Flat Clustering ($K = 3$)

CLUSTER #1: $D_5, D_6, D_9, D_2, D_3, D_{11}$
CLUSTER #2: D_4, D_7, D_{12}
CLUSTER #3: D_1, D_8, D_{10}

(b) Hierarchical Clustering

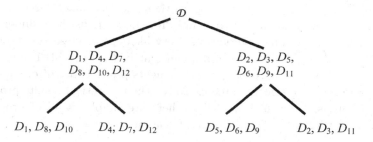

Fig. 12.4. The flat and the hierarchical clustering paradigms

Random Projections[58–61] is a simple and powerful dimension reduction technique that uses suitably scaled random matrix with independent, normally distributed entries to project data into low-dimensional spaces. This technique has already been found to be a computationally efficient, yet sufficiently accurate method for dimensionality reduction in different areas.[62–65] The procedure to get a random projection is straightforward and arises from the Johnson-Lindenstrauss (JL) lemma.[58] The lemma states that any n point set lying in L-dimensional Euclidean space can be embedded into a R-dimensional space, with $R \geq O(\varepsilon^{-2}\ln(n))$, without distorting the distances between any pair of points by more than a factor $1\pm\varepsilon$, where $\varepsilon \in (0, 1)$.

Over the years, the probabilistic method has allowed for the original proof of Johnson and Lindenstrauss to be greatly simplified, while at the same time giving conceptually simple randomized algorithms for constructing the embedding.[59–61] Using matrix notation, one can formalize the embedding operation as follows:

$$\mathbf{H} = \mathbf{PX} \qquad (12.14)$$

where $\mathbf{X}$ is the original set of n, L-dimensional observation, $\mathbf{H}$ is the projection of the data into a lower, R-dimensional subspace, and $\mathbf{P}$ is the random matrix providing an embedding that satisfies the JL lemma. In principle, (12.14) is a projection only if $\mathbf{P}$ is orthogonal, so to preserve the similarities between the original vectors in the low-dimensional space. In very high-dimensional spaces, however, it is possible to save computation time by avoiding orthogonalization without affecting significantly the quality of the projection matrix. As pointed out in the work by Hecht-Nielsen,[66] in a high-dimensional space there exists a much larger number of almost orthogonal than orthogonal directions. Thus, high-dimensional vectors having random directions are very likely to be close to orthogonal.

Obviously, the choice of the random matrix $\mathbf{P}$ in (12.14) is one of the key points of interest. Although the elements p_{ij} of $\mathbf{P}$ are often Gaussian distributed, the present research exploited the theoretical results proposed by Achlioptas,[67] which showed that there are simpler ways of producing Random Projections. Thus, $\mathbf{P}$ can be generated as follows:

$$p_{ij} = \sqrt{\frac{3}{R}} \cdot \begin{cases} +1 \text{ with probability } 1/6 \\ 0 \quad \text{ with probability } 2/3 \\ -1 \text{ with probability } 1/6 \end{cases} \qquad (12.15)$$

In this work, random projections for reduction in dimensionality are applied to the term-by-document matrix that results from working out vector $\mathbf{v}\prime(\bar{D}_i)$ for every $D_i \in \mathcal{D}$ (step 3.a of the pseudocode). Therefore, $\mathbf{X}$ is a set of n_D observation lying in a n_T –dimensional space and $\mathbf{P}$ is a $R \times n_T$ matrix computed as indicated above.

12.4.3. *Computational complexity*

In general, the computational complexity of a document clustering framework is determined by two elements: the clustering algorithm and the procedure supporting the document indexing phase, which may exploit a dimensionality reduction technique to address the problem of curse of dimensionality, as discussed above.

The proposed framework uses k-means as clustering algorithm. The time complexity of the k-means algorithm is $O(nkl)$, where n is the number of patterns, k is the number of clusters and l is the number of iterations of the training phase. While k-means is the most popular algorithm in document clustering due to its simplicity and efficiency, other clustering techniques have also been applied to this task: Self Organizing Maps (SOMs), Expectation-Maximization (EM), fuzzy clustering, etc. In fact, the time complexity of those algorithms is comparable or even greater.

Table 12.1. Time complexity of the most popular dimensionality reduction techniques

Dimensionality Reduction Technique	Computational Cost
RP	$O(Rn_T n_D)$
LSI	$O(22n_T^3 + 4n_T n_D^2)$
LPI	$O(22n_T^3 + 4n_T n_D^2 + R^3)$
NMF	$O(qRn_T n_D)$

The choice of the document indexing model can indeed affect the overall computational complexity of the clustering framework. In this regard, Table 12.1 reports the time complexity of the Random-Projections technique along with the time complexities of other popular dimensionality reduction techniques exploited by document indexing models: Latent Semantic Index (LSI), Locality Preserving Indexing (LPI), and Nonnegative Matrix Factorization (NMF). Here, R denotes the dimensionality of the eventual low-dimensional space, while q is the number of iterations performed in the NMF procedure. Table 12.1 shows that Random Projections outperforms both the LSI and the LPI reduction models in terms of computational complexity: the LSI model is based on the computationally demanding SVD; the LPI model combines a Principal Component Analysis (PCA) with a generalized eigenvector problem.

On the other hand, both the time complexities of RP and NMF are linear in n_T (number of terms) and n_D (number of documents). However, NMF suffers from some crucial issues. First, the factorization is not unique; furthermore, different types of nonnegative matrix factorizations exist, which arise from using different cost functions and exploiting (or not) a regularization procedure.

12.5. Experimental Results

Two real-world benchmarks provided the experimental domains for the proposed document-clustering framework: the Reuters database[21] and the largest real email corpus in the public domain, the Enron mail dataset.[22] The former was chosen to assess the method performance on a public source of information, which represents a typical framework of today's trends in data gathering and analysis for security and intelligence. The latter dataset made it possible to validate the operation of the clustering principle in a set of complex scenarios involving non-trivial security issues.

The Reuters-21578 corpus includes 21,578 documents, which appeared on the Reuters newswire in 1987. One or more topics have been manually added to each document. Actually, the whole database involves 135 different topics derived from economic subject categories; indeed, only 57 topics have at least twenty occurrences. The Reuters-21578 corpus represents a standard benchmark for content-based document management. This paper exploits such corpus to show that the document clustering framework based on kernel k-means provide an effective tool to generate consistent structures for information access and retrieval.

On the other hand, the Enron mail dataset provides a reference corpus to test text-mining techniques that address intelligence applications.[23] The Enron mail corpus was posted originally on Internet by the Federal Energy Regulatory Commission (FERC) during its investigation on the Enron case. FERC collected a total of 619.449 emails from 158 Enron employees, mainly senior managers. Each message included: the email addresses of the sender and receiver, date, time, subject, body and text. The original set suffered from document integrity problems, hence an updated version was later set up by SRI International for the CALO project. Eventually, William Cohen from Carnegie Mellon University put the cleaned dataset online[22] for researchers in March 2004. Other processed versions of the Enron corpus have been made available on the web, but were not considered in the present work because the CMU version made it possible fair comparison of the obtained results with respect to established, reference corpora in the literature.

The set of messages covered a widest range of topics, originating from a vast community of people who did not form a closed set. A few people wished to conceal both the extent of their connections and the contents of their discussions; at the same time, by far the large majority of messages were completely innocent. As a result, the Enron data set provided a good experimental domain to evaluate the ability of a text mining framework in a 'needle-in-a-haystack' scenario, which closely resembled a typical situation in security-related applications such as counterterrorism.[23]

12.5.1. *Reuters-21578*

The experimental session based on the Reuters-21578 database involved a corpus $\mathcal{D}_R$ including 8.267 documents out of the 21.578 originally provided by the database. The eventual corpus $\mathcal{D}_R$ was obtained by adopting the criterion already used in the work of Cai et al.[40] First, all the documents with multiple topics were discarded. Then, only the documents associated to topics having at least 18 occurrences have been included in $\mathcal{D}_R$. As a result, the corpus featured 32 topics.

The clustering performance of the proposed methodology was evaluated by analyzing the results obtained in three experiments. In the experiments, a flat clustering paradigm partitioned the documents in $\mathcal{D}_R$, by using three different settings of the metric weight parameter, $\alpha=\{0.3, 0.5, 0.7\}$, as per (12.7). When adopting $\alpha=0.3$ or $\alpha=0.7$ in (12.7), either component $\Delta^{(f)}$ or $\Delta^{(b)}$, was predominant; in the experiment featuring $\alpha=0.5$, the quantities $\Delta^{(f)}$ and $\Delta^{(b)}$ evenly contributed to the measured distance between each pair of documents.

Table 12.2 outlines the results obtained with the setting $\alpha = 0.3$. The performances of the proposed clustering framework were evaluated by using the *purity* parameter. Let N_k denote the number of elements lying in a cluster C_k and let N_{mk} be the number of elements of the class I_m in the cluster C_k. Then, the purity $pur(k)$ of the cluster C_k is defined as follows:

$$pur(k) = \frac{1}{N_k} \max_m (N_{mk}) \qquad (12.16)$$

The overall purity of the clustering results is defined as follows:

$$purity = \sum_k \frac{N_k}{N} \cdot pur(k) \qquad (12.17)$$

where N is the total number of elements.

The purity parameter was preferred to other measures of performance (*e.g.* the F-measures) because it is widely accepted in machine learning classification problems.[25]

The evaluations were conducted with different number of clusters K, ranging from 20 to 100. For each experiment, four quality parameters are presented:

- the overall purity, $purity_{OV}$, of the clustering result;
- the lowest purity value $pur(k)$ over the K clusters;
- the highest purity value $pur(k)$ over the K clusters;

- the number of elements (*i.e.* documents) associated to the smallest cluster.

Tables 12.3 and 12.4 reports the results obtained with $\alpha = 0.5$ and $\alpha = 0.7$, respectively.

As expected, experimental results showed that overall purity increased when the number of clusters, K, increased. The value of the overall purity seems to indicate that clustering performances improved when setting $\alpha = 0.3$. Thus empirical outcomes confirmed the effectiveness of the proposed document distance measure, combining the conventional content-based similarity with a behavioral similarity criterion.

Table 12.2.   Clustering performances obtained on Reuters-21578 with $\alpha=0.3$

Number of clusters	Overall purity	$pur(k)$ minimum	$(pur)(k)$ maximum	Smallest cluster
20	0.712108	0.252049	1	109
40	0.77138	0.236264	1	59
60	0.81154	0.175	1	13
80	0.799685	0.181818	1	2
100	0.82666	0.153846	1	1

Table 12.3.   Clustering performances obtained on Reuters-21578 with $\alpha=0.5$

Number of clusters	Overall purity	$pur(k)$ minimum	$pur(k)$ maximum	Smallest cluster
20	0.696383	0.148148	1	59
40	0.782267	0.222467	1	4
60	0.809121	0.181818	1	1
80	0.817467	0.158333	1	1
100	0.817467	0.139241	1	2

Table 12.4.   Clustering performances obtained on Reuters-21578 with $\alpha=0.7$

Number of clusters	Overall purity	$pur(k)$ minimum	$pur(k)$ maximum	Smallest cluster
20	0.690577	0.145719	1	13
40	0.742833	0.172638	1	6
60	0.798718	0.18	1	5
80	0.809483	0.189655	1	2
100	0.802589	0.141732	1	4

A detailed analysis of the clustering performances attained by the proposed framework can be drawn from the graphs presented in Figure 12.5. The graphs report the cumulative distribution of the cluster purity for the different experiments listed in Table 12.2 (only the experiment with $K = 20$ is not included). The reported results showed that, in every experiment, 70% of the obtained clusters exhibited a purity greater than 0.6; furthermore, 50% of the clusters scored a purity greater than 0.9. The reliability of the present document-clustering scheme was indeed confirmed when counting the documents lying in clusters having a purity of 1.0. With an overall number of clusters $K = 40$, a set of 2,575 documents (*i.e.*, 31% of the total number of documents) were assigned to those clusters; when using $K = 100$, that percentage increased to 35% (2,950 documents).

A final set of experiments involved the clustering scheme exploiting random projections for a reduction in dimensionality, as introduced in Sec. 12.4. This analysis addressed the critical aspect concerning the trade off between clustering accuracy and computational complexity. Such a problem is common in all text-mining applications and can prove especially relevant when using the k-means clustering algorithm. The performance of this clustering scheme was evaluated on the corpus $\mathcal{D}_R$ by setting $\alpha = 0.3$; the dimension of the eventual reduced space was set to $R = 500$ and $R = 100$. Table 12.5 and Table 12.6 report the results obtained with these set up by varying the desired number of clusters K.

Unsurprisingly, the clustering performances obtained by exploiting dimension reduction were slightly inferior to those attained by the conventional clustering scheme (Table 12.2). Indeed, one should take into account that by setting $R = 500$ the original term-by-document matrix had been reduced of a factor 100. Nonetheless, Table 12.5 and Table 12.6 show that the overall purity attained by the model was satisfactory even in the presence of a substantial reduction in dimensionality.

These results can be compared with those obtained on the same dataset by the clustering framework proposed by Cai et al.,[40] which introduced a clustering scheme combining the conventional k-means algorithm with a dimensionality reduction model based on the Locality Preserving Index (LPI). The results presented in that work[40] showed that the LPI-based clustering scheme, although computationally demanding (as per Table 12.1), can outperform other well-known methodologies, such as LSI-based clustering and spectral clustering algorithms.

When applied to the Reuters database, the LPI-based clustering scheme attained an average purity of 0.77;[40] in that work, evaluations were conducted with different number of clusters, ranging from two to ten. Thus,

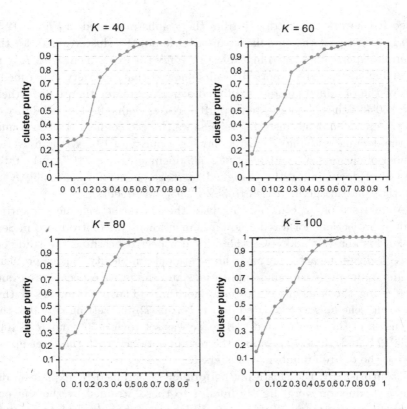

Fig. 12.5.   The cumulative distributions of the cluster purity for the experiments reported in Table 12.1

the clustering performances of the LPI-based clustering are slightly better than those obtained by the proposed clustering scheme (Table 12.5 and Table 12.6), which exploits random projections for dimensionality reduction. However, as anticipated in Sec. 12.3, the scheme based on random projections outperforms the LPI reduction model in terms of computational complexity: while dimensionality reduction by using random projections is supported by a straightforward matrix multiplication (as per 12.13), the LPI scheme is actually based on the computationally expensive Singular Valued Decomposition (SVD).[40] Therefore, the dimension reduction model based on random projections proposed in the present work seems to guarantee a satisfactory tradeoff between performance and complexity.

The effectiveness of the proposed document-clustering framework was eventually confirmed by a comparison with the document-clustering model

Table 12.5. Clustering performances obtained on Reuters-21578 with $\alpha=0.3$ and dimension reduction ($R=$ 500) by random projections

Number of clusters	Overall purity	$pur(k)$ minimum	$pur(k)$ maximum	Smallest cluster
20	0.70231	0.126386	1	32
40	0.709084	0.117647	1	2
60	0.731221	0.182109	1	1
80	0.726019	0.121145	1	1
100	0.692029	0.158004	1	1

Table 12.6. Clustering performances obtained on Reuters-21578 with $\alpha=0.3$ and dimension reduction ($R=$ 100) by random projections

Number of clusters	Overall purity	$pur(k)$ minimum	$pur(k)$ maximum	Smallest cluster
20	0.666626	0.106776	1	31
40	0.69723	0.115813	1	2
60	0.705213	0.149718	1	1
80	0.721785	0.11674	1	1
100	0.739204	0.137662	1	1

using nonnegative matrix factorization (NMF) introduced by Shahnaz et al.[41] When applied to the Reuters database, the NMF-based model attained an overall purity superior to 0.7 only in experimental sessions[41] involving 6 topics (or less) out of the 135 originally included in the database. Therefore, the prediction accuracy obtained by the model introduced in this chapter outperformed the one attained by the NMF-based model.

12.5.2. *Enron dataset*

The experimental session based on the Enron mail corpus involved two different experiments. The first experiment exploited the dataset made available on the web by Ron Bekkerman from the University of Massachusetts Amherst. The dataset[68] collects email from the directories of seven former Enron employees: *beck-s, farmer-d, kaminski-v, kitchen-l, lokay-m, sanders-r* and *williams-w3*. Each of these users had several thousand messages, with *beck-s* having more than one hundred folders. The goal of the first experiment was to evaluate the ability of the proposed clustering framework to extract key elements from a heterogeneous scenario, in which one cannot rely on a set of predefined topics. All the seven folders were processed to remove non-topical folders such as *all_documents, calendar, contacts, deleted_items*, *discussion_threads*, *inbox*, *notes_inbox*, *sent*, *sent_items* and *sent_mail*.

For the purpose of increasing complexity, Bekkerman's dataset was augmented by including the email folder of one of the former executives of Enron, Vice President Sara Shackleton. The underlying hypothesis was that email contents might also be characterized by the role the mailbox owner played within the company. Toward that end, when applying the clustering algorithm, only the 'body' sections of the emails were used, and sender/receiver, date/time info were discarded.

Table 12.7.   Results of the first experiment on the Enron dataset

Cluster ID	Size	Most frequent words
1	1825	ect, Kaminski, research, Houston, manag, energy
2	8416	deal, hpl, gas
3	1881	Kitchen, deal, gas
4	1210	dbcaps97data, database, iso, error
5	1033	epmi, mmbtu, California, gas, northwest
6	2094	ect, manag, risk, trade, market
7	1239	deal, work, meet
8	1522	message, email, http, subject
9	1091	market, energy, trade, price, share, stock, gas, dynegi
10	4044	ect, Shackleton, agreement, trade, isda

The experiment involved 24,355 emails. Table 12.7 reports on the results obtained by this experiment and shows the terms that characterize each of the clusters provided by the clustering framework. For each cluster, the most descriptive words between the twenty most frequent words of the cluster are listed; reported terms actually included peculiar abbreviations: "ect" stands for Enron Capital & Trade Resources, "hpl" stands for Houston Pipeline Company, "epmi" stands for Enron Power Marketing Inc, "mmbtu" stands for Million British Thermal Units, "dynegi" stands for Dynegy Inc, a large owner and operator of power plants and a player in the natural gas liquids and coal business, which in 2001 made an unsuccessful takeover bid for Enron. The results reported in Table 12.7 showed that the document clustering attained some significant outcomes. First, cluster no. 10 grouped a considerable portion of the emails ascribed to the Shackleton subset: most frequent words indeed confirm that the word "Shackleton" appears several time in the email bodies, as well as the term "isda," which stands for International Swaps and Derivatives Association. It is worth noting that the term "isda" never appeared in the list of the most frequent terms of the other nine clusters. Another significant outcome concerned clusters no. 7 and no. 8, which seemed to group all emails that did not deal with technical topics. At the same time, both clusters no. 1 and cluster no. 3 related to Enron employees, Kaminski and Kitchen, respectively. When analyzing cluster no. 4, it turned out that it gathered the email notifications automatically sent by a database server, which were collected in a subfolder in the mailbox of *williams-w3*.

The second experiment aimed at estimating the ability of the proposed framework to group messages by the same author when considering body text only. This experiment ultimately aimed at verifying the application of text mining technologies in an intelligence-analysis environment, in which fake identities may be bypassed by associating messages to the original authors. Thus the clustering algorithm was tested on a dataset collecting all the emails included in the folder "sent" of six Enron employees randomly selected: *symes-k, namec-g, lenhart-m, delainey-d, rogers-b*. Eventually, the corpus included 6,618 emails body; obviously, all information concerning the email addresses of senders/receivers was discarded.

The graph in Figure 12.6 shows the results obtained in this experiment; the x-axis gives the number of clusters, whereas the y-axis reports on the classification error (an error was detected when ascribing a message to the wrong author). The obtained figures proved the effectiveness of the proposed clustering methodology, which scored a classification error of 15% (*i.e.* 1,043 emails) when using 60 clusters for the partitioning. Moreover, the analysis of the eventual clusters led to interesting outcomes.

In the 60-clusters partitioning, fifteen clusters were assigned, after the calibration procedure, to the author *lenhart-m*. Those clusters actually shared also a great part of the terms included in their own list the most frequent words; but, surprisingly enough, those terms were *weekend, tonight, party, golf, gift, ticket, happy, softball, hotmail, jpg, msn, love, game, birthday, celebrate adult, drink, pool*. Hence, the unsupervised clustering procedure revealed that a significant portion of the emails included in the "Sent" folder of the author *lenhart-m* did not deal with themes related to the working activity. Indeed, such outstanding result can be double checked by actually analyzing the emails provided in the Enron database.

12.6. Conclusions

Text mining provides a valuable tool to deal with large amounts of unstructured text data. Indeed, in security applications text-mining technologies

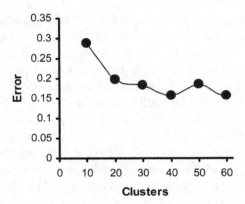

Fig. 12.6.　The results of the second experiment on the Enron database

can automate, improve and speed up the analysis of existing datasets, with the goal of preventing criminal acts by the cataloguing of various threads and pieces of information, which would remain unnoticed when using traditional means of investigation.

Within the text mining environment, document clustering represents one of the most effective techniques to organize documents in an unsupervised manner. Nonetheless, the design of a document-clustering framework requires one to address other crucial aspects in addition to the choice of the specific clustering algorithm to be implemented. A major characteristic of the representation paradigm of text documents is the high dimensionality of the feature space, which imposes a big challenge to the performance of clustering algorithms. Furthermore, the definition of the underlying distance measure between documents is critical for getting meaningful clusters.

The hybrid document-clustering approach proposed in this chapter mostly addresses such issues by combining the specific advantages of content-driven processing with the effectiveness of an established pattern-recognition grouping algorithm. Two crucial novelty aspects characterize the proposed approach. First, distances between documents are worked out by a semantic-based hypermetric. The specific approach integrates a content-based with a user-behavioral analysis, as it takes into account both lexical and style-related features of the documents at hand. Secondly, the core clustering strategy exploits a kernel-based version of the conventional k-means algorithm to group similar documents; hence, the model exploits the implicit normalization of RBF kernel functions while embedding semantic information in the whole mechanism.

The present research tackled indeed the problem of curse of dimensionality by considering an advanced approach in the vector-space paradigm, which applied Johnson-Lindenstrauss-type random projections for a reduction in dimensionality before clustering. The analysis focused in particular on the critical aspect concerning the trade off between clustering accuracy and computational complexity, which is a general issue in all text-mining applications, and can be particularly relevant when using k-means for document clustering.

Experimental results indeed confirmed the consistency of the proposed framework. The hybrid document-clustering approach proved effective when dealing with a standard benchmark for content-based document management. Furthermore, it attained remarkable performances with an experimental domain resembling the kind of data collected as part of counterterrorism efforts.

References

1. H. Chen and F. Y. Wan, Artificial Intelligence for Homeland Security, *IEEE Trans. Intelligent Systems,*. **20**(5) (September/October, 2005).
2. H. Chen, W. Chung, J. Xu, G. Wang, Y. Qin, and M. Chau, Crime data mining: a general framework and some examples, *IEEE Trans. Computer.* **37**(4), 50–56, (2004).
3. J. W. Seifert. Data Mining and Homeland Security: An Overview. Technical report, CRS Report RL31798, (2007). www.epic.org/privacy/fusion/crs-dataminingrpt.pdf.
4. J. Mena, *Investigative Data Mining for Security and Criminal Detection.* (Butterworth-Heinemann, 2003).
5. B. Schneier. Why data mining wont stop terror. http://www.wired.com/politics/security/commentary/securitymatters/2006/03/70357.
6. K. Taipale, Data Mining And Domestic Security: Connecting The Dots To Make Sense Of Data, *The Columbia Science And Technology Law Review.* **V**, 1–83, (2003).
7. G. Petasis, V. Karkaletsis, G. Paliouras, I. Androutsopoulos, and C. Spyropoulos. Ellogon: A New Text Engineering Platform. In *Proc. 3rd International Conference on Language Resources and Evaluation (LREC-2002)*, pp. 72–78, Las Palmas, Canary Islands, Spain, (2002).
8. D. Ferrucci and A. Lally, UIMA: An Architectural Approach to Unstructured Information Processing in the Corporate Research Environment, *Natural Language Engineering.* **10**(3-4), 327–348 (September, 2004).
9. F. Sebastiani. Text Mining and its Applications to Intelligence, CRM and

KM. In ed. A. Zanasi, *Text Categorization.* WIT Press, (2005).

10. D. Sullivan, *Document warehousing and text mining.* (John Wiley and Sons, 2001).

11. W. Fan, L. Wallace, S. Rich, and Z. Zhang, Tapping the power of text mining, *Communications of the ACM.* **49**(9), 76–82 (September, 2006).

12. R. Popp, T. Armour, T. Senator, and K. Numrych, Countering terrorism through information technology, *Communications of the ACM.* **47**(3), 36–43 (March, 2004).

13. B. Goertzel and J. Venuto. Accurate SVM Text Classification for Highly Skewed Data Using Threshold Tuning and Query-Expansion-Based Feature Selection. In *Proc. International Joint Conference on Neural Networks,* pp. 1220–1225, Vancouver, BC, Canada (July 16-21, 2006).

14. N. Beebe and G. Dietrich, Digital forensic text string searching: Improving information retrieval effectiveness by thematically clustering search results, *Digital Investigation.* **4**, 49–54 (September, 2007).

15. A. Zanasi, Ed., *Mining and its Applications to Intelligence, CRM and KM.* (WIT Press, 2007).

16. S. C. Johnson, Hierarchical Clustering Scheme, *Psychometrika.* **32**(3), 241–254, (1966).

17. Y. Linde, A. Buzo, and R. Gray, An algorithm for vector quantizer design, *IEEE Trans. Commun.* **COM-28**, 84–95 (January, 1980).

18. S. Lloyd, Least squares quantization in PCM, *IEEE Trans. Inf. Theory.* **28** (2), 127–135, (1982).

19. J. Shawe-Taylor and N. Cristianini, *Kernel Methods for Pattern Analysis.* (Cambridge University Press, Cambridge, 2004).

20. G. Biau, L. Devroye, and G. Lugosi, On the Performance of Clustering in Hilbert Spaces, *IEEE Trans. on Information Theory.* **54**(2), 781–790 (February, 2008).

21. Reuters. 21578 Text Categorization Collection. UCI KDD Archive.

22. Enron. The Enron Email Dataset. http://www-2.cs.cmu.edu/~enron/.

23. C. Workshop on Link Analysis and Security. http://research.cs.queensu.ca/home/skill/proceedings/, (2005). Newport Beach, California, USA.

24. M. Hearst. What Is Text Mining. http://www.sims.berkeley.edu/~hearst/textmining.html.

25. C. D. Manning, P. Raghavan, and H. Schtze, *Introduction to Information Retrieval.* (Cambridge University Press, 2008).

26. D. D. Lewis and K. S. Jones, Natural language processing for information retrieval, *Communications of the ACM.* **39**, 92–101, (1996).

27. R. Baeza-Yates and B. Ribiero-Neto, *Modern Information Retrieval.* (ACM Press, New York, 1999).

28. G. Salton, A. Wong, and L. Yang, A vector space model for information retrieval, *Journal Amer. Soc. Inform. Sci.* **18**, 613–620, (1975).

29. M. Berry and M. Browne, *Understanding Search Engines: Mathematical Modeling and Text.* (SIAM, 2005).

30. G. Salton and C. Buckley, Term-weighting approaches in automatic text retrieval, *Information Processing and Management.* **24**, 513–523, (1988).

31. G. Salton, G., and C. Buckley, Improving retrieval performance by relevance feedback, *Journal of the American Society for Information Science.* **41**(4), 288–297, (1990).

32. M. Xie, H. Wang, and T. N. Goh, Quality dimensions of Internet search engines, *Journal of Information Science.* **24**(5), 365–372, (1998).

33. A. K. Jain and R. C. Dubes, *Algorithms for Clustering Data.* (Prentice Hall, 1988).

34. S. Ridella, S. Rovetta, and R. Zunino, Plastic algorithm for adaptive vector quantization, *Neural Computing and Applications.* **7**(1), 37–51, (1998).

35. V. Vapnik, *The Nature of Statistical Learning Theory.* (Springer, 2000), 2nd edition edition.

36. B. Tang, M. Shepherd, E. Milios, and M. Heywood. Comparing and Combining Dimension Reduction Techniques for Efficient Text Clustering. In *International Workshop on Feature Selection for Data Mining - Interfacing Machine Learning and Statistics, in conjunction with 2005 SIAM International Conference on Data Mining*, Newport Beach, California (April, 2005).

37. I. S. Dhillon. Co-clustering documents and words using bipartite spectral graph partitioning. In *Proceedings of the seventh ACM SIGKDD international conference on Knowledge Discovery and Data Mining*, pp. 269–274, New York, USA, (2001). ACM.

38. D. H, H. Mannila, and P. Smyth, *Principles of Data Mining.* (MIT Press, Cambridge, MA).

39. M. Berry, S. Dumais, and G. W. OBrien, Using linear algebra for intelligent information retrieval, *SIAM Review.* **37**(4), 573–595, (1995).

40. D. Cai, X. He, and J. Han, Document Clustering Using Locality Preserving Indexing, *IEEE Transaction on knowledge and data engineering.* **17**(12), 1624–1637 (December, 2005).

41. F. Shahnaz, M. W. Berry, V. P. Pauca, and R. J. Plemmons, Document clustering using nonnegative matrix factorization, *Information Processing and Management.* **42**, 373–386, (2006).

42. J. Shlens. A Tutorial on Principal Component Analysis. `http://www.snl.salk.edu/~shlens/pub/notes/pca.pdf`.

43. I. Dhillon, Y. Guan, and B. Kulis. A unified view of Kernel kmeans, Spectral Clustering and Normalized Cuts. Technical Report UTCS Technical Report TR-04-25, University of Texas at Austin, Department of Computer Sciences, Austin, TX 78712 (February, 2005).

44. G. Qian, S. Sural, Y. Gu, and S. Pramanik, Similarity between Euclidean and cosine angle distance for nearest neighbor queries, *Proceedings of the 2004 ACM symposium on Applied computing.* pp. 1232–1237, (2004).

45. L. Jing, M. K. Ng, and J. Z. Huang, An Entropy Weighting k-Means Algorithm for Subspace Clustering of High-Dimensional Sparse Data, *IEEE Transactions on knowledge and data engineering.* **19**(8), 1026–1041, (2007).

46. M. W. Berry and M. Castellanos, *Survey of Text Mining II.* (Springer, 2008).

47. A. Hotho, A. Nürnberger, and G. Paass, A brief survey of text mining, *LDV Forum - GLDV Journal for Computational Linguistics and Language Technology.* **20**(1), 19–62, (2005).

48. Y. J. Horng, S. M. Chen, Y. C. Chang, and C. H. Lee, A New Method for Fuzzy Information Retrieval Based on Fuzzy Hierarchical Clustering and Fuzzy Inference Techniques, *IEEE Transactions on fuzzy systems.* **13**(2), 216–228 (April, 2005).

49. W. C. Tjhi and L. Chen, A heuristic-based fuzzy co-clustering algorithm for categorization of high-dimensional data, *Fuzzy Sets and Systems.* **159**(4), 371–389, (2008).

50. K. M. Hammouda and M. S. Kamel, Efficient phrase-based document indexing for web document clustering, *IEEE Transactions on Knowledge and Data Engineering.* **16**(10), 1279–1296, (2004).

51. H. Chim and X. Deng, Efficient Phrase-based Document Similarity for Clustering, *IEEE transaction on knowledge and data engineering.* **20**(9), 1217–1229 (September, 2008).

52. O. Zamir and O. Etzioni, Grouper: A Dynamic Clustering Interface to Web Search Results, *Computer Networks.* **31**(11-16), 1361–1374, (1999).

53. L. Dey, A. Rastogi, and S. Kumar, Generating Concept Ontologies through Text Mining Web Intelligence, *Proc. 2006 IEEE/WIC/ACM International Conference on Web Intelligence.* pp. 23 – 32 (December, 2006).

54. M. Girolami, Mercer kernel based clustering in feature space, *IEEE Trans. Neural Networks.* **13**(3), 780–784, (2002).

55. J. Mercer, *Functions of positive and negative type and their connection with the theory of integral equations.* (Philos. Trans. Roy. Soc., London, 1909).

56. B. Scholkopf and A. Smola, *Learning with Kernels: Support Vector Machines, Regularization, Optimization and Beyond.* (MIT Press, Cambridge, MA, 2002).

57. J. Shawe-Taylor and N. Cristianini, *Kernel Methods for Pattern Analysis.* vol. W. Johnson and J. Lindenstrauss, (Cambridge University Press, 2004).

58. W. Johnson and J. Lindenstrauss, Extensions of Lipsdchitz maps into a Hilbert space, *Contemporary Mathematics.* **26**, 189–206, (1984).

59. P. Frankl and H. Maehara, The Johnson-Lindenstrauss lemma and the sphericity of some graphs, *Journal of Combinatorial Theory.* **B 44**, 355–362, (1988).

60. P. Frankl and H. . Maehara, Some geometric applications of the beta distribution, *Annals of the Institute of Statistical Mathematics.* **42**, 463–474, (1990).

61. S. Dasgupta and A. Gupta, An elementary proof of a theorem of johnson and lindenstrauss, *Random Structures and Algorithms.* **22**, 60–65, (2003).

62. A. Bertoni and G. Valentini. Random projections for assessing gene expression cluster stability. In *Proc. IJCNN05*, vol. 1, pp. 149–154, (2005).

63. N. Goel, G. Bebis, and A. V. Nefian. Face recognition experiments with random projections. In *Biometric Technology for Human Identification II, Proc SPIE*, vol. 5779, pp. 426–437 (March, 2005).

64. J. Lin and D. Gunopulos. Dimensionality Reduction by Random Projection and Latent Semantic Indexing. In *In Proc. of SDM*, San Francisco, CA, (2003).

65. E. Bingham and H. Mannila. Random projection in dimensionality reduc-

tion: Applications to image and text data. In *Proceedings of the Seventh ACM SIGKDD International Conference on Knowledge Discovery and Data Mining*, pp. 245–250, (2001).

66. R. Hecht-Nielsen. Context vectors: general purpose approximate meaning representations self-organized from raw data. In eds. J. Zurada, R. M. II, and C. Robinson, *Computational Intelligence:Imitating Life*, p. 4356. IEEE Press, (1994).

67. D. Achlioptas, Database-friendly random projections, *Symposium on Principles of Database Systems (PODS)*. pp. 274–281, (2001).

68. R. Bekkerman, A. McCallum, and G. Huang. Automatic Categorization of Email into Folders: Benchmark Experiments on Enron and SRI Corpora. Technical Report IR-418, CIIR Technical Report, (2004). http://www.cs.umass.edu/~ronb/papers/email.pdf.

Chapter 13

Genetic Algorithms for Designing Network Security Protocols

Luis Zarza[1,2], Jordi Forné[1], Josep Pegueroles[1], Miguel Soriano[1]

[1] *Universidad Politécnica de Cataluña, Departamento de Ingeniería Telemática, Jordi Girona 1-3 Campus Nord C3 08034 Barcelona, España {luisz, jforne, josep, soriano}@entel.upc.edu*

[2] *Universidad Tecnológica Mixteca, Inst. de Electrónica y Computacin, Carretera Huajuapan-Acatlima, km. 2.5, Huajuapan, Oaxaca, México luisz@entel.upc.edu*

The design of cryptographic and security protocols for new scenarios and applications can be computationally expensive. Examples of these can be sensor or mobile ad-hoc networks where thousands of nodes can be involved. In such cases, the aid of an automated tool generating protocols for a predefined problem can be of great utility. This work uses the genetic algorithms (GA) techniques for the automatic design of security networked protocols. When using GA for optimizing protocols two aspects are critical: the genome definition and the evaluation function. We discuss how security protocols can be represented as binary strings and can be interpreted as security protocols; moreover we define several basic criteria for evaluating security protocols. Finally, we present the software we developed for generating secure communications protocols and show some examples and obtained results.

Contents

13.1. Introduction

Security mechanisms are mandatory in current data communications protocols across unsecured media such as the Internet. It is not easy to determine whether a communication protocol complies with the relevant security requirements, mainly in complex scenarios, such as group communications in sensor networks, where hundreds of entities can be involved.

The methodologies used to study the security of communications protocols have been improved gradually and include automated techniques. These have already proved to be effective for analyzing and detecting whether security protocols are vulnerable to common and some less common types of attack; and research is being carried out into the possible use of artificial intelligence techniques to design cryptographic and security protocols. In this study we propose the use of Genetic Algorithms (GA) to provide information needed to generate and optimize security protocols.

Genetic algorithms are based on Darwin's Theory of Evolution and have become widely used as problem solving techniques. They are used to solve problems which cannot be solved analytically or are highly complex. In GAs, possible solutions are represented as codified individuals so that their code can be recombined and modified. Consequently, the individuals evolve to such an extent that at least one can be considered a good solution to the problem.

Several conditions must be satisfied when GAs are applied. Firstly, it must be possible to represent all possible solutions using the defined code and to interpret each one as a specific solution. Secondly, the algorithm must be capable of evaluating each solution by assigning a value that indicates how "good" the solution is. In general, GAs use one or more weighted criteria to evaluate the characteristics of proposed solutions and produce a global value for each individual.

In this work we follow the above mentioned conditions to apply GA to the problem of designing optimal security protocols.

We can consider a security protocol as a simple series of messages exchange among the different parts of a system. Each message must carry information identifying the sender, the receiver, the transmitted data and the keys used. Some or all of the messages are coded. Hence, the representation of the security protocols is constructed with definitions from series of bits that described each of the components (binary strings).

The following aspects must be considered when designing the binary representation of protocols for their genetic evolution:

- The search space represented by all possible combinations of bits will include all possible solutions of the problem.
- The binary representation must be as small as possible to limit the size of the search space.
- Each point in the search space must be clearly interpretable as a valid protocol, even though it may not be "good".

To evaluate the fitness of a security protocol we must take into account fundamental aspects such as the amount of data to be transmitted and the measures required to prevent malicious parties from accessing the data. An optimal protocol must also prevent redundancies and minimize the number of resources used during the required operations.

Protocols are analyzed and a numeric value is obtained. This number indicates how suitable each protocol is for solving the problem (fitness function). In the case of security protocols, certain aspects must be considered to determine whether the protocol complies securely and efficiently with the communication objectives.

The rest of this chapter is organized as follows. Section 13.2 reviews the principles of Genetic Algorithms applied to solve complex problems. Section 13.3 introduces the characteristics of security protocols definition in order to study how they can be represented as binary strings. Section 13.4 presents state of the art work in automatic generation of security protocols. Sections 13.5 and 13.6 describe our work on the use of Genetic Algorithms for automatic security protocols design. First we define the genotype and relate it to the binary strings interpretation. Then we systematize evaluation of individuals of the search space and define parameters and values of the fitness function. Finally, Section 13.7 concludes.

13.2. Genetic algorithms

J. H. Holland established the principles of genetic algorithms,[1] inspired by the book "The Genetical Theory of Natural Selection" written by the evolutionary biologist R. A. Fisher.[2] Holland began his work in 1962 and presented the findings in "Adaptation in Natural and Artificial Systems", published in 1975.[1] Holland proposed that complex problems should be approached in the same way that natural systems adapt during evolutionary processes. The basic aim of his work was to design artificial systems that can replicate as natural beings. Thus, each element in a population would represent a possible (not optimal) solution, and new elements would be generated according to the rules of "natural selection" as a means of reaching an optimal solution. David Goldberg conducted research into production line problems and was the first engineer to apply successfully the principles proposed by Holland.[3]

In general, the application of genetic algorithms can be considered a metaheuristic technique.[4] Genetic algorithms comprise a series of computational procedures designed to imitate important aspects of biological evolution. They first evaluate a random population and then construct a subsequent generation by increasing the reproductive capabilities of individuals whose gene interpretation (phenotype) better satisfies the objectives.[5]

13.2.1. Definitions and terminology

For the sake of clarity, we introduce some of the terminology and definitions that will be used throughout the paper.

Genetic algorithm: an adaptive search procedure based on principles derived from evolution in natural populations.[6,7] *Population*: a set of individuals existing at a given moment in time, from which a selection will be made to create the individuals of a new set or population.[7]

Individual: a data structure that represents a possible solution of the problem.[6,7]

Genotype: a numerical representation of an individual used for storage, recombination and mutation. It is also known as genetic code.

Phenotype: the set of features that characterize an individual, which can be obtained by interpreting the corresponding genotype.

13.2.2. *General characteristics of genetic algorithms*

Genetic algorithms have been used most frequently for solving optimization problems and have proved to be very efficient. However, not all optimization problems can be solved using this technique, and the following requirements must be satisfied for the algorithm to function effectively:[8]

- The optimal solution should be at least one of a finite number of possible proposals.
- An aptitude function for evaluating proposals must be defined (fitness function).
- The proposals must be codified so that they are easy to implement in the computer.

The first requirement is very important because if the search space is not limited the genetic evolution could be lost into a infinite space so it might never find the optimal solution (not even through an exhaustive search).[9]

The fitness function is critical in our systems because it assigns numerical values that can be used to examine the difference between proposals.[10] This function is a key contribution of this work. One of the most important goals in our proposal is to overcome the inherent difficulty of developing this function, particularly if we consider that the optimal solution is unknown. The fitness function design must include criteria that identify the positive or negative aspects of the proposals. Consequently, according to the result of the fitness function some proposals will be "punished" and others "rewarded"; the latter group will be more likely to reproduce and will therefore propagate to converge towards the optimal solution.

Each genotype is an element in the search space whose interpretation points to a particular phenotype, which is a proposed solution. Each possible solution described by a phenotype must be the interpretation of at least one genotype. The difficulty in the third point is how to define this relationship between the numerical sequence (genotypes) and the proposed solutions (phenotypes).[11] The relationship is shown in Figure 13.1.

13.2.3. *Search space*

The protocol search is performed through a series of binary sequences that represent the protocols. Any binary string of a specified size must be interpretable as a formally correct protocol, even though it could not be a valid

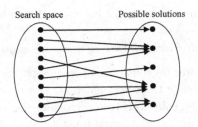

Fig. 13.1.   Relationship between the search space and the set of possible solutions.

solution for the problem. In the interpretation method used in this study, each binary sequence must be divided into messages which, in turn, must be subdivided into groups of bits that indicate the source and destination of each message, the message load and the keys employed (if any). This can be seen in Figure 13.2, which shows a binary string divided into two messages, each of which specifies the sender, the receiver, the data (1 indicates which of the data known by the sender are included in the message), and the possible keys (key1, key2 and key3). Modular arithmetic (modulo 3) is applied to the bits indicating the sender and receiver so that the total number does not exceed the number of entities involved. The interpretation of the first message in the example suggests that A sends to B the message X_a coded with the key K_{ab}.

	send	recv	data	key1	key2	key3	send	recv	data	key1	key2	key3
# bits	2	2	8	3	3	3	2	2	8	3	3	3
genoma	01	00	00000010	000	001	000	00	01	00000010	001	000	000

oper	mod 3	mod 3					mod 3	mod 3				
	1	0					0	1				

interpret	A	B	Xa	-	Kab	-	B	A	Xb	Kab	-	-

Fig. 13.2.   Example of interpretation of a genome in a 2 message protocol.

13.2.4. *Operation of a simple genetic algorithm*

A simple genetic algorithm can be formally represented as follows:

(1) generate initial population, G(0);

(2) evaluate G(0);

(3) $t:=0$;

(4) REPEAT{

    (a) $t:=t+1$;

    (b) generate G(t) using G(t-1);

    (c) evaluate G(t);

(5) }UNTIL find a solution;

First, the initial population is constructed as a set of character strings that represent proposed solutions to the problem. Next, the fitness function is applied to assess the benefits of each individual, which are combined on the basis of their aptitude to produce the next generation (presumably, most of the "best" solutions will be selected). This sequence can then be iterated until the best solution of all those reached meets our expectations.

The population is a set of symbol strings of fixed length L. The symbols belong to an alphabet Σ. Each string, or genome, represents a possible solution to a problem. Each string, or individual, must have a value that reflects its adaptation capability, which indicates how close it is to solving the problem. This value is represented by f and defined by the following expression:

$$\Sigma^L \rightarrow \mathbb{R}^+ \cup 0 \qquad (13.1)$$

13.2.4.1. *Selection phase*

This phase ensures that the features for subsequent generations are propagated in such a way that the algorithm continues to converge towards the optimal solution.

There are many selection techniques, which can be differentiated according to the likelihood that the best individuals will be maintained from one generation to the next:[12]

(1) *Population model.* The whole population is generated from the crossings of selected individuals.

(2) *Steady-state model.* Two individuals are selected with a probability that is directly proportional to their fitness. When they are crossed, a new individual is generated to replace an old individual, which is selected with a probability that is inversely proportional to its fitness. This technique allows individuals to coexist with their ancestors.[6]

(3) *Elitist selection.* This technique guarantees that the fittest individuals are copied from one generation to the next. A number of individuals (the "best") are simply copied to the next generation, but they are also considered as potential parents of new individuals.

Other selection techniques consider parameters such as the values used to define the probability that an individual will be selected, because this probability can be related directly to the fitness value (carrousel selection), or to a sequential numeric rank, which is a number assigned to each individual according to its fitness (rank selection). In addition, the discriminating power of the selection can increase with the average fitness to magnify the fitness differences (scaled selection).[13]

We also consider selection in stages, in which the best individuals in different sub-groups are matched (match selection), and selection in rounds, in which the least fit individuals are discarded in the first rounds to reduce the computational load (hierarchical selection).

13.2.4.2. *Modification phase*

In this phase genetic operators are applied to selected individuals to generate new elements in the search space, which presumably inherit the best characteristics of individuals from the previous generation. The main genetic operators are combination and mutation.

- *Combination*: the data from the genotypes of two selected individuals are combined and portions from each one are copied into two new individuals. The combination operator is the most important operator in genetic algorithms. A simple example of this operation is shown in Figure 13.3.

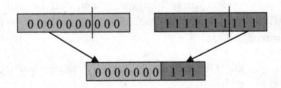

Fig. 13.3.   Combination operation.

- *Mutation*: individuals are selected according to a predefined mutation probability (different from selection probability), and some data in their genotypes are changed according to a different predefined mutation probability for characters. Mutation is a secondary operator intended to maintain the diversity of the population and therefore considers parts of the search space.[6,7] An example of this operator is shown in Figure 13.4.

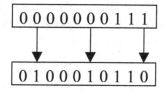

Fig. 13.4. Mutation operation.

13.2.4.3. *Evaluation phase*

Each individual in the population must be evaluated. The evaluation consists in determining a value that represents the suitability of the individuals for solving the problem. Although the optimal solution is not known, there must be some criteria for determining whether one solution is better than others, and this must be represented by numeric values so that individuals can be compared objectively. Although the evaluation function is crucial in genetic algorithms and its nature is closely related to internal aspects of the problem to be solved, its operation is defined separately to the genetic operators.

13.2.5. *Genetic algorithms and learning*

Genetic algorithms have been applied in many fields, including automatic learning,[14] problem solving in task scheduling and the development of neuronal networks,[15] and supervised learning (that is, to generate a set of rules from examples to determine the class to which an individual belongs).[6] There are two main criteria for solving these types of problems:

- What an individual represents.
- How objects are represented.

The first criterion has been considered in two ways in the literature, each based on a particular school for rule generation:

- *Michigan*.[16] Individuals represent individual rules, so the solution to the problem is given by the whole population. In this approach the meaning of each individual's evaluation must be redefined because the fitness of the solution is dependent on the whole population.
- *Pittsburgh*.[17] Each individual is a rule set, so each individual is a solution. This approach matches the classic scheme of genetic algorithms because each individual is a solution.

According to objects representation, there are two basic types of representations, which influence the definition of the genetic operator in different ways:

- *Classic*. Individuals are represented with binary strings, the length of which can vary. This is a minimalist approach that does not differ considerably from general genetic algorithms, although some work is required to determine the appropriate binary representation for problem.
- *Ad hoc*. The representation is closer to the problem to be solved, that is, the characteristics of the individuals are described almost directly by values. This approach is more efficient but requires modifications to the genetic operators.

We based our work on the Pittsburgh approach because we consider individuals as contending protocols. In the Michigan approach the individuals would either have to be considered as messages and, therefore, part of a protocol, or could be interpreted as entities that know their own protocols and try to communicate with others. In this case, each entity could try to convince others to adopt its protocol, but this remains open to debate.

We apply the classic object representation approach to examine the genetic operations and their operational parameters. The ad hoc approach could be used in later research.

13.3. Security protocols

Once we have reviewed the principles of Genetic Algorithms, we should take a close approach to Security protocols nature in order to adapt them to the GA rules.

Security protocols are designed to provide secure communication within an insecure network. The security requirements in this type of network include the following:[18]

- *Confidentiality.* An intruder must not be able to receive a message that is intended for another recipient.
- *Authentication.* A part must be able to confirm that a received message was sent by the indicated sender.
- *Integrity.* It must be possible to guarantee that a received message has not been altered or damaged.
- *Non-repudiation.* If an entity has sent a message, it will not be able to deny it later.

In cryptographic protocols, all or some of the messages can contain encrypted data.

The cryptographic protocol evaluation must return a value that indicates the fitness of the messages, which can be determined by considering the following critical characteristics:

- Whether the protocols permit non-authorized entities to access confidential data.
- Whether a part has received or understood a message that whose content it should know.
- Whether messages can be transmitted redundantly.
- Whether the receiver can verify the authenticity of the message sender.
- Whether the receiver can demonstrate that the sender knows the content of the transmitted message.

Depending on the field in which the protocol is applied, certain additional parameters or requirements may need to be defined. If a protocol complies with the requirements listed above, we can consider that it solves the problem. However, when many different protocols can solve the problem we can introduce additional requirements to see which protocol reaches the optimal solution:

- Only a small number of messages should be transmitted.
- Less coding should be used.
- Fewer resources should be used to encode and transmit large messages.
- Coding should use symmetric keys instead of public keys as this reduced the resources required.

Cryptographic techniques are used in a wide range of applications, so associated protocols are developed continuously. Consequently, a protocol that is successful when it is introduced but may later be revealed to be flawed. Potential flaws include the susceptibility to changes that may be introduced to deceive an entity.

Additional characteristics may take into account the following parameters:

- The number of parts that must be communicated.
- The availability of one or more certifying authorities.
- The possibility that one or more of the parts involved could act maliciously.
- The possible need to minimize the use of resources in one or more of the parts involved (asymmetric resources).
- The reliability of the certifying authority.

13.3.1. *Conventions*

As stated by Abadi and Needham,[19] the following basic principles must be considered when designing cryptographic protocols:

- The content of a message must clearly state its purpose so that there is only one possible interpretation. It should be possible to write the message in natural language.
- The conditions upon which a message must act must be clearly defined so when it is revised it can be seen that it is acceptable or not.
- The meaning of the codification and the way in which it is applied must be clearly defined.
- The method by which the timelines of the messages are proved and the meaning of temporal information must be clearly explained.

Standard notation must be adopted. Abadi and Needham formalized a notation that has become widely used: symbols such as A and B represent the communicating entities, S represents a server, or certifying authority, T is a timestamp, N represents a nonce (a quantity generated to test data freshness), K is a key and K^{-1} is its inverse. If a symmetric key algorithm is applied, K and K^{-1} are the same. In public-key cryptosystems, it is assumed that K^{-1} is the secret key and K is the public key. $\{X\}_K$ represents X encrypted by K, so any entity that knows $\{X\}_K$ and K^{-1} can obtain X.

Consider the following message:

$$Message4 : B \rightarrow A : \{T_a + 1\}K_{ab} \tag{13.2}$$

This example shows the fourth message from a protocol, in which B sends to A the timestamp T_a incremented by 1, encrypted with the key K_{ab}. It can be inferred from the subscripts in this notation that T_a was generated by A and that K_{ab} is a key for communicating A with B. We can also deduce that K_a is the public key for A.

It should be stressed that the message in the example does not guarantee that A will receive the message from B; it will be sent, but the message could be lost, corrupted or received in a different order to that intended by the protocol designer.

13.4. State of art

The evaluation of security protocols and application of metaheuristics have been considered in previous studies in the literature. There are several main lines of research in the field of protocol evaluation: the oldest and most common uses state exploration, whereas new approaches use techniques such as belief logic, theorem proving based on the Dolev-Yao model,[20] and type verification.

13.4.1. *State exploration*

In this method, a tool is used to define the state space and search for paths across it that represent successful attacks by intruders.

This method has been expanded to include additional components such as model verifiers, including general-purpose model verifiers, specific purpose model verifiers and theorem probing.

The NRL analyzer presented by Meadows[21] models protocols as interactions between a set of machine states. It tests the security of the protocol by specifying insecure states and applying exhaustive search or test techniques to the machine models to demonstrate that these states cannot be reached. Millen and Meadows developed a high-level language for applying formal analytical methods to test the security of cryptographic protocols. This language is used in the CAPSL[22] tool developed by the United States Navy.

Fiore and Abadi[23] proposed an algorithm for analyzing symbolic models that operates by restricting the infinite number of traces caused by the unbounded inputs from the environment to a finite number, even for a finite number of processes that describe a protocol. When this algorithm is applied, a protocol is presented as a process, which is the parallel composition of the parts of the protocol. 1.1

13.4.2. *Belief logic*

Clark and Jacob[24] showed how evolutionary search, with genetic algorithms, can be used to evolve protocols by means of the BAN logic. The BAN logic, developed by Burrows, Abadi and Needham[25] can be used to reason about protocol security. With BAN logic, a message exchange is performed according to beliefs or principals by applying a set of inference rules to modify the belief state of each entity. BAN logic assumes that entities are honest. Before the inference rules are applied, each message is probed for violations, such as the transmission of open messages (without encryption). If violations are detected, the message is simply ignored.

The genome structure proposed by Clark and Jacob contains the following components: initial conditions indicated by six bits that specify the entities that share keys, and 1 bit for each additional belief of each entity; senders and receivers of M messages; and message components, consisting of indices that refer to the beliefs of the sender.

The initial conditions for each protocol can evolve, which means that the solution can establish the initial conditions that the protocol requires in order to work correctly. The initial conditions can also be imposed in specific problems so that the condition indicated by the genome is ignored.

The genome interpretation process consists of a series of operations. Messages from principals that do not share a key are discarded. Next, a mode T operation is applied to the indices of transmitted beliefs, where T is the number of beliefs known by the sender. Finally, the BAN inference rules are applied to define new beliefs.

In contrast to Clark and Jacob, in our work we do not discard message exchange between entities that do not share a key. Instead, we assign a low grade so that the entities can evolve and overcome this limitation. The module function is not applied to the number of data known by the sender, because new data could be acquired while the protocol is being executed. For the evaluation of the protocols we do not use the BAN logic, but an algorithm for registering the information exchanged between parts, including information about how the data were acquired.

Clark and Jacob proposed to evaluate the protocols on the basis of several criteria related to the status of the defined objectives (goal beliefs required by each entity). The criteria are:

- *Early Credit.* Goals achieved early are assigned a better value.
- *Uniform Credit.* The same value is assigned to all goals achieved.
- *Delayed Gratification.* Late goals are assigned a better value.
- *Advanced Delay Gratification.* A better value is assigned to late goals but no value is assigned to goals achieved during the initial exchange.
- *Uniform Delay Gratification.* No credit is given for goals achieved early, but later weights are equal and positive.
- *Destination Judgment.* The number of goals achieved is counted, irrespective of when or where they are achieved.

The results obtained with this proposal suggest that the technique is plausible.

Meadows[26] claims that belief logics such as BAN are weaker than state exploration because they operate at a higher level of abstraction.

13.4.3. *Genetic programming*

Pavel Ocenasek[27] suggested that general evolutionary processes should be followed but also introduced a specialized form of genetic algorithm referred to as genetic programming. This technique makes no distinction between the genome and the phenotype, as in the ad hoc approach described above. The genetic operations are carried out directly on the solution, instead of a binary representation, as Koza explains in.[28] Ocenasek considered that genetic programming is necessary because security protocols have different sizes. Consequently, he developed tree-shaped structures in which the operations carried out by the protocols are indicated. However, Ocenasek also explained that operations such as crossover considerably alter the meanings of the protocol operations. In genetic algorithms, small changes in a genotype must produce small changes in a phenotype. Therefore, Ocenasek suggested that a heuristic was needed to define which sub-trees could be exchanged without altering the semantics of the instruction sequence.

We do not consider genetic programming in this study. Although the protocols have different sizes, we suggest that there are segments in the genomes whose interpretation will produce invalid or empty messages that will be ignored, but which will be included in the code transmitted to new individuals. This "sleeping" code is valuable because it can combine or mutate to form a valid message for a good protocol. In addition, the way in which data is represented in a message provides versatility without requiring the protocol size to be changed, because the messages can contain either simple data or all of the information known by the sender.

13.5. Genome definition and interpretation

Genetic algorithms use strings of symbols to represent individuals, which are the protocols to be considered. The strings are known as genomes or chromosomes. The individuals that provide the best results are identified through a process in which the genomes are modified, the data are mixed, and values from different parts are exchanged. The interpretation of each genome produces a phenotype consisting of a series of characteristics that describe an individual and, for the purposes of the present work, a protocol. In this case, the phenotype is composed of a set of messages that are exchanged by the entities. Each message specifies the source and destination of the message, the data transmitted and the encryption keys used in the case of encrypted data.

The search space is a set of all possible combinations of the symbols that make up genomes. For a specific problem, the size of the genomes is defined and the search space is limited. Importantly, the search space increases exponentially with genome size, which is why genetic algorithms are used for the search procedure instead of performing an exhaustive of the entire space, which would take an unreasonable amount of time. The search space must be minimized even when genetic algorithms are used, although it is important to ensure that protocols that could solve the problem efficiently are not omitted. Next, we present our proposal for the genotype definition and how it can be interpreted as a security protocol.

13.5.1. *The binary sequence*

To define the meaning of a genotype, as it is interpreted, we need to establish the parts of the protocol and the amount of data required to describe it.

Each protocol consists of a set of messages that are exchanged by the entities involved. Each message contains the following information:

- *Sender*. The entity that sent the message.
- *Receiver*. The intended recipient of the message.
- *Data*. The information to be transmitted.
- *Key*. The keys used to encrypt the information, if any.

At this point in our research we are not considering messages which have parts coded and other parts not coded. We split partially coded messages and treat them as separate messages. We will consider partially coded messages in future work.

13.5.1.1. *Sender and receiver*

For the sender and receiver fields, the total number of entities involved in the problem must be known, although spy entities are not included because they cannot be considered as a sender or receiver.

In protocols for solving easy problems, data exchange between two entities A and B or secure data exchange using a certification authority can use two bits for the source and two bits for the destination of each message. If two or three entities participate, modular arithmetic ($mod2$ or $mod3$) can be applied when interpreting the genotype to ensure that all bit combinations points to a valid entity.

In general, the number of bits required for N entities is $roof(log_2(N))$, this is, the greater or equal integer closer to x such as $2^x \geq N$. In advanced protocols, certain combinations could be assigned a special meaning, such as "directed to nobody" or "directed to all". Therefore, the number of bits required would be $roof(log_2(N+2))$, although this would only apply to the receiver because "all" or "nobody" cannot be used to designate the sender.

If messages need to be transmitted to groups of entities, the initial conditions of the groups and their respective members could be indicated in tables. The number of bits required would be $roof(log_2(N + G + 2))$, where G is the number of groups. Table 13.1 shows an example of a table for specifying the receiver when the A, B and CA (certification authority) entities are considered, adding "nobody", "all" and two groups. A group cannot send a message, so $mod(N)$ should be applied for the source and $mod(N + 2 + G)$ for the destination.

Another approach, instead of using static tables (Table 13.1), is the use of a dynamic set, included in the genome, so each solution includes how groups of entities are defined (the definition of groups evolved too).

For example, if we have 4 entities, A, B, C, D and groups G_1, G_2, G_3 and G_4, we need 3 bits to specify the receiver. If each message can include any of A, B, C and D, and any of the groups G_1, G_2, G_3 and G_4, we need 8 bits for message (one per possible receiver). Including a group inside a group allows creating hierarchical trees of groups. For example, consider the following groups:

Table 13.1. Example
of Code for Specifying
Receiver

Code	Interpretation
000	A
001	B
010	CA
011	A,CA
100	A,B
101	nobody
110	all
111	-

$G_1 : A, B$

$G_2 : C, D$

$G_3 : G_1, G_2$

$G_4 : (empty)$

If we allow each possible solution to have an adaptable group definition, we need 8 bits (4 for entities and 4 for other groups) for each receiver, adding a total of 32 bits for genome. Of course the groups can't be senders, so we need 2 bits for the sender, and 3 bits for the receiver in each message. As an example, the bits needed to produce the previous groups are:

```
11000000 00110000 00001100 00000000
```

meaning:

```
AB------ --CD---- ----G1G2-- --------
```

If a group contains itself, this can be ignored.

13.5.1.2. *Data*

Each message can transmit various data elements simultaneously. These data elements can be keys or texts. Eights bits can be used to indicate which of the data known by the sender must be transmitted. Bits that indicate data which does not exist at the source will be ignored. If all eight bits are zero, the message will be empty and the protocol will ignore it.

Each entity can know a variable number of data elements. In simple problems with N entities, in the worst case, each entity could know N public keys, one private key, $N - 1$ symmetric keys, one data element to transmit and one data element to be received. Each possible known data could be sent, so there must be a bit for each of them on each message.

Consequently, the maximum number of data elements that an entity can know is $3 + N + N - 1 = 2N + 2$. If $N = 3$, each entity could know eight data elements. The genome size should be minimized to limit the search space.

An entity could know a larger volume of data if private keys are transmitted, but this is not desirable and the protocols would be assigned a low fitness score. Therefore, no more than eight data elements need to be transmitted.

The size of the genome code does not depend on the number of messages transmitted.

13.5.1.3. *Keys*

The order in which the data are encrypted affects the outcome, so the keys used are identified, ordered, and assigned three bits each that indicate which of the data elements known by the sender is used as a key. Text sent by a user is prohibited and cannot be considered as a key. A key field with three zeros indicates that there is no key. If the three key fields are filled with zeros, the message is not encrypted prior to transmission. Consequently, keys can only be selected from the first seven data elements known by the source. Extra bits can be added to extend the range. Key trees and group keys require a more complex management structure. These types of cases should be analyzed using GAs because although advanced protocols could be discovered, they must have a correct genome structure.

13.5.1.4. *Structure*

We can infer from the information given above that each protocol message requires fours bits to indicate the sender and receiver, eight bits to indicate the data to be sent, and nine bits to indicate the keys used. Therefore, each message must have a total length of 21 bits.

If a protocol with two messages is needed to solve a given problem, 42 bits will be required. Figure 13.2 contains an example of this structure and its interpretation, although the data known by the entities are not shown.

Genomes can have more complex structures than simple binary chains. Genetic algorithms can be defined for genomes constructed from several chains (helix) of non-binary symbols. Of course, genomes can also be defined with a single helix of binary symbols to reduce complexity and improve performance. Multiple helixes are useful when the environment (*i.e.* the problem to solve) changes over time.

13.5.2. *From the binary sequence to the genome*

Once we have defined the genome structure for representing protocols in the search space, we then need to establish criteria for converting any binary string of the specified size into a security protocol.

There is a special relationship between the genome set (search space) and the phenotype set (protocols).

It must be possible to interpret each genome to produce a phenotype (that is, a valid protocol, even if it is not useful). The phenotype is valid if it contains valid characteristics for a protocol, although it may not be useful if does not transport any data or if it is assigned a very low fitness score.

Two different genomes could generate the same phenotype. This cannot occur in other search spaces for other types of problems, but it is unavoidable when searching for security protocols, because the number of messages that a good protocol will have is not known but a reasonable number amount of messages must be defined, so good protocols could contain ignored (invalidated) messages. Since some protocols may contain ignored messages, certain genomes could be differentiated only by ignored messages and would therefore produce the same phenotype.

The same valid messages could come from segments of different genomes, because these could contain invalid references to keys and data that are ignored.

13.5.2.1. *Genome structure*

In the field of genetic algorithms, a genome can be described as a set of N series of symbols of the same size, each of which is constructed from a series of symbols with values in a certain range. In genetic biology, each series of symbols is called a helix because the data series are twisted like helixes. This type of geometric structure does not exist in genetic algorithms, but data from the helix can be processed because they are contained in a front-to-front configuration.

13.5.2.2. *Genome interpretation*

The following steps must be carried out to obtain the phenotype from a genome interpretation:

Each i-th bit of the dominant binary chain is obtained by adding values at the i-th position of each helix and applying an exclusive-OR operation (i.e, applying modulo 2 arithmetic)..

The binary string is segmented into N messages of 21 bits. These N messages represent the data exchange between entities.

Each message is defined with two bits for the sender, two bits for the receiver, eight bits for the data contained in the message, and nine bits to specify the keys. If two bits are used to specify the source and the destination there can be four possible entities. Modular arithmetic can be applied to the number of entities to reduce the message waste. Each bit of data in the message indicates the presence or absence of data known by sender. The nine bits that specify keys must be subdivided into three groups of three bits each. Each group specifies one of the seven data elements known by the sender as an encryption key. A group 000 indicates that there is no key. Each message can either remain unencrypted or be encrypted up by three keys.

This process is shown in Figure 13.1 for a two-message protocol, where the interpretation produces the following protocol:

$$Message1 : A \to B : \{X_a\}K_{ab} \qquad (13.3)$$

$$Message2 : B \to A : \{X_b\}K_{ab} \qquad (13.4)$$

13.5.3. *Analysis for genome construction*

Once we have seen how to generate and interpret the genome, we will analyze how the length of the structure affects the search performance.

One of the most important design criteria is the total length of the genome. This is critical if we consider that the size of the search space increases exponentially when genome length grows linearly, so the time needed to conduct an exhaustive search of all possible solutions will also increase exponentially with the size of the search space and the size of each genome.

The time taken to analyze each genome increases slightly when genetic algorithms are used, due to the overhead introduced by the genetic operations. However, in this case only a very small portion of the search space needs to be explored. In some cases the system produces a slightly worse solution due to the presence of a local maximum. Small changes in values produce worse solutions. The incidence of local maxima can be reduced by adjusting the parameters in the evaluation function.

Figure 13.5 shows the time needed to solve problems with between two and five messages with an exhaustive search and with genetic algorithms. Figure 13.6 shows the time taken by genetic algorithms as the number of

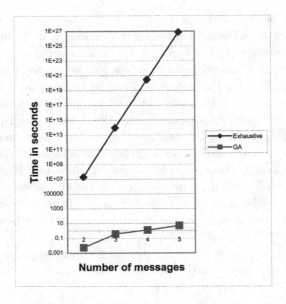

Fig. 13.5.   Time required with exhaustive search and with genetic algorithms.

messages increases. The times increase exponentially for both techniques, but the increase is greater for the exhaustive search. In figure 13.5 the time scale is logarithmic. Figure 13.6 shows that even with genetic algorithms the time grows exponentially.

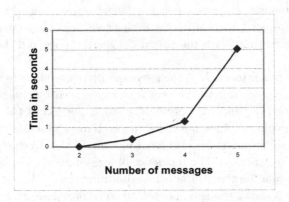

Fig. 13.6.   Time required with genetic algorithms as number of messages increases.

This result is especially relevant if we take into account that complex protocols (large number of parts involved, large number of keys to be considered, etc.) increase the length of the genotype. The longer the genotype is the longest is the time needed to perform the exhaustive or GA search. However, the GA search will be much faster than the exhaustive one.

13.6. Security protocol evaluation: towards the fitness function

Security protocols evaluation is a very difficult task that often identifies major weaknesses in widely used protocols. Each new weakness discovered highlights the complexity of security protocols and proves that much more research needs to be carried out before we can understand them fully. The methodology applied in this study is based on the assumption that all of the entities could be listening to the network and trying to decode all messages.

The evaluation methodology must be carefully designed and take into account the following points:

- The elements that must be evaluated to determine the "fitness" of the protocol
- The way in which these elements are detected
- The value that should be assigned to each element.

13.6.1. *Aspects to evaluate*

Next we present the aspects we included for consideration in the fitness function:

13.6.1.1. *Number of goals achieved*

A problem definition must specify the data that the entities must acquire securely. Each data element acquired by an entity must be accounted for positively. Some data may not be acquired correctly, which leads to the following conclusions:

It is assumed that all entities listen to the network, so they should know when certain data are not intended for them. If data are acquired incorrectly despite this knowledge, the protocol does not work correctly.

Each data element is evaluated to verify the authenticity of the sender. If this cannot be guaranteed, the protocol is not good enough.

Goals achieved must be counted, but data that are known indirectly (non-intended) or that are non-authenticated (not encrypted with a key known only by the sender, and perhaps the receiver and a trusted authority) must be assigned a lower value.

13.6.1.2. *Leaked data*

Data known by non-authorized entities reveal data leakage, and protocols that allow leakages must be penalized by losing points. These types of protocols are not good solutions but must not be eliminated, because parts of them could produce good protocols when combined with parts of others.

13.6.1.3. *Number of data acquired redundantly*

Data acquired redundantly incur a penalty for the protocol. Protocols in which this occurs could solve the problem, but the redundancies could be improved by further evolution.

13.6.1.4. *Data acquired by keys received later than the data*

Some entities could receive data before the encryption keys required to decrypt them. However, simple protocols are more effective when the key is received first. Therefore, points are subtracted when protocols decode data with a key received later than the data itself.

13.6.1.5. *Number of messages in the protocol*

Points must be subtracted when protocols use large numbers of messages, as ideal protocols are simple and use resources efficiently.

13.6.1.6. *Transmission of large and small messages*

In initial tests we found that proposed protocols used the certifying authority to transmit messages to their destination, instead of distributing the necessary keys. The certifying authority is not a relay for messages, and duplicate transmission of large messages is a waste of resources. Therefore, instead of simply forbidding the transmission of large messages to the authority, points should be deducted for each transmission of large messages to prevent the waste.

13.6.1.7. *Public and symmetric keys*

Some data must be secret or require authentication, whereas other data do not need to be encrypted or authenticated. Public key algorithms have a much higher computational cost than symmetric algorithms, which is particularly important when portable devices are used because they have limited computing capabilities and power supplies. Consequently, symmetric keys should be used whenever possible, particularly when sending large messages and no keys should be used when they are not strictly necessary. Therefore, points must be subtracted for protocols that use symmetric keys, and many more points must be deducted when public keys are used.

13.6.1.8. *Encoding large and small messages*

The penalties for using symmetric and public keys should take into account the size of the data to be encoded. We consider two sizes: small for keys, and large for user data.

13.6.2. *Detecting the elements to be evaluated*

In this study we identify the elements to be evaluated as messages are exchanged. Therefore, each message is considered for each entity, because it is assumed that all entities listen to the network. Each entity will be analyzed to determine whether it can read the message; if it can, the new data must be recorded to show whether it was intended for the entity and whether it was authenticated. If the data was received redundantly, a counter is increased.

If an entity receives a key that could be used to decode a coded message received previously, a complex record of pending decryptions could be kept. However, for the sake of simplicity, a flag is activated to indicate that the entity has acquired at least one new key that could be used to decode previous messages. There are two flags: one to indicate that at least one unsuccessful attempt has been made to decode a coded message, and another to indicate that there is at least one new key that could be used to decode the message. If both flags are activated after all of the messages have been presented to each entity, the entire process is repeated.

It is critical to record the number of data elements obtained during the first run for each entity and each message and to ignore new data in possible messages to send, because this would alter the meaning of the protocol at this stage. During the first run a count is kept of the number of valid messages, the number and type of keys used, and the number of large and small messages. There is also an accumulator for adding the defined weights of large and small messages, which are then multiplied by the defined weights of public and symmetric keys to determine the encryption cost.

Once the tracking has been completed, the results must be combined.

To determine the number of goals achieved, the list of expected data is compared with the data obtained, taking into account the conditions in which they were acquired (*i.e.* directed and/or authenticated). Data that were not received correctly force a deduction.

Data leakages are verified by counting the number of data elements received that were not in desired list.

13.6.3. *Setting the weight of each element to be evaluated*

The following criteria must be taken into account when protocols are evaluated:

- The critical criteria that determine whether a protocol is valid:
- The goals are achieved
- There are no leakages
- The criteria that determine whether a protocol is optimal:
- There are no redundancies
- The number of messages is minimal
- The cost of transmitting large and small messages is minimal
- The cost of encrypting large and small messages is minimal
- The cost of encrypting messages using public and symmetric keys is minimal

Consequently, fairly high values should be assigned to the critical criteria so that they become more important as the solutions evolve.

When assigning values to the critical criteria, a preference must be established between a protocol that achieves the desired goals (data to be transmitted) but leaks data to unauthorized entities or a protocol that prevents leakages but does not transmit all of the required data. It is obviously vital to prevent leakages, so leakages must be penalized at least as heavily as unachieved goals.

The criteria that determine whether a protocol is optimal can be relatively flexible according to the design objectives in each case, although it should always be taken into account that more resources are needed to transmit large messages, to encrypt large messages, and to encrypt messages with symmetric keys.

13.6.4. *Definition of proper values for weights*

The weights were gradually defined and adjusted as we monitored the number of evaluations required to reach optimal protocols for solving the proposed problems. However, the weights had to be formalized so we conducted additional tests and took a large number of measurements to verify the values assigned.

In the tests, we grouped the parameters by type and analyzed the behaviour of the system by varying the values and observing the mean number of evaluations needed to find the optimal protocol.

A mean of 239.098 evaluations were needed to find an optimal protocol for two entities that used a certifying authority to authenticate public keys and which could also use a symmetric key. The number of evaluations required increased and decreased when different weights were changed.

13.6.5. *Applied values and their results*

We applied the criteria described above and obtained a series of values which can be used to evaluate the results of the proposed protocols. The following values were selected:

- *FITADD = 40* Value to be added for each correct data element at the desired destination.
- *FITRED = 2* Value to be subtracted for each redundancy.
- *FITLEAK = 40* Value to be subtracted for each data element acquired by a non-authorized entity.
- *FITLATE = 5* Value to be subtracted for each data decrypted with a key received late.
- *FITNMES = 1* Cost of each message. This value will be subtracted for each message transmitted.
- *FITMESGR = 3* Cost of transmitting a large message (user data). This value will be subtracted.
- *FITMESPE = 1* Cost of transmitting a small message (keys).
- *FITENCRK = 1* Cost of encoding with a symmetric key.
- *FITENCRP = 8* Cost of encoding with a public key.
- *FITENCR_GR = 5* Cost of encoding large data.
- *FITENCR_PE = 1* Cost of encoding small data.

The last four elements are calculated for each message as follows:

- The number of small is data multiplied by FITENCR_PE.
- The product is added to the number of large data multiplied by FITENCR_GR.
- The result is multiplied by the sum of FITENCRK and FITENCRP because there are both symmetric and public keys.

This gives the cost of encoding a message. The total for all messages is calculated and then subtracted from the total cost.

For example, if the transmitted data is $\{\{X_a, X_b, K_{ab}\}K_b\}Ks^{-1}$, the encoding cost is:

$$(2\times\text{FITENCR\_GR}+1\times\text{FITENCR\_PE})\times(\text{FITENCRK}+\text{FITENCRP}) =$$
$$(2\times5+1\times1)\times(1+8) = 11\times9 = 99$$

This value must be subtracted from the total. Let us consider different examples:

13.6.5.1. *Example 1*

(1) *Problem*: A and B must exchange X_a and X_b using a symmetric key K_{ab} known by both.

(2) *Different individuals of the search space*:

    (a) The following example is a possible non-correct protocol to be evaluated:

        Message 1 B → A: $\{X_b, K_{ab}\}K_{ab}$

        Message 2 A → B: X_a, K_{ab}, X_b

    (b) The following example is a possible correct but non-optimal protocol

        Message 1 B → A: $\{X_b\}K_{ab}$

        Message 2 A → B: $\{X_a, K_{ab}\}K_{ab}$

        Message 3 A → B: $\{K_{ab}\}K_{ab}$

    (c) The following example is a possible correct and optimal protocol:

        Message 1 B → A: $\{X_b\}K_{ab}$

        Message 2 A → B: $\{X_a\}K_{ab}$

(3) *Analysis*

The data acquired, including the spy entity C, are as follows for the different cases:

    (a) A: X_b in mode 3 (directed and authenticated)

        B: X_a in mode 2 (directed but not authenticated)

       C: X_a, K_{ab}, X_b in mode 0 (not directed and not authenticated)
- (b) A: X_b in mode 3 (directed and authenticated)
  - B: X_a in mode 3 (directed and authenticated)
  - C: (nothing).
- (c) A: X_b in mode 3 (directed and authenticated)
  - B: X_a in mode 3 (directed and authenticated)
  - C: (nothing).

(4) *Evaluation*

- (a) Fitness function: 280 - 120 - 6 - 0 - 2 - 11 - 6 = 135.
  Detail of evaluation:
  Goals achieved: $((3+1)+(2+1)) \times 40 = 280$ (acquired by A and B).
  Data leaked: $3 \times 40 = 120$ (known by C).
  Redundant data: $3 \times 2 = 6$ (K_{ab} was already known by A, K_{ab} and X_b were already known by B).
  Keys received after coded data: $0 \times 5 = 0$.
  Cost for the total number of messages: $2 \times 1 = 2$.
  Cost for large and small messages: $3 \times 3 + 2 \times 1 = 11$ (bigs: X_b, X_a, X_b , small: K_{ab}, K_{ab}).
  Total cost of encryption: $(1 \times 5 + 1 \times 1) \times 1 = 6$ (a small message and a large message encoded with a symmetric key).
- (b) Fitness function: 320 - 0 - 4 - 0 - 3 - 8 - 12 = 293.
  Detail of evaluation:
  Goals achieved: $((3+1)+(3+1)) \times 40 = 320$ (acquired by A and B).
  Leaked data: $0 \times 40 = 0$ (no undesired data were acquired).
  Redundant data: $2 \times 2 = 4$ (K_{ab} was already known by B but was transmitted twice).
  Keys received after coded data: $0 \times 5 = 0$.
  Cost for the total number of messages: $3 \times 1 = 3$
  Cost for large and small messages: $2 \times 3 + 2 \times 1 = 8$ (large: X_b, X_a, small: K_{ab}, K_{ab}).
  Total cost of encryption: $(1 \times 5) \times 1 + (1 \times 5 + 1 \times 1) \times 1 + (1 \times 1)$ $\times 1 = 12$ (a large message, a small message with a large one, and a small message, all encoded with a symmetric key).
- (c) Fitness function: 320 - 0 - 0 - 0 - 2 - 6 - 10 = 302.
  Detail of evaluation:
  Goals achieved: $((3+1)+(3+1)) \times 40 = 320$ (acquired by A and

B).
Leaked data: $0 \times 40 = 0$ (no undesired data were acquired).
Redundant data: $0 \times 2 = 0$ (no redundancies).
Keys received after coded data: $0 \times 5 = 0$
Cost for the total number of messages: $2 \times 1 = 2$
Cost for large and small messages: $2 \times 3 + 0 \times 1 = 6$ (large: X_b, X_a, small: no one).
Total cost of encryption: $(1 \times 5) \times 1 + (1 \times 5) \times 1 = 10$ (a large message, a small message with a large one, and a small message, all encoded with a symmetric key).

13.6.5.2. *Example 2*

(1) *Problem*: A and B must exchange X_a and X_b using an authority to obtain public keys, although symmetric keys can also be used.
(2) *Possible solution* (individual in the search space)
Message 1 C $\to$ B: $\{X_a\}K_c^{-1}$
Message 2 C $\to$ A: $\{X_b\}K_c^{-1}$
Message 3 A $\to$ B: $\{\{K_{ab}\}X_b\}K_a^{-1}$
Message 4 A $\to$ B: $\{X_a\}K_{ab}$
Message 5 B $\to$ A: $\{X_b\}K_{ab}$
(3) *Analysis* The data acquired, including the spy entity D, are:
A: P_b, X_b in mode 3 (directed and authenticated)
B: P_a, K_{ab}, X_a in mode 3 (directed and authenticated)
C: (nothing)
D: (nothing)
(4) *Evaluation* Fitness function: $800 - 0 - 0 - 0 - 5 - 9 - 42 = 744$.
Goals achieved: $((3+1)+(3+1)+(3+1)+(3+1)+(3+1)) \times 40 = 800$ (acquired by A and B).
Leaked data: $0 \times 40 = 0$ (no undesired data were acquired).
Redundant data: $0 \times 2 = 0$ (no redundancies).
Keys received after coded data: $0 \times 5 = 0$.
Cost for the total number of messages: $5 \times 1 = 5$.
Cost for large and small messages: $2 \times 3 + 3 \times 1 = 9$ (large: X_b, X_a, small: P_a, P_b, K_{ab}).
Total encryption cost: $(1 \times 1) \times 8 + (1 \times 1) \times 8 + (1 \times 1) \times (8+8) + (1 \times 5) \times 1 + (1 \times 5) \times 1 = 42$ (two small messages coded with private key, one small message encoded with public and private keys, and two large messages encoded with symmetric keys).

13.7. Conclusions

Computers running genetic algorithms can solve problems without having to explore all possible solutions. However, the search space must be designed carefully so that all potentially good solutions are considered but it remains reasonably small.

We defined a genome structure for representing security protocols, taking into account the information needed to describe suitable protocols. We indicated several important considerations for representing advanced protocols such as binary strings.

We examined the impact of the search space size on the number of analyses required to carry out an exhaustive search and the effectiveness of genetic algorithms, and found that GAs are promising tools for synthesizing security protocols.

A series of parameters and values were defined for evaluating security protocols. We applied the values in a series of tests and recorded the time needed to find an optimal protocol for the problems proposed.

The evaluation revealed that genetic algorithms are useful tools for generating security protocols. Improved algorithms will be capable of generating more complex protocols for solving problems such as group communications over sensor networks.

We have also developed a software tool that uses metaheuristic genetic algorithms to create cryptographic protocols.[29]

References

1. J. H. Holland, *Adaptation in Natural and Artificial Systems*. (University of Michigan Press, 1975).
2. R. A. Fisher, *The Genetical Theory of Natural Selection*. (Oxford University Press, USA, 2000). ISBN 0198504403.
3. D. Goldberg, *Genetic Algorithms for Search, Optimization, and Machine Learning*. (Addison-Wesley, 1989).
4. Z. Michalewicz and D. B. Fogel, *How to Solve It: Modern Heuristics*. (Springer, 2004). ISBN 3540224947.
5. D. A. Coley, *An Introduction to Genetic Algorithms for Scientists and Engineers*. (World Scientific Publishing Company, 1997). ISBN 9810236026.
6. A. Moreno, E. Armengol, J. Béjar, and L. Belanche, *Aprendizaje Automtico*. (Ediciones UPC, 1994).
7. J. R. Koza. Survey of genetic algorithms and genetic programming. In *WESCON'95. Conference record Microelectronics Communications Technol-*

ogy Producing Quality Products Mobile and Portable Power Emerging Technologies, (1995).

8. T. Back, *Evolutionary Algorithms in Theory and Practice: Evolution Strategies.* (Oxford University Press, 1996). ISBN 0195099710.

9. G. Greenwood and Q. Zhu. Convergence in evolutionary programs with self-adaptation. In *Evol. Comput.*, vol. 9, pp. 147–157, (2001).

10. A. Baresel, H. Sthamer, and M. Schmidt. Fitness function design to improve evolutionary structural testing. In *Proceedings of the Genetic and Evolutionary Computation Conference*, pp. 1329–1336 (Jul, 2002).

11. B. Sendho, M. Kreutz, and W. V. Seelen. A condition for the genotype-phenotype mapping: Causality. In *The Seventh International Conference on Genetic Algorithm.* Morgan Kauman, (1997).

12. D. E. Goldberg and K. Deb. A comparative analysis of selection schemes used in genetic algorithms. In *Foundations of Genetic Algorithms*, pp. 69–93. Morgan Kaufmann, (1991).

13. M. Srinivas and L. M. Patnaik, Genetic algorithms: A survey, *IEEE Computer.* **27**(6), 17–26, (1994).

14. T. Mitchell, B. Buchanan, G. DeJong, T. Dietterich, P. Rosenbloom, and A. Waibel. Machine learning. In *Annual Review of Computer Science*, vol. 4, pp. 417–433, (1990).

15. H. Kitano, Designing neural networks using genetic algorithms with graph generation system, *Complex Systems Journal.* **4**, 461–476, (1990).

16. J. H. Holland, *Escaping Brittleness: The Possibilities of General-Purpose Learning Algorithms Applied to Parallel Rule-Based Systems.* 1986.

17. S. F. Smith. Flexible learning of problem solving heuristics through adaptive search. In *Proc. 8th IJCAI*, (1983).

18. W. Stallings, *Cryptography And Network Security: Principles and Practice.* (Pearson, 2006).

19. M. Abadi and R. Needham, Prudent engineering practice for cryptographic protocols, *IEEE Transactions on Software Engineering.* **22**, 122–136, (1996).

20. D. Dolev and A. Yao, On the security of public key protocols, *Information Theory, IEEE Transactions on.* **29**(2), 198–208, (1983).

21. C. Meadows, Applying formal methods to the analysis of a key management protocol, *Journal of Computer Security.* **1**, (1992).

22. S. Brackin, C. Meadows, and J. Millen. Capsl interface for the nrl protocol analyzer. In *ASSET '99: Proceedings of the 1999 IEEE Symposium on Application - Specific Systems and Software Engineering and Technology*, p. 64, Washington, DC, USA, (1999). IEEE Computer Society.

23. M. Fiore and M. Abadi. Computing symbolic models for verifying cryptographic protocols. In *In Proc. of the 14th Computer Security Foundation Workshop (CSFW14*, pp. 160–173. IEEE, Computer Society Press, (2001).

24. J. A. Clark and J. L. Jacob. Searching for a solution: Engineering tradeoffs and the evolution of provably secure protocols. In *SP '00: Proceedings of the 2000 IEEE Symposium on Security and Privacy*, pp. 82–95, Washington, DC, USA, (2000). IEEE Computer Society. ISBN 0-7695-0665-8.

25. M. Burrows, M. Abadi, and R. Needham, A logic of authentication, *ACM*

Trans. Comput. Syst. **8**(1), 18–36, (1990).

26. C. Meadows, Formal methods for cryptographic protocol analysis: emerging issues and trends, *IEEE Journal on Selected Areas in Communications.* **21** (1), 44–54 (Jan, 2003).

27. P. Ocenasek and M. Sveda, An approach to automated design of security protocols, *IEEE Proceedings of the International Conference on Networking, International Conference on Systems and International Conference on Mobile Communications and Learning Technologies (ICNICONSMCL'06).* pp. 77–77 (Apr, 2006).

28. J. R. Koza, *Genetic programming as a means for programming computers by natural selection.* (MIT Press, 1992).

29. L. Zarza. Network security protocols design tool by means of genetic algorithms. http://isg.upc.es/ga/.

Chapter 14

Evolving Strategy-Based Cooperation in Wireless Mobile Ad Hoc Networks

Marcin Seredynski[1], Pascal Bouvry[1] and Mieczyslaw A. Klopotek[2]

[1] *University of Luxembourg,*
Faculty of Sciences, Technology and Communication,
6, rue Coudenhove Kalergi, L-1359, Luxembourg, Luxembourg,
{marcin.seredynski,pascal.bouvry}@uni.lu

[2] *Polish Academy of Sciences, Institute of Computer Science,*
ul. Ordona 21, 01-237 Warsaw, Poland,
klopotek@ipipan.waw.pl

A wireless mobile ad hoc network (MANET) consists of a number of devices forming a temporary network that operates without support of a fixed infrastructure. The correct operation of such a network requires some cooperation on the level of packet forwarding by participating devices. On the other hand, distributed nature of a system, lack of a single authority, absence of incentives for packet forwarding and limited battery resources may lead to a noncooperative behavior that causes degradation of the network throughput. This work provides an analysis of a potential for emergence of cooperation in MANETs by means of multi-disciplinary approach. This kind of approach uses concepts concerning cooperation developed in evolutionary biology (direct and indirect reciprocity) and tools like genetic algorithms and evolutionary game theory. The work demonstrates how MANETs can be secured against selfish behavior with a new distributed reputation-based cooperation enforcement system. The evolutionary game-theoretic approach is used as a frame to explore the performance of such a system. Detailed simulation studies prove that selfish behavior becomes unattractive when a certain number of devices follows the proposed forwarding strategy.

Contents

14.1. Introduction

Recent advances in portable computers such as laptops and PDAs brought
the development of wireless communication technologies. Inexpensive wireless network interface devices such as wireless LANs are becoming a standard in nowadays portable computer devices. The fourth generation architecture is expected to include mobile ad hoc networks (MANETs), self-
organized networks composed of devices (referred to as nodes) equipped
with wireless communications and network capability.[1] Such networks do
not rely on any fixed architecture and nodes act as both routers and hosts.
Two devices can directly communicate with each other only when they are
located within their radio range. Otherwise, the communication should rely
on packet forwarding by other intermediate nodes, thus network is based
on the cooperation of its participants. Typically, MANETs are not admin-
istrated by a single authority, therefore it is not possible to impose any
security policies or enforce cooperative behavior.

The proper functioning of MANETs requires nodes to share *packet forwarding* responsibility. Nodes are said to *cooperate* when they forward
packets on behalf of other network participants. Nodes reluctant to packet
forwarding are referred to as *selfish nodes*. Most of devices run on batter-
ies. As a result, energy conservation is a critical issue. This means that
the risk that nodes would act selfishly in order to conserve their battery by
discarding packets received for forwarding is very high. As shown in the
literature, such a behavior can be a serious threat to the existence of the
network.[2-4] The problem of selfish behavior appears in civilian application
networks, where nodes belong to different authorities. In such networks
nodes are not motivated to cooperate.[5] No classical security mechanism

can help counter such a misbehavior.[6]

In MANETs cooperation and security are closely linked with each other. A network that is protected from attacks is called a *secure network*, while a network that is resistant to a strategic behavior of users is called a *strategy-proof* network. The most important difference between the two models is as follows: a malicious attacker wants to jeopardize the operation of the network while a selfish user wants to exploit it.[7]

Typical civilian MANETs are self-organizing which means that they operate without any external management.[8] Global behavior of such networks emerges form local interactions among nodes.[8,9] In such networks *a priori* trust relationships most probably do not exist. There is also no reason to assume that nodes are seeking the "common good". Nodes will behave rationally by pursuing their *self interest* and trying to use the network without sharing their resources (battery, computational power, etc.) to help others. A common solution to this problem is a *reputation-based cooperation enforcement system*: nodes are equipped with a *reputation system* combined with a *response mechanism*.[6,10–14] Each node keeps reputation ratings of other network participants. Upon receipt of a packet for forwarding, the node checks the reputation of the node that originated the packet (referred to as sender). Only packets originated by cooperative node will be forwarded. This approach enforces cooperation because selfish nodes cannot use the network for their own purposes, unless they contribute to the packet forwarding. A good survey of cooperation enforcement systems with a game theoretical analysis can be found in.[13,15–17]

When designing the reputation system one has to decide what kind of actions should be regarded as good and what kind of actions as bad. Discarding packets is an obvious candidate, but this is not the only way of saving battery life. The other way is to switch the wireless networking interface into *sleep mode*. In such a mode a node is unavailable for any network duties. This is by far the most efficient way of conserving energy as the power consumption is about 98% lower comparing to the consumption in *idle mode*[18]. Entering sleep mode is very tempting, because such a behavior will be unnoticed by other network participants. In our opinion, activity - measured in terms of the number of packets forwarded by a node is an important factor that has to be taken into account when evaluation a reputation of a node. Network participants should be rewarded not only on the basis the ratio of packets forwarded to packets discarded but also on the basis of the number of packets forwarded (activity).

In this chapter we propose a new reputation-based cooperation enforcement system that aims at securing MANETs against the selfish behavior of its participants. The forwarding decision is based on trust and activity levels of the sender. Traditional tools to model MANETs are not suitable to describe a high level property like cooperation[13] because human behavioral and social factors seem to be at the heart of these new types of problems. Such networks cannot be represented as a parametric situation because an optimal behavior of a node depends on the behavior of others. This is why in order to model the evolution of behavior of the network equipped with the proposed cooperation enforcement system we propose an evolutionary game-theoretic approach. The network is described as a game in which nodes (referred later to as players) are independent decision makers. The system presented in this chapter is an improved version of our works presented in.[19,20] The main changes include a new reputation system and modification of the utility function of the game describing the packet forwarding in MANETs.

The rest of the chapter is organized as follows. The next section introduces the cooperation enforcement system and the framework of the evolutionary approach for its evaluation. Then in Section 14.3 experimental results are provided. Finally, the conclusions are drawn in Section 14.4.

14.2. Cooperation enforcement system

The general idea of the proposed cooperation enforcement system is as follows: nodes collect *reputation data* about the behavior of other network participants. Next, on basis of such data two reputation metrics called *trust* and *activity* are calculated. Afterwards, these metrics are used by a *forwarding strategy*, which defines whether to forward or discard a packet from a sender with a given reputation. The strategic interaction is assumed to be one-on-one interaction between sender and forwarders, which means that intermediate nodes base their forwarding decisions on the reputation of the source node and not on the reputation of other (previous) forwarders.

A performance of a player using a particular strategy is a function not only of his strategy, but also strategies of other players, thus it is not an optimization problem but a gaming problem. In such problems there is no single strategy that may be successfully applied in all networking environments. In order to solve this problem an evolutionary game theory-based model is proposed. Instead of carrying out a perfect rational process in which each player has a common knowledge of perfect rationality, strategies emerge from a learning process in which players find that some strategies perform better that others. The evolutionary game theoretical approach can be seen as having two games referred to as *inner* and *outer games.*[21] The former can be viewed as a classical game where players interact with each other using their strategies and receive payoffs. The later game is where evolution takes place: player's payoffs are translated into changes in strategy frequencies.

The scheme of the proposed framework is shown in Figure 14.1. From evolutionary game-theoretical point of view it can be divided into two parts referred to as *networking part* (inner game) and *evolutionary part* (outer game). The first part describes MANETs equipped with the reputation-based *cooperation enforcement system* and *strategy evaluation tools*, which model network traffic and utility of players. This part captures the inner game in which players interact with each other (by forwarding packets). The strategy evaluation tools consist of a *Network Traffic Simulator* (NTS) and a *Packet Forwarding Game* (PFG). The NTS simulates network traffic as some nodes act as senders and some as forwarders, while the PFG distributes utility to players that use a particular strategy. The PFG can be viewed as a game-theoretical interpretation of strategic interactions in the NTS. The second part of the framework can be seen as the outer game serving as an optimization agent. This game captures an evolutionary perspective of the behavior of MANET equipped with the proposed cooperation enforcement system. The mechanism used as the optimization agent is a classical genetic algorithm (GA). These two parts are dynamically linked. Strategies are first evaluated by means of NTS and PFG and then they evolve by means of GA: more successful strategies proliferate while less successful strategies become less common. GA also introduces variations between strategies (by means of crossover and mutation operators).

The distributed cooperation enforcement system assumes that the following components are implemented by each node willing to participate in the system:

- *reputation system* responsible for collection of reputation data about behavior of other nodes and assignment of trust and activity levels on the basis of such data
- *response mechanism (incentive system)* represented by a *forwarding strategy.*

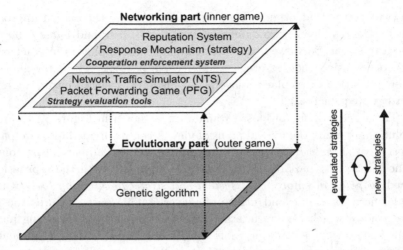

Fig. 14.1.   Framework of the evolutionary game-theoretical approach for analysis of the cooperation enforcement system.

14.2.1. *Assumptions and performance metrics*

The following assumptions about the properties of MANETs are made: there are no *a priori* trust relations between nodes entering the MANET. The network layer is based on a reactive, source routing protocol. It means that sender places in the header of the packet a sequence of intermediate nodes that the packet should follow on its way to the destination. Nodes use an omni-directional antenna with a similar radio range. The bi-directional communication between nodes and promiscuous mode of the wireless interface are assumed. Nodes have the ability to recognise each other and memorize their mutual interactions. These assumptions can be found in most of the works in the related area (e.g,[3,6,11]). In this work we only consider a packet forwarding function as a networking duty, however the system can be extended to other network services that also require cooperation.

The following performance metrics describing the performance of a player using a particular strategy are used throughout this work: *utility*, a *success rate*, an *overall network cooperation level* and a *forwarding rate*. *Utility* describes preferences of a node by referring to the amount of welfare that such a node derives from an event. The utility is used by the evolutionary part of the framework (see Section 14.2.5). A fraction of packets originated by *ith* node that successfully reached the destination is called a *success rate* (sr). It is defined as:

$$sr_i = \frac{npr_i}{nps_i} \qquad (14.1)$$

where nps_i is a total number of packets originated by ith node and npr_i is a number of these packets that reached the destination. An *overall network cooperation level* is an average success rate of all nodes in the network. Node i can also compute a *forwarding rate* of jth node (fr_j), which is defined as:

$$fr_j = \frac{req\_acc_j}{req\_acc_j + req\_dsc_j} \qquad (14.2)$$

where req_acc_j and req_dsc_j are numbers of packets forwarded and discarded, respectively by jth node.

14.2.2. *Reputation system*

The reputation data collection is performed in the following way: due to the wireless nature of the communications in MANETs nodes can be equipped with a *watchdog mechanism*[3] that enables them to verify whether a packet was successfully delivered to the destination. A node that asks another node to forward a packet can verify by means of a *passive acknowledgement*[22] whether the asked node is actually accepting the forwarding request. An example is shown in Figure 14.2: node p_1 wants to send packets to node p_5 via intermediate nodes p_2, p_3 and p_4. First, p_1 sends packets to p_2 and next it verifies by means of the passive acknowledgment whether p_2 received and then forwarded packets to node p_3. The concept of the passive acknowledgment is as follows: p_2 is in the radio range of p_1, thus p_1 is in the range of p_2. When p_2 forwards packets from p_1 to p_3, it sends data into open air. It means that this transmission can be overheard by node p_1. It enables node p_1 to confirm that node p_2 forwarded packets to node p_3. If communication fails (for instance node p_4 decides to discard the packet as in the given example) such an event is recorded by node p_3. In this case node p_3 informs node p_2 about selfish behavior of p_4 and then p_2 forwards this message to the sender (source node). As a results, reputation systems of nodes p_1, p_2 and p_3 are updated with the events - "packet forwarded by p_2", "packet forwarded by p_3" and "packet discarded by p_4". The detailed analysis of the watchdog mechanism can be found in.[3]

The reputation data is classified into two types referred to as a *personal reputation data* and a *general reputation data*. The former takes into account only information about packets originated by a node itself while in the latter status of packets originated by other nodes is taken into account.

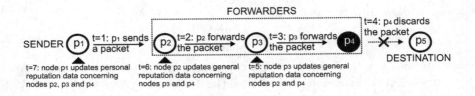

Fig. 14.2.   Reputation data update example: communication between nodes p_1 and p_5 failed because packet was discarded by node p_4.

It means that if a node is in a role of a sender then it will collect personal reputation data and if a node is in a role of forwarder it will collect general reputation data. For instance, in the example shown in Figure 14.2 the information about selfish action performed by node p_4 is processed as the personal reputation data by node p_1 (since action of node p_4 concerns packets originated by node p_1), while nodes p_2 and p_3 process it as the general reputation data.

When designing a reputation system one has to decide what kind of actions should be regarded as good and what kind of actions as bad. Reputation is context dependent, it can be treated as a vector in which each entry corresponds to a certain context. In the proposed system reputation data collected by nodes is processed into two metrics called *trust* and *activity*. Each of them can have assigned one of four discrete values ranging from 1 to 4 allocated on the basis of calculations on available reputation data. In general, trust is related to the ratio of packets forwarded by a node to packets received for forwarding by such a node, while activity is related to the total number of packets forwarded by a node. In MANETs both metrics used together are good indicators of reliability and fairness of a behavior of a given node. Routing packets through nodes having a reputation of often being in sleep mode is risky because such nodes might not be available (by remaining in idle mode) at right time, thus will not receive the forwarding request. The same goes with with distrusted nodes: even if such nodes receive packets it is vert likely they will not forward it. The exact assignment of trust and activity values to the given node is relative to the behavior of others: when node i wants to calculate the trust and activity levels of node j it compares certain performances of that node to the network average (average performance value of all known nodes).

For instance, if node i wanted to calculate the activity level of node j it would have to do the following: first, to calculate the average (req_acc_{avr}), minimum (req_acc_{min}) and maximum (req_acc_{max}) numbers of packets forwarded by all know nodes. Next, calculate two values called *low activity level bound* (A_L) and *high activity level bound* (A_H) as follows:

$$A_L = req\_acc_{min} + \frac{req\_acc_{avr} - req\_acc_{min}}{2} \qquad (14.3)$$

$$A_H = req\_acc_{avr} + \frac{req\_acc_{max} - req\_acc_{avr}}{2} \qquad (14.4)$$

Afterwards, one of four activity levels is then allocated to *jth* node on the basis of comparison of the number of packets forwarded by such a node (req_acc_j) with these values:

- if $req\_acc_j <= A_L$ then set activity to 1,
- if $req\_acc_j > A_L$ and $req\_acc_j <= req\_acc_{avr}$ then set activity to 2,
- if $req\_acc_j > req\_acc_{avr}$ and $req\_acc_j <= A_H$ then set activity to 3,
- if $req\_acc_j > A_H$ then set activity to 4.

Computation of the trust level is very similar to the calculation of activity. The criterion of the number of packets forwarded is replaced with the forwarding rate. Firstly, forwarding rate of *jth* node (fr_j), average (fr_{avr}), minimum (fr_{min}) and maximum (fr_{max}) forwarding rates of all know nodes are calculated. Then, *low* (T_L) and *high trust level bounds* (T_H) are calculated in a similar way as A_L and A_H (using forwarding rates instead of numbers of accepted forwarding requests):

$$T_L = fr_{min} + \frac{fr_{avr} - fr_{min}}{2} \qquad (14.5)$$

$$T_H = fr_{avr} + \frac{fr_{max} - fr_{avr}}{2} \qquad (14.6)$$

Afterwards, one of four trust levels is allocated to *jth* node as follows:

- if $fr_j <= T_L$ then set trust to 1,
- if $fr_j > T_L$ and $fr_j <= fr_{avr}$ then set trust to 2,
- if $fr_j > fr_{avr}$ and $fr_j <= T_H$ then set trust to 3,
- if $fr_j > T_H$ then set trust to 4.

Trust level is computed using personal reputation data, while activity is calculated using both, personal and general reputation data.

14.2.3. *Selection of best paths: path rating mechanism*

If a source node has more than one path available to the destination it will choose the one with the best rating which is calculated as a multiplication of all known forwarding rates of all nodes belonging to the route. An unknown node has the forwarding rate set to 0.5. Path rating is calculated using personal reputation data. If such data are unavailable then general reputation data is used.

14.2.4. *Response mechanism: forwarding strategy*

An action set for a node receiving a forwarding request is as follows: $\{F, D\}$ where "F" stands for the action "forward the packet" and "D" for "discard the packet". The exact action is defined by a *strategy* which is a rule that tells which action to choose against a packet sent by a node with a given reputation (represented in terms of trust and activity reputation metrics). An example of the strategy is shown in Figure 14.3. Four levels are defined for each metric, in consequence 16 possible combinations of these levels exist. Decisions in each case are represented by positions no. $0 - 15$, while the last position defines the action against packets originated by an unknown node.

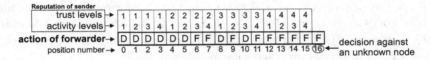

Fig. 14.3.   Coding of the strategy

14.2.5. *Packet Forwarding Game*

We define a *Packet Forwarding Game* (PFG) as a sequence of packet relays from a source node to a destination node via some intermediate nodes: the source node requests intermediate nodes to forward its packets along the route. The players are the sender (that originated a packet) and forwarders that received the packet for forwarding. Each player is said to play *his own game* when being a source of a packet and is said to be a *participant of other players' game* when acting as an intermediate node. As soon as the game is played out (either the packet reached the destination or any of the forwarders discarded it) all nodes that received the packet for forwarding receive payoffs. The exact values of payoffs depend on the decisions they made and on their trust and activity levels held in the sender. Generally, the greater trust/activity levels are the greater payoff is received by *ith* node forwarding the packet originated by *jth* node. High trust and activity levels held by *ith* node in *jth* node mean that in the past *jth* node forwarded a significant number of packets for *ith* node. Thus, it is more likely that such a node will be used in the future as an intermediate node, which means that reciprocating in order to gain reputation with that node will likely pay off in the future. On the other hand, when a node decides to discard a packet it will be rewarded for saving its battery life. The lesser the reputation of the sender is the greater payoff for discarding a forwarding request is received. Since path rating mechanism is used (by senders), building good reputation with selfish nodes is not rational. The exact payoff received by *ith* node for forwarding a packet oryginated by jth node (pf_{ij}) is calculated as follows:

$$pf_{ij} = tr_{ij} * ac_{ij}^2 \qquad (14.7)$$

where tr_{ij} and ac_{ij} are trust and activity levels, respectively, held by *ith* node in *jth* node. Payoffs for discarding packets are a mirror of the forwarding ones. For instance, payoff for discarding a packet originated by a node with a lowest defined trust and activity levels is equal to the payoff for forwarding a packet originated by a node with a highest reputation level. Payoff function for forwarders is show in Figure 14.4.

reputation of sender / action of forwarder	trust 1 activity				trust 2 activity				trust 3 activity				trust 4 activity				unknown
	1	2	3	4	1	2	3	4	1	2	3	4	1	2	3	4	
packet forwarded	1	4	9	16	2	8	18	32	3	12	27	48	4	16	36	64	2
packet discarded	64	32	18	12	48	27	9	4	36	16	8	2	32	12	3	1	1
	payoff values for forwarding or discarding a packet sent by a node with a given reputation (trust/activity)																

Fig. 14.4.   Payoff function for forwarding and discarding a packet send by a node with a given reputation.

As soon as all PFG are finished the utility of each player is derived from the following performance measures of players:

- total payoffs received for forwarding and discarding packets
- success rate (defined in Section 14.2.1)
- forwarding efficiency (defined below)

- discarding efficiency (defined below).

In order to compute the utility of a player (evaluation of his strategy) values of the two additional metrics, *forwarding efficiency* and *discarding efficiency* are calculated. The *forwarding efficiency* (f_{eff}) of a player indicates how close was the actual average payoff obtained by such a player for a packet forwarded to the maximum defined value for such an event. It is calculated as follows:

$$f_{eff} = \frac{pf\_tot}{req\_acc * pf\_max} \qquad (14.8)$$

where *pf_tot* is a total payoff received for forwarding, *req_acc* is a number of packets forwarded by such a player and *pf_max* is a maximum defined payoff for forwarding a single packet (according to the payoff function shown in Figure 14.4 *pf_max* is equal to 64). For instance, if the value of f_{eff} was equal to 1 it would mean that player was forwarding only packets originated by players with the highest possible trust and activity values.

The *discarding efficiency* (d_{eff}) of a player indicates how close was the actual average payoff obtained by such a player for a packet discarded to the maximum defined value for such an event. It is calculated as follows:

$$d_{eff} = \frac{pd\_tot}{req\_dsc * pd\_max} \qquad (14.9)$$

where *pd_tot* is a total payoff received for discarding, *req_dsc* is a total number of packets discarded by such a player and *pd_max* is a maximum defined payoff for discarding a single packet (according to the payoff function shown in Figure 14.4 *pd_max* is equal to 64). For instance, if the value of d_{eff} was equal to 1 it would mean that such a player was discarding only packets originated by players with the lowest possible trust and activity values.

Finally, the utility of *ith* node (μ_i) is calculated with the following utility function:

$$\mu_i = sr * \frac{pf\_tot * f_{eff} + pd\_tot * d_{eff}}{req\_acc} \qquad (14.10)$$

where *sr* is a success rate of a node.

14.2.6. *Evaluation of strategies*

A *Network Traffic Simulator* (NTS) represents a network composed of a finite population of N nodes. It serves as a tool to evaluate forwarding strategies. Time is divided into R *rounds*. Each round is composed of several *forwarding session slots*. During a single slot one PFG is played. In every round each node initiates a single forwarding session (plays its own PFG) exactly once, thus each round is composed of N forwarding session slots. Intermediate and destination nodes are chosen randomly in each forwarding session. The NTS itself can be described with the following steps:

Algorithm #1: NTS scheme

(1) specify i (source node) as $i := 1$, N as a number of players participating in the NTS and R as a number of rounds
(2) randomly select player j (destination of the packet) and intermediate nodes, forming several possible paths to the destination
(3) for each available path calculate its rating and select the path with the best rating
(4) play the PFG (described in Section 14.2.5)
(5) update payoffs of nodes that received the packet for forwarding
(6) update the reputation data among all game participants
(7) if $i < N$, then choose the next player $i := i + 1$ and go to the step 2. Else go to the step 8
(8) if $r < R$, then $r := r + 1$ and go to the step 1 (next round). Else stop the NTS
(9) calculate utility of each player as described in Section 14.2.5.

14.2.7. *Scheme of the evolutionary approach for analysis of behavior of the network*

The networking part is composed of the cooperation enforcement system and strategy evaluation tools (NTS and PFG). Its goal is to simulate MANET in order to evaluate forwarding strategies (as described in the previous section). Each player uses a single strategy, which is first evaluated in the networking part. Next, set of strategies of all players (called population of strategies) is processed by the outer game represented by GA. The GA receives as an input evaluated strategies (strategies with assigned utility). The representation of a forwarding strategy used by GA (candidate solution from GAs' point of view) is straightforward. Each position of

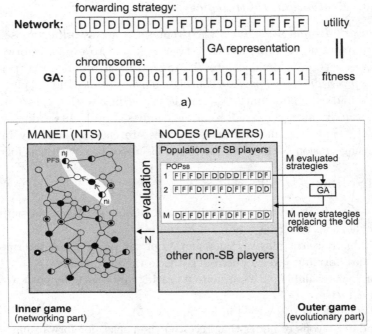

a)

b)

Fig. 14.5.   GA representation of a candidate solution (a). Evaluation and evolution of strategies (b).

a strategy is simply represented as a bit (gene) of the chromosome where "1" represents an action "F" (forward packet) and "0" an action "D" (discard packet) (see Figure 14.5a). The utility assigned to strategies in the networking part (by PFG) is now referred to as a fitness. GA returns a new set of strategies that replaces the pervious one. The process is repeated for a predefined number of times (referred to as generations). Since each player uses a single strategy, terms strategy and players are used interchangeably. The proposed evolutionary approach is visualized in Figure 14.5b.

Players that use the reputation-based forwarding strategies are called SB players. Other types of players (that use other forwarding approach) are defined later. SB players form a *population* denoted as POP_{SB} of a size

M. A detailed scheme of the evolutionary process is as follows:
Algorithm #2: evolutionary scenario scheme

- **step 1: initialization of SB-type players** - randomly generate M strategies constituting the population of SB-type players (POP_{SB})
- **step 2: initialization of NTS with players** - load SB players (that were not yet evaluated) as well as other types of players to NTS (according to some specified distribution). The number of all players loaded to NTS is N
- **step 3: evaluation in NTS** - run the NTS with selected players as described in Section 14.2.6
- **step 4:** if some players of the POP_{SB} have not yet been evaluated in the NTS then go to the step 2, otherwise go to step 5
- **step 5: evolutionary phase** - apply GA on the current population of SB-type players and create a new population of players replacing the previous one (see below, **algorithm #3**)
- **step 6: check stop condition** - if steps 2-5 were repeated predefined number of steps (generations) stop the algorithm. Otherwise repeat steps $2 - 5$.

The scheme of GA is as follows:
Algorithm #3: GA scheme

- **step 1 - selection:** select the $M/2$ pairs of strategies using the tournament selection
- **step 2 - GA operators:** obtain new population of strategies by applying crossover and mutation operators to each of $M/2$ selected pairs (standard one-point crossover and uniform bit flip mutation are used). Mutation and crossover probabilities are given as parameters.

14.2.8. *Underlying mechanisms*

According to the presented proposal the enforcement of cooperation is based on the forwarding strategy coupled with the reputation system. Forwarding decision is made primary on the basis of personal reputation data as the use of general reputation is limited to calculation of activity. As a result, cooperation is mainly based on the mechanism of *direct reciprocity*[23] which assumes that individuals have a sufficiently large chance to meet again. Direct reciprocity leads to *reciprocal altruism* in which one node provides a benefit to another without expecting any immediate return of it, however favor provided by one node to another should be reciprocated in the future. Strategy defines the sort of goodness that enables sustaining exchange of altruism. If general reputation data was more significant, then discarding packets by forwarders would involve an additional cost defined in terms of decrease of their reputation in eyes of other forwarders. Whenever personal reputation is used, action of forwarders affect their reputation only in the eyes of senders. However, if network is larger or the mobility of nodes is limited then use of personal reputation data might not be sufficient as selfish nodes might easily escape punishment. In such a case, the mechanism underlying cooperation is *indirect reciprocity*.[24-26] Such a mechanism refers to the emergence of cooperation in groups where a chance to meet again between two individuals is very little. In such a case one node acts as a donor of forwarding service while the other as its recipient. The reason why cooperation can emerge in such environment is because forwarders assess senders by using social information (represented here by general reputation data).

14.3. Computational experiments

The analysis of the cooperation issues in MANETs was carried out in several *test scenarios* that define the distribution of various types of players participating in the NTS (described below). The scheme for a single run of the test scenario is performed according to the evolutionary scenario scheme described in Section 14.2.7. The outcome of each test scenario is the performance of the network in the last generation of the evolutionary scheme.

14.3.1. *Types of players in the NTS*

Six types of players participating in the network (NTS) differing in goals and approach towards packet forwarding were defined: *Strategy-Based* players (denoted as *SB*), *Adaptive Sleeping* players (*AS*), *Adaptive Forwarding* players (*AF*), *Cooperative* players (*C*) and two types of selfish players - *Selfish Player 1* and *2* (*SF1* and *SF2*). Strategy-Based player forwards packets according to his trust and activity-based strategy. He represents a type of player that for some reasons cannot stay in sleep mode (for instance expects to receive packets addressed to himself for the most of the time). The remaining types of players forward packets without taking into account the reputation of sender. The *AS* forwards all packets, however whenever his success rate is greater then 0.4 he enters sleep mode (such a player can afford to do so because he mainly uses short duration communication scenarios). The *AF* does not sleep at all (for the same reasons as SB). He forwards packets whenever his success rate drops below 0.4. The *C* type of player never sleeps and accepts all forwarding requests. The Selfish Player 1 *SF*1 is always in idle mode, however he discards all intermediate packets. Selfish Player *SF*2 also stays in idle mode, but forwards packets with probability 0.5. All players try to send the same number of packets (by playing the same number of their own PFG). Properties of each type of player are summarized in Table 14.1. All types of players use the path rating mechanism when they act as senders.

Table 14.1. Types of nodes participating in the NTS and settings of test scenarios.

Type of player	Forwarding approach	Sleep mode	s_1[a]	s_2[b]	s_3[c]
Strategy-Based (SB)	reputation based	never	10	20	40
Adaptive Sleep (AS)	forward if in idle mode	if $sr > 0.4$	10	5	4
Adaptive Forwarding (AF)	if $sr < 0.4$	never	10	5	4
Cooperative (C)	always forward	never	10	5	4
Selfish 1 (SF1)	always discard	never	10	15	4
Selfish 2 (SF2)	forward with prob. 0.5	never	10	10	4

[a] distribution of players in scenario 1 (s_1), [b] distribution of players in scenario 2 (s_2), [c] distribution of players in scenario 3 (s_3).

14.3.2. *Conditions of experiments*

The parameter specifications of GA and NTS used in the experiments are shown in Table 14.2. The NTS is composed of 60 nodes of a different type.

Table 14.2. Parameters values.

POP_{SB} size (M)	NTS size (N)	R[b]	cp [c]	mp [d]	ng [e]	nr [f]
50	60	600	0.9	0.001	100	60

[b] number of rounds in NTS, [c] crossover probability, [d] mutation probability, [e] number of generations, [f] number of runs of each scenario.

Three scenarios of experiments denoted as s_1, s_2 and s_3 were performed. Their settings are shown in Table 14.1 (last three columns). In scenario 1 the network was composed of the equal number of all types of players. In scenario 2 two types of players dominated the network: one third of the network was composed of SB-type players and one-fourth of SF1 players. In the last scenario SB players were the majority (around 67% share of the network) while all remaining types of players had about 8% share each. Each scenario was repeated 60 times (referred to as runs). The values of performance metrics of each type of player were calculated as the arithmetic mean over the values of all runs. In each run the initial population of strategies of SB players was generated randomly.

14.3.3. *Results*

The following overall network cooperation levels were obtained: 26% in scenario 1, 15% in scenario 2 and 64% in scenario 3 (see Section 14.2.1 for description of performance metrics). The performances of players in scenario 1 (according to their type) are shown in Table 14.3.

Table 14.3.   Performances of players according to their type in scenario 1.

Type of player	Success rate	npf[a]	fr[b]
Strategy-Based (SB)	0.27	0	0
Adaptive Sleep (AS)	0.25	1247	1.0
Adaptive Forwarding (AF)	0.25	1239	0.95
Cooperative (C)	0.25	1252	1.0
Selfish 1 (SF1)	0.27	0	0
Selfish 2 (SF2)	0.26	456	0.5

[a] number of packets forwarded, [b] forwarding rate.

One can see that performances of all types of players were very similar in terms of the achieved success rate (around 0.26, meaning that 26% of packets reached the destitation). However, the participation level to forwarding duties varied from one type to another. SB-type players did not participate to packet forwarding at all as their forwarding rate was very close to 0. It means that the evolved strategies of such players were "always defect". They adapted to the environment and decided that behaving selfishly (as SP2-type players) is the best (rational) choice. Players of type AS, AF and C forwarded a significant number of packets (around 1200), but they did not receive any reward for that. Due to insufficient number of SB players the defense against selfish behavior was not created: SB players decided that in such an environment the best is to act selfishly. The situation was different in scenario 2, where one third of the network was composed of SB-type players. The results of that scenario are shown in Table 14.4.

Table 14.4.   Performances of players according to their type in test scenario 2.

Type of player	Success rate	npf[a]	fr[b]
Strategy-Based (SB)	0.17	271	0.3
Adaptive Sleep (AS)	0.17	987	1.0
Adaptive Forwarding (AF)	0.16	989	0.99
Cooperative (C)	0.17	1066	1.0
Selfish 1 (SF1)	0.09	0	0
Selfish 2 (SF2)	0.09	350	0.5

[a] number of packets forwarded, [b] forwarding rate.

This time the success rates of both types of selfish players was very low, below 0.04. Other types of players obtained the success rate around 0.17. Again, as in scenario 1, the contribution level varied from one type of player to another. This time, SB player were more cooperative: each SB player forwarded on average 271 packets. However, this was still way below the values of other non-selfish players that forwarded from 987 (AS) to 1066 (C) packets. The reason why selfish players obtained lower success rates than other types of players was due to the fact that SB players differentiated their forwarding decisions on the basis of the reputation of the source. Although their average forwarding rate was 0.3 (see Table 14.4) the detailed forwarding rates concerning particular types of players varied, ranging from 0 to 0.49 (see Table 14.5).

Table 14.5.   Forwarding rates of Strategy-Based players concerning packets of other types players in all test scenarios.

	SB	AS	AF	C	SF1	SF2
Scenario 1:	0	0	0	0	0	0
Scenario 2:	0.47	0.49	0.47	0.49	0	0.02
Scenario 3:	1.0	0.78	0.7	1.0	0	0

The forwarding rate concerning packets originated by selfish players was very close to 0, while concerning packets originated by other types of players was between 0.47 and 0.49. The SF2 players forwarded on average more packets than SB players, however they did not consider the reputation of the source node (meaning that they forwarded packets for selfish players as well). Since SB players evaluate reputation mainly on the basis of personal reputation, forwarding packets for non-SB players did not improve the reputation of forwarders seen by SB players. The reason why the over-all network cooperation levels was so low was due to the large presence of SF2 players. This level was greatly improved (by reaching 64%) in scenario 3, where the network was dominated by SB players. The performances of players in this scenario are shown in Table 14.6. The cooperation enforcement system proved to be successful as the success rates of selfish players of both types dropped to 0.04. SB players improved their success rates to 0.76 and decided to actively participate to forwarding duties (1629 packets forwarded). Only C players contributed more to packet forwarding. This time there was a clear relationship between the level of contribution to network duties and the achieved success rate. The SB and C players forwarded more packets than other types, which was reflected in their success rates.

Table 14.6. Performances of players according to their type in test scenario 3.

Type of player	Success rate	npf[a]	fr[b]
Strategy-Based (SB)	0.76	1629	0.92
Adaptive Sleep (AS)	0.41	694	1.0
Adaptive Forwarding (AF)	0.32	1473	0.95
Cooperative (C)	0.76	1822	1.0
Selfish 1 (SF1)	0.04	0	0
Selfish 2 (SF2)	0.04	568	0.5

[a] number of packets forwarded, [b] forwarding rate.

As in the previous scenario, forwarding rates of SB players differed from one type of the source requesting the forwarding service to another (see Table 14.5). Cooperative players received at least forwarding rate equal to 0.7. The forwarding differentiation made by SB players, which resulted from the application of the reputation-based strategy can be seen as an efficient investment of reputation. Other types of players did not take into account the reputation of the source and as a result their efficiency (defined as a ratio of packets forwarded to the obtained success rate) was lower that the one of SB players.

These three scenarios demonstrated that the efficiency of cooperation enforcement was related to the share of the network by SB and SF1 players. Whenever the number of players that followed the reputation-based forwarding was very low, or the number of selfish players was high, the cooperation enforcement system could not be created. In such a case, SB players applied a selfish strategy and as a result such players saved battery life. Other types of players that contributed to packet forwarding in such an environment did not receive any reward for their cooperative behavior.

14.4. Conclusions

With the communication paradigm of MANETs new problems that are difficult to tackle with conventional methods have emerged. A distributed nature of a system, lack of a single authority and limited battery resources lead to a noncooperative behavior at the level of packet forwarding that causes degradation of the network throughput. Attempts to use traditional techniques to solve cooperation issues in MANETs left many important problems unsolved, and often not addressed. The main reason is that human behavioral and social factors seam to be at the heart of these new types of problems. In this chapter a different approach towards solving the problem of selfish behavior was proposed. The introduced cooperation enforcement system was assessed using a new evaluation scheme based on evolutionary game theory. The system was designed in a way that cooperation was mainly based on the mechanism of direct reciprocity, which led to reciprocal altruism among network participants. In scenarios, where the number of nodes following the proposed approach was greater than the number of selfish nodes the network was successfully secured against noncooperative behavior.

References

1. J. Liu and I. Chlamtac. Mobile Ad Hoc Networking with a view of G4 Wireless: Imperatives and Challenges. In eds. S. Basagni, M. Conti, S. Giordano, and I. Stojmenovic, *Mobile Ad Hoc Networking*, chapter 1, pp. 1–45. Wiley-IEEE Press, (2004).
2. L. Buttyan and J. P. Hubaux. Nuglets: a Virtual Currency to Stimulate Cooperation in Self-Organized Mobile Ad Hoc Networks. Technical Report DSC/2001/001, Swiss Federal Institute of Technology, (2001).
3. S. Marti, T. Giuli, K. Lai, and M. Baker. Mitigating routing misbehavior in mobile ad hoc networks. In *Proc. ACM/IEEE 6th International Conference on Mobile Computing and Networking (MobiCom 2000)*, pp. 255–265, (2000).
4. P. Michiardi and R. Molva. Simulation-based Analysis of Security Exposures in Mobile Ad Hoc Networks. In *Proc. European Wireless Conference*, (2002).
5. L. Buttyan and J. P. Hubaux, Stimulating Cooperation in Self-Organizing Mobile Ad Hoc Networks, *Mobile Networks and Applications*. **8**(5), 579–592, (2003).
6. P. Michiardi and R. Molva. CORE: A COllaborative REputation mecha-

nism to enforce node cooperation in Mobile Ad Hoc Networks. In *Proc. 6th Conference on Security Communications, and Multimedia (CMS 2002)*, pp. 107–121, (2002).

7. J. P. Hubaux and et al. Cooperation In Wireless Networks. http://winet-coop.epfl.ch/. Accessed on February 2008.

8. J. P. Hubaux, L. Buttyan, and S. Capkun. The Quest for Security in Mobile Ad Hoc Networks. In *Proc. 2nd ACM international symposium on Mobile ad hoc networking and computing*, pp. 146–155. ACM, (2001).

9. F. Dressler. Self-Organization in Ad Hoc Networks: Overview and Classification. Technical Report Technical Report 02/06, University of Erlangen, Dept. of Computer Science 7 (March, 2006).

10. S. Buchegger and J. Y. L. Boudec. The Effect of Rumor Spreading in Reputation Systems for Mobile Ad-Hoc Networks. In *Proc. Workshop on Modeling and Optimization in Mobile, Ad Hoc and Wireless Networks (WiOpt 2003)*, pp. 131–140, (2003).

11. S. Buchegger and J. Y. L. Boudec. Performance Analysis of the CONFIDANT Protocol. In *Proc. 3rd International Symposium on Mobile Ad Hoc Networking and Computing (MobiHoc 2002)*, pp. 226–236, (2002).

12. S. Buchegger and J. Y. L. Boudec, Self-Policing Mobile Ad Hoc Networks by Reputation Systems, *IEEE Communications Magazine, Special Topic on Advances in Self-Organizing Networks*. **43**(7), 101–107, (2005).

13. S. Giordano and A. Urpi. Self-Organized and Cooperative Ad Hoc Networking. In eds. S. Basagni, M. Conti, S. Giordano, and I. Stojmenovic, *Mobile Ad Hoc Networking*, chapter 13, pp. 355–371. Wiley-IEEE Press, (2004).

14. Q. He, W. Dapeng, and P. Khosla. SORI: a Secure and Objective Reputation-Based Incentive Scheme for Ad-hoc Networks. In *Proc. Wireless Communications and Networking Conference (WCNC 2004)*, vol. 2, pp. 825–830, (2004).

15. K. Mandalas, D. Flitzanis, G. Marias, and P. Georgiadis. A Survey of Several Cooperation Enforcement Schemes for MANETs. In *Proc. Fifth IEEE International Symposium on Signal Processing and Information Technology*, pp. 466–471. IEEE, (2005).

16. G. F. Marias, P. Georgiadis, D. Flitzanis, and K. Mandalas, Cooperation enforcement schemes for MANETs: A survey, *Wireless Communications and Mobile Computing*. **6**(3), 319–332, (2006).

17. P. Michiardi and R. Molva, Analysis of coalition formation and cooperation strategies in mobile ad hoc networks, *Ad Hoc Networks*. **3**(2), 193–219, (2005).

18. L. Feeney and M. Nilsson. Investigating the Energy Consumption of a Wireless Network Interface in an Ad Hoc Networking Environment. In *Proc. The IEEE Conference on Computer Communications (INFOCOM 2001)*, pp. 1548–1557, (2001).

19. M. Seredynski, P. Bouvry, and M. A. Klopotek. Performance of a Strategy Based Packets Forwarding Performance of a Strategy Based Packets Forwarding in Ad Hoc Networks. In *Proc. The Third International Conference on Availability, Security and Reliability (ARES 2008)*, pp. 1036–1043. IEEE Computer Society (March, 2008).

20. M. Seredynski, P. Bouvry, and M. A. Klopotek. Preventing Selfish Behavior in Ad Hoc Networks. In *Proc. Congress on Evolutionary Computation (CEC 2007)*, pp. 3554 – 3560. IEEE Computer Society, (2007).
21. T. L. Vincent and J. S. Brown, *Evolutionary Game Theory, Natural Selection and Darwinian Dynamics.* (Cambridge University Press, 2005).
22. J. Jubin and J. D. Turnow, The DARPA packet radio network protocols, *Proceedings of the IEEE.* **75**(1), 21–32, (1987).
23. R. L. Trivers, The Evolution of Reciprocal Altruism, *The Quarterly Review of Biology.* **46**(1), 35–57 (March, 1971).
24. R. D. Alexander, *The Biology of Moral Systems.* (Aldine Transaction, 1987).
25. M. Nowak and K. Sigmund, The Dynamics of Indirect Reciprocity, *Journal of Theoretical Biology.* **194**(4), 561–574, (1988).
26. O. Leimar and P. Hammerstein, Evolution of Cooperation Through Indirect Reciprocity, *Proceedings of the Royal Society of London B.* **268**, 745–753, (2001).

Acknowledgements to the Referees

We gratefully acknowledge the referees who reviewed the respective chapters found in the book. The list is given below.

Gildas Avoine
Pascal Bouvry
Jordi Castellà-Roca
Valentina Ciriani
Rinku Dewri
Josep Lluis Ferrer
Jordi Forné
Paolo Gastaldo
Ana Isabel González-Tablas
Jordi Herrera
Hiroaki Kikuchi
Victor Korobitsin
Bing Lu
Jesús Manjón
Josep Maria Mateo-Sanz

Sadaaki Miyamoto
Antonio Moreno
Jordi Nin
Roberto Di Pietro
Domènec Puig
Matthias Schmid
Francesc Sebé
Francesc Serratosa
Miquel Soriano
Claudio Soriente
Vicenç Torra
Aida Valls
Zhenke Yang
Fan Zhang
Zonghua Zhang

A special thank goes to Arnau Gavaldà, Jesús Manjón and Glòria Pujol for helping in editing and disseminating this book.

Disclaimer and Acknowledgements

This work was partly supported by the Spanish Ministry of Education through projects TSI2007-65406-C03-01"E-AEGIS" and CONSOLIDER CSD2007-00004 "ARES", and by the Government of Catalonia under grant 2005 SGR 00446.

Author Index

Subject Index